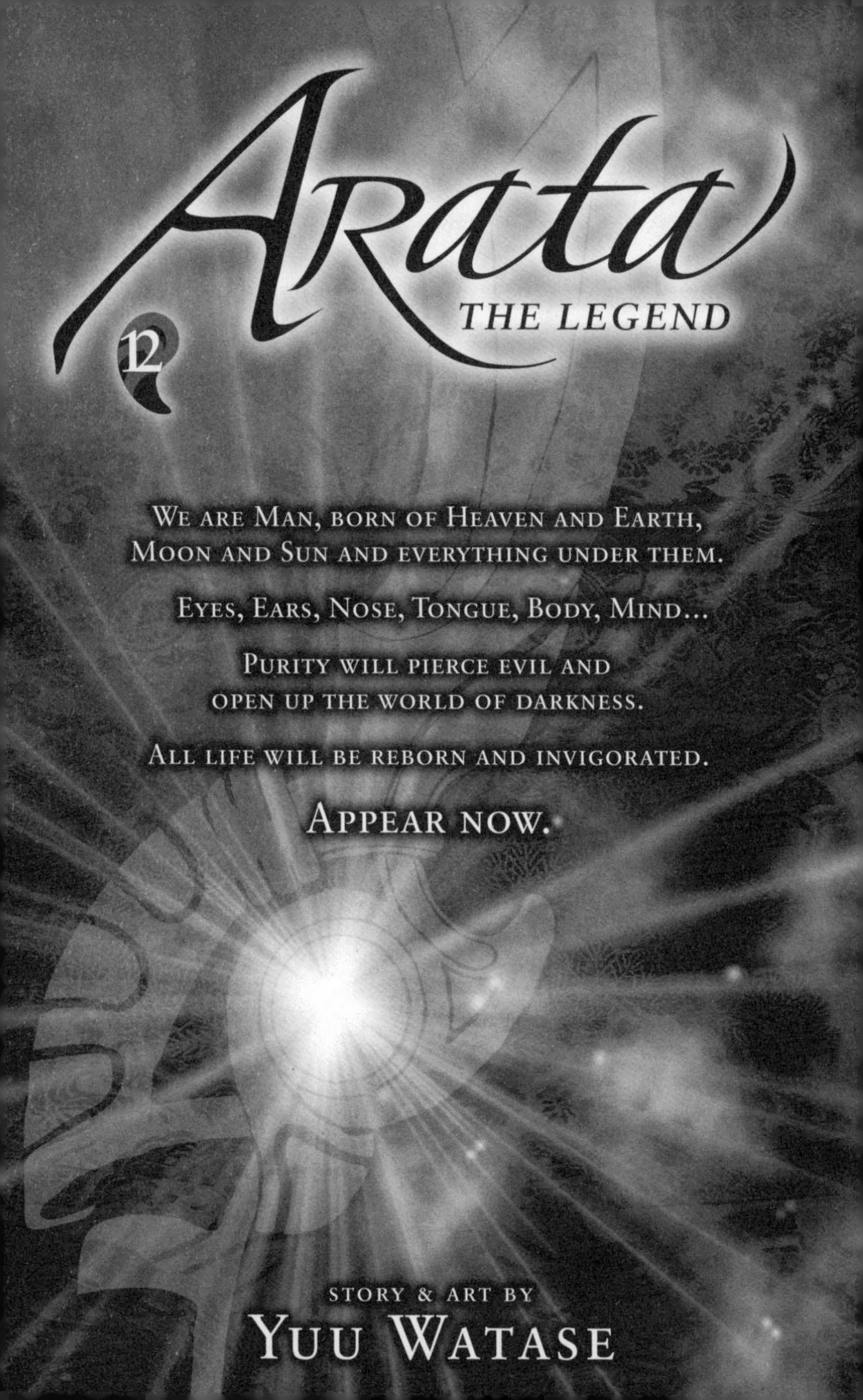
Arata
THE LEGEND
12
We are Man, born of Heaven and Earth,
Moon and Sun and everything under them.
Eyes, Ears, Nose, Tongue, Body, Mind...
Purity will pierce evil and
open up the world of darkness.
All life will be reborn and invigorated.
Appear now.
STORY & ART BY
Yuu Watase

Arata
THE LEGEND

CHARACTERS

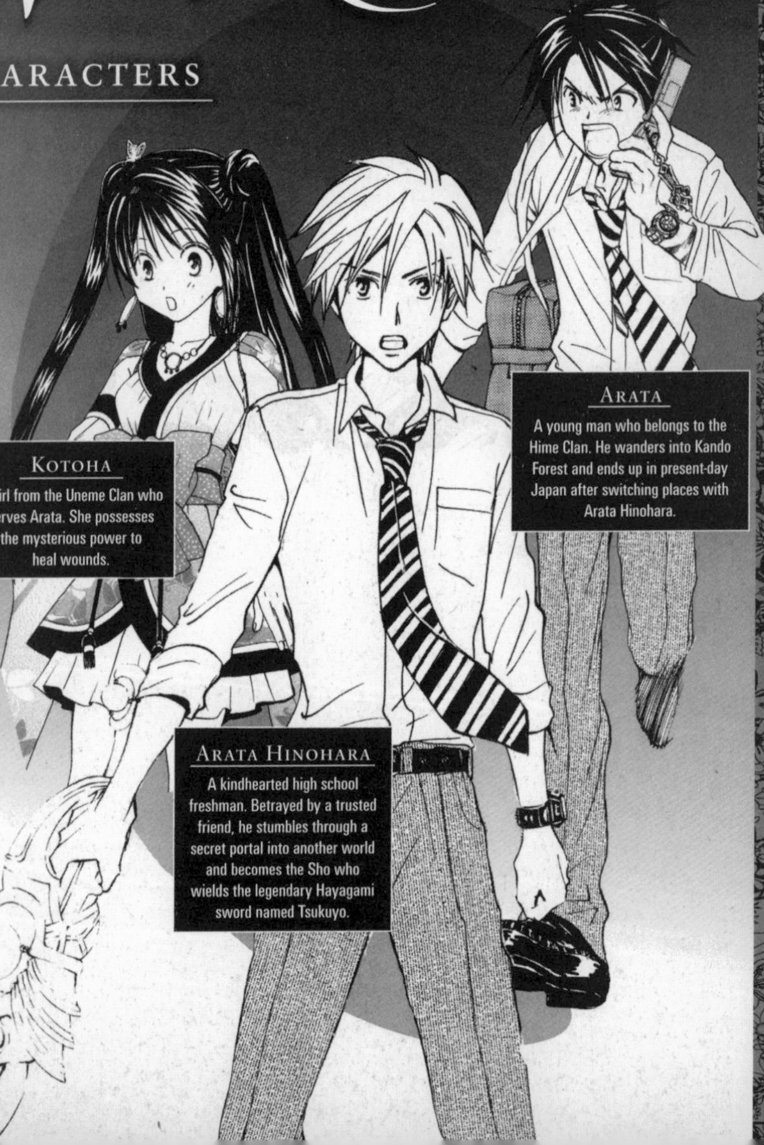

ARATA
A young man who belongs to the Hime Clan. He wanders into Kando Forest and ends up in present-day Japan after switching places with Arata Hinohara.

KOTOHA
A girl from the Uneme Clan who serves Arata. She possesses the mysterious power to heal wounds.

ARATA HINOHARA
A kindhearted high school freshman. Betrayed by a trusted friend, he stumbles through a secret portal into another world and becomes the Sho who wields the legendary Hayagami sword named Tsukuyo.

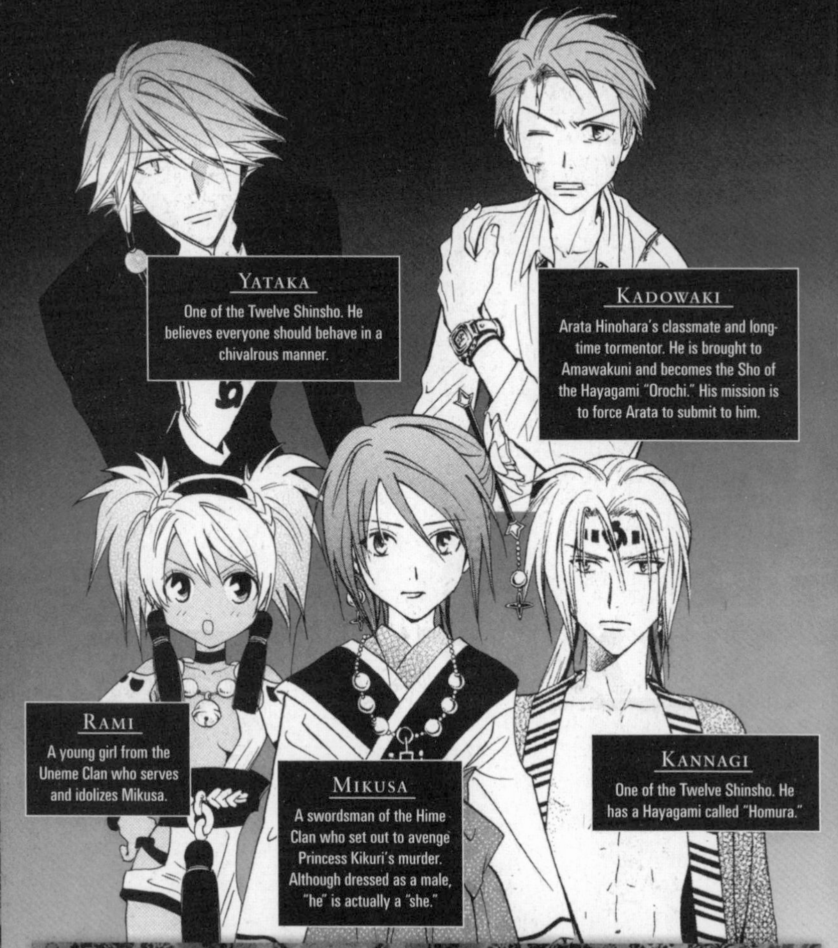
YATAKA
One of the Twelve Shinsho. He believes everyone should behave in a chivalrous manner.
KADOWAKI
Arata Hinohara's classmate and long-time tormentor. He is brought to Amawakuni and becomes the Sho of the Hayagami "Orochi." His mission is to force Arata to submit to him.
RAMI
A young girl from the Uneme Clan who serves and idolizes Mikusa.
MIKUSA
A swordsman of the Hime Clan who set out to avenge Princess Kikuri's murder. Although dressed as a male, "he" is actually a "she."
KANNAGI
One of the Twelve Shinsho. He has a Hayagami called "Homura."

THE STORY THUS FAR

Betrayed by his best friend, Arata Hinohara—a high school student in present-day Japan—wanders through a portal into another world where he and his companions journey onward to deliver his Hayagami sword "Tsukuyo" to Princess Kikuri who lingers in a state between life and death.

Hinohara discovers that his foe, the Shinsho Yataka, and Princess Kikuri were once sweethearts and that Yataka still loves her deeply. When Yataka is won over by Hinohara's kindness and strength, he begs Hinohara to save the princess and offers to submit to him. However, Hinohara's Tsukuyo rejects Yataka's submission. Yataka then joins Hinohara and company on their journey despite a bit of friction with Kannagi. Later, the other Arata in Japan tells Hinohara that Imina Oribe actually belongs to the Hime Clan. Hinohara then discovers that the person Oribe switched places with was Mikusa!

Meanwhile, Kadowaki presents Akachi with a deadly proposal...

12

Arata
THE LEGEND

CONTENTS

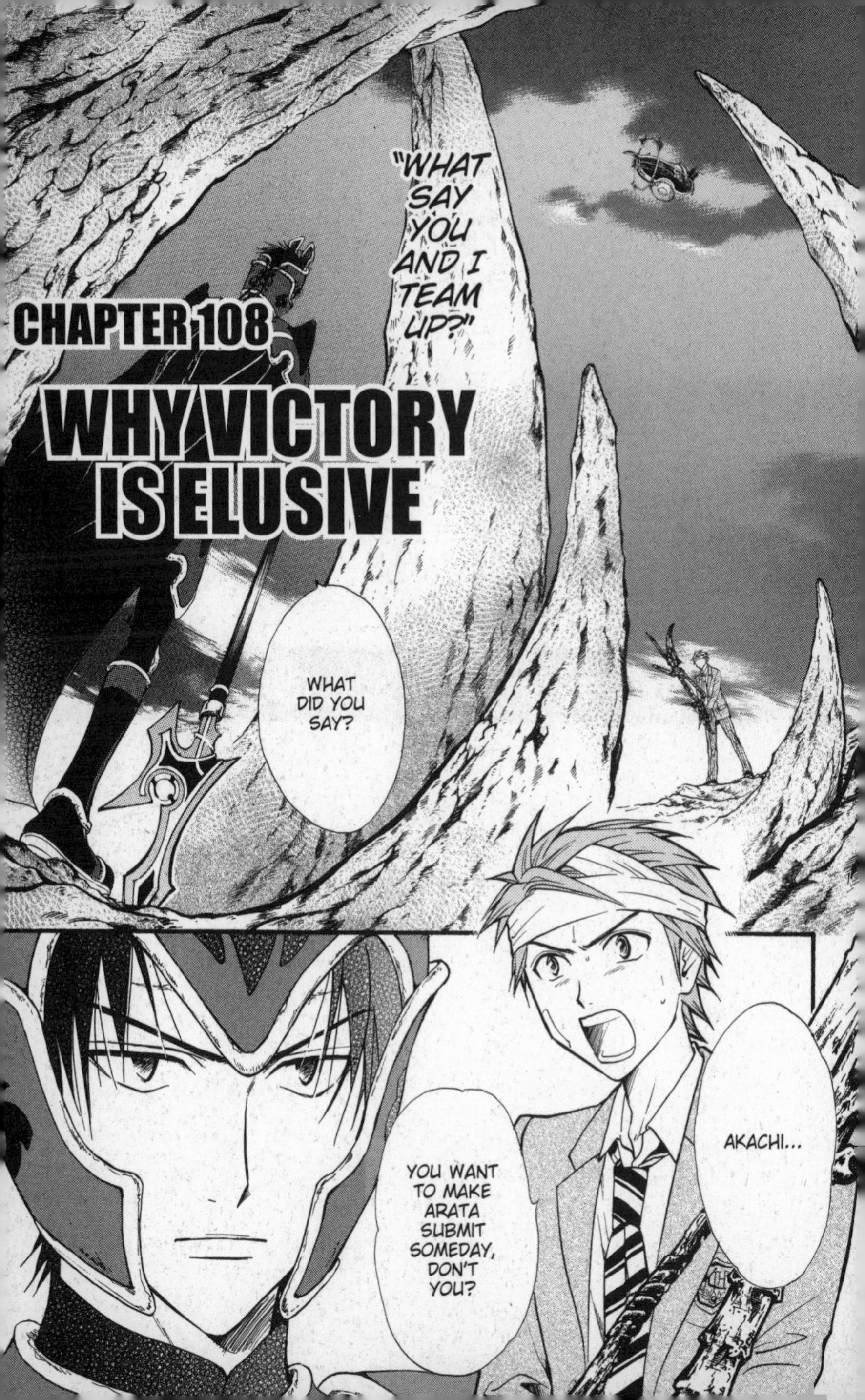
"WHAT SAY YOU AND I TEAM UP?"
CHAPTER 108
WHY VICTORY IS ELUSIVE
WHAT DID YOU SAY?
AKACHI...
YOU WANT TO MAKE ARATA SUBMIT SOMEDAY, DON'T YOU?

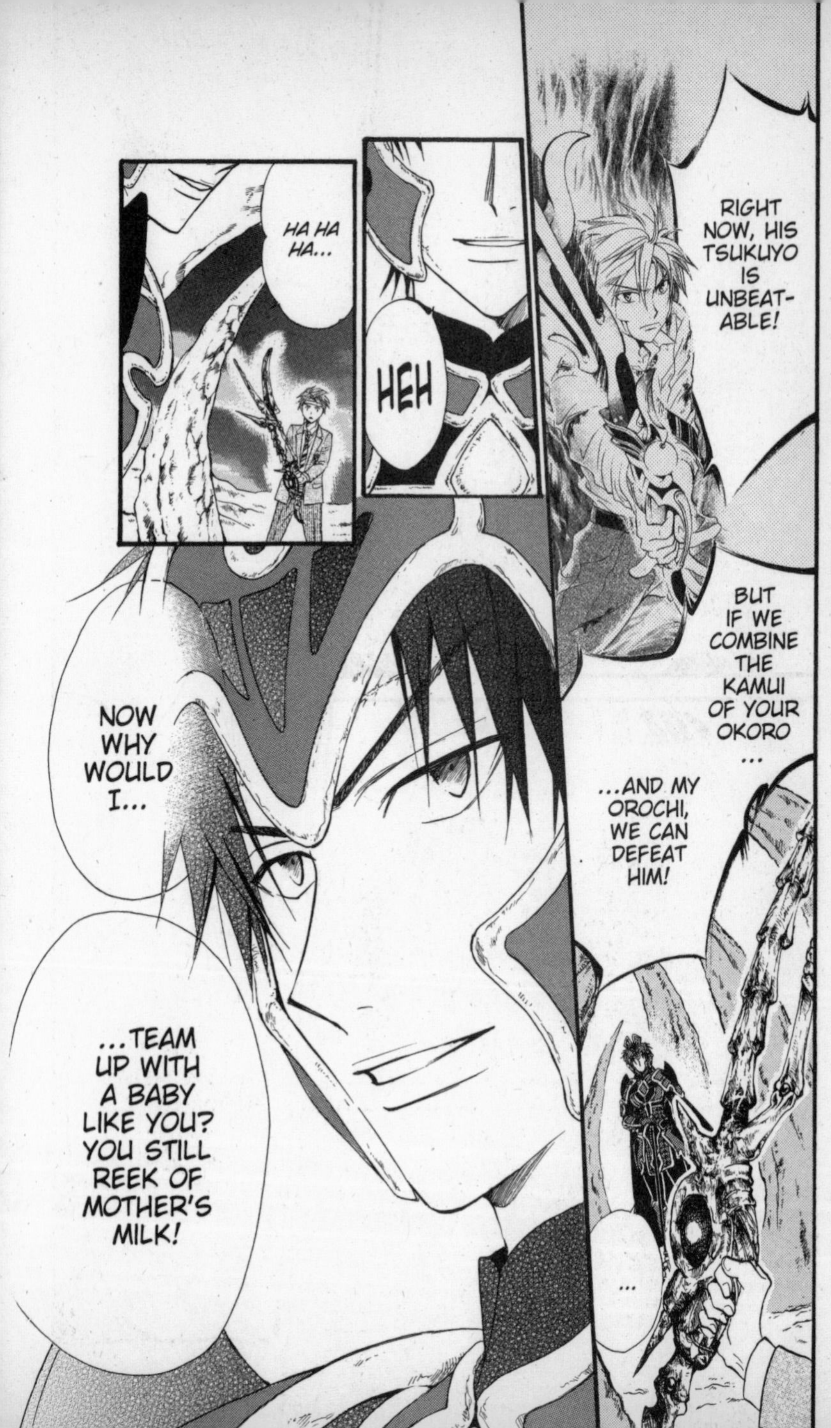
RIGHT NOW, HIS TSUKUYO IS UNBEAT-ABLE!
BUT IF WE COMBINE THE KAMUI OF YOUR OKORO...
...AND MY OROCHI, WE CAN DEFEAT HIM!
...
HEH
HA HA HA...
NOW WHY WOULD I...
...TEAM UP WITH A BABY LIKE YOU? YOU STILL REEK OF MOTHER'S MILK!

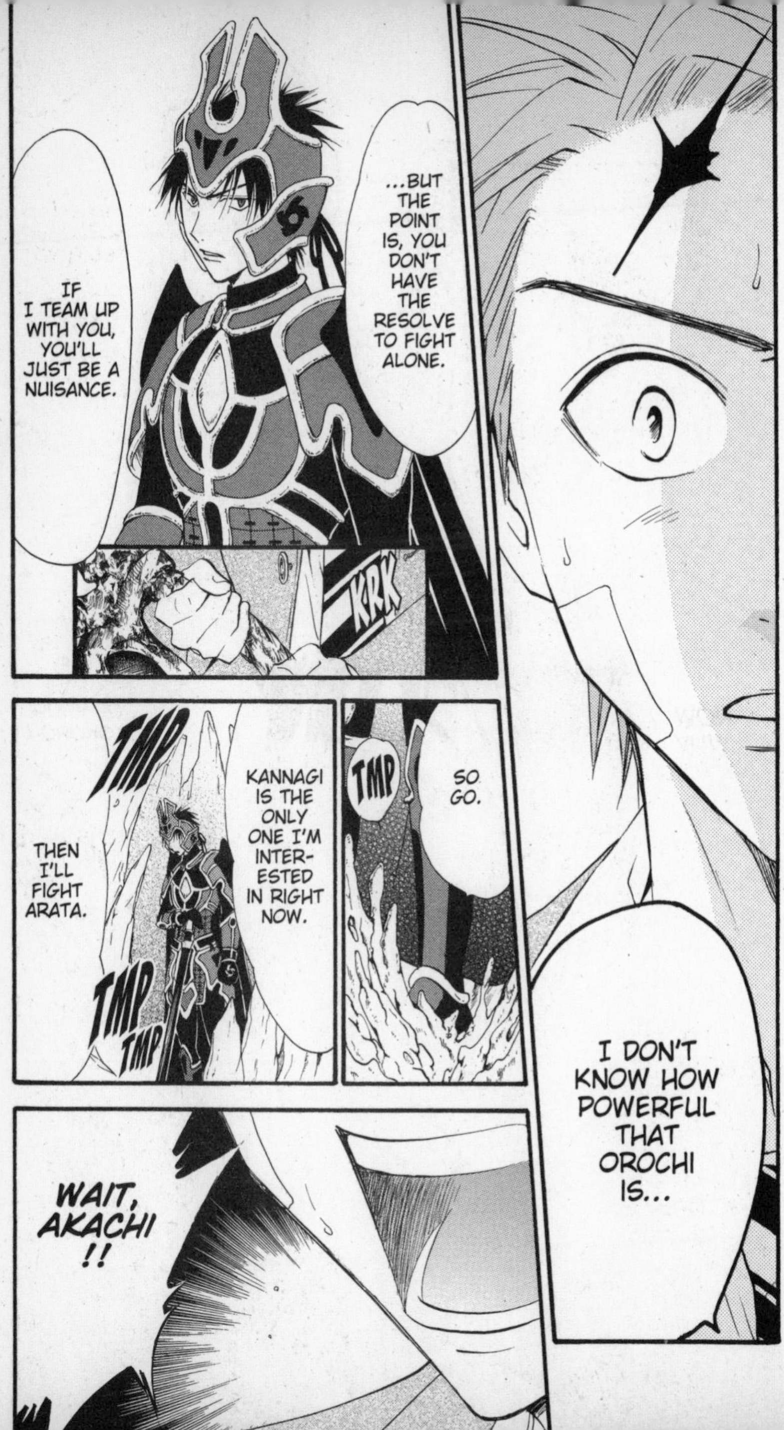
I DON'T KNOW HOW POWERFUL THAT OROCHI IS...
...BUT THE POINT IS, YOU DON'T HAVE THE RESOLVE TO FIGHT ALONE.
IF I TEAM UP WITH YOU, YOU'LL JUST BE A NUISANCE.
KRK
TMP
SO GO.
KANNAGI IS THE ONLY ONE I'M INTER-ESTED IN RIGHT NOW.
TMP
THEN I'LL FIGHT ARATA.
TMP
TMP
TMP
WAIT, AKACHI!!

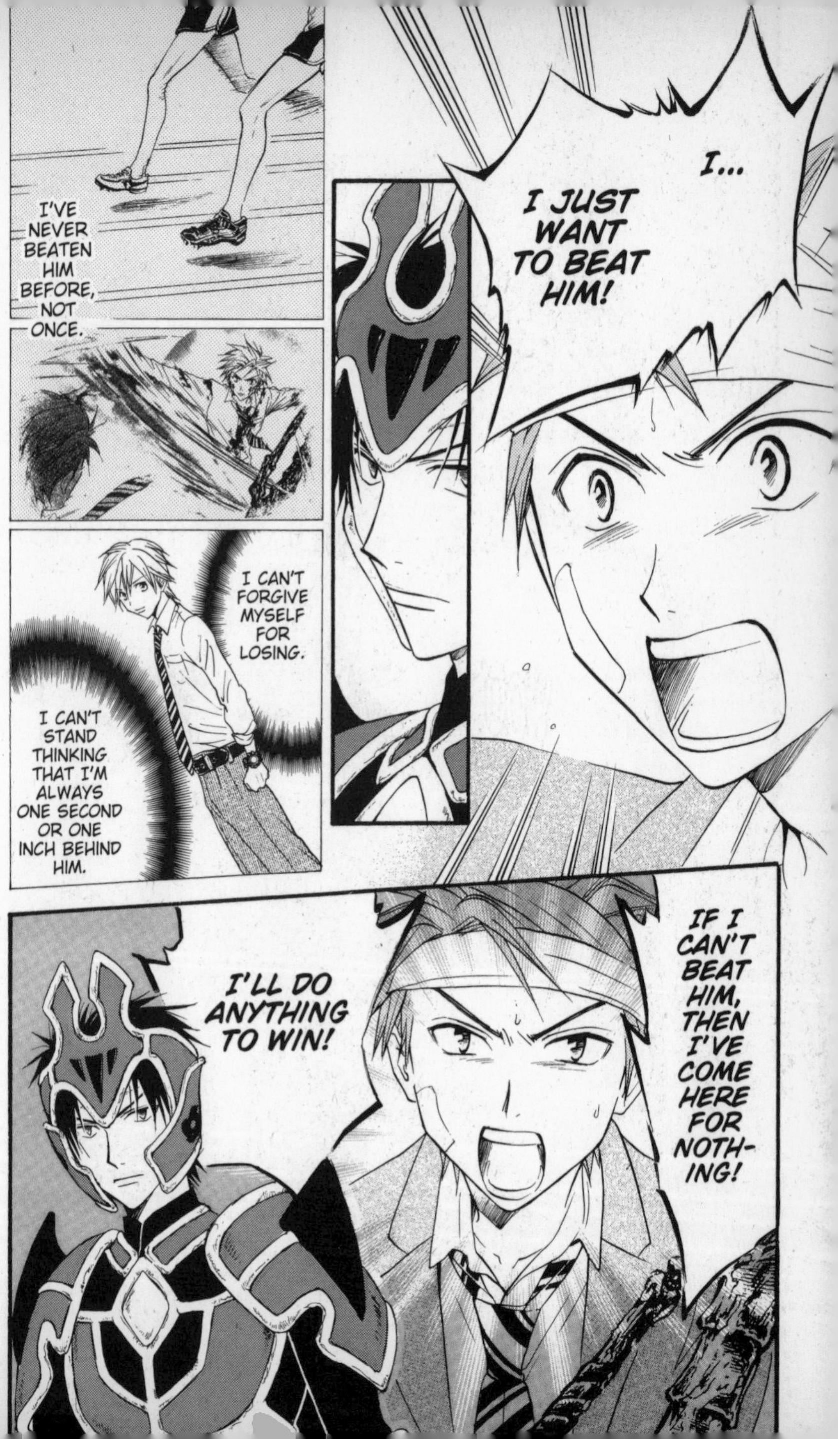
I...
I JUST WANT TO BEAT HIM!
I'VE NEVER BEATEN HIM BEFORE, NOT ONCE.
I CAN'T FORGIVE MYSELF FOR LOSING.
I CAN'T STAND THINKING THAT I'M ALWAYS ONE SECOND OR ONE INCH BEHIND HIM.
IF I CAN'T BEAT HIM, THEN I'VE COME HERE FOR NOTH-ING!
I'LL DO ANYTHING TO WIN!

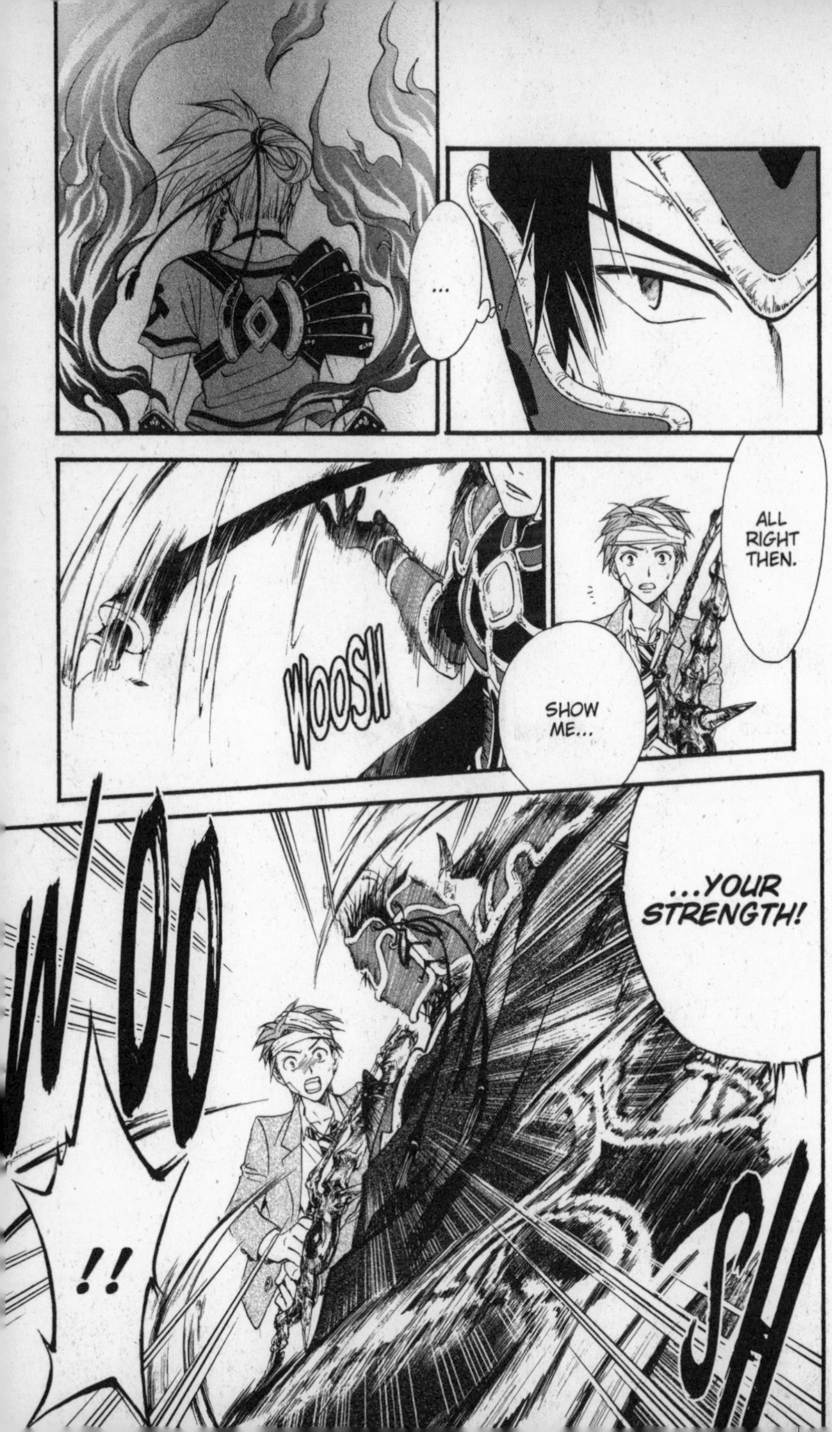
...
ALL RIGHT THEN.
SHOW ME...
WOOSH
...YOUR STRENGTH!
WOOSH
!!

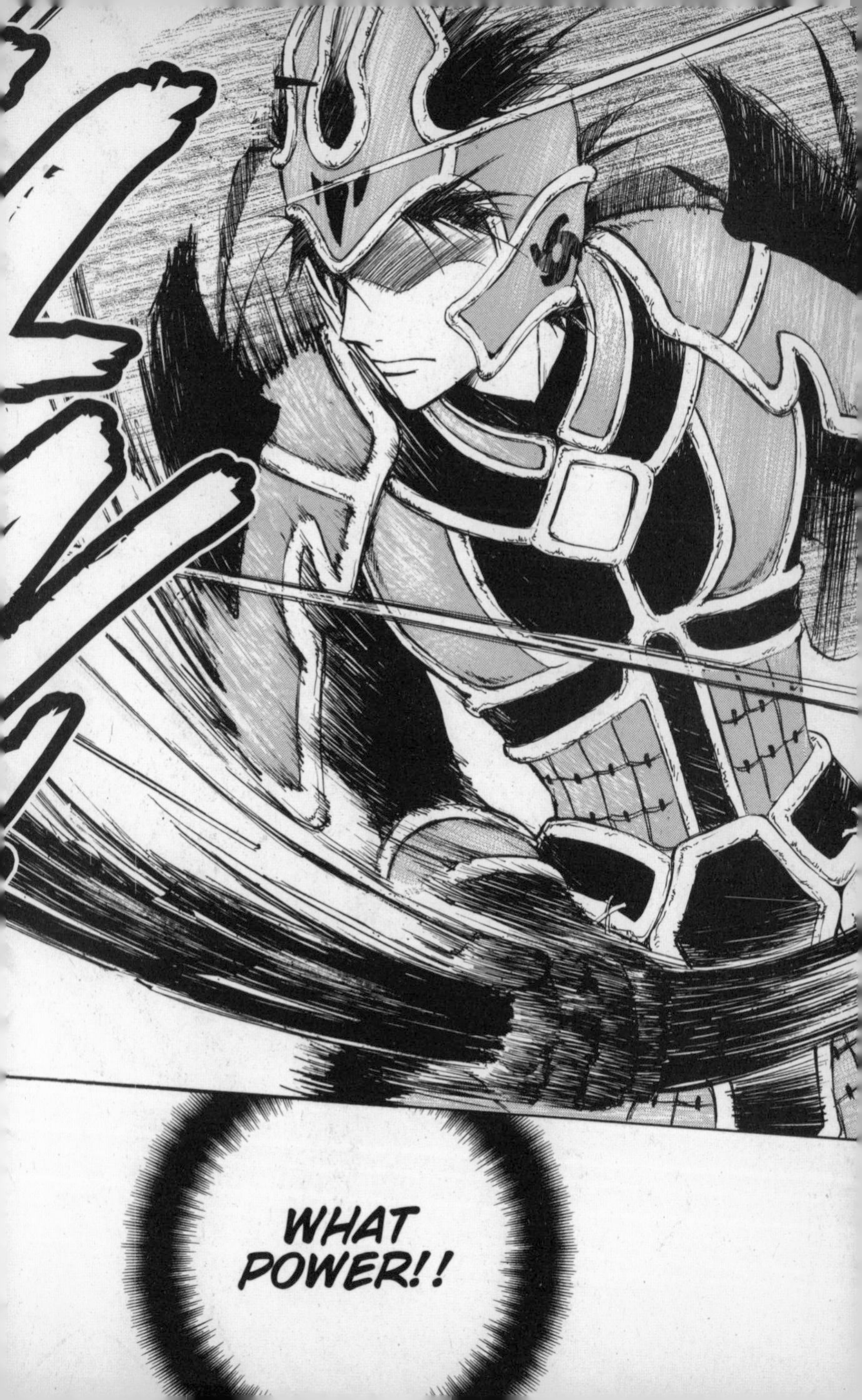
WHAT POWER!!

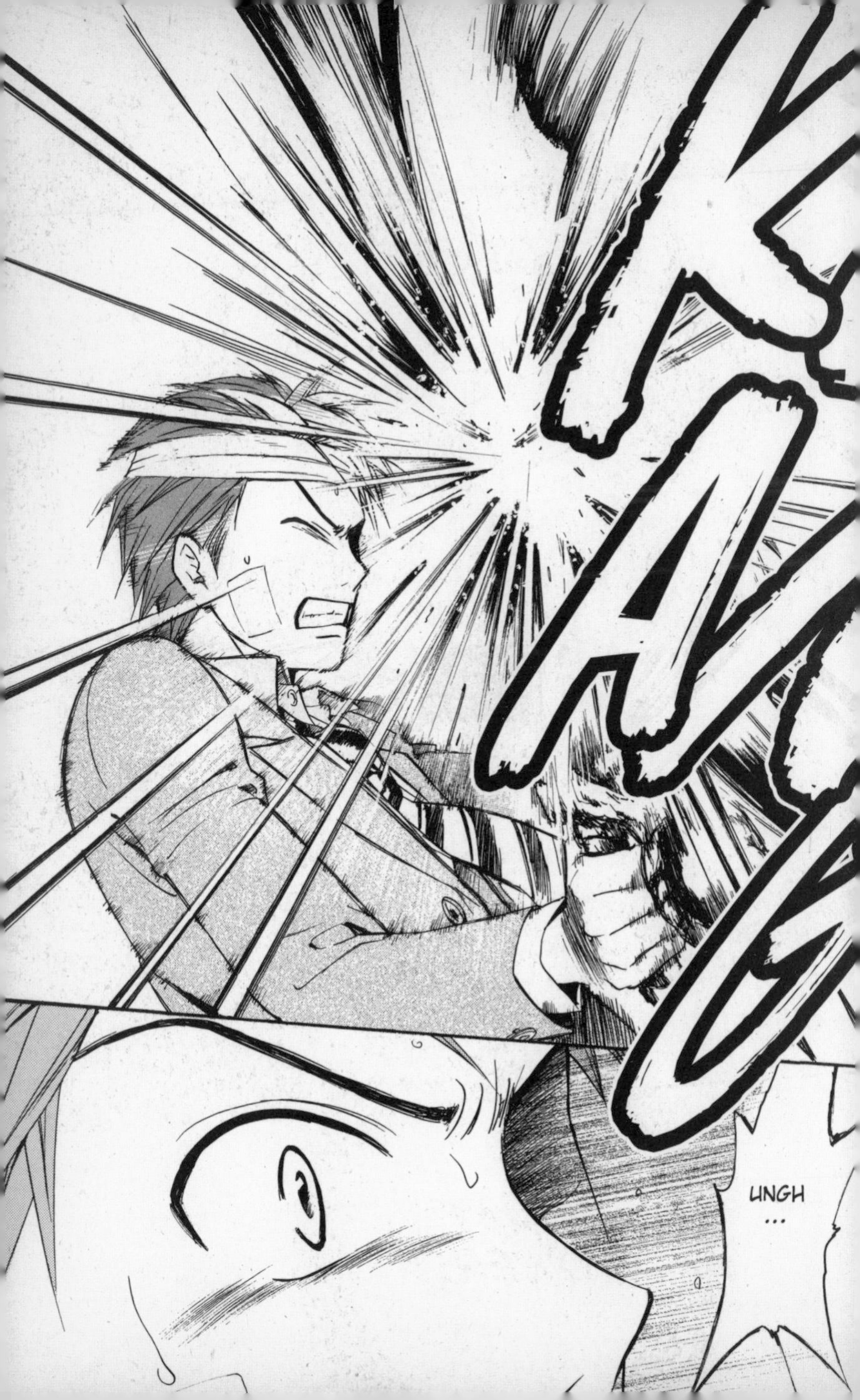
UNGH
...

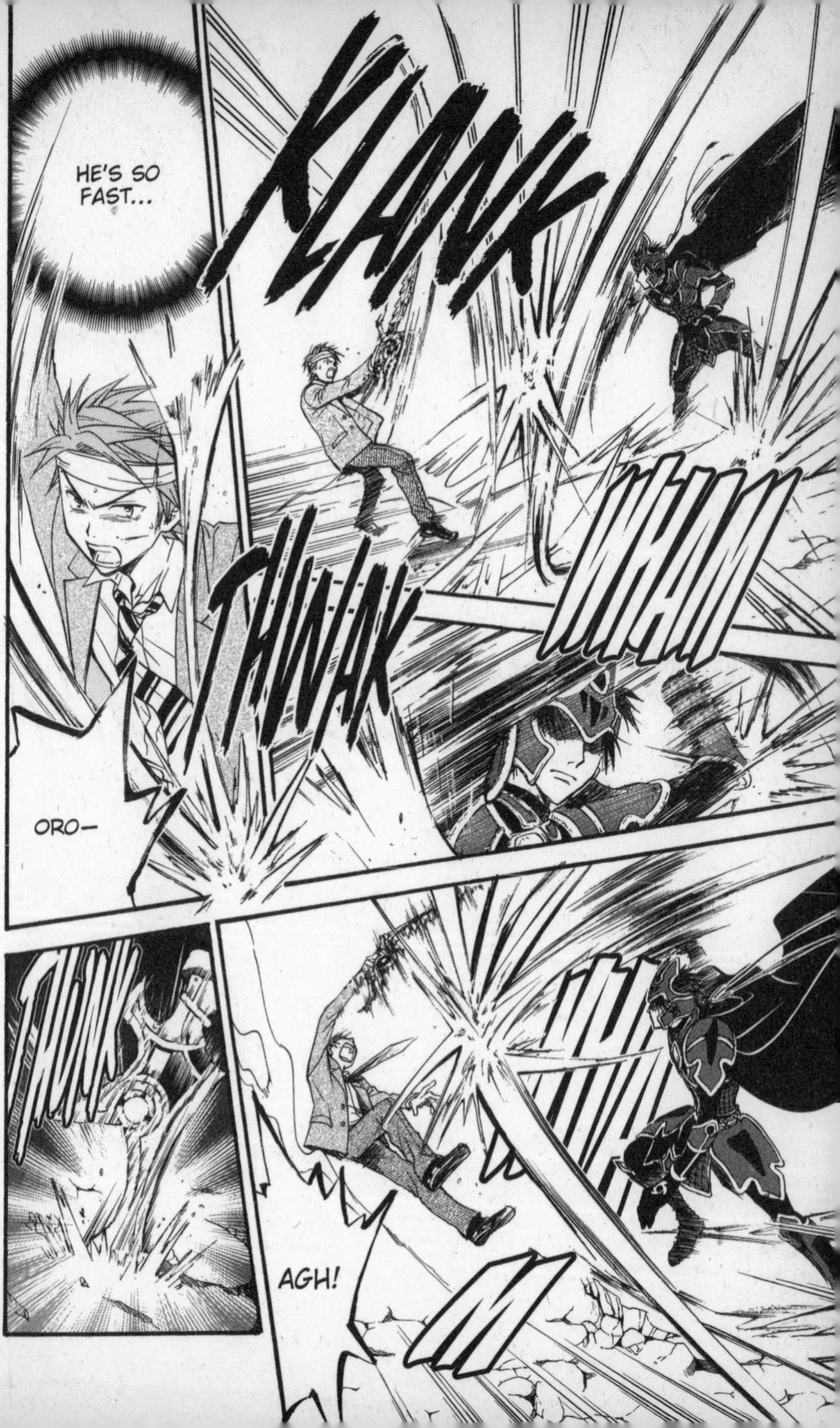
KLANK
HE'S SO FAST...
WHAM
THWAK
ORO—
AGH!

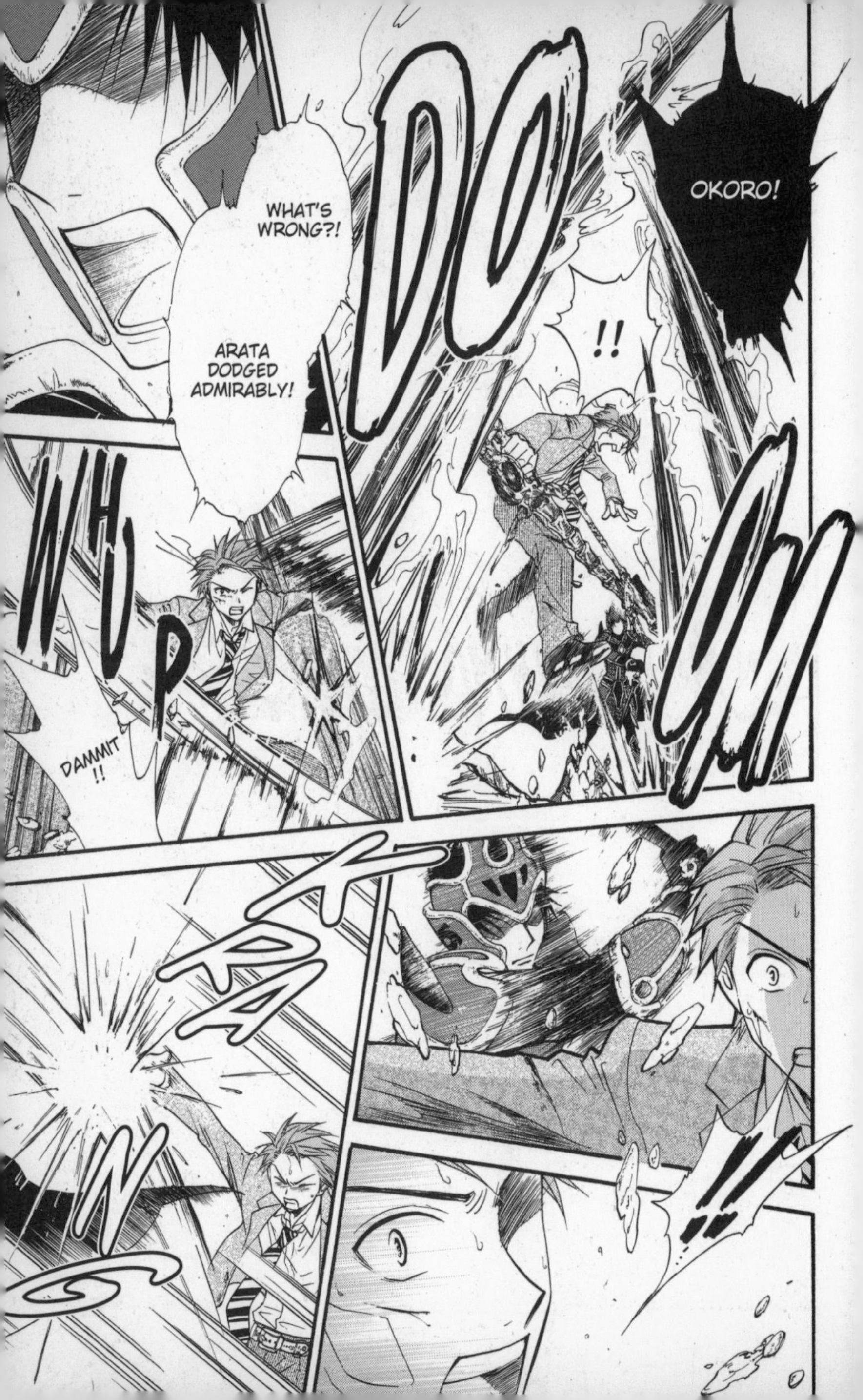
OKORO!
DOOM
!!
WHAT'S WRONG?!
ARATA DODGED ADMIRABLY!
WHUP
DAMMIT !!
!!

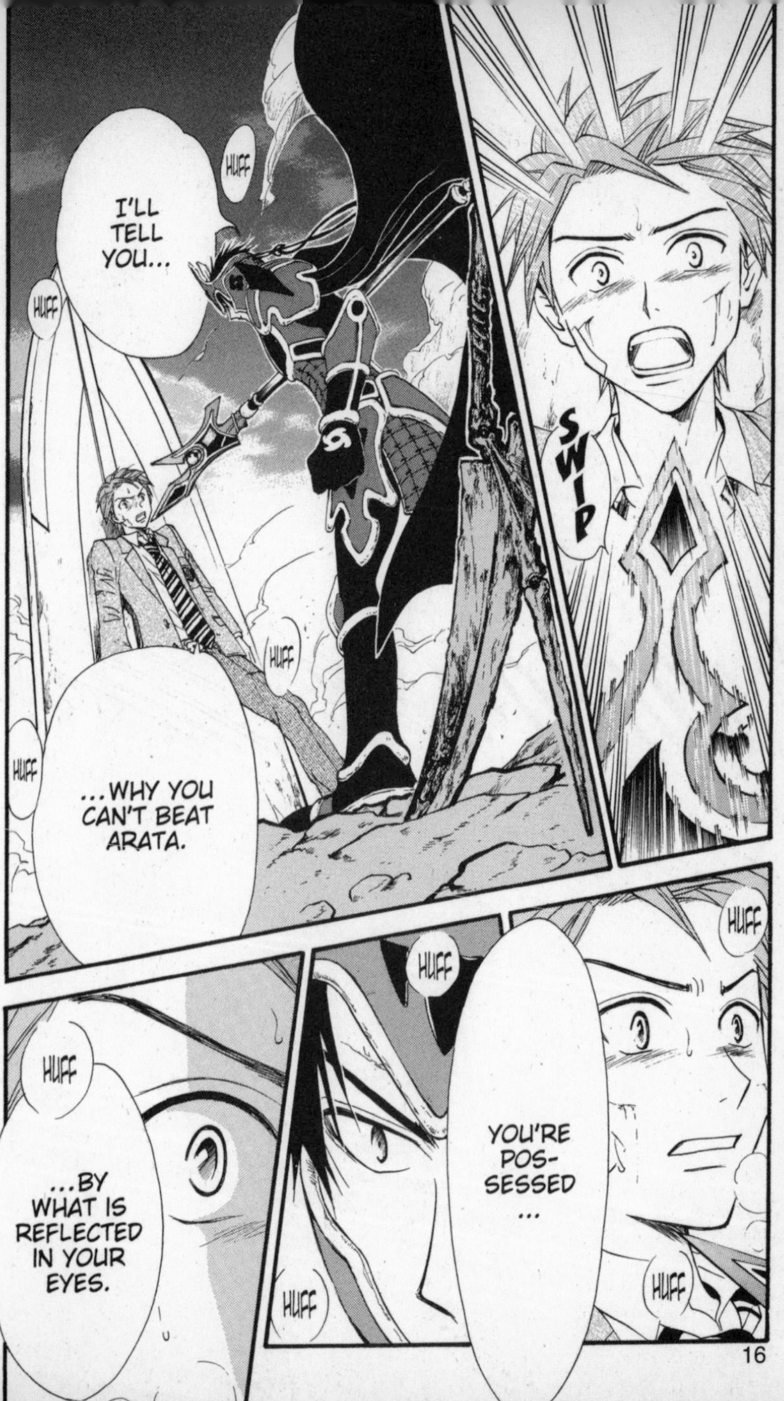
SWIP
HUFF
I'LL TELL YOU...
HUFF
HUFF
HUFF
...WHY YOU CAN'T BEAT ARATA.
HUFF
YOU'RE POS-SESSED ...
HUFF
HUFF
HUFF
HUFF
...BY WHAT IS REFLECTED IN YOUR EYES.

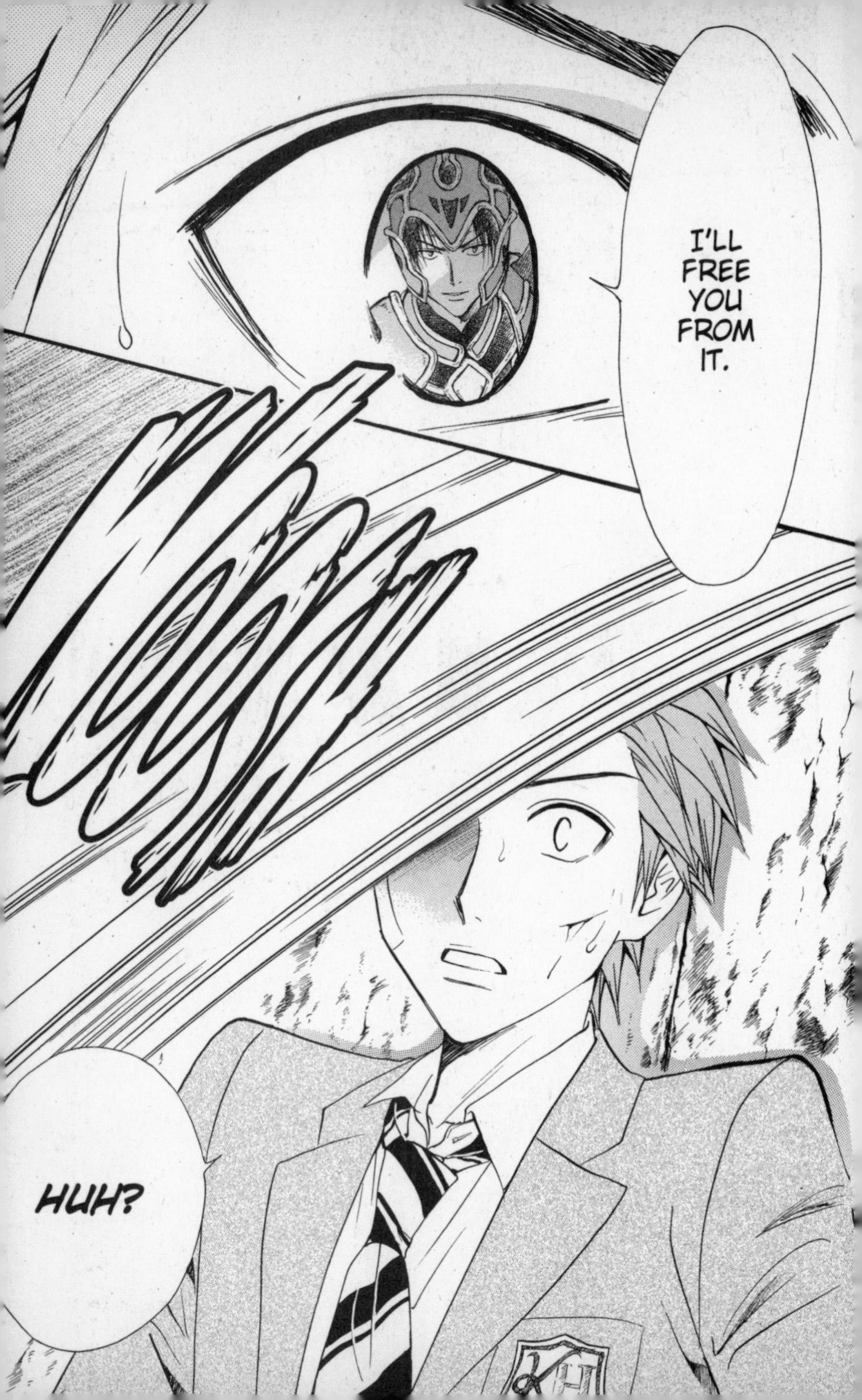
I'LL FREE YOU FROM IT.
HUH?

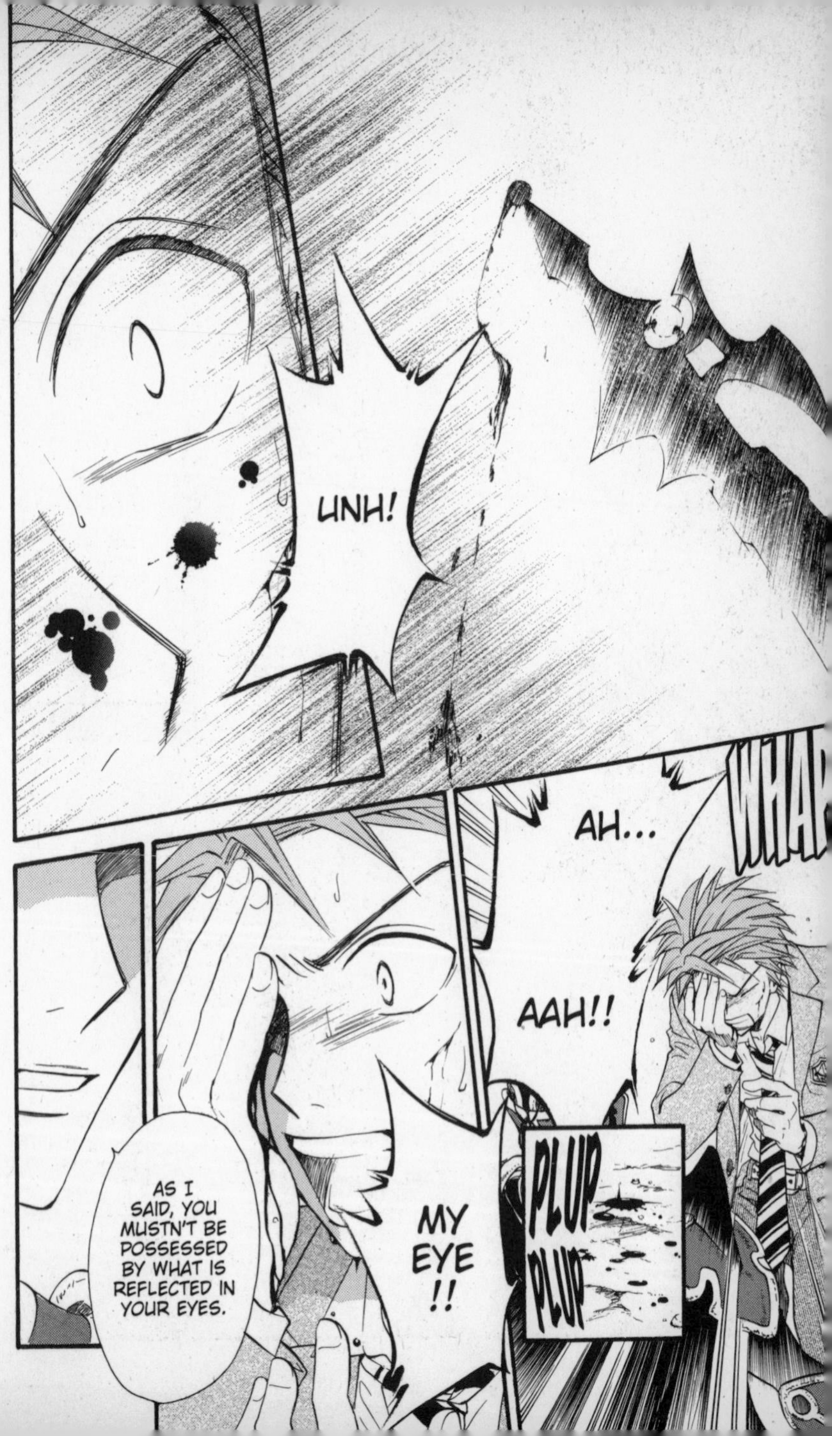
UNH!
WHA
AH...
AAH!!
PLUP PLUP
MY EYE!!
AS I SAID, YOU MUSTN'T BE POSSESSED BY WHAT IS REFLECTED IN YOUR EYES.

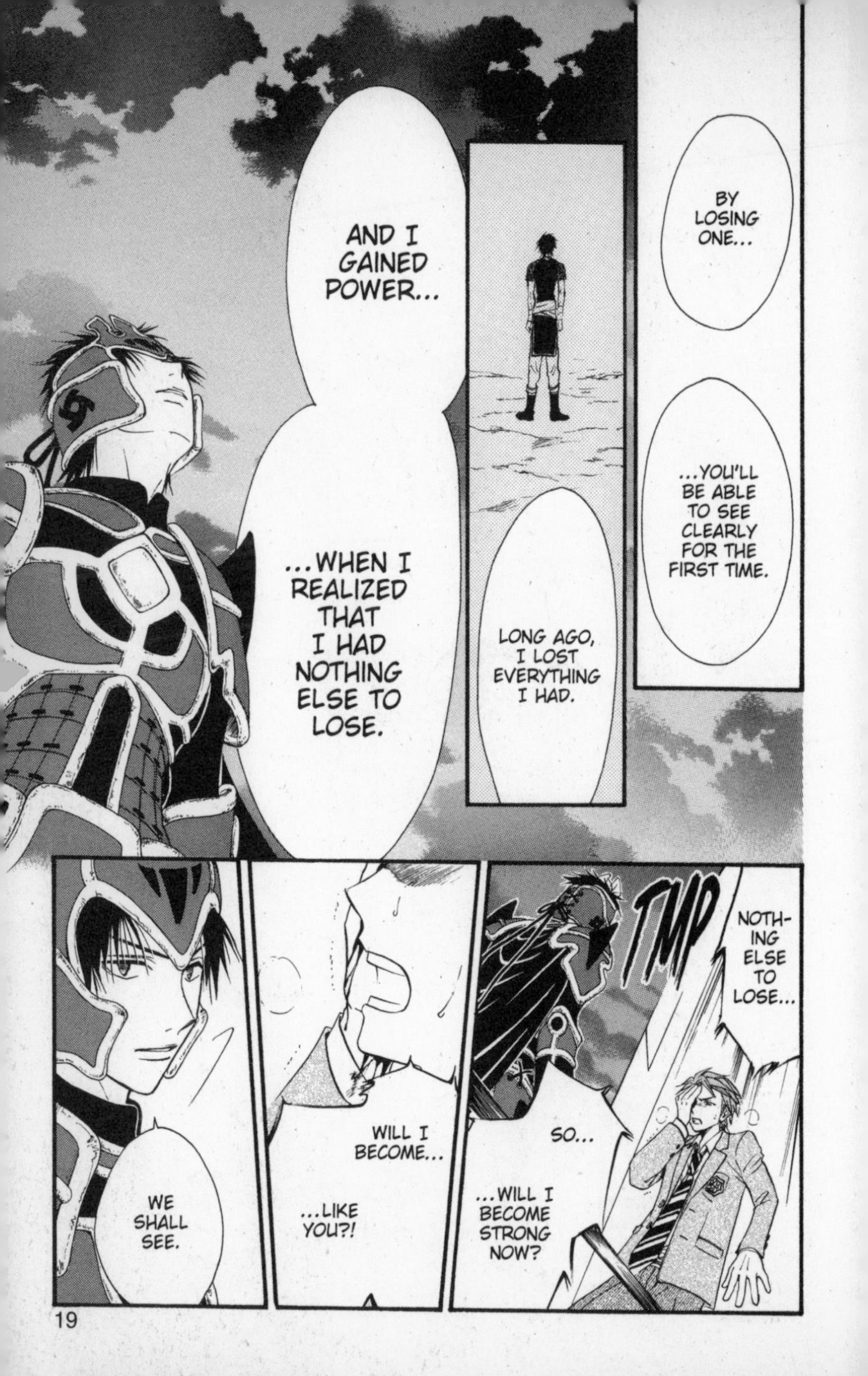
BY LOSING ONE...
...YOU'LL BE ABLE TO SEE CLEARLY FOR THE FIRST TIME.
LONG AGO, I LOST EVERYTHING I HAD.
AND I GAINED POWER...
...WHEN I REALIZED THAT I HAD NOTHING ELSE TO LOSE.
NOTHING ELSE TO LOSE...
TMP
SO...
...WILL I BECOME STRONG NOW?
WILL I BECOME...
...LIKE YOU?!
WE SHALL SEE.

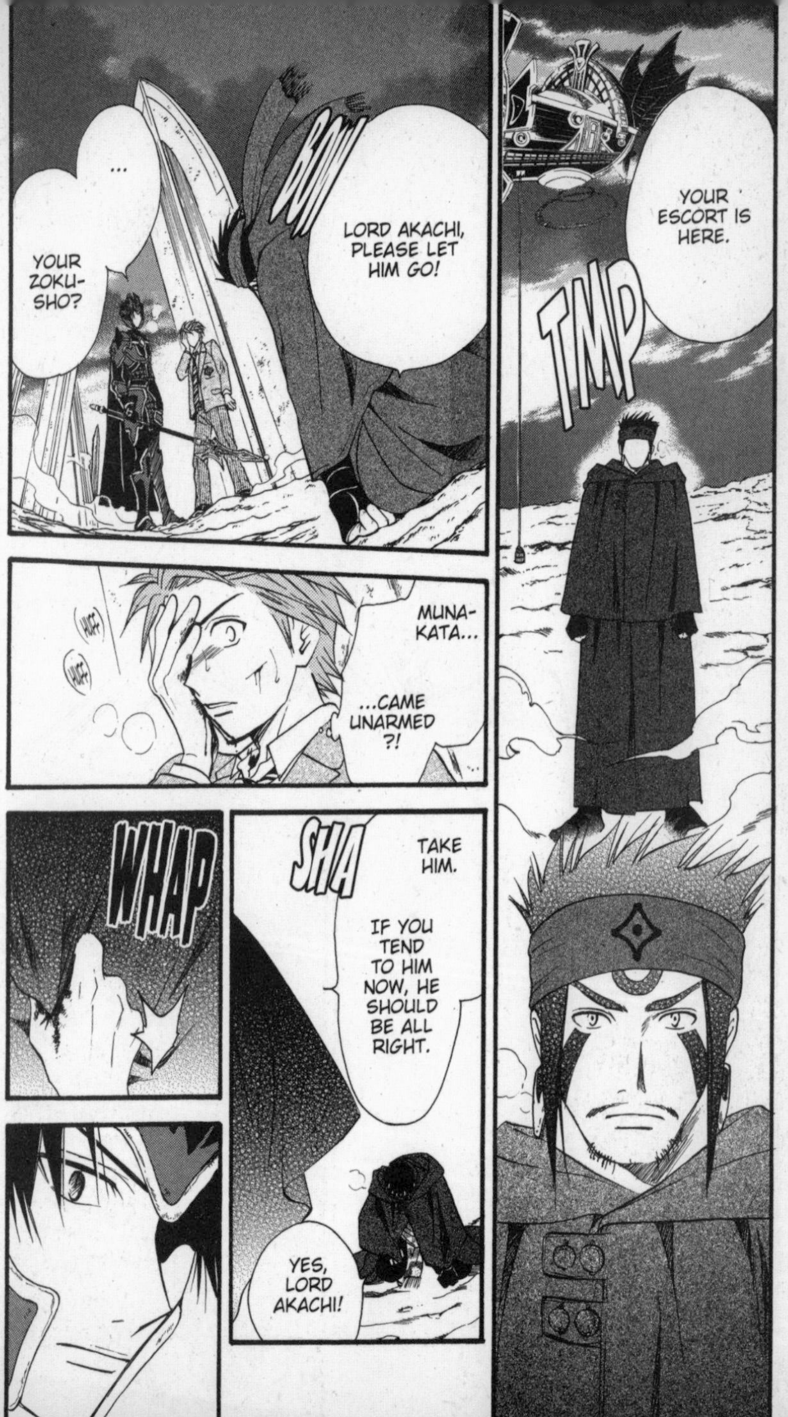
YOUR ESCORT IS HERE.
TMP
BOW
LORD AKACHI, PLEASE LET HIM GO!
...
YOUR ZOKU-SHO?
MUNA-KATA...
...CAME UNARMED?!
HUFF
HUFF
SHIA
TAKE HIM.
IF YOU TEND TO HIM NOW, HE SHOULD BE ALL RIGHT.
YES, LORD AKACHI!
WHAP

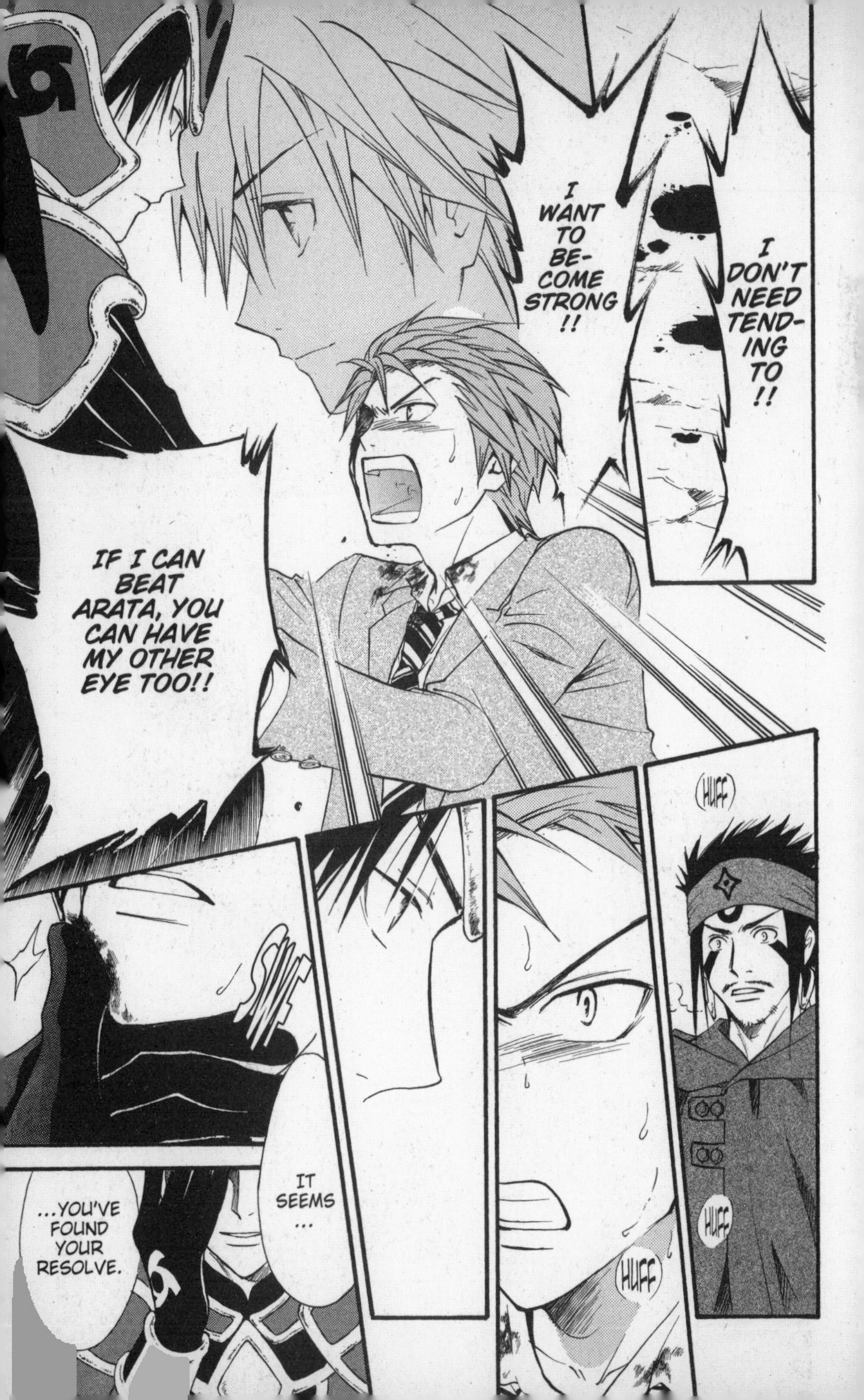
I DON'T NEED TENDING TO!!
I WANT TO BECOME STRONG!!
IF I CAN BEAT ARATA, YOU CAN HAVE MY OTHER EYE TOO!!
(HUFF)
HUFF
HUFF
IT SEEMS...
...YOU'VE FOUND YOUR RESOLVE.

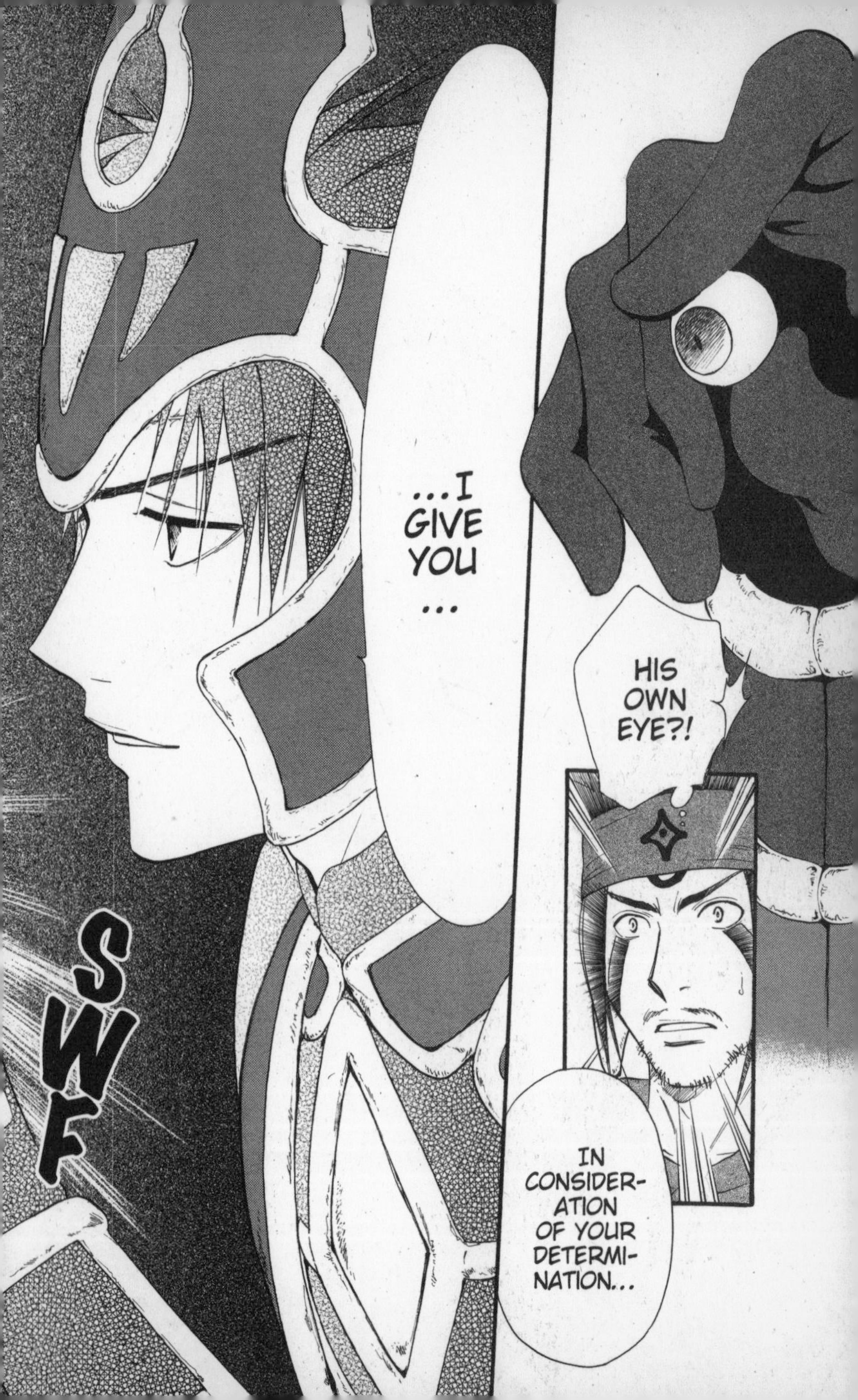
HIS OWN EYE?!
IN CONSIDERATION OF YOUR DETERMINATION...
...I GIVE YOU...
SWF

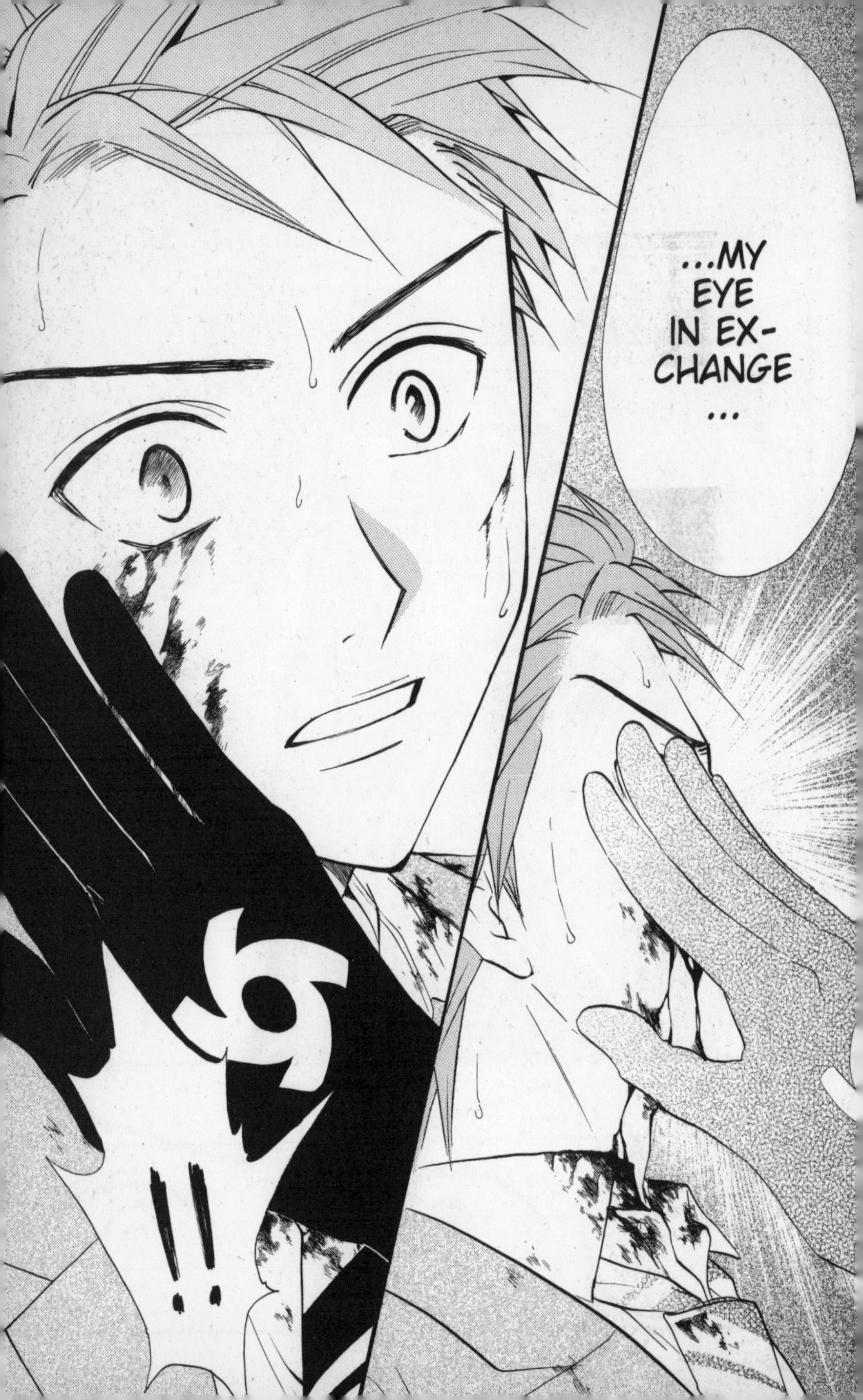
...MY EYE IN EX-CHANGE ...
!!

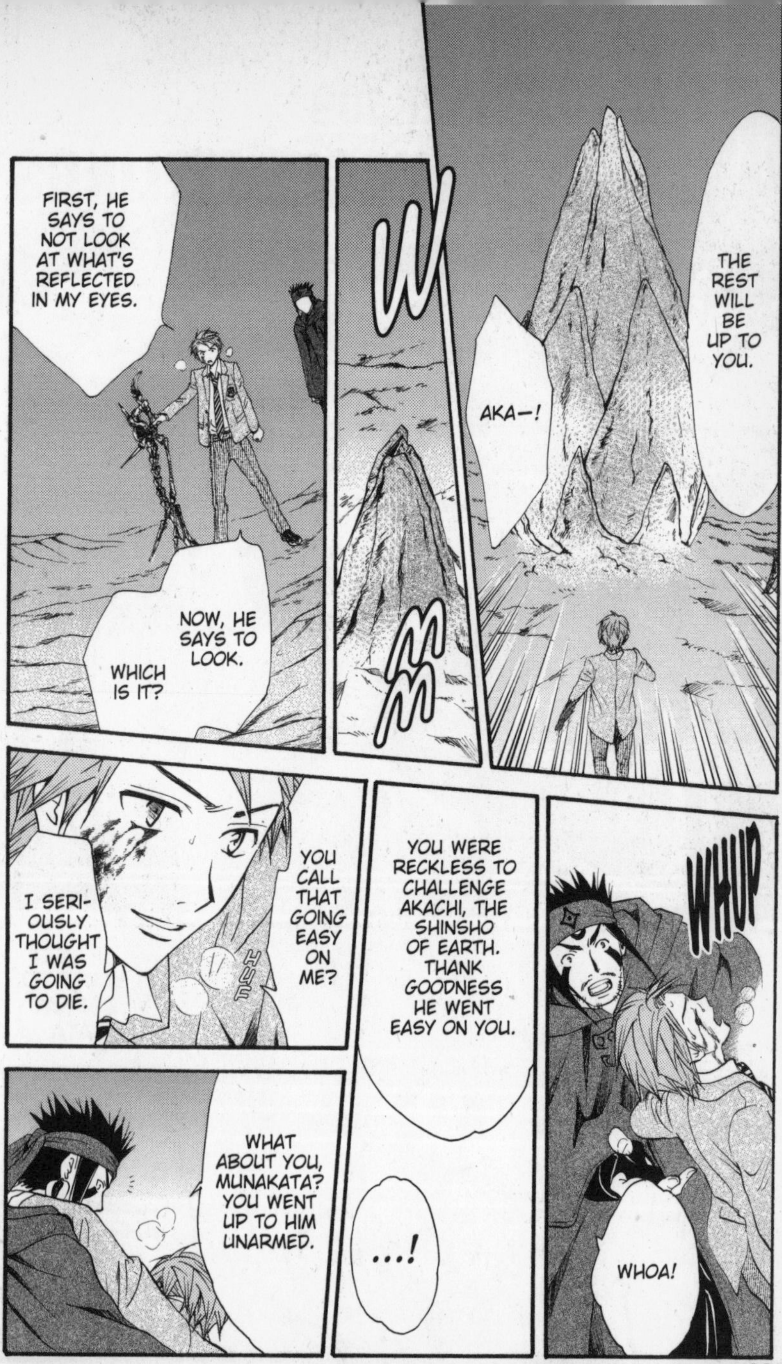
THE REST WILL BE UP TO YOU.
AKA—!
FIRST, HE SAYS TO NOT LOOK AT WHAT'S REFLECTED IN MY EYES.
NOW, HE SAYS TO LOOK.
WHICH IS IT?
WHUP
WHOA!
YOU WERE RECKLESS TO CHALLENGE AKACHI, THE SHINSHO OF EARTH. THANK GOODNESS HE WENT EASY ON YOU.
...!
YOU CALL THAT GOING EASY ON ME?
HUF
I SERI-OUSLY THOUGHT I WAS GOING TO DIE.
WHAT ABOUT YOU, MUNAKATA? YOU WENT UP TO HIM UNARMED.

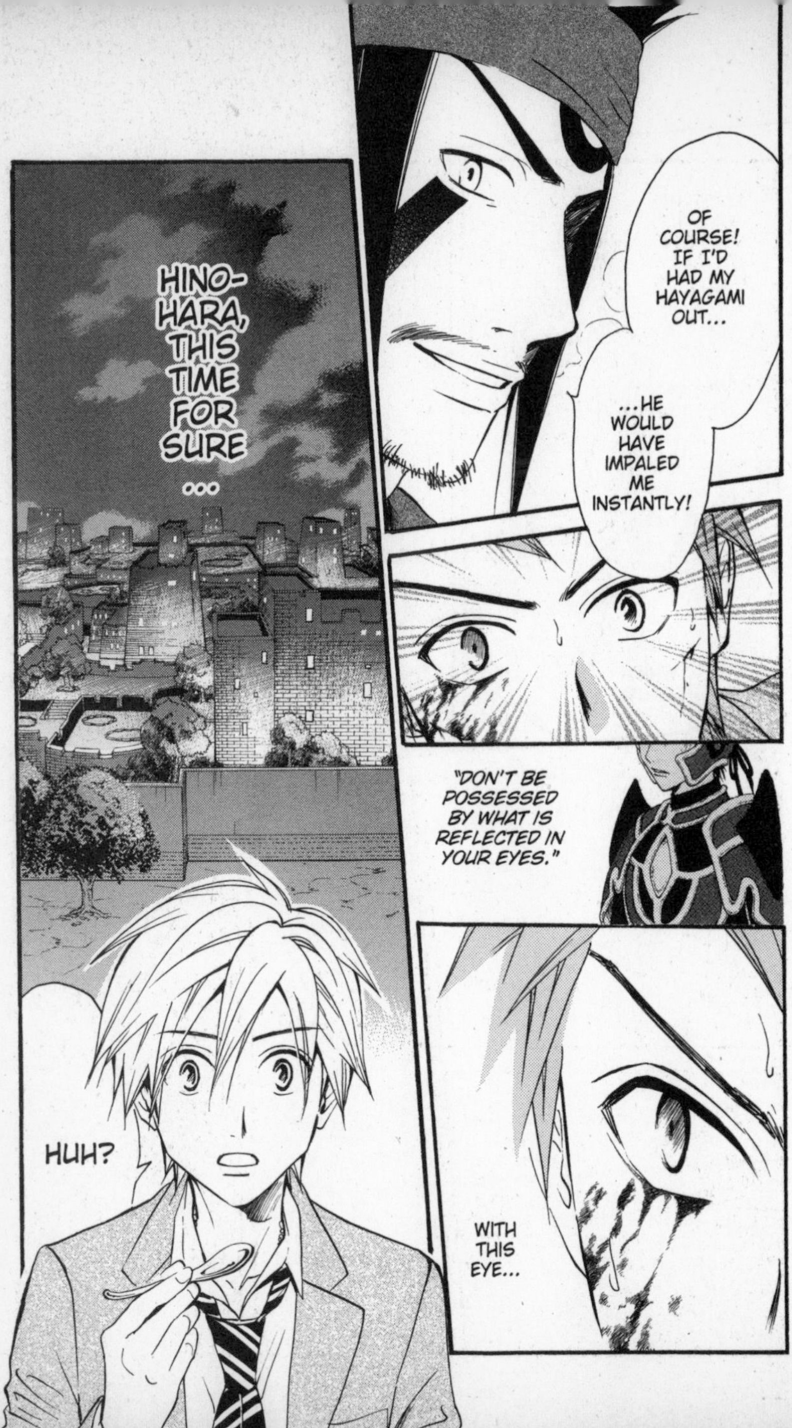
OF COURSE! IF I'D HAD MY HAYAGAMI OUT...
...HE WOULD HAVE IMPALED ME INSTANTLY!
"DON'T BE POSSESSED BY WHAT IS REFLECTED IN YOUR EYES."
WITH THIS EYE...
HINO-HARA, THIS TIME FOR SURE...
HUH?

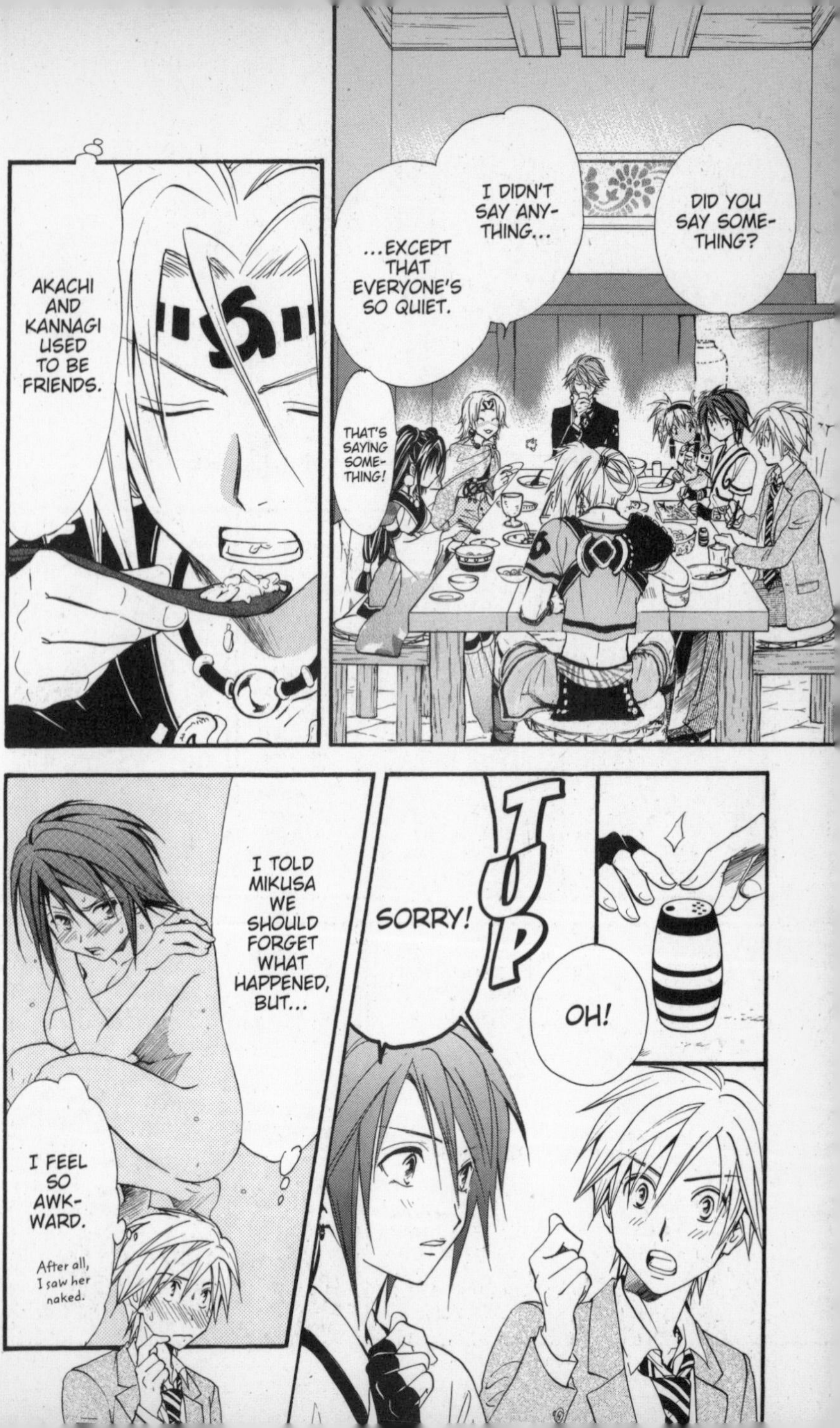
DID YOU SAY SOME-THING?
I DIDN'T SAY ANY-THING...
...EXCEPT THAT EVERYONE'S SO QUIET.
THAT'S SAYING SOME-THING!
AKACHI AND KANNAGI USED TO BE FRIENDS.
OH!
TUP
SORRY!
I TOLD MIKUSA WE SHOULD FORGET WHAT HAPPENED, BUT...
I FEEL SO AWK-WARD.
After all, I saw her naked.

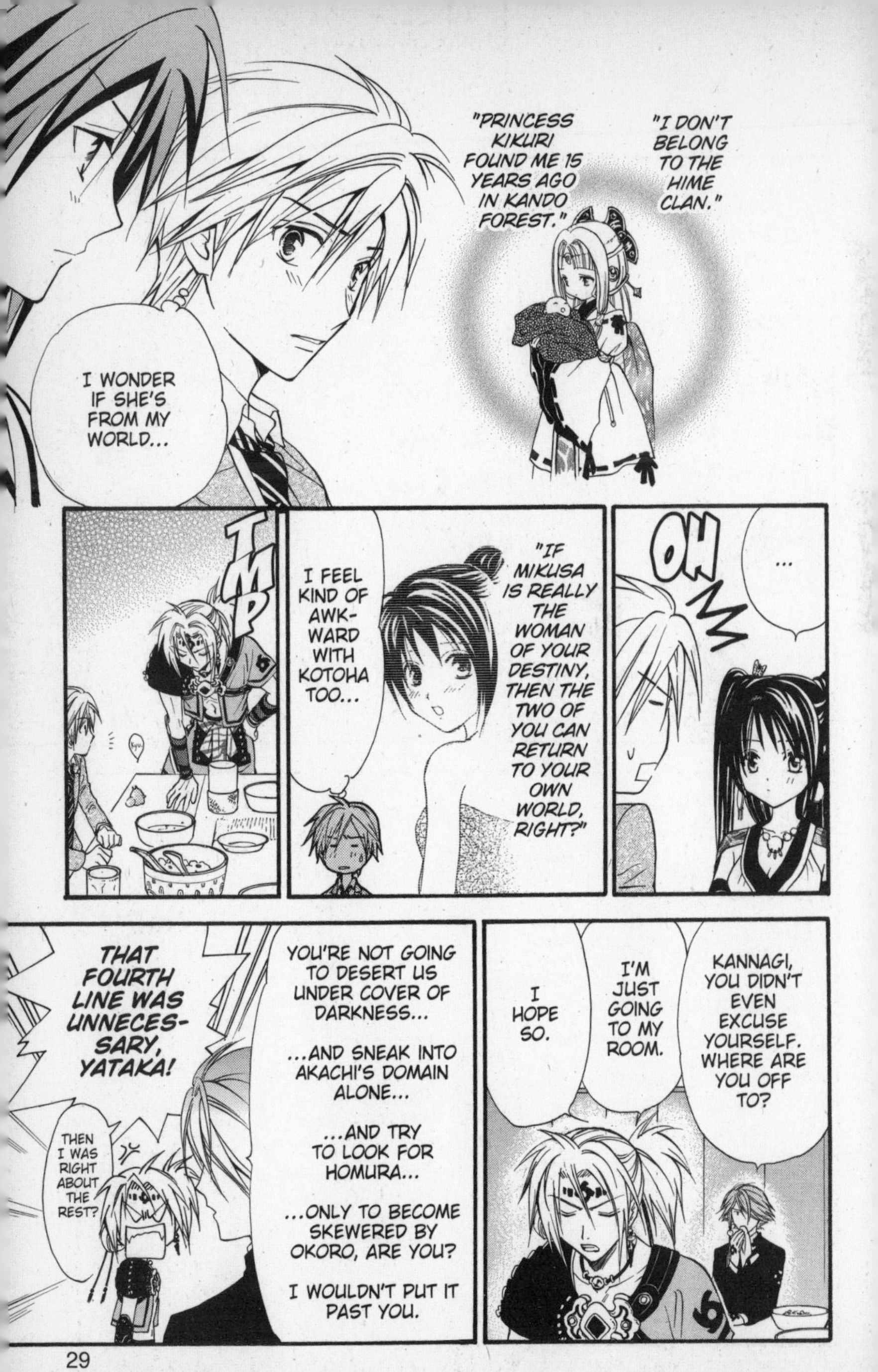
"I DON'T BELONG TO THE HIME CLAN."
"PRINCESS KIKURI FOUND ME 15 YEARS AGO IN KANDO FOREST."
I WONDER IF SHE'S FROM MY WORLD...
...
OHM
"IF MIKUSA IS REALLY THE WOMAN OF YOUR DESTINY, THEN THE TWO OF YOU CAN RETURN TO YOUR OWN WORLD, RIGHT?"
I FEEL KIND OF AWK-WARD WITH KOTOHA TOO...
TMP
Kyu
KANNAGI, YOU DIDN'T EVEN EXCUSE YOURSELF. WHERE ARE YOU OFF TO?
I'M JUST GOING TO MY ROOM.
I HOPE SO.
YOU'RE NOT GOING TO DESERT US UNDER COVER OF DARKNESS... ...AND SNEAK INTO AKACHI'S DOMAIN ALONE... ...AND TRY TO LOOK FOR HOMURA... ...ONLY TO BECOME SKEWERED BY OKORO, ARE YOU? I WOULDN'T PUT IT PAST YOU.
THAT FOURTH LINE WAS UNNECES-SARY, YATAKA!
THEN I WAS RIGHT ABOUT THE REST?

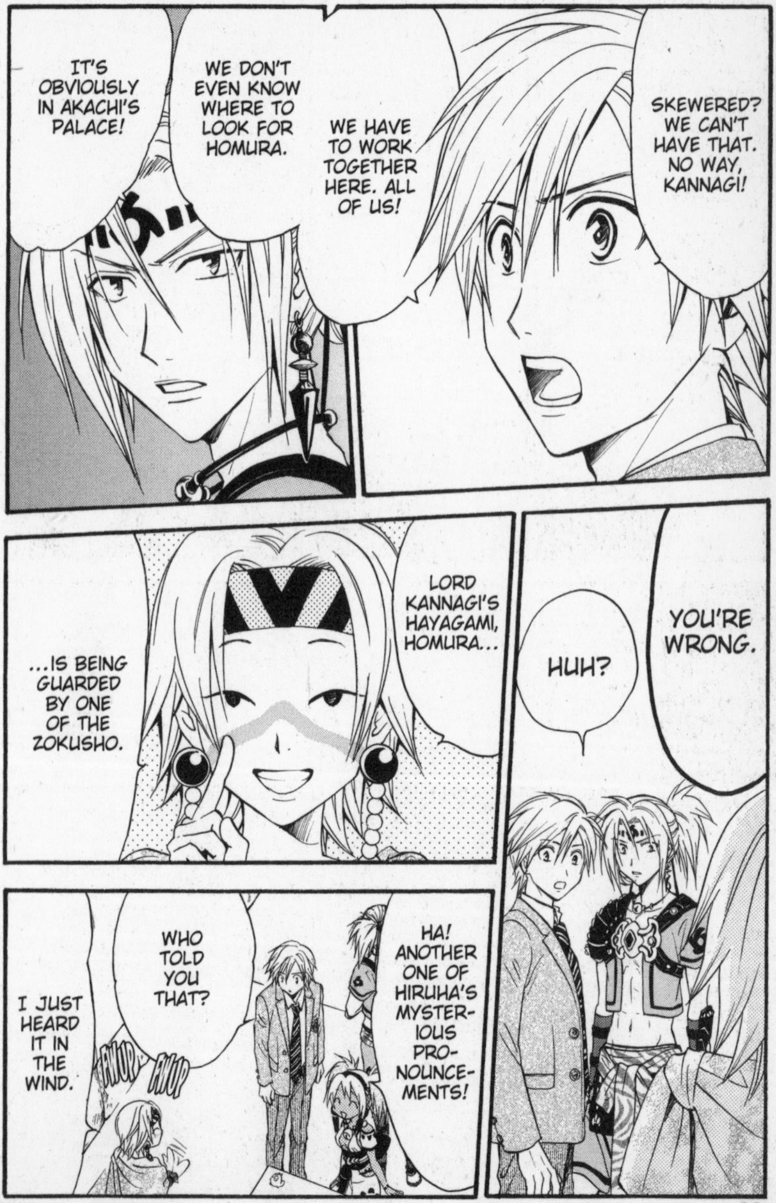
SKEWERED? WE CAN'T HAVE THAT. NO WAY, KANNAGI!
WE HAVE TO WORK TOGETHER HERE. ALL OF US!
WE DON'T EVEN KNOW WHERE TO LOOK FOR HOMURA.
IT'S OBVIOUSLY IN AKACHI'S PALACE!
YOU'RE WRONG.
HUH?
LORD KANNAGI'S HAYAGAMI, HOMURA...
...IS BEING GUARDED BY ONE OF THE ZOKUSHO.
HA! ANOTHER ONE OF HIRUHA'S MYSTERIOUS PRONOUNCEMENTS!
WHO TOLD YOU THAT?
I JUST HEARD IT IN THE WIND.

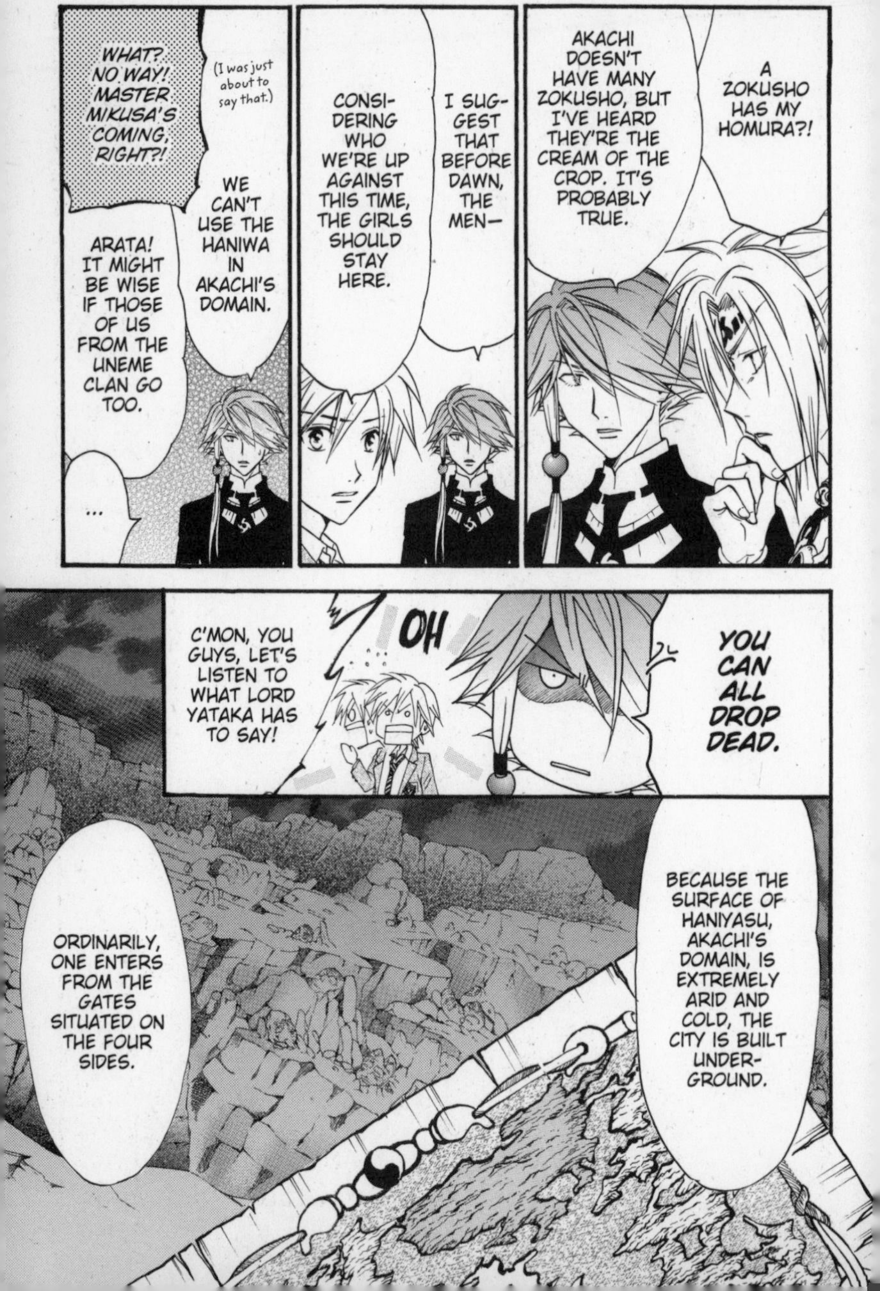
A ZOKUSHO HAS MY HOMURA?!
AKACHI DOESN'T HAVE MANY ZOKUSHO, BUT I'VE HEARD THEY'RE THE CREAM OF THE CROP. IT'S PROBABLY TRUE.
I SUGGEST THAT BEFORE DAWN, THE MEN—
CONSIDERING WHO WE'RE UP AGAINST THIS TIME, THE GIRLS SHOULD STAY HERE.
WE CAN'T USE THE HANIWA IN AKACHI'S DOMAIN.
(I was just about to say that.)
WHAT? NO WAY! MASTER MIKUSA'S COMING, RIGHT?!
ARATA! IT MIGHT BE WISE IF THOSE OF US FROM THE UNEME CLAN GO TOO.
...
YOU CAN ALL DROP DEAD.
OH
C'MON, YOU GUYS, LET'S LISTEN TO WHAT LORD YATAKA HAS TO SAY!
BECAUSE THE SURFACE OF HANIYASU, AKACHI'S DOMAIN, IS EXTREMELY ARID AND COLD, THE CITY IS BUILT UNDERGROUND.
ORDINARILY, ONE ENTERS FROM THE GATES SITUATED ON THE FOUR SIDES.

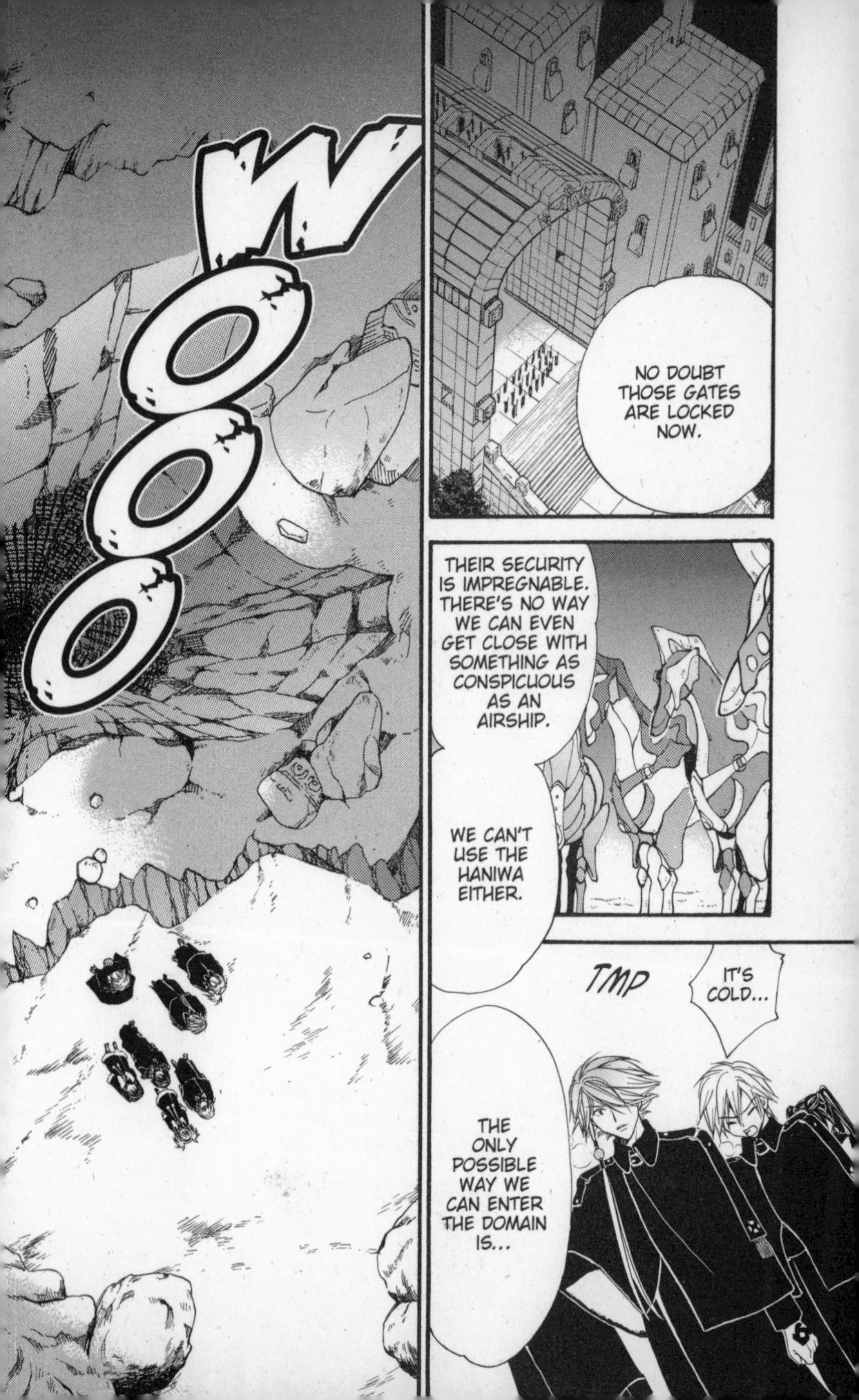
NO DOUBT THOSE GATES ARE LOCKED NOW.
THEIR SECURITY IS IMPREGNABLE. THERE'S NO WAY WE CAN EVEN GET CLOSE WITH SOMETHING AS CONSPICUOUS AS AN AIRSHIP.
WE CAN'T USE THE HANIWA EITHER.
IT'S COLD...
TMP
THE ONLY POSSIBLE WAY WE CAN ENTER THE DOMAIN IS...
WOOO

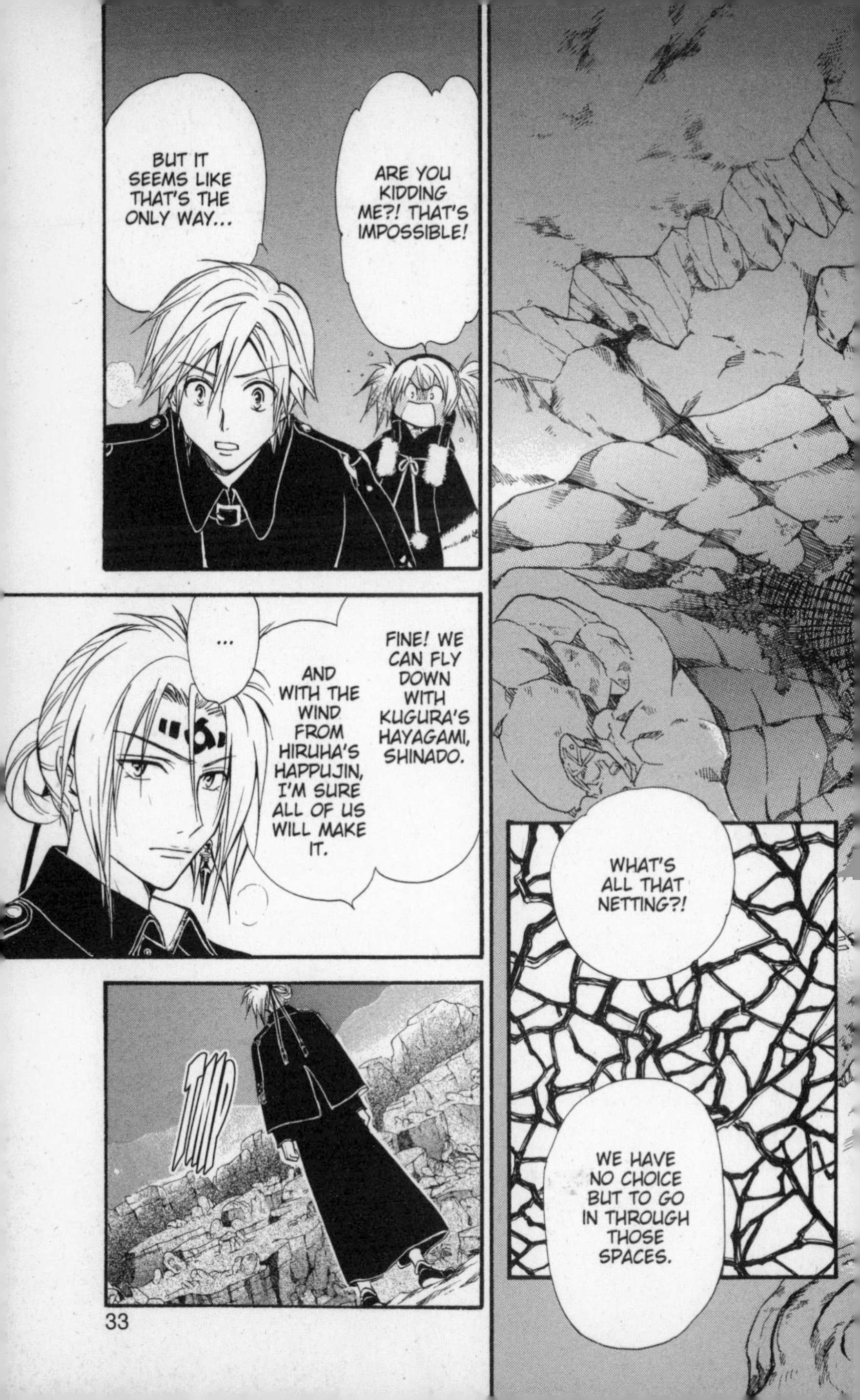
WHAT'S ALL THAT NETTING?!
WE HAVE NO CHOICE BUT TO GO IN THROUGH THOSE SPACES.
ARE YOU KIDDING ME?! THAT'S IMPOSSIBLE!
BUT IT SEEMS LIKE THAT'S THE ONLY WAY...
FINE! WE CAN FLY DOWN WITH KUGURA'S HAYAGAMI, SHINADO.
AND WITH THE WIND FROM HIRUHA'S HAPPUJIN, I'M SURE ALL OF US WILL MAKE IT.
...

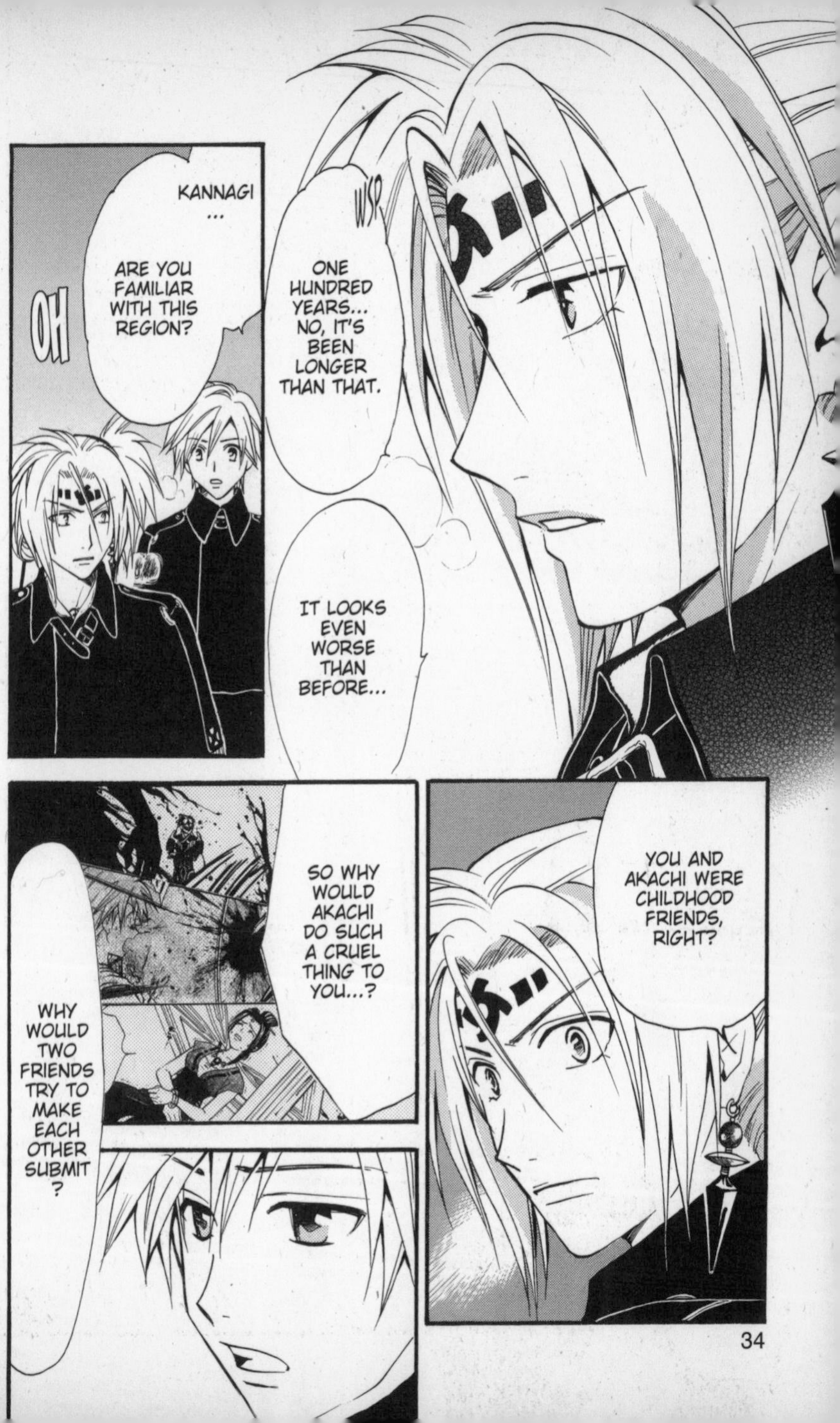
WSP
ONE HUNDRED YEARS... NO, IT'S BEEN LONGER THAN THAT.
IT LOOKS EVEN WORSE THAN BEFORE...
KANNAGI ...
ARE YOU FAMILIAR WITH THIS REGION?
OH
YOU AND AKACHI WERE CHILDHOOD FRIENDS, RIGHT?
SO WHY WOULD AKACHI DO SUCH A CRUEL THING TO YOU...?
WHY WOULD TWO FRIENDS TRY TO MAKE EACH OTHER SUBMIT ?

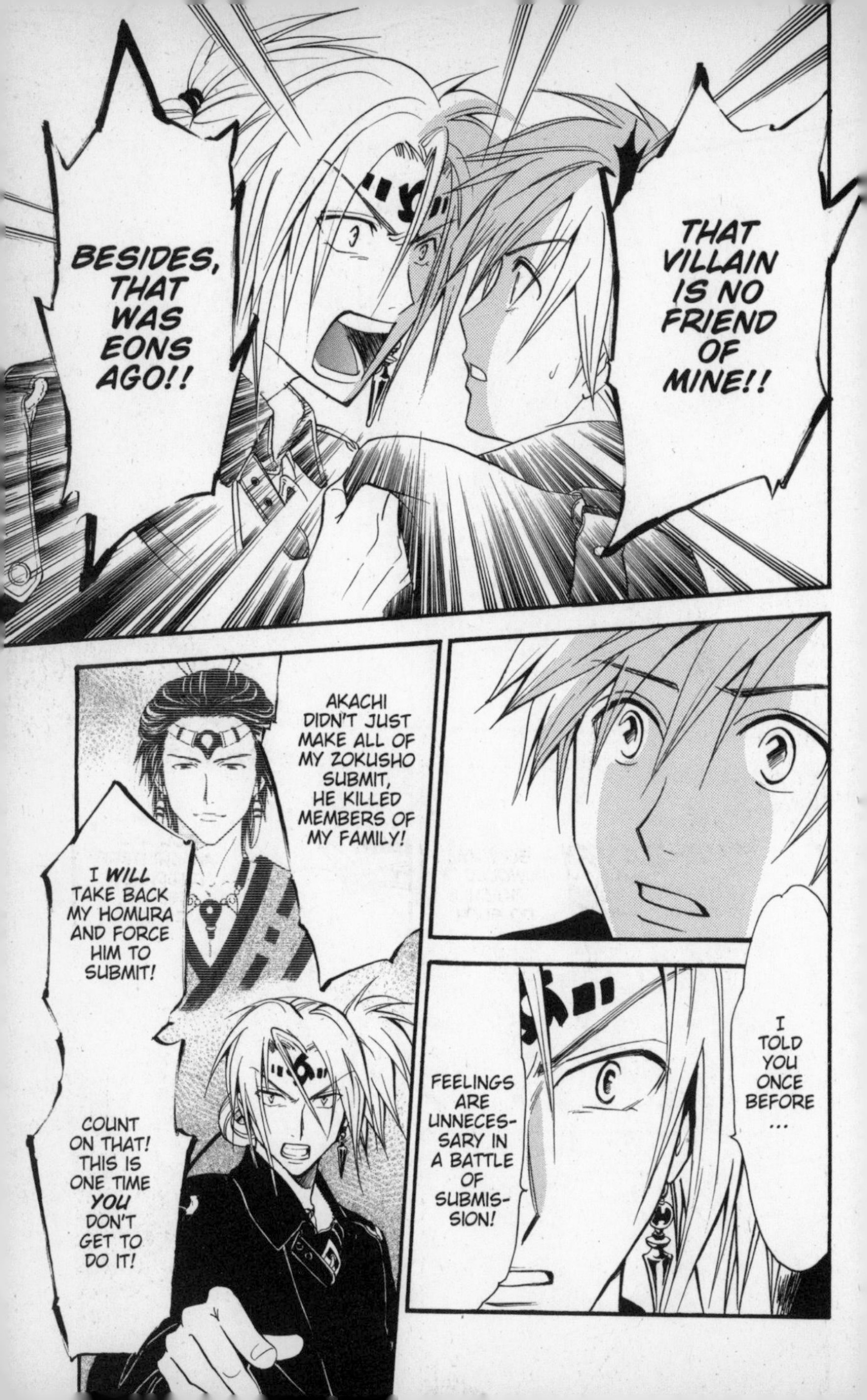
THAT VILLAIN IS NO FRIEND OF MINE!!
BESIDES, THAT WAS EONS AGO!!
I TOLD YOU ONCE BEFORE...
FEELINGS ARE UNNECES-SARY IN A BATTLE OF SUBMIS-SION!
AKACHI DIDN'T JUST MAKE ALL OF MY ZOKUSHO SUBMIT, HE KILLED MEMBERS OF MY FAMILY!
I *WILL* TAKE BACK MY HOMURA AND FORCE HIM TO SUBMIT!
COUNT ON THAT! THIS IS ONE TIME *YOU* DON'T GET TO DO IT!

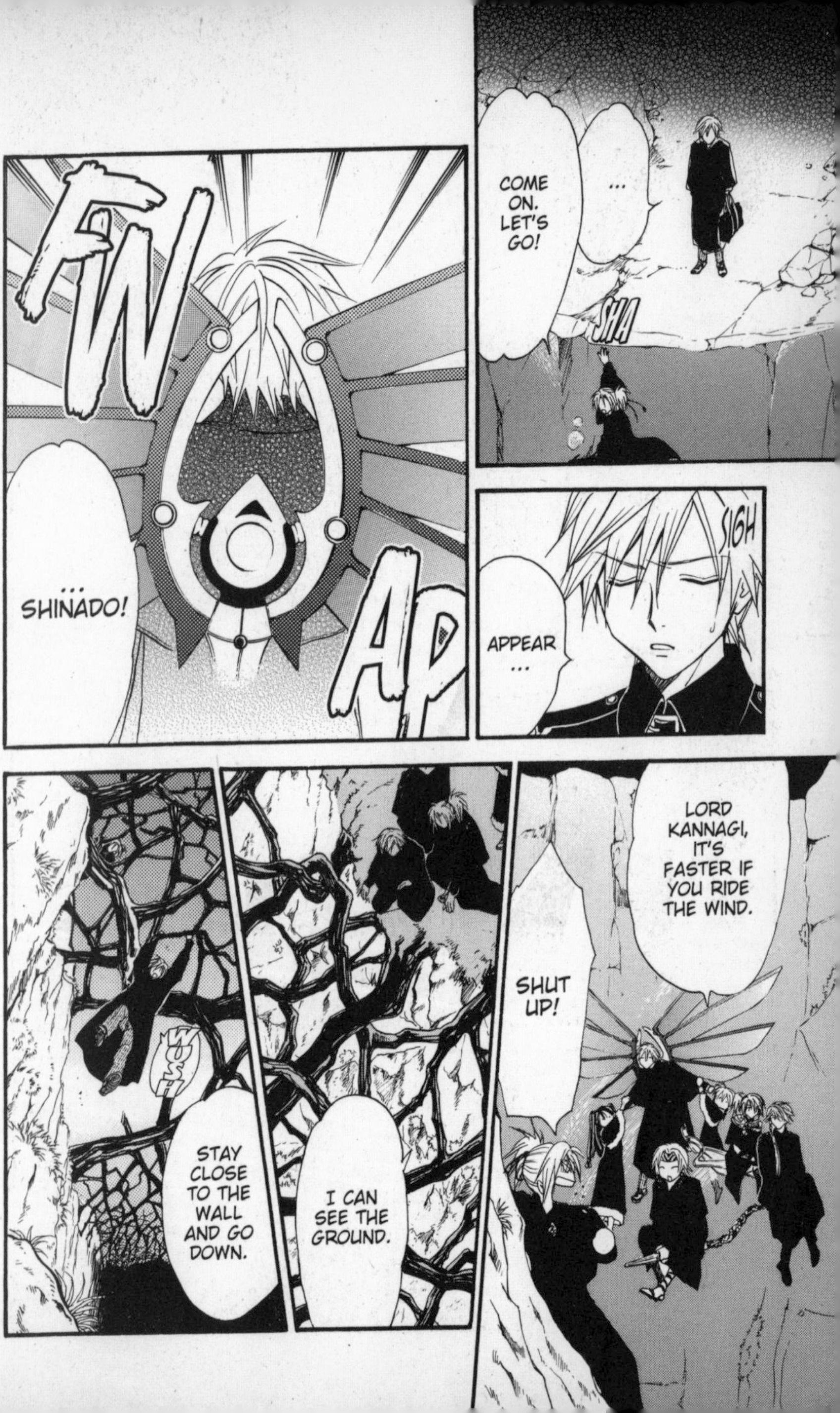
...
COME ON. LET'S GO!
SHA
SIGH
APPEAR...
FW
...SHINADO!
AP
LORD KANNAGI, IT'S FASTER IF YOU RIDE THE WIND.
SHUT UP!
I CAN SEE THE GROUND.
WUSH
STAY CLOSE TO THE WALL AND GO DOWN.

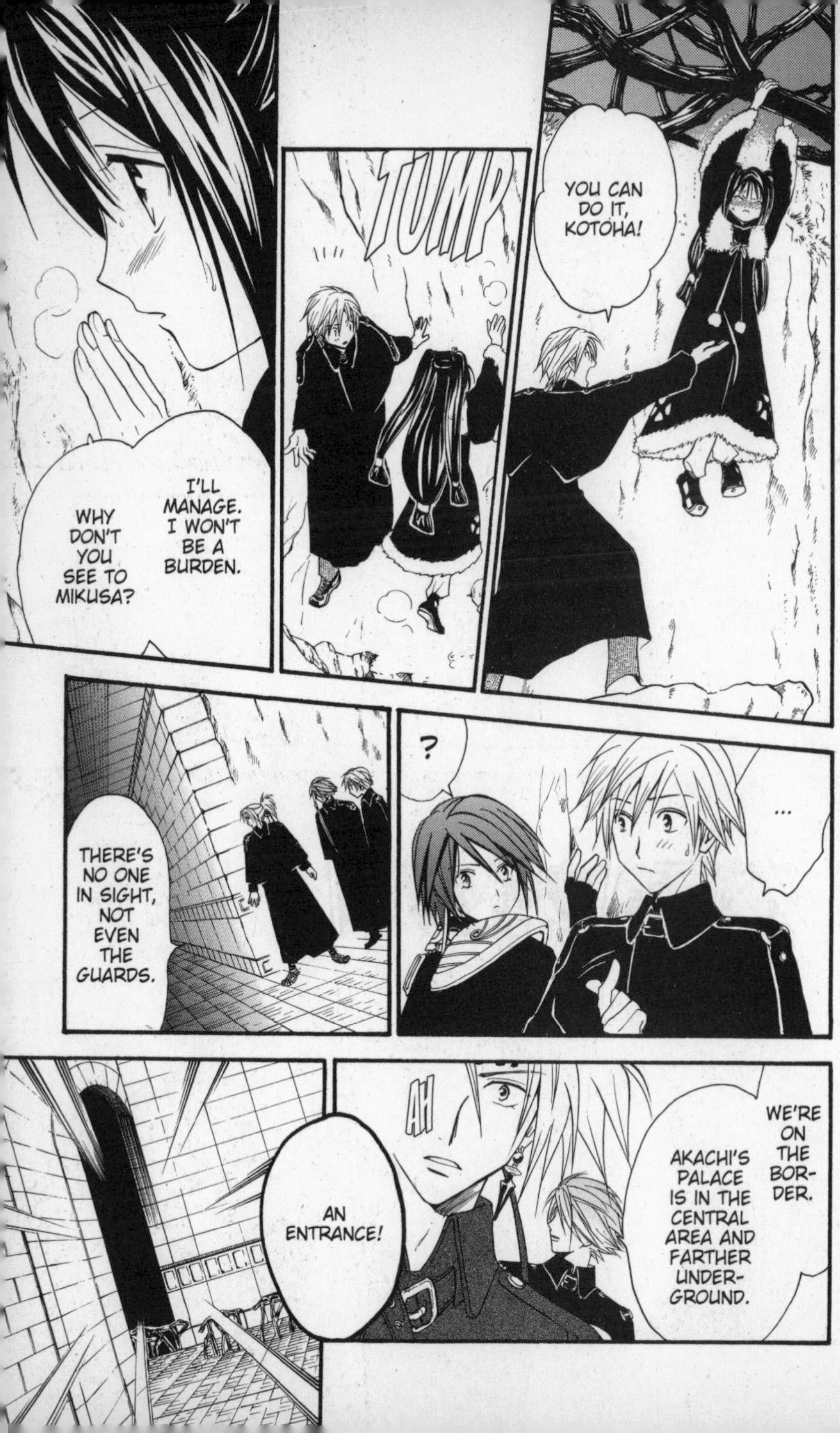
YOU CAN DO IT, KOTOHA!
JUMP
I'LL MANAGE. I WON'T BE A BURDEN.
WHY DON'T YOU SEE TO MIKUSA?
?
...
THERE'S NO ONE IN SIGHT, NOT EVEN THE GUARDS.
WE'RE ON THE BORDER.
AKACHI'S PALACE IS IN THE CENTRAL AREA AND FARTHER UNDERGROUND.
AH
AN ENTRANCE!

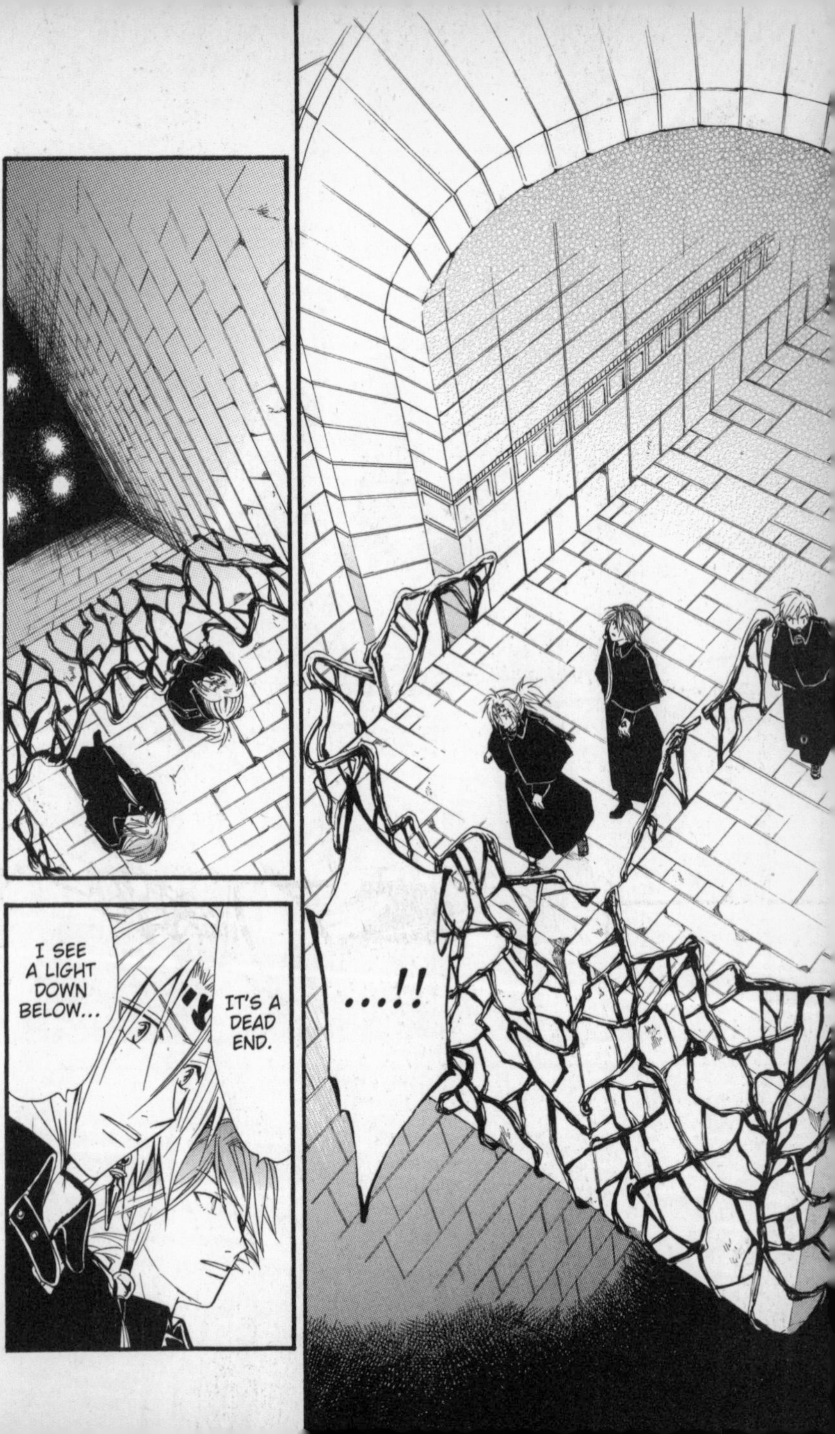
...!!
IT'S A DEAD END.
I SEE A LIGHT DOWN BELOW...

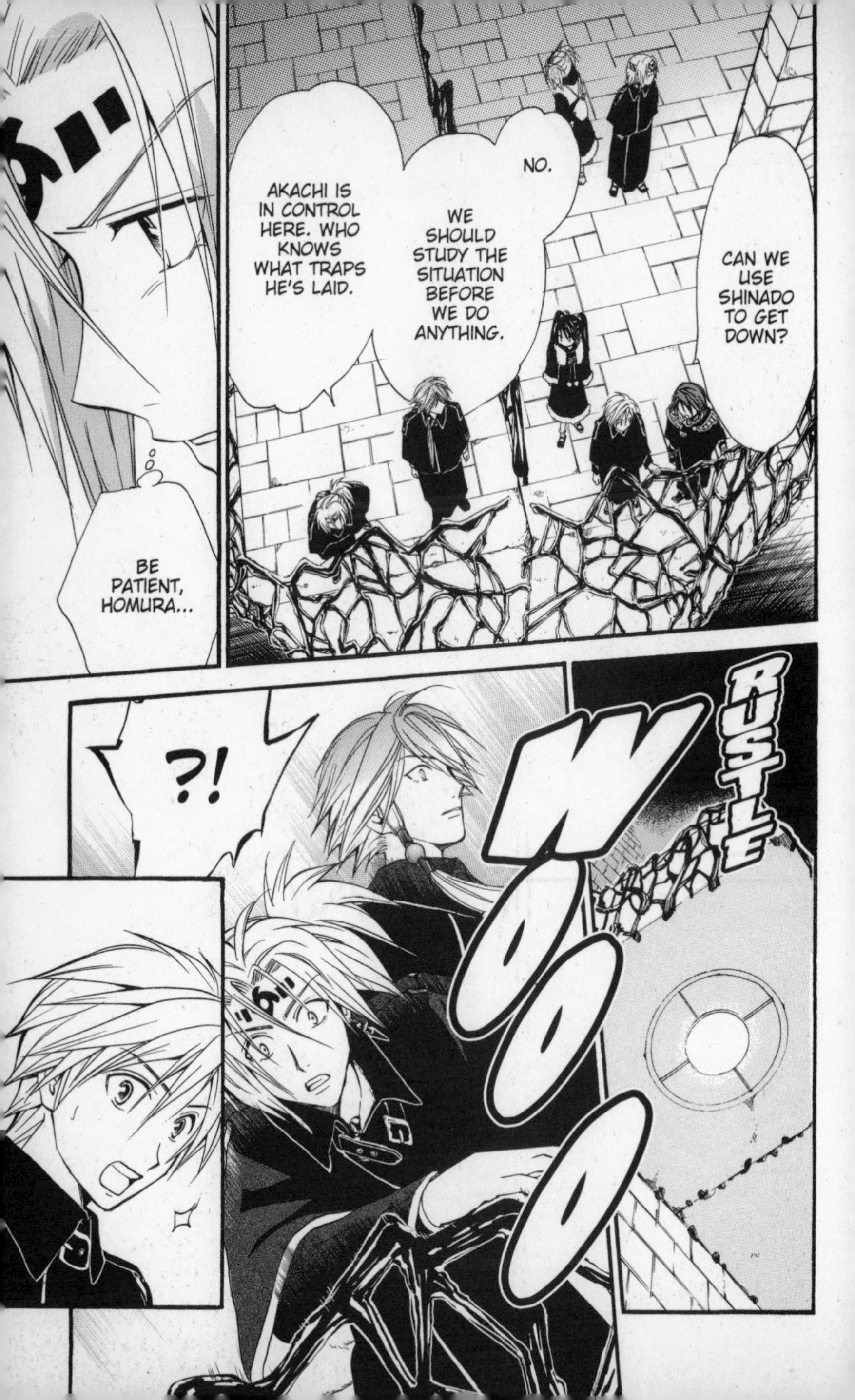
CAN WE USE SHINADO TO GET DOWN?
NO.
WE SHOULD STUDY THE SITUATION BEFORE WE DO ANYTHING.
AKACHI IS IN CONTROL HERE. WHO KNOWS WHAT TRAPS HE'S LAID.
BE PATIENT, HOMURA...
RUSTLE
WOOOO
?!

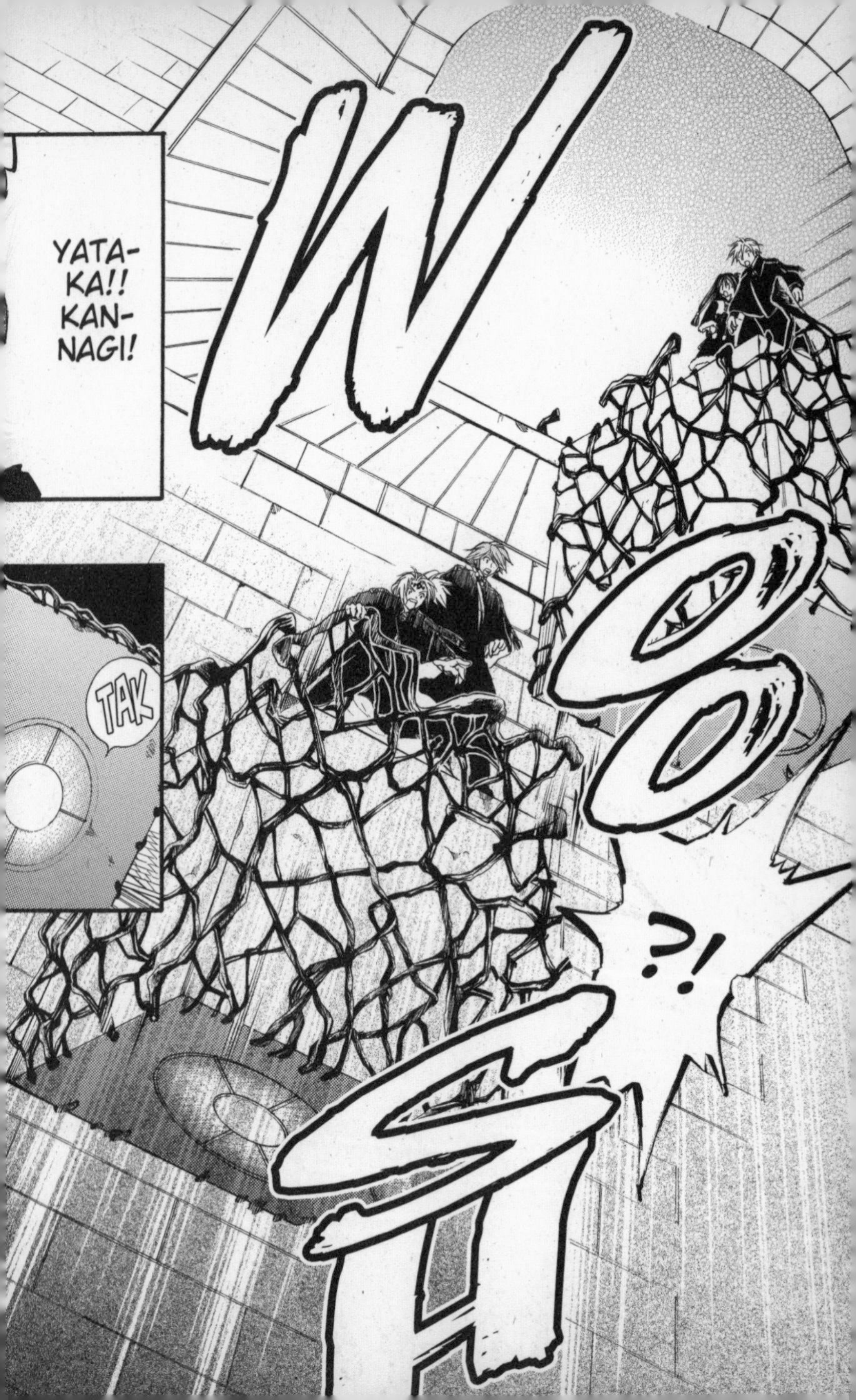
WOOSH
?!
YATA-KA!! KAN-NAGI!
TAK

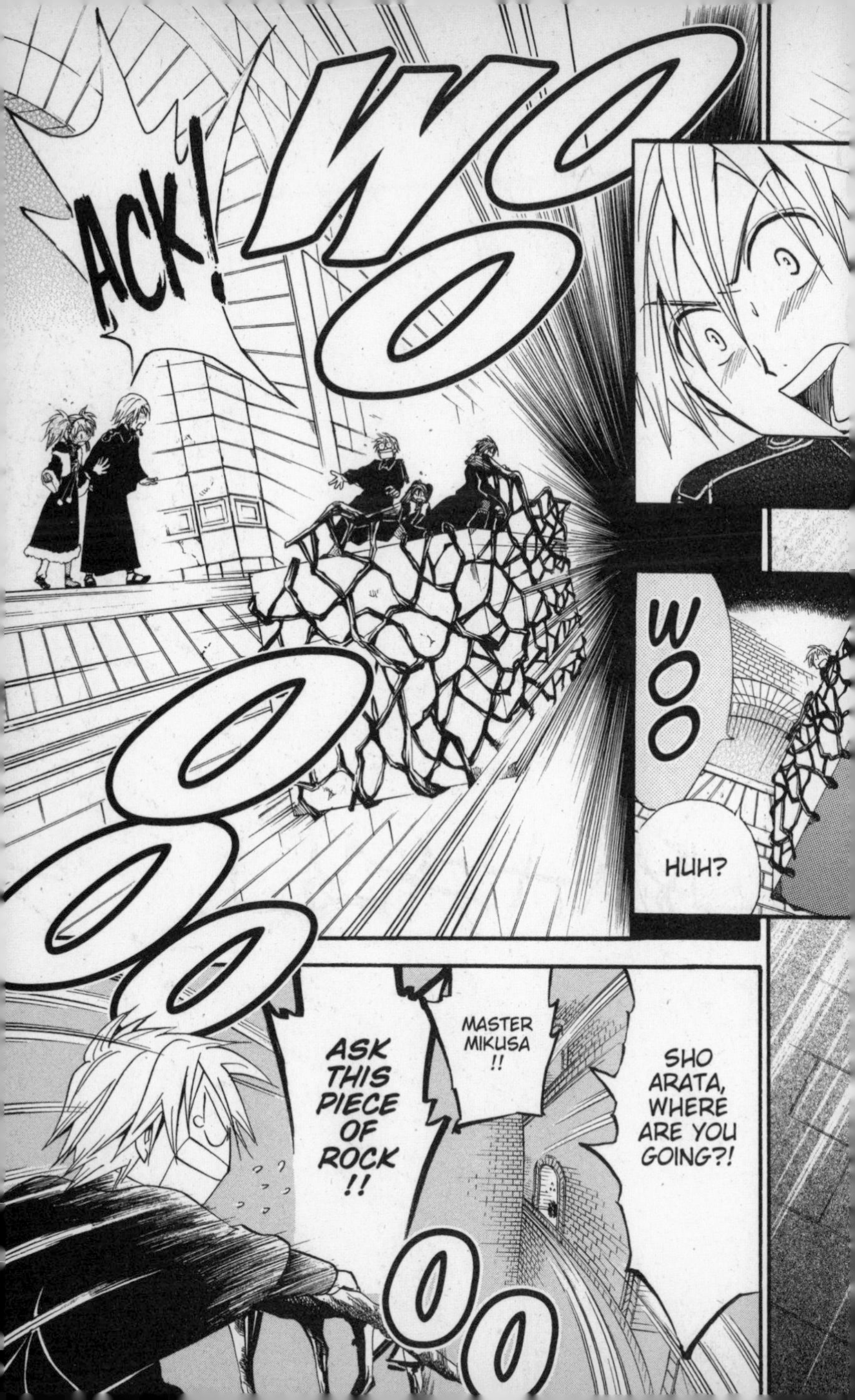

WOO
HUH?
WOOOO
ACK!
SHO ARATA, WHERE ARE YOU GOING?!
MASTER MIKUSA !!
ASK THIS PIECE OF ROCK !!
OOO

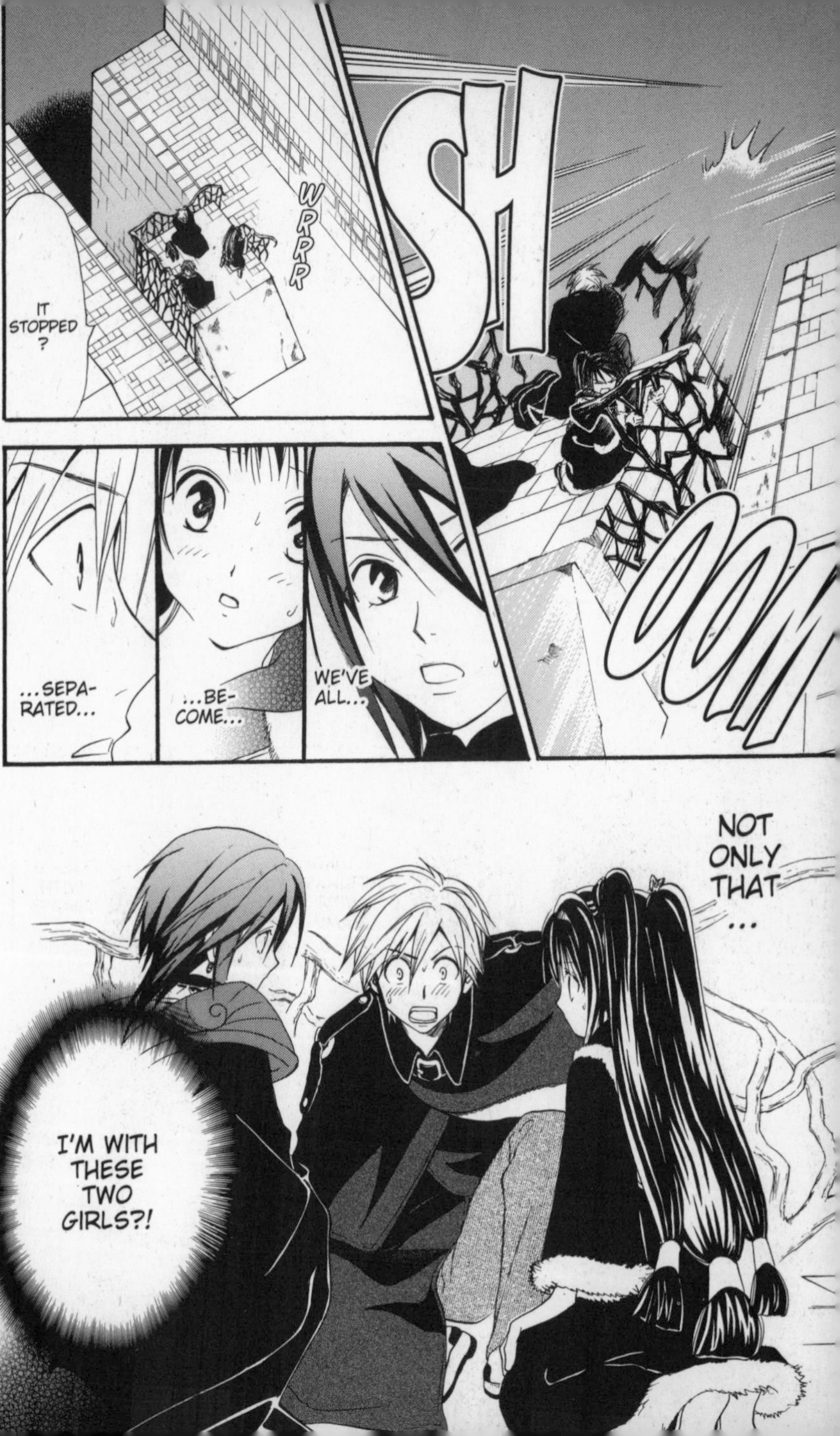
SH
OOM
WRRR
IT STOPPED?
WE'VE ALL...
...BE-COME...
...SEPA-RATED...
NOT ONLY THAT...
I'M WITH THESE TWO GIRLS?!

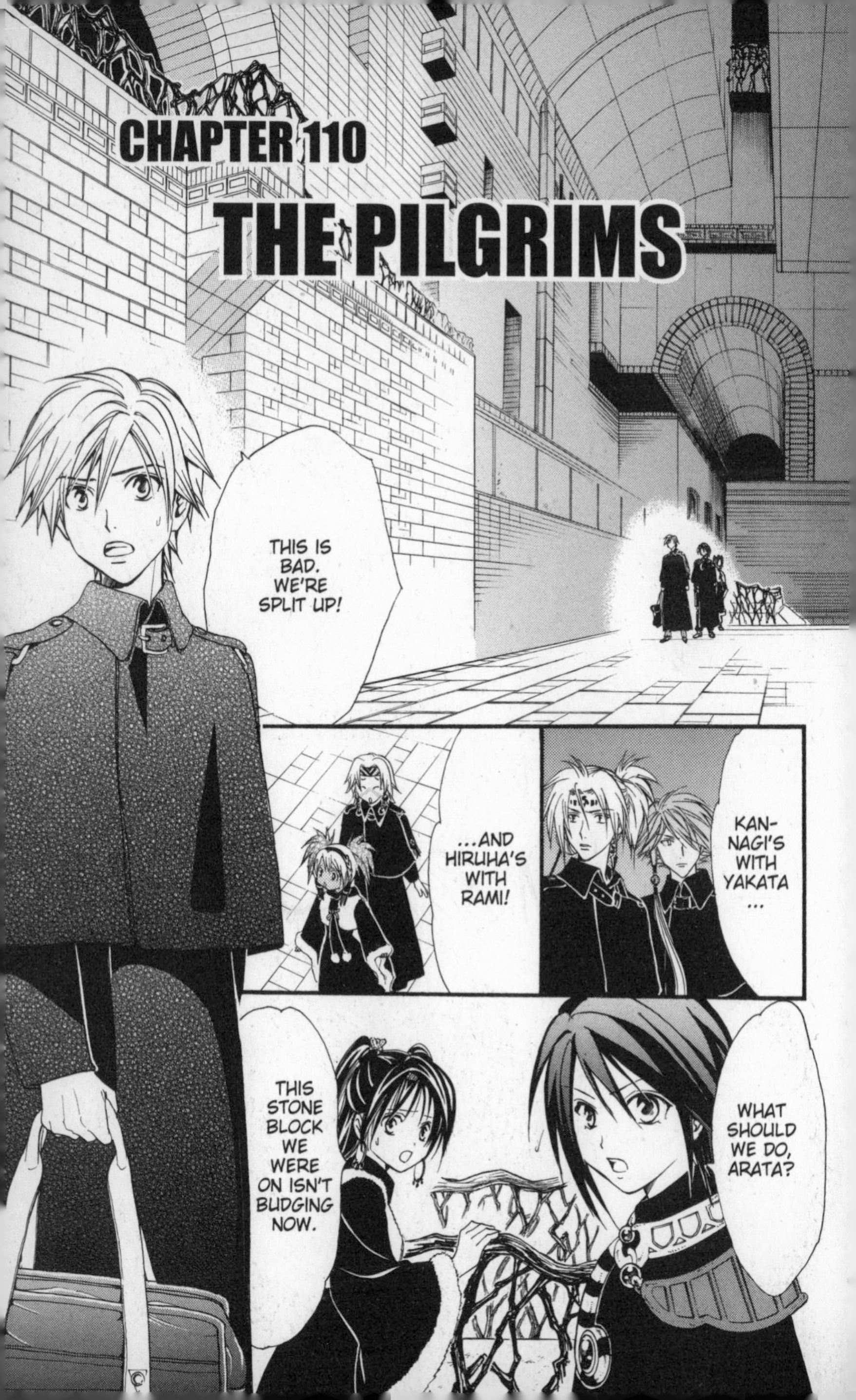
CHAPTER 110
THE PILGRIMS
THIS IS BAD. WE'RE SPLIT UP!
KAN-NAGI'S WITH YAKATA...
...AND HIRUHA'S WITH RAMI!
WHAT SHOULD WE DO, ARATA?
THIS STONE BLOCK WE WERE ON ISN'T BUDGING NOW.

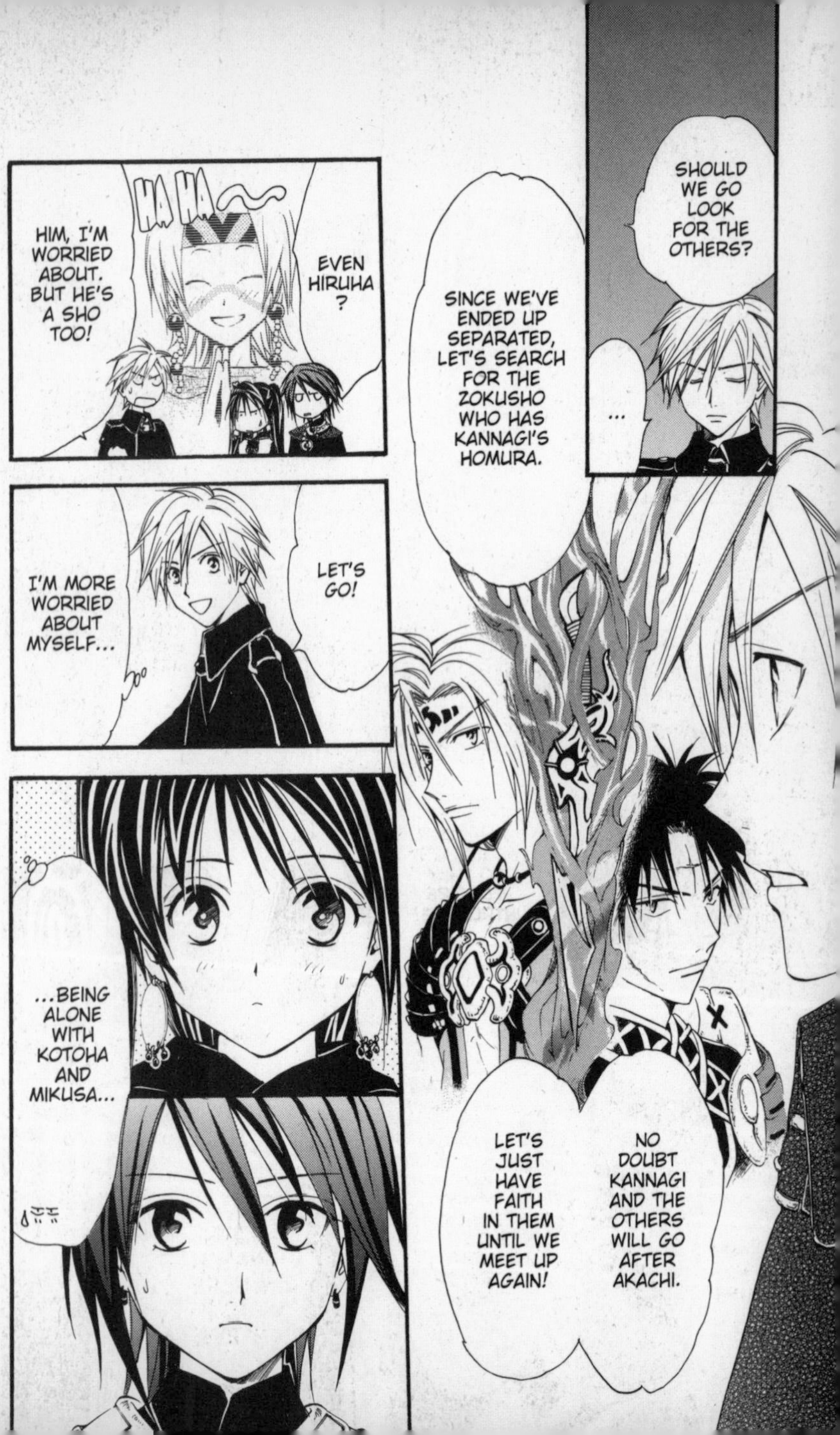
SHOULD WE GO LOOK FOR THE OTHERS?
...
SINCE WE'VE ENDED UP SEPARATED, LET'S SEARCH FOR THE ZOKUSHO WHO HAS KANNAGI'S HOMURA.
NO DOUBT KANNAGI AND THE OTHERS WILL GO AFTER AKACHI.
LET'S JUST HAVE FAITH IN THEM UNTIL WE MEET UP AGAIN!
HA HA~
EVEN HIRUHA?
HIM, I'M WORRIED ABOUT. BUT HE'S A SHO TOO!
LET'S GO!
I'M MORE WORRIED ABOUT MYSELF...
...BEING ALONE WITH KOTOHA AND MIKUSA...

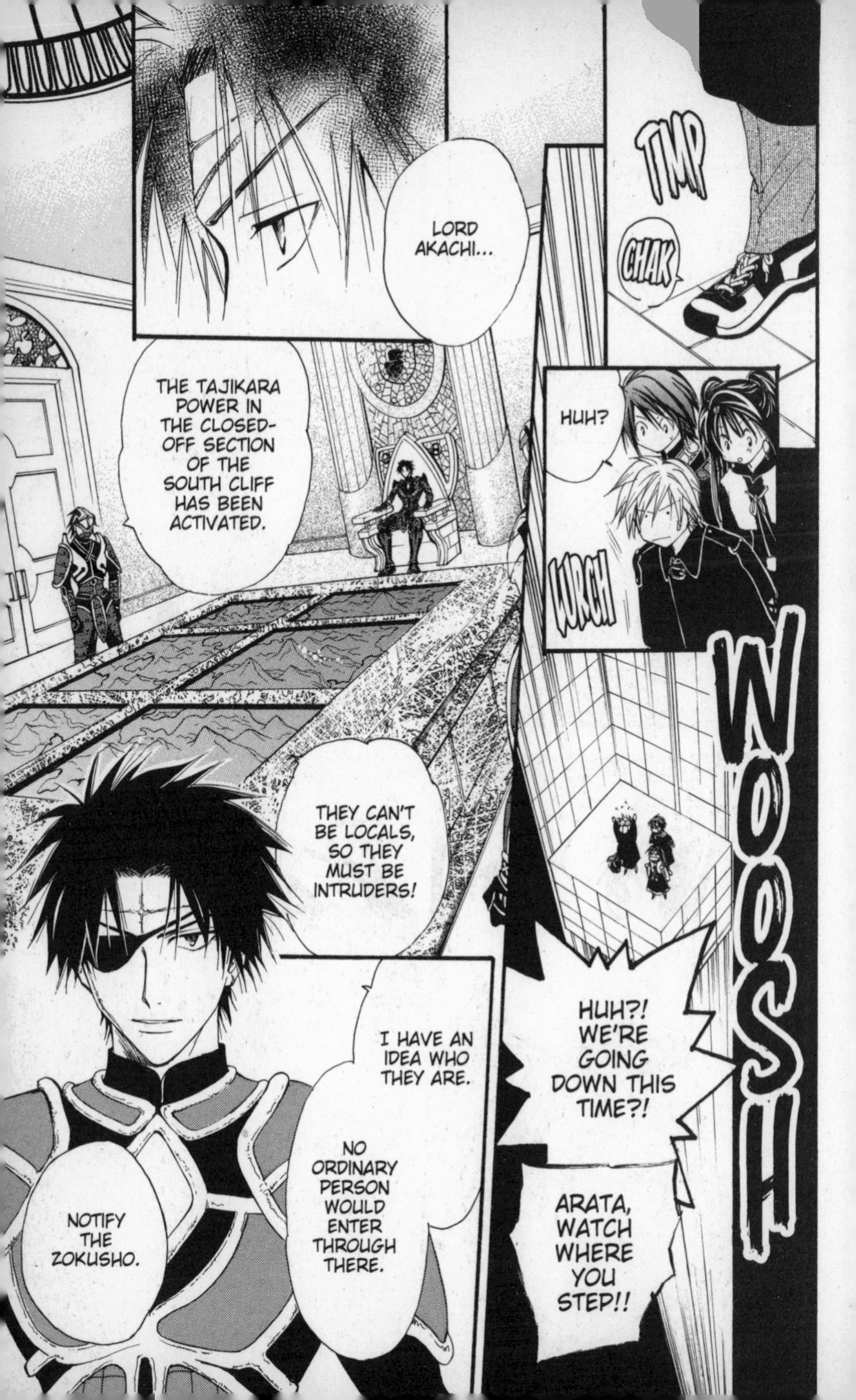
TMP
CHAK
HUH?
WORCH
WOOSH
HUH?! WE'RE GOING DOWN THIS TIME?!
ARATA, WATCH WHERE YOU STEP!!
LORD AKACHI...
THE TAJIKARA POWER IN THE CLOSED-OFF SECTION OF THE SOUTH CLIFF HAS BEEN ACTIVATED.
THEY CAN'T BE LOCALS, SO THEY MUST BE INTRUDERS!
I HAVE AN IDEA WHO THEY ARE.
NO ORDINARY PERSON WOULD ENTER THROUGH THERE.
NOTIFY THE ZOKUSHO.

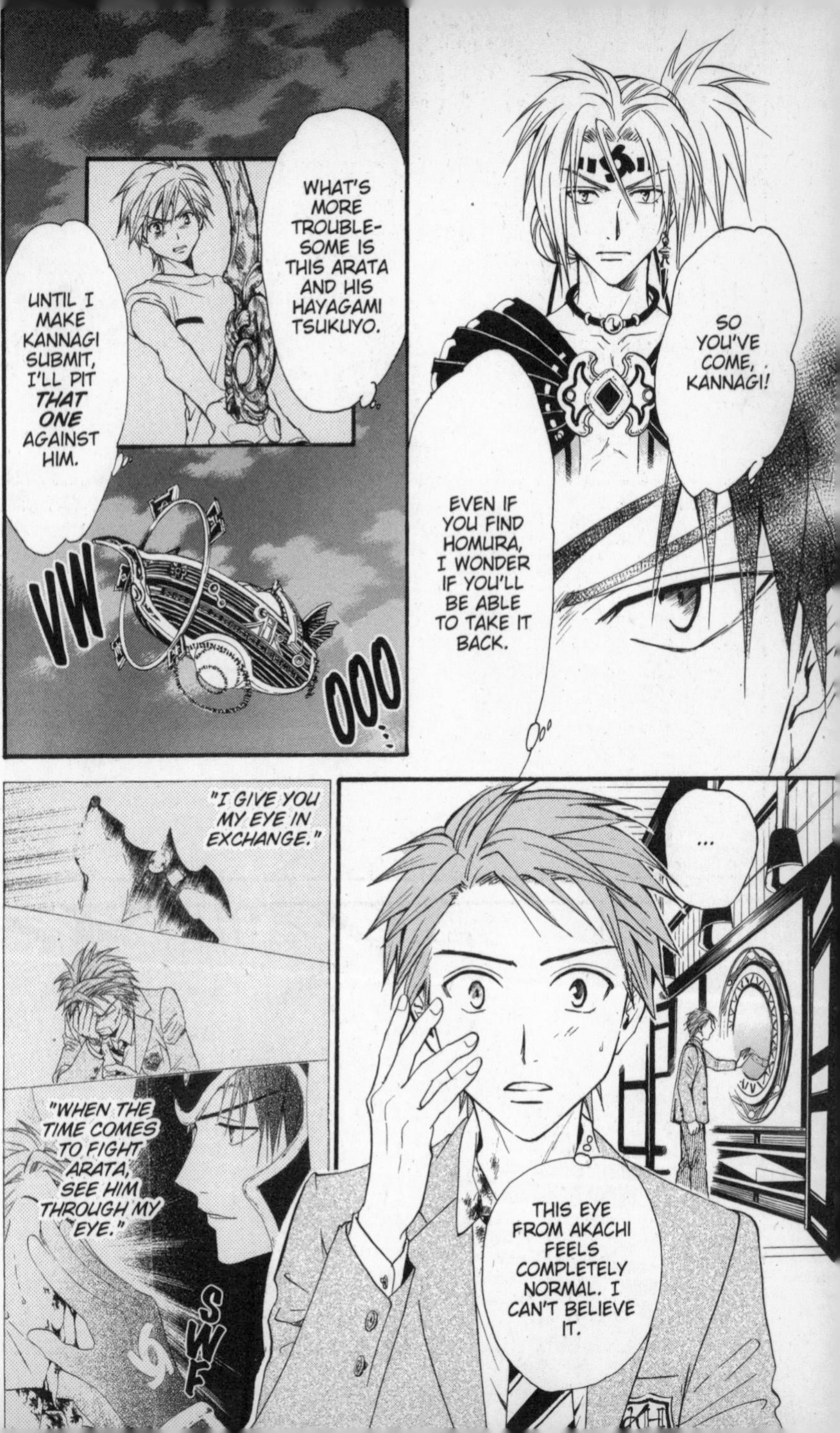
SO YOU'VE COME, KANNAGI!
EVEN IF YOU FIND HOMURA, I WONDER IF YOU'LL BE ABLE TO TAKE IT BACK.
WHAT'S MORE TROUBLE-SOME IS THIS ARATA AND HIS HAYAGAMI TSUKUYO.
UNTIL I MAKE KANNAGI SUBMIT, I'LL PIT *THAT ONE* AGAINST HIM.
VWOOO
...
THIS EYE FROM AKACHI FEELS COMPLETELY NORMAL. I CAN'T BELIEVE IT.
"I GIVE YOU MY EYE IN EXCHANGE."
"WHEN THE TIME COMES TO FIGHT ARATA, SEE HIM THROUGH MY EYE."
SWF

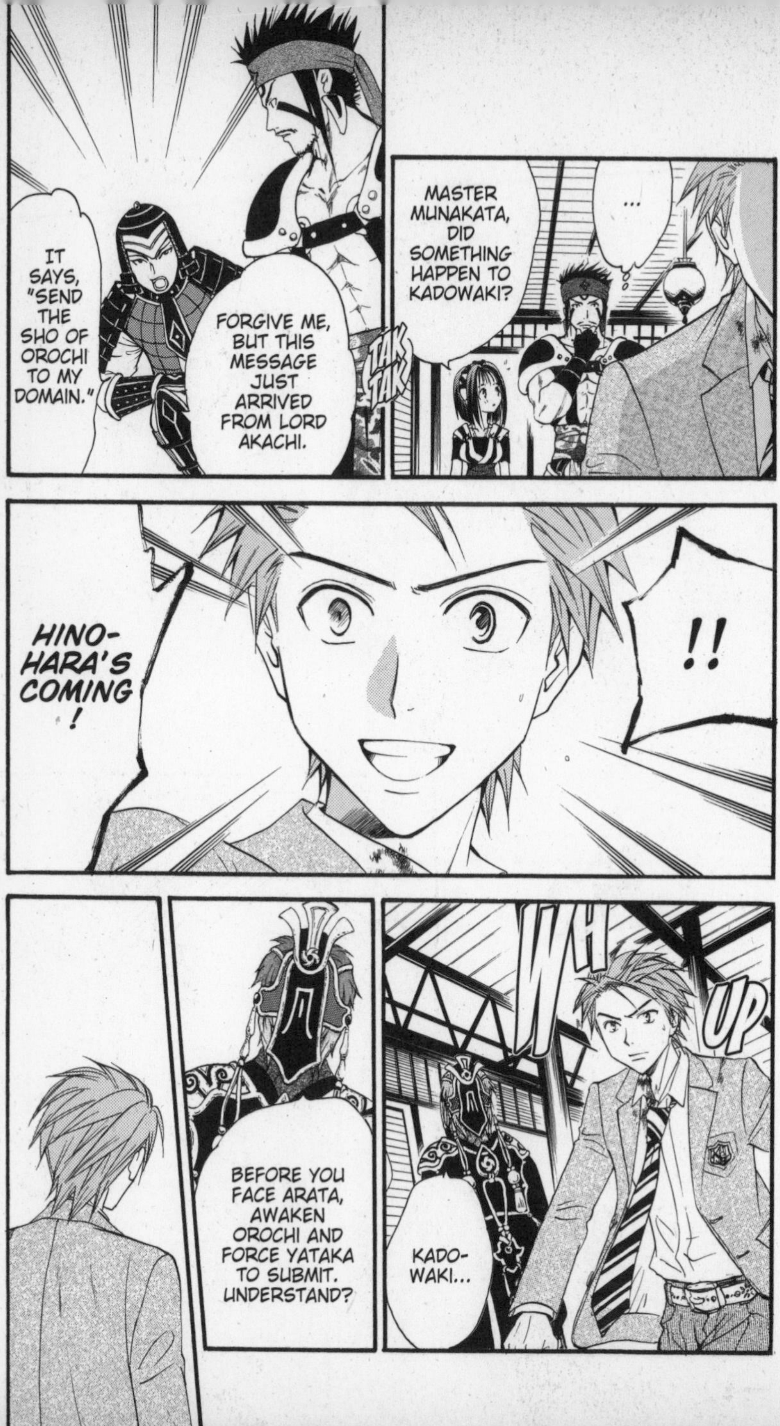
...
MASTER MUNAKATA, DID SOMETHING HAPPEN TO KADOWAKI?
TAK TAK
FORGIVE ME, BUT THIS MESSAGE JUST ARRIVED FROM LORD AKACHI.
IT SAYS, "SEND THE SHO OF OROCHI TO MY DOMAIN."
!!
HINO-HARA'S COMING!
WHUP
KADO-WAKI...
BEFORE YOU FACE ARATA, AWAKEN OROCHI AND FORCE YATAKA TO SUBMIT. UNDERSTAND?

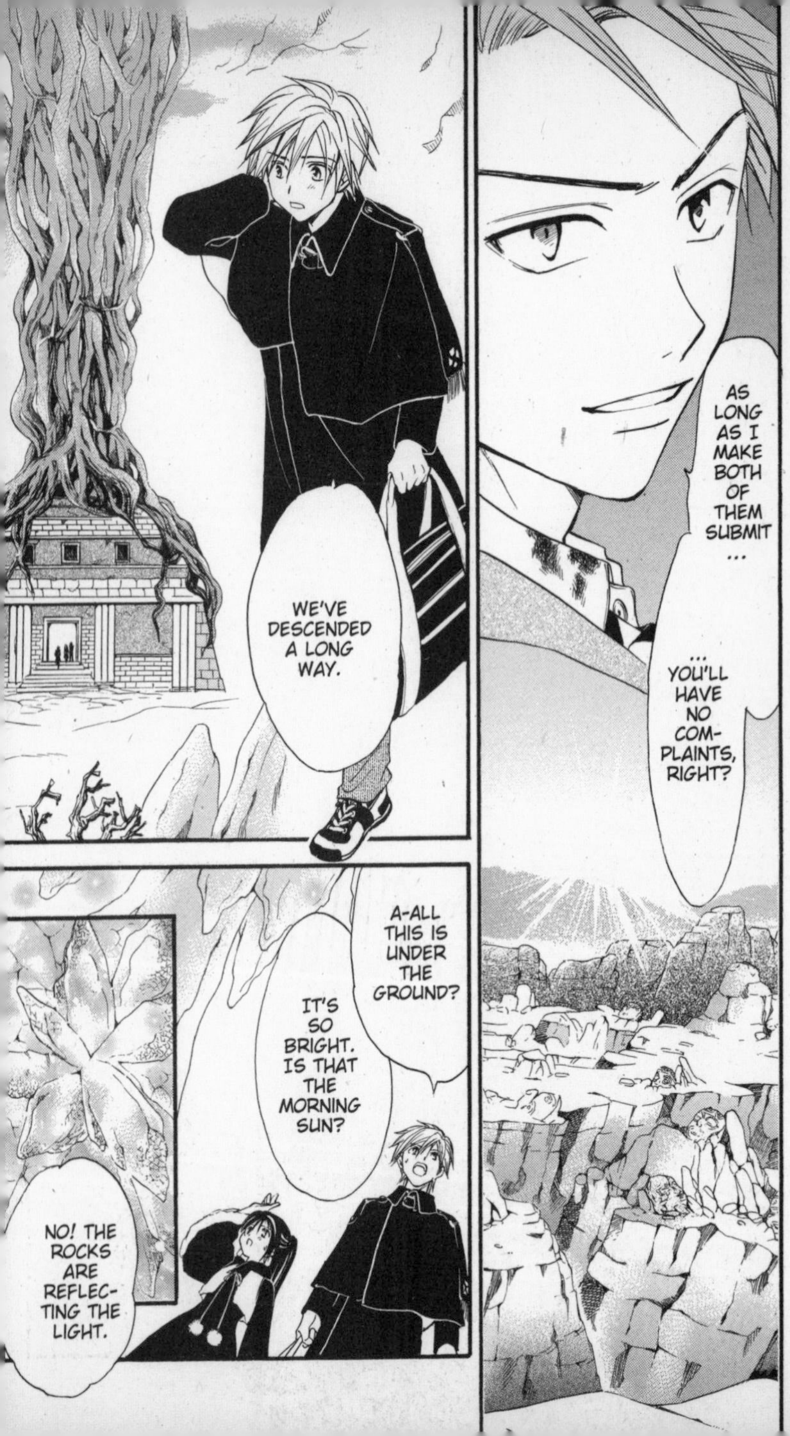
AS LONG AS I MAKE BOTH OF THEM SUBMIT...
...YOU'LL HAVE NO COMPLAINTS, RIGHT?
WE'VE DESCENDED A LONG WAY.
A-ALL THIS IS UNDER THE GROUND?
IT'S SO BRIGHT. IS THAT THE MORNING SUN?
NO! THE ROCKS ARE REFLECTING THE LIGHT.

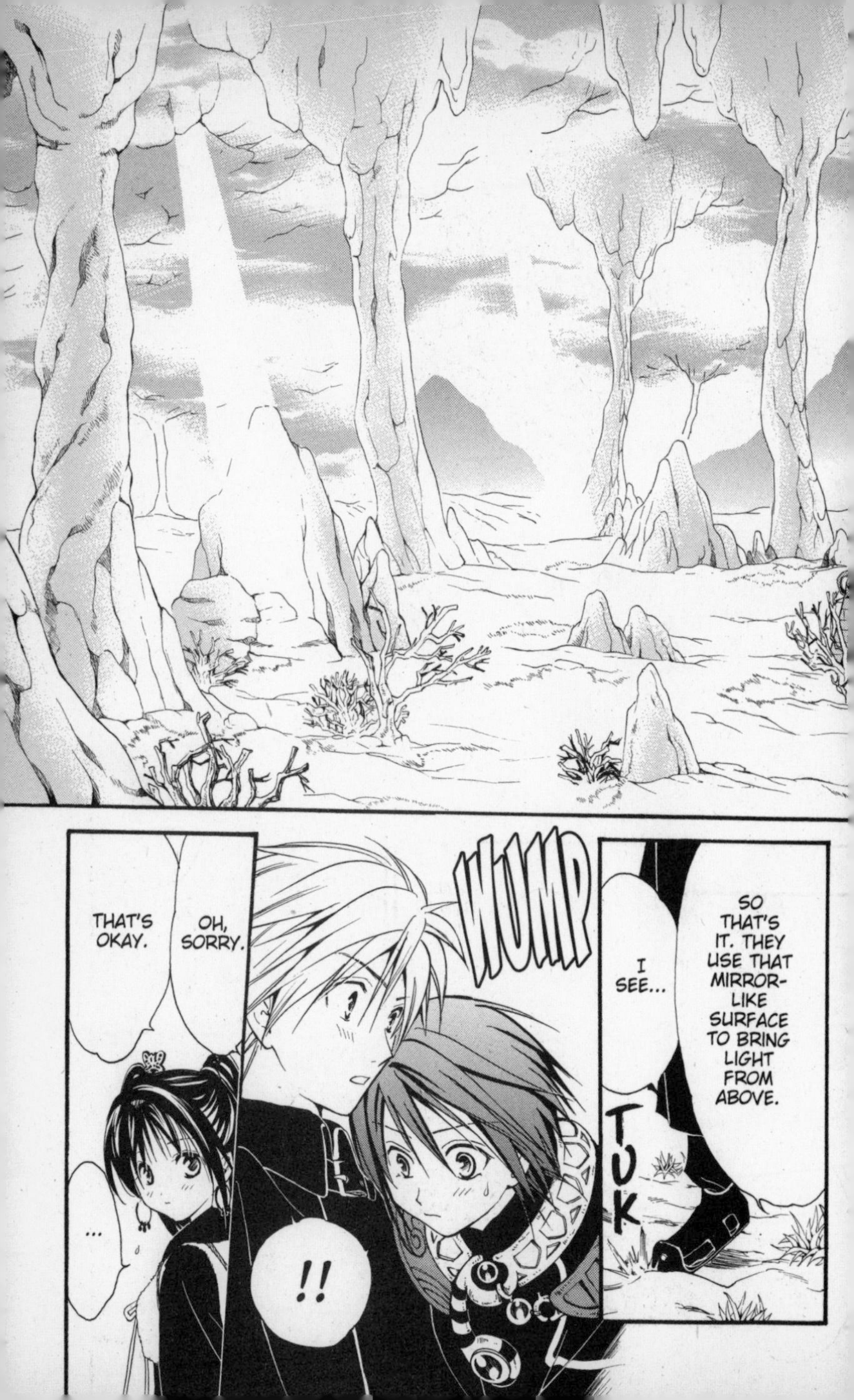
SO THAT'S IT. THEY USE THAT MIRROR-LIKE SURFACE TO BRING LIGHT FROM ABOVE.
I SEE...
TUK
WUMP
OH, SORRY.
THAT'S OKAY.
!!
...

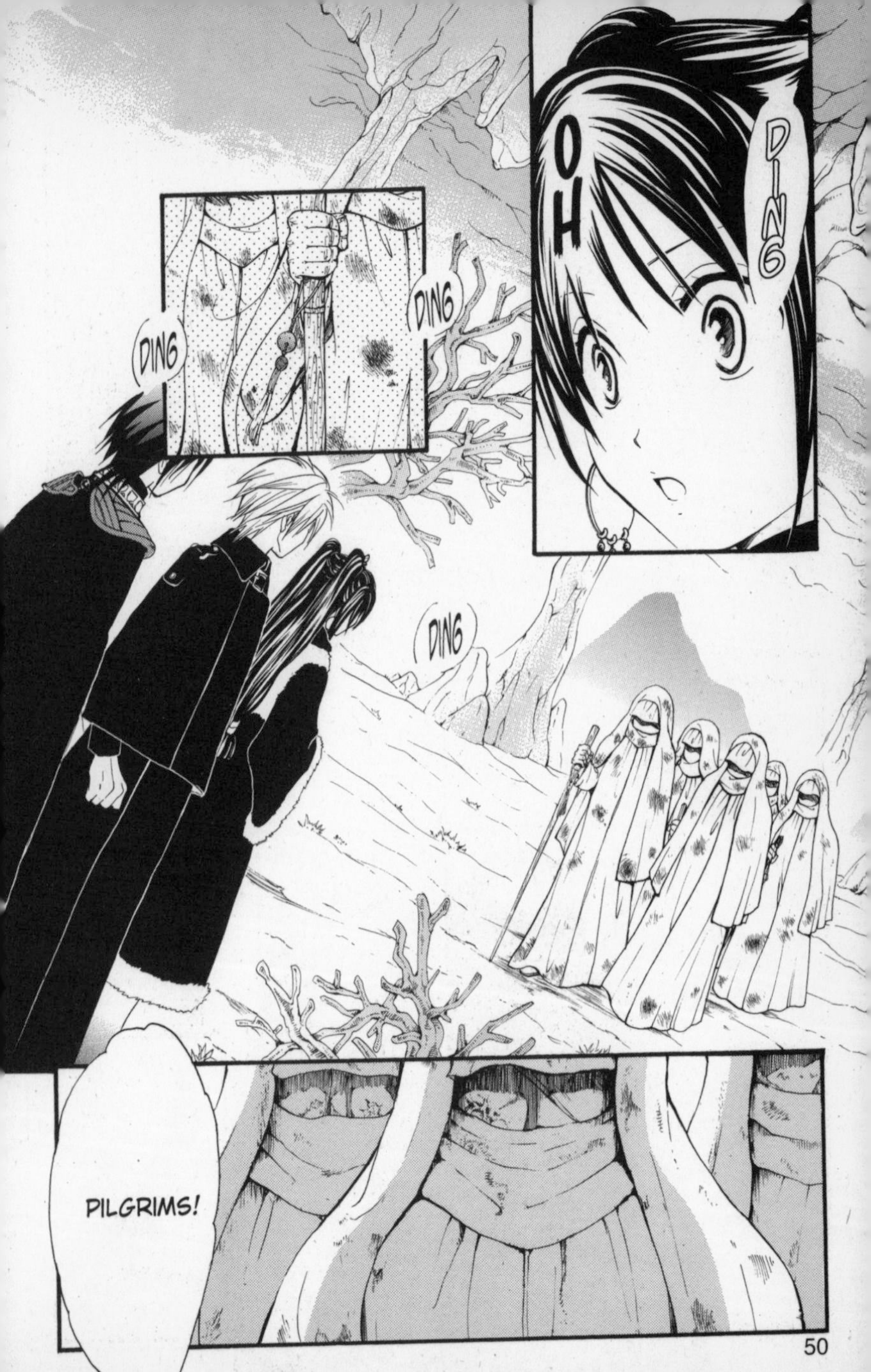
DING DING
OH
DING
DING
DING
PILGRIMS!

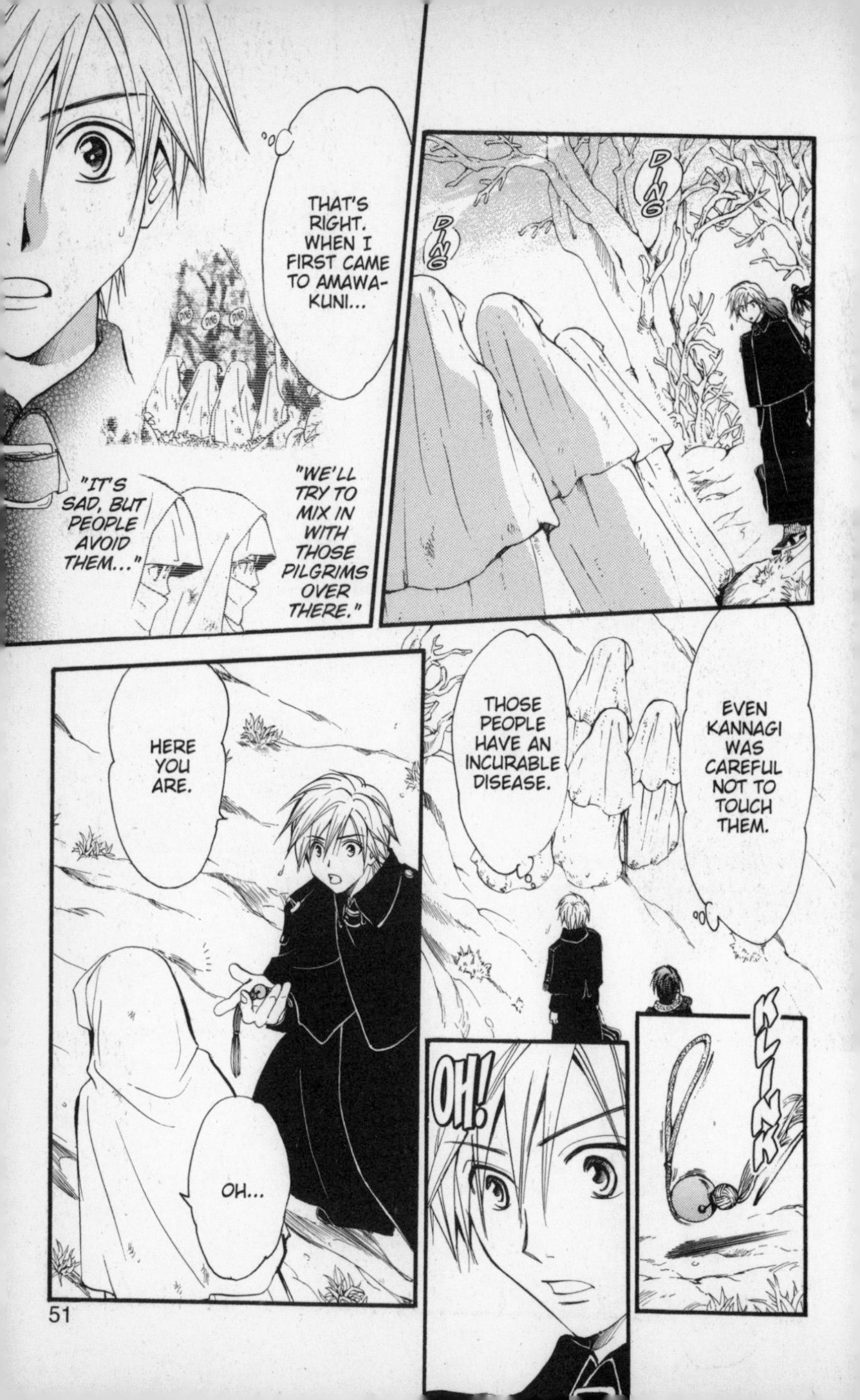
DING
DING
THAT'S RIGHT. WHEN I FIRST CAME TO AMAWA-KUNI...
DING DING DING
"WE'LL TRY TO MIX IN WITH THOSE PILGRIMS OVER THERE."
"IT'S SAD, BUT PEOPLE AVOID THEM..."
EVEN KANNAGI WAS CAREFUL NOT TO TOUCH THEM.
THOSE PEOPLE HAVE AN INCURABLE DISEASE.
KLINK
OH!
HERE YOU ARE.
OH...

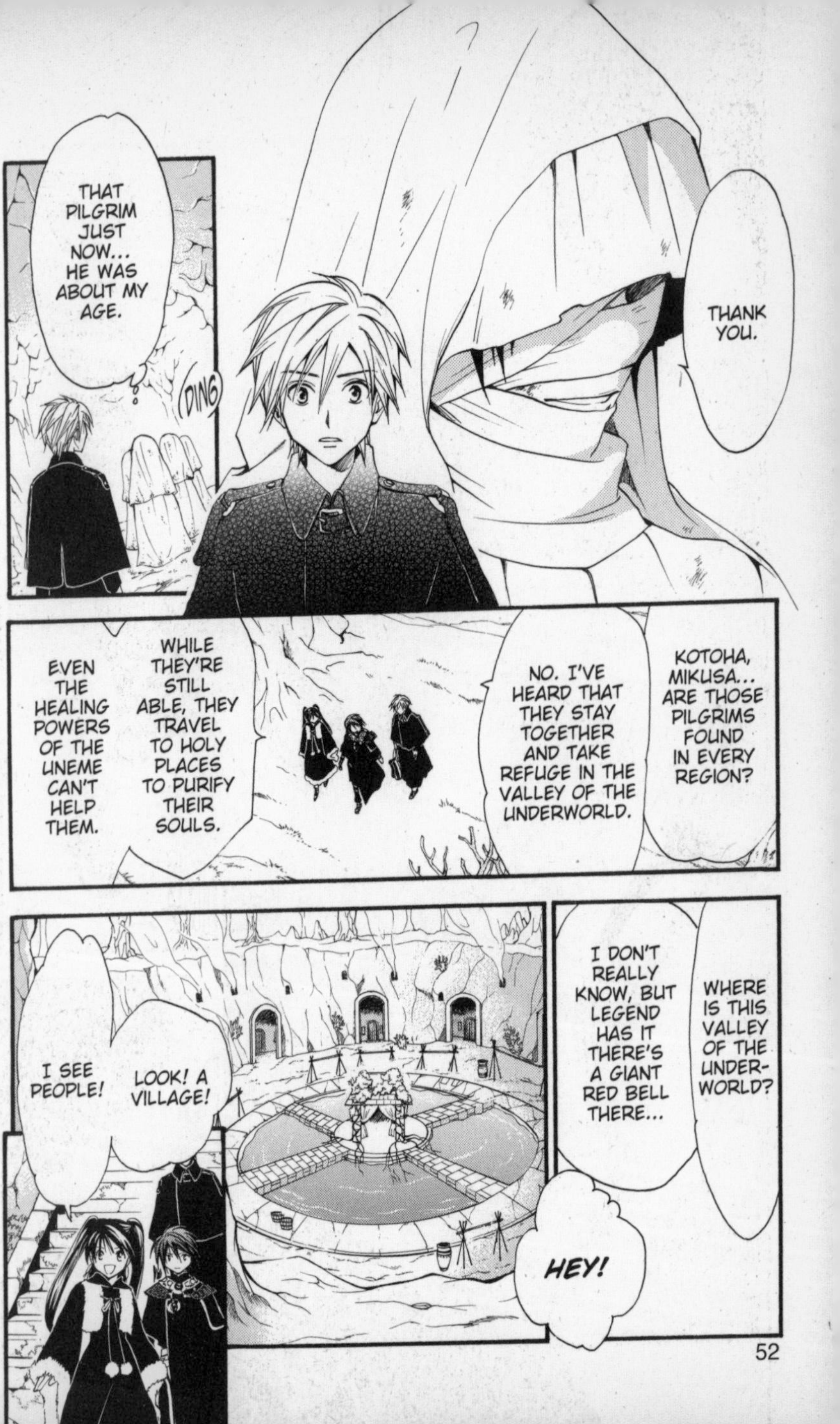
THANK YOU.
DING
THAT PILGRIM JUST NOW... HE WAS ABOUT MY AGE.
KOTOHA, MIKUSA... ARE THOSE PILGRIMS FOUND IN EVERY REGION?
NO. I'VE HEARD THAT THEY STAY TOGETHER AND TAKE REFUGE IN THE VALLEY OF THE UNDERWORLD.
WHILE THEY'RE STILL ABLE, THEY TRAVEL TO HOLY PLACES TO PURIFY THEIR SOULS.
EVEN THE HEALING POWERS OF THE UNEME CAN'T HELP THEM.
WHERE IS THIS VALLEY OF THE UNDER-WORLD?
I DON'T REALLY KNOW, BUT LEGEND HAS IT THERE'S A GIANT RED BELL THERE...
HEY!
LOOK! A VILLAGE!
I SEE PEOPLE!

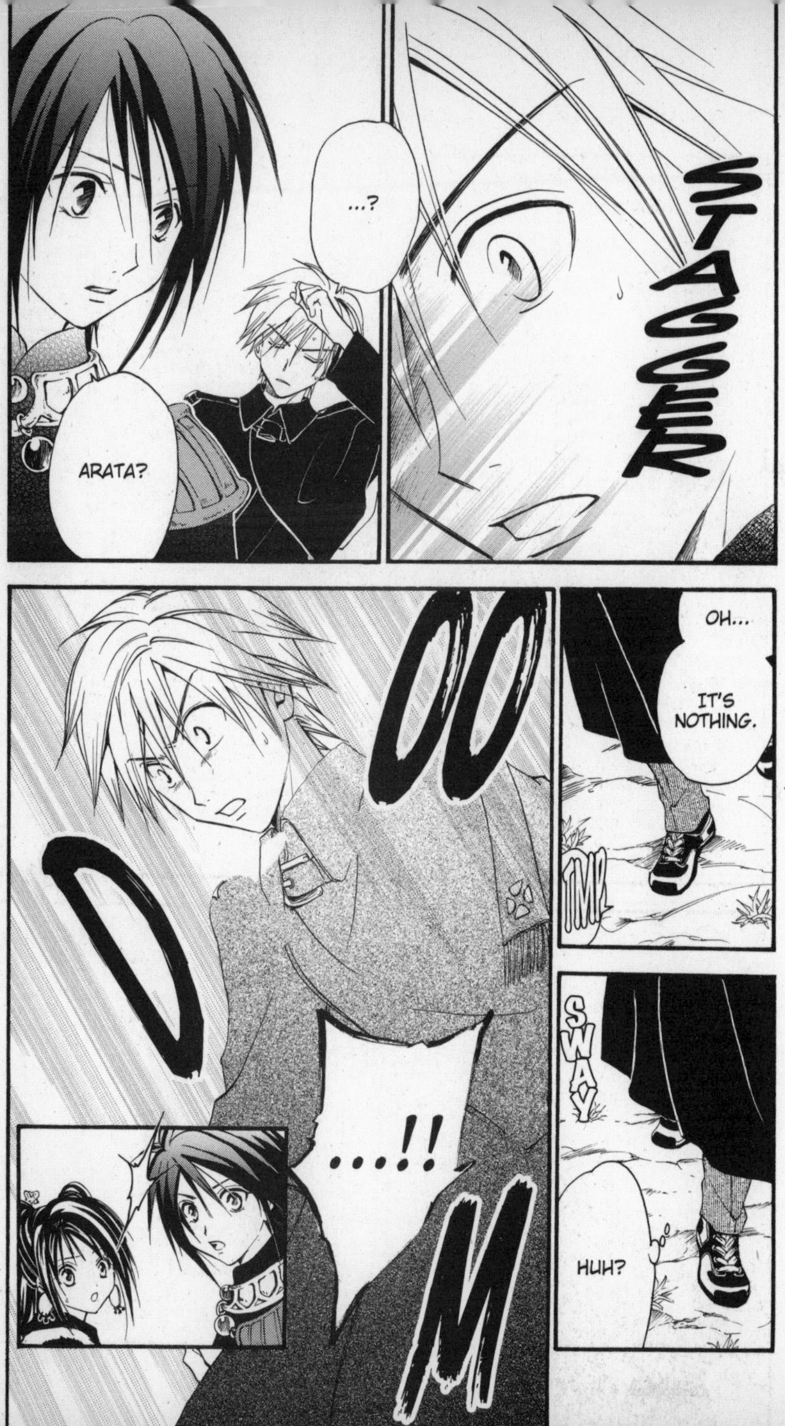
STAGGER
...?
ARATA?
OH...
IT'S NOTHING.
TMP
SWAY
HUH?
DOOM
...!!

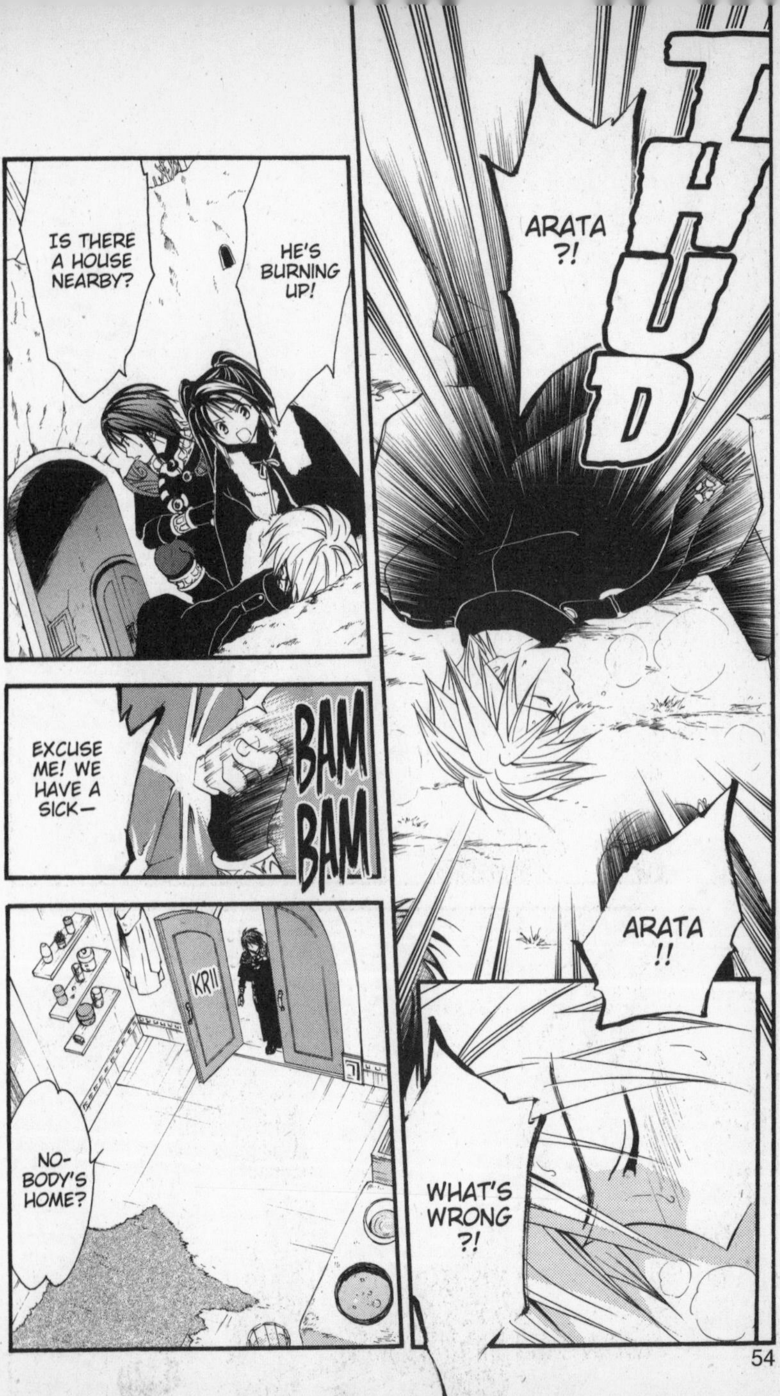
THUD
ARATA?!
ARATA!!
WHAT'S WRONG?!
HE'S BURNING UP!
IS THERE A HOUSE NEARBY?
BAM BAM
EXCUSE ME! WE HAVE A SICK—
KRII
NO-BODY'S HOME?

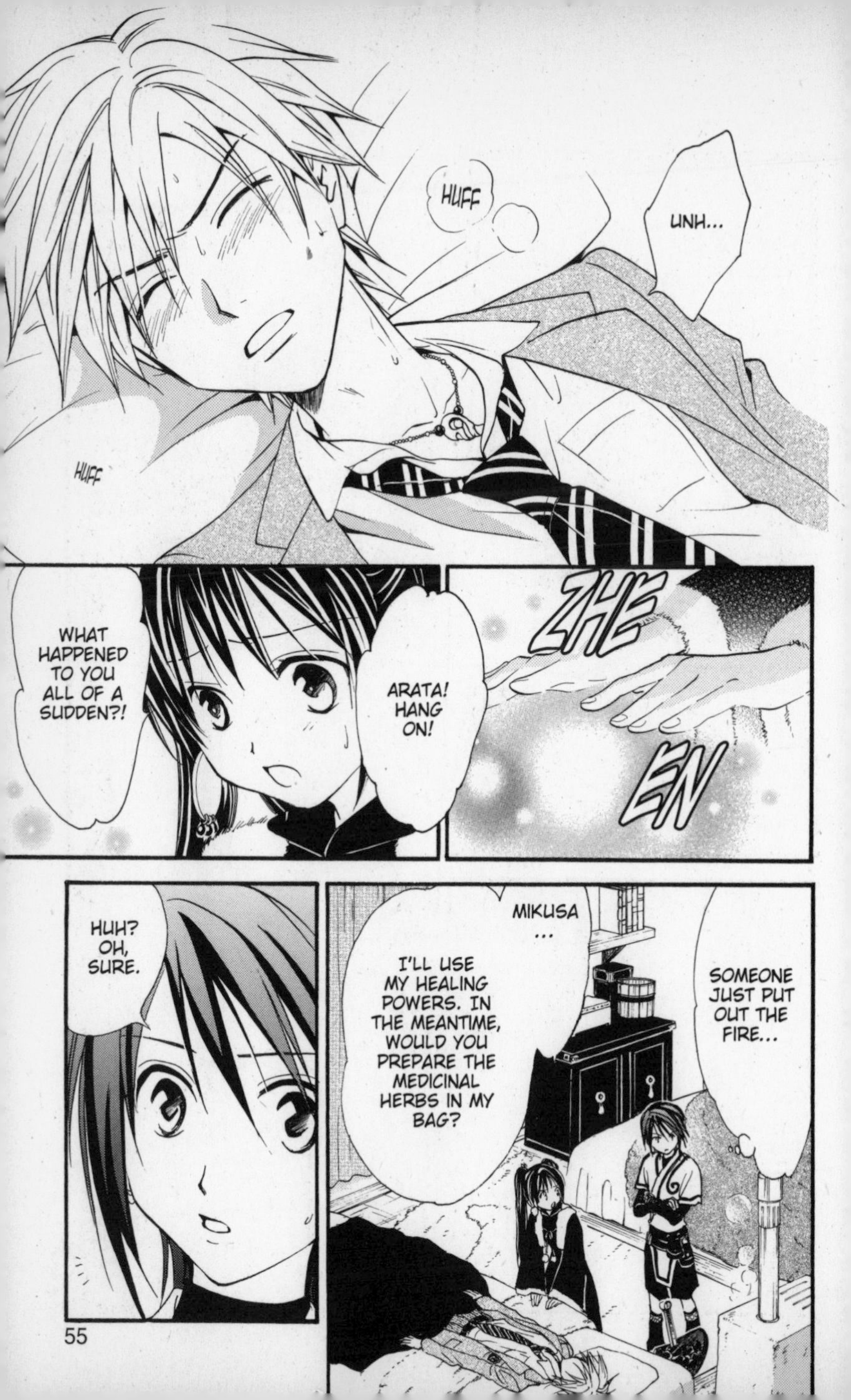
UNH...
HUFF
HUFF
ARATA! HANG ON!
WHAT HAPPENED TO YOU ALL OF A SUDDEN?!
SOMEONE JUST PUT OUT THE FIRE...
MIKUSA...
I'LL USE MY HEALING POWERS. IN THE MEANTIME, WOULD YOU PREPARE THE MEDICINAL HERBS IN MY BAG?
HUH? OH, SURE.

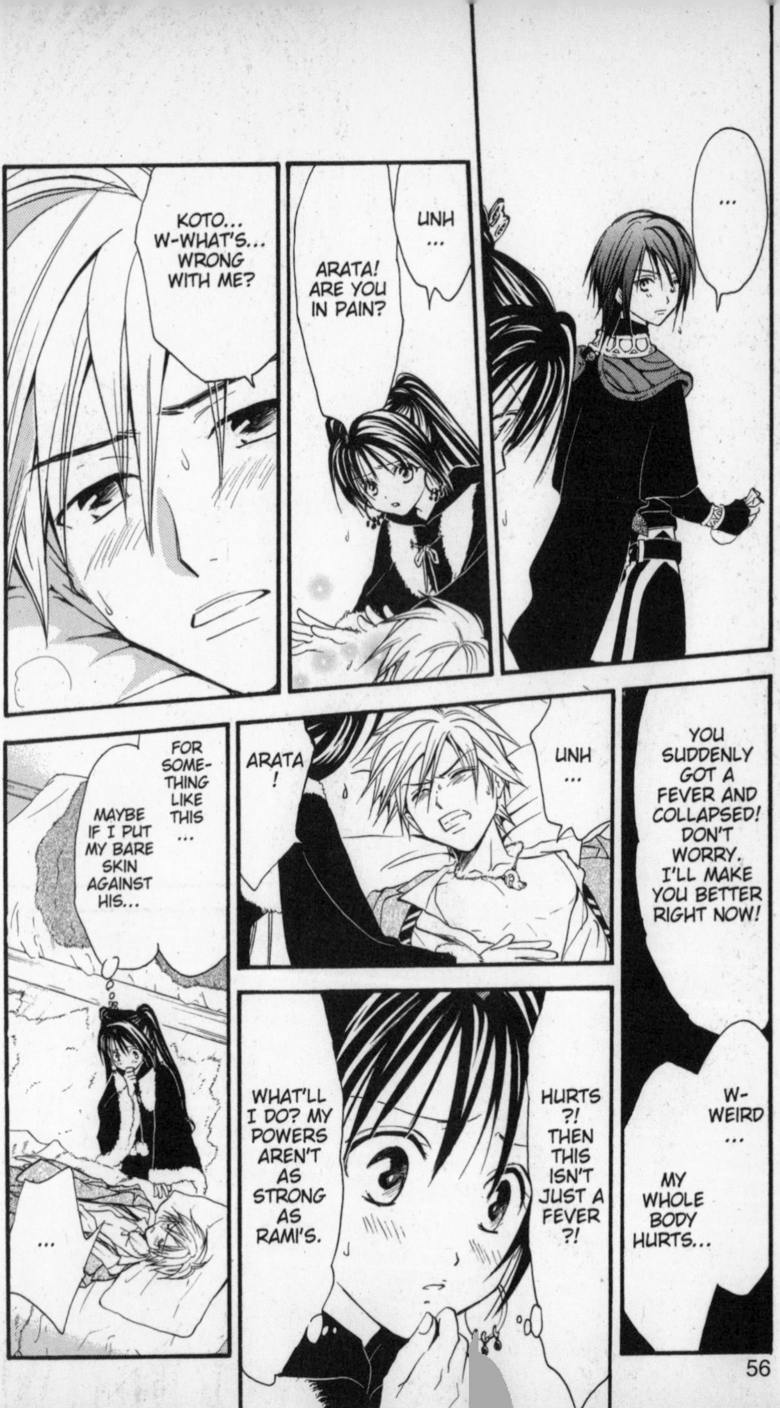
...
UNH ...
ARATA! ARE YOU IN PAIN?
KOTO... W-WHAT'S... WRONG WITH ME?
YOU SUDDENLY GOT A FEVER AND COLLAPSED! DON'T WORRY. I'LL MAKE YOU BETTER RIGHT NOW!
W-WEIRD ...
MY WHOLE BODY HURTS...
UNH ...
ARATA!
HURTS?! THEN THIS ISN'T JUST A FEVER?!
WHAT'LL I DO? MY POWERS AREN'T AS STRONG AS RAMI'S.
FOR SOME-THING LIKE THIS ...
MAYBE IF I PUT MY BARE SKIN AGAINST HIS...
...

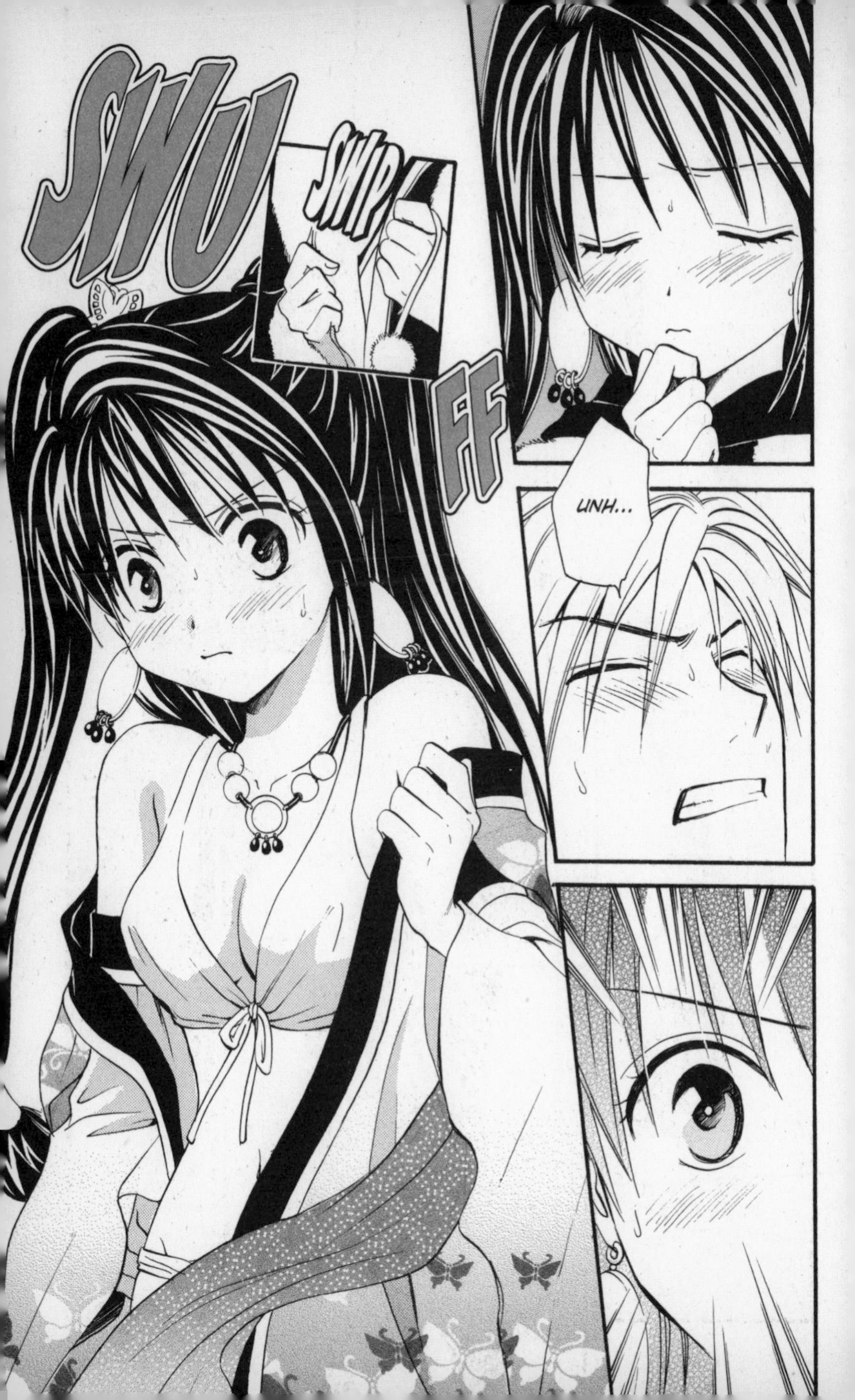
SWI
SWIRL
FF
UNH...

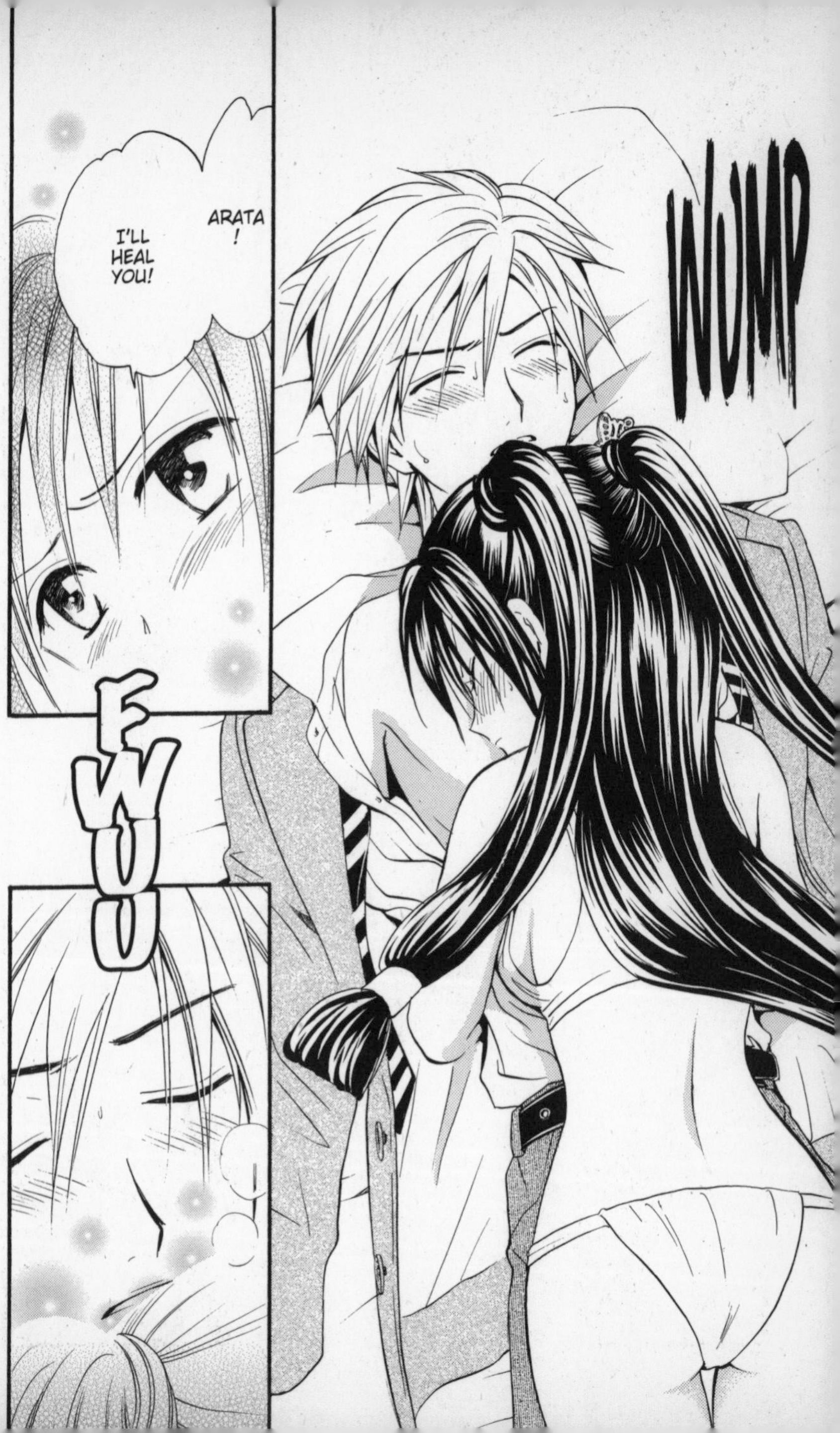
WUMP
ARATA! I'LL HEAL YOU!
FWUU

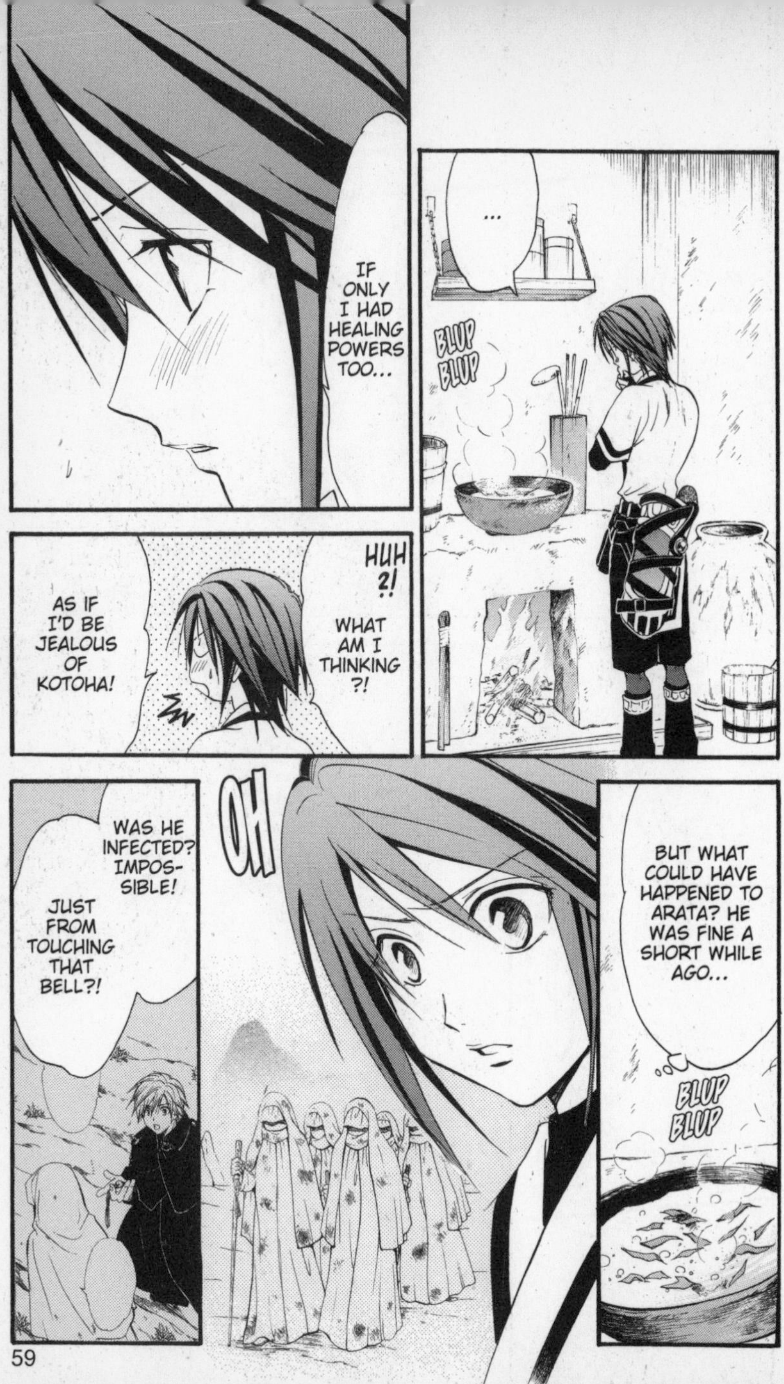
...
BLUP BLUP
IF ONLY I HAD HEALING POWERS TOO...
HUH?!
WHAT AM I THINKING?!
AS IF I'D BE JEALOUS OF KOTOHA!
BUT WHAT COULD HAVE HAPPENED TO ARATA? HE WAS FINE A SHORT WHILE AGO...
BLUP BLUP
OH
WAS HE INFECTED? IMPOSSIBLE!
JUST FROM TOUCHING THAT BELL?!

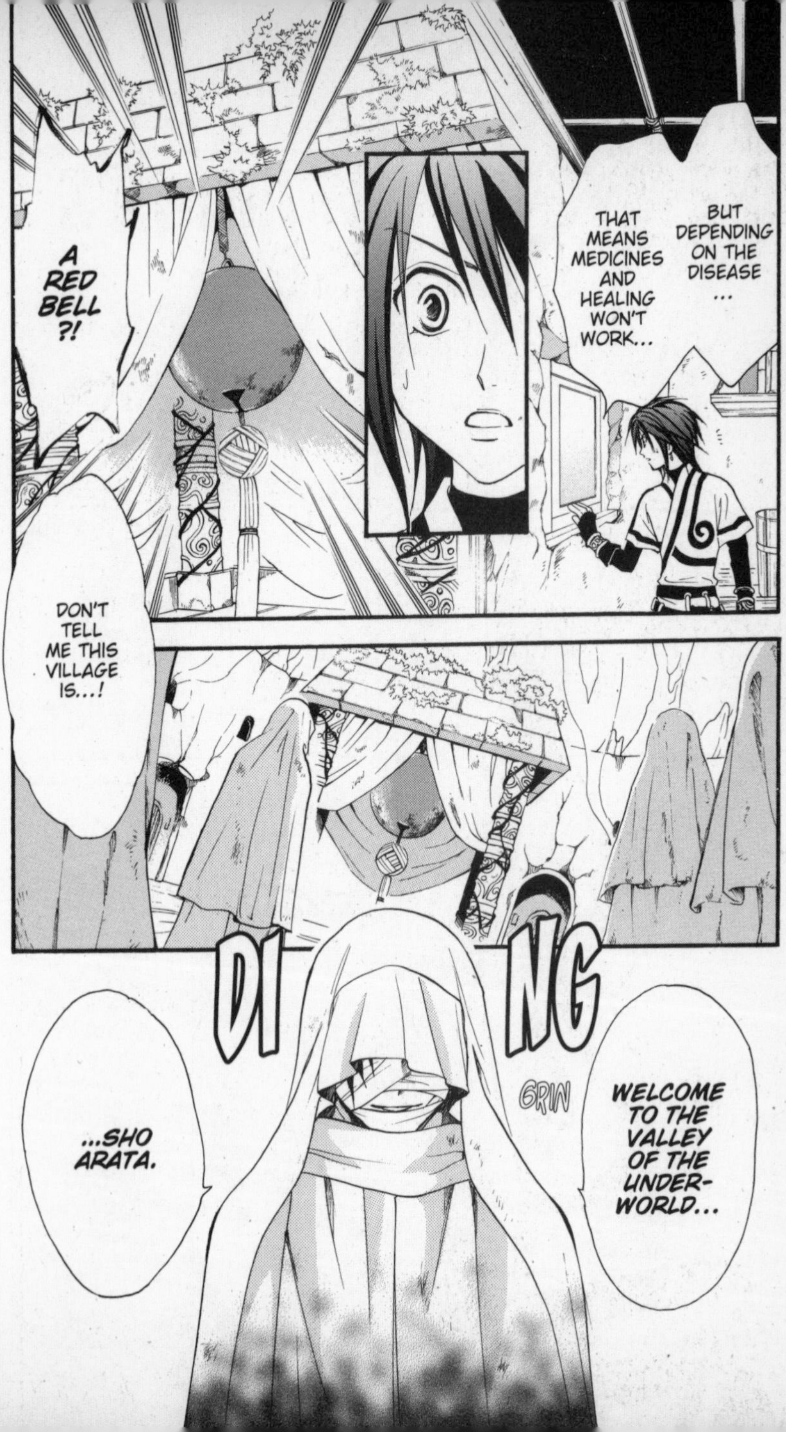
BUT DEPENDING ON THE DISEASE...
THAT MEANS MEDICINES AND HEALING WON'T WORK...
A RED BELL?!
DON'T TELL ME THIS VILLAGE IS...!
DING
GRIN
WELCOME TO THE VALLEY OF THE UNDER-WORLD...
...SHO ARATA.

CHAPTER 111
THE MYSTERY OF ARATA'S COLLAPSE

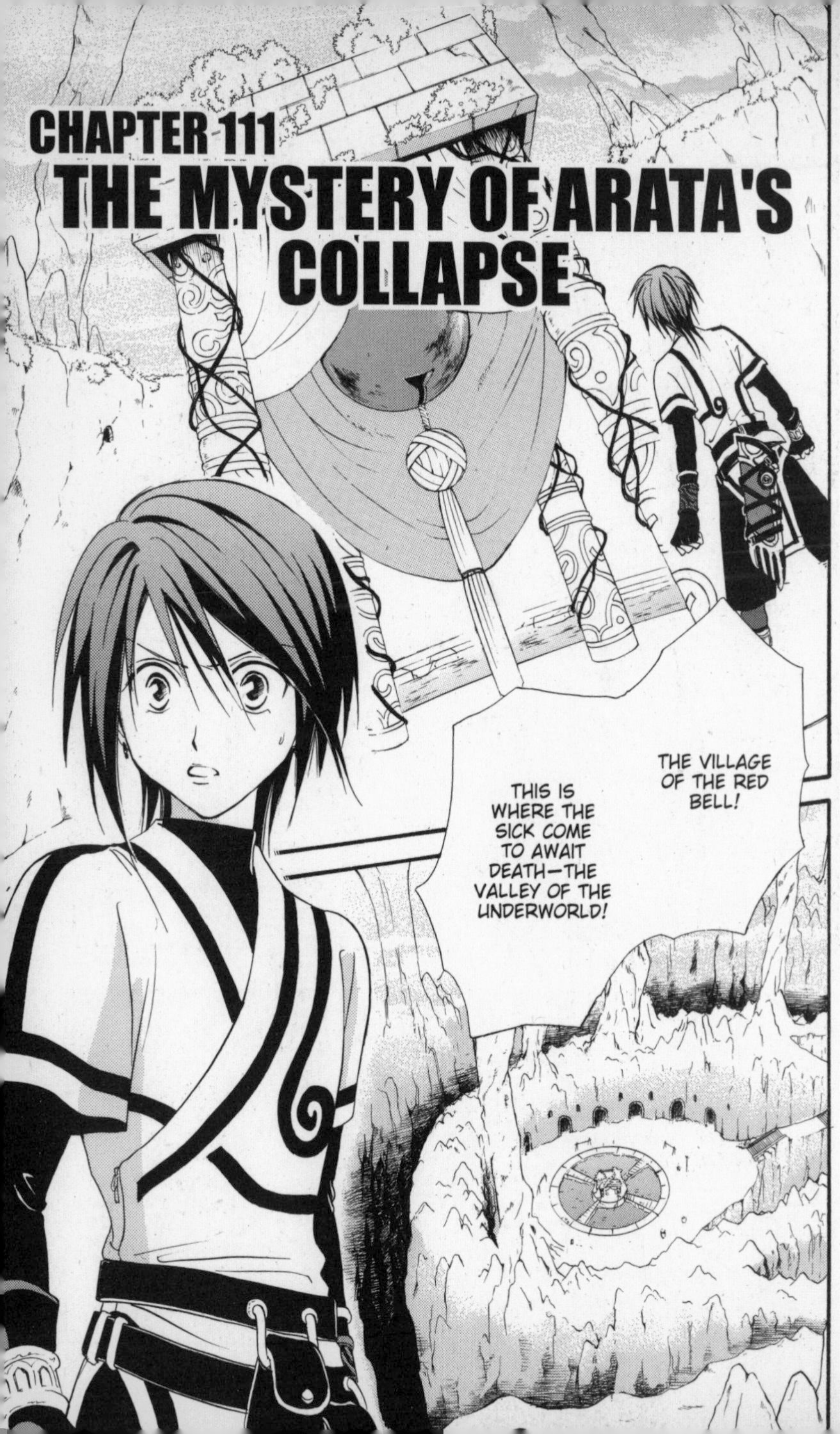
THE VILLAGE OF THE RED BELL!
THIS IS WHERE THE SICK COME TO AWAIT DEATH—THE VALLEY OF THE UNDERWORLD!

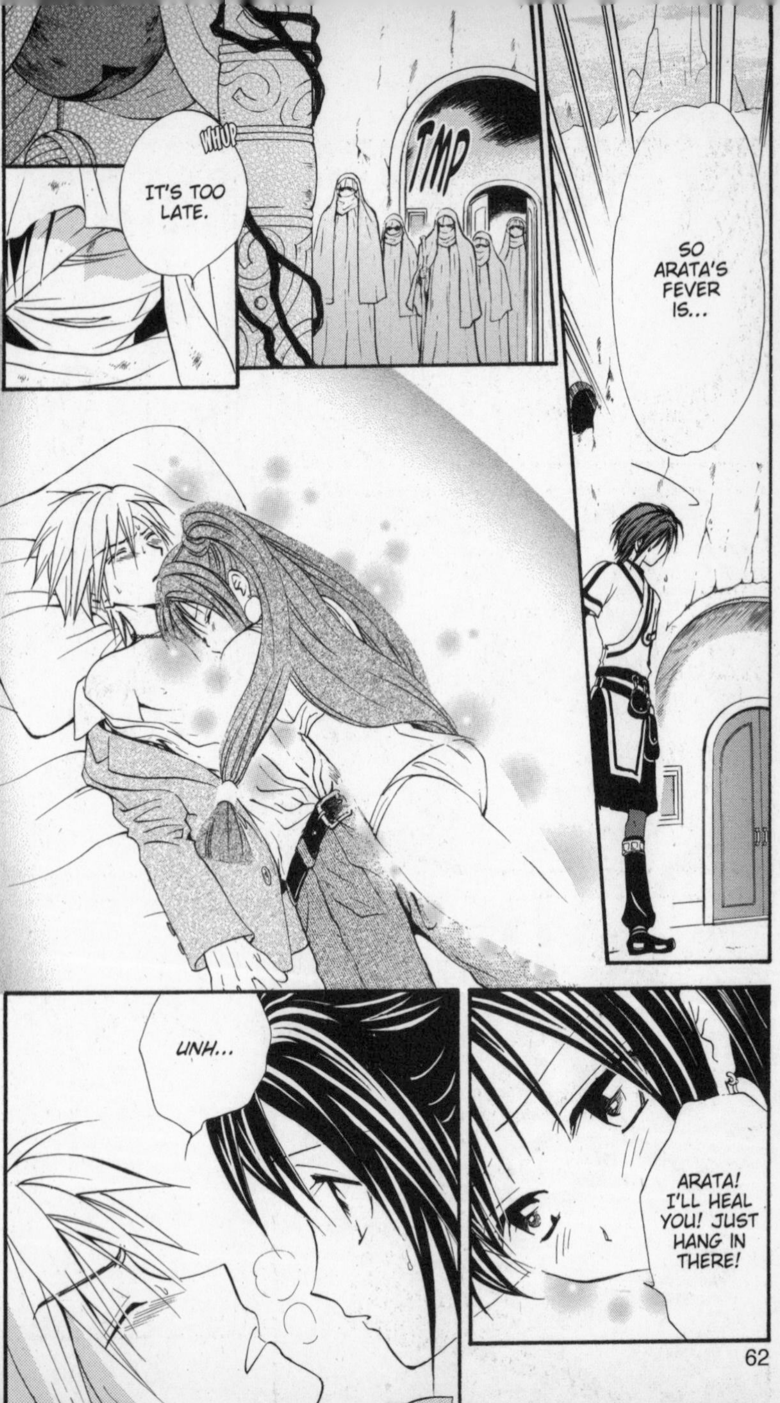
SO ARATA'S FEVER IS...
TMP
WHUP
IT'S TOO LATE.
ARATA! I'LL HEAL YOU! JUST HANG IN THERE!
UNH...

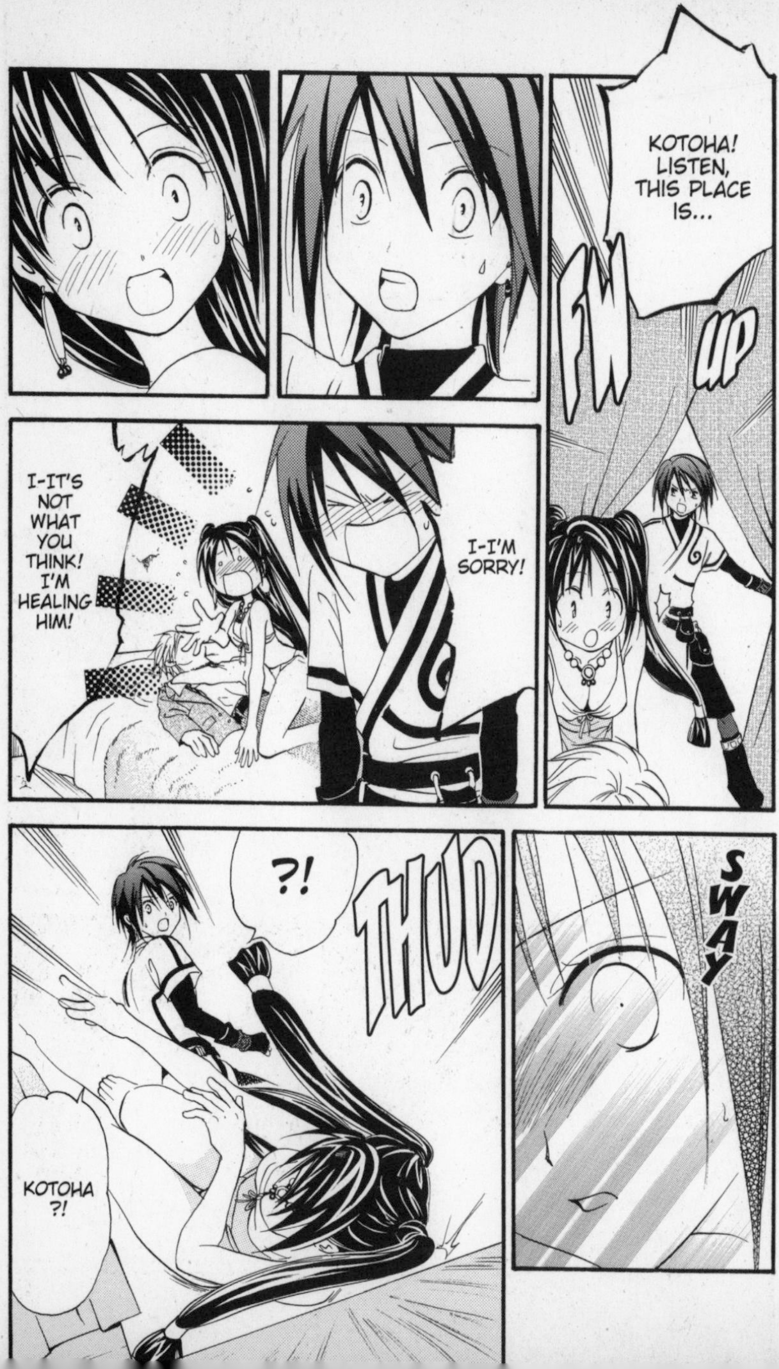
KOTOHA! LISTEN, THIS PLACE IS...
FW UP
I-I'M SORRY!
I-IT'S NOT WHAT YOU THINK! I'M HEALING HIM!
SWAY
THUD
?!
KOTOHA ?!

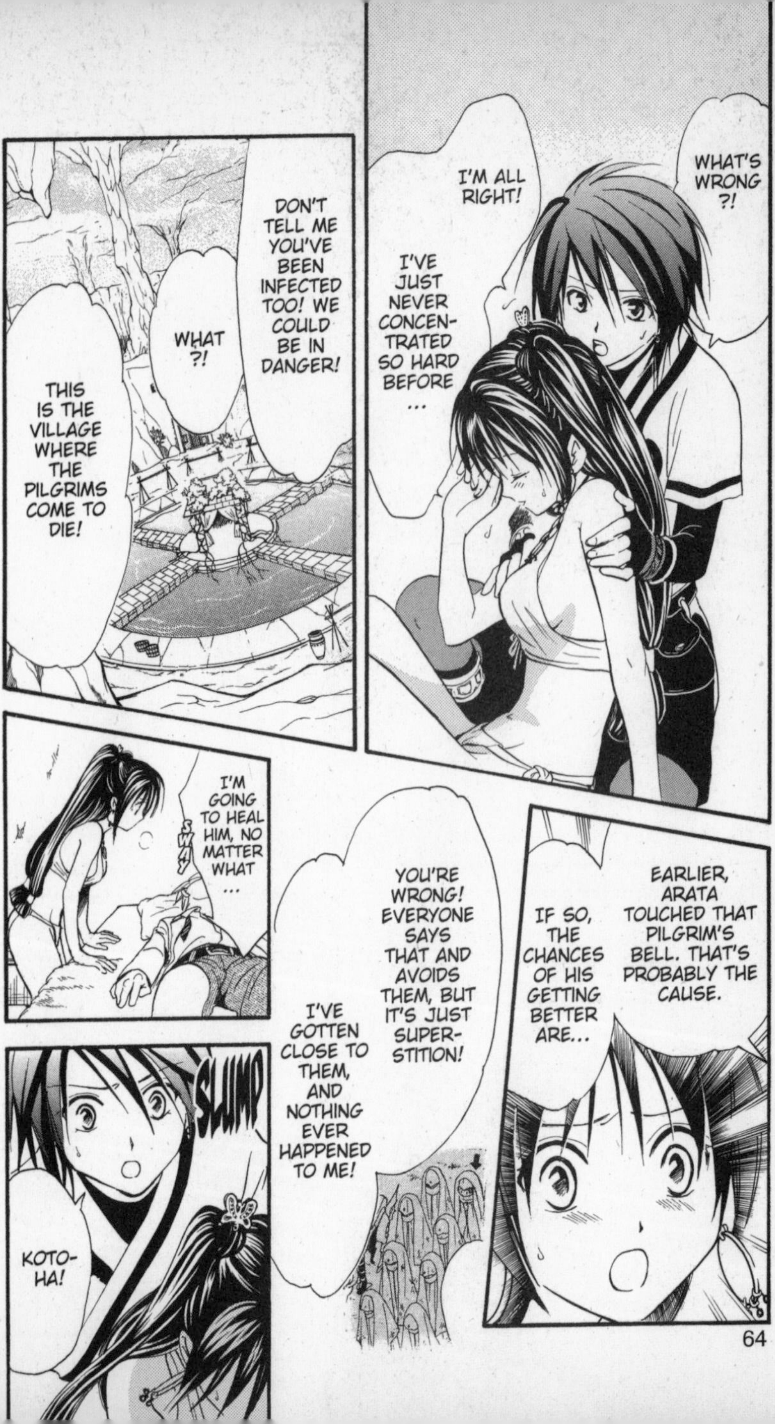
WHAT'S WRONG ?!
I'M ALL RIGHT!
I'VE JUST NEVER CONCENTRATED SO HARD BEFORE ...
DON'T TELL ME YOU'VE BEEN INFECTED TOO! WE COULD BE IN DANGER!
WHAT ?!
THIS IS THE VILLAGE WHERE THE PILGRIMS COME TO DIE!
EARLIER, ARATA TOUCHED THAT PILGRIM'S BELL. THAT'S PROBABLY THE CAUSE.
IF SO, THE CHANCES OF HIS GETTING BETTER ARE...
YOU'RE WRONG! EVERYONE SAYS THAT AND AVOIDS THEM, BUT IT'S JUST SUPERSTITION!
I'VE GOTTEN CLOSE TO THEM, AND NOTHING EVER HAPPENED TO ME!
I'M GOING TO HEAL HIM, NO MATTER WHAT ...
SWAY
SLUMP
KOTO-HA!

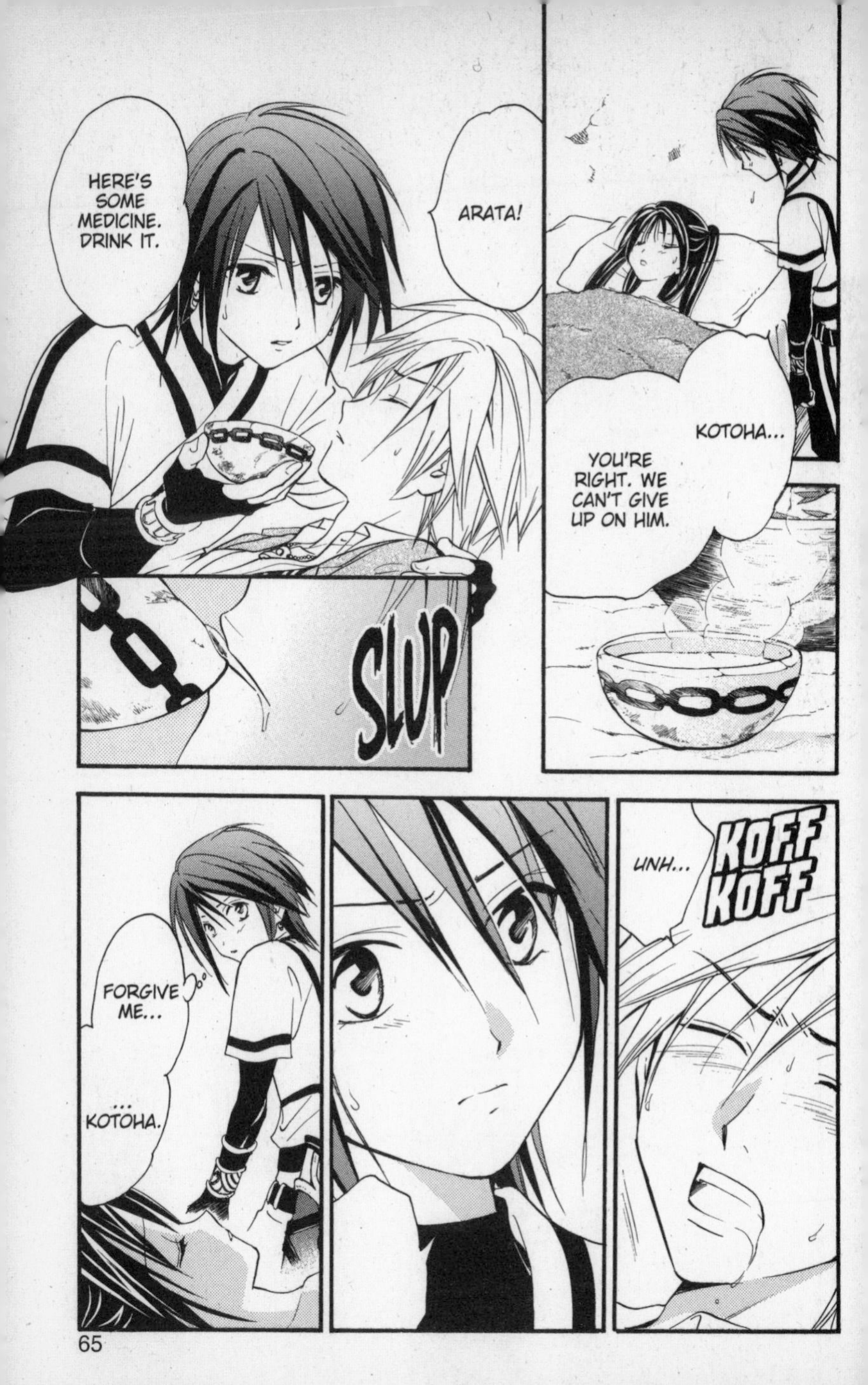
KOTOHA...
YOU'RE RIGHT. WE CAN'T GIVE UP ON HIM.
ARATA!
HERE'S SOME MEDICINE. DRINK IT.
SLUP
UNH...
KOFF KOFF
FORGIVE ME...
... KOTOHA.

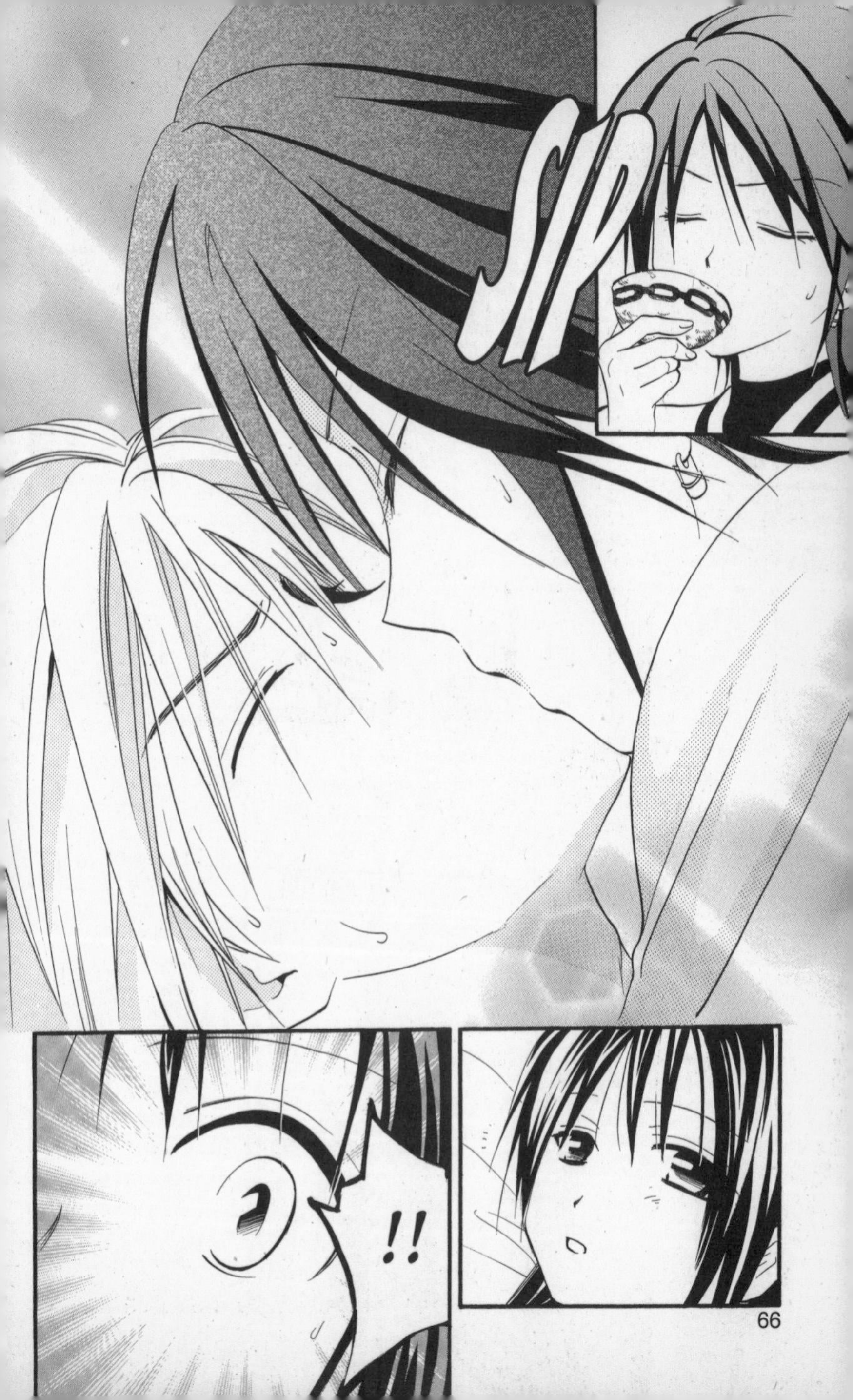
SIP
...
!!

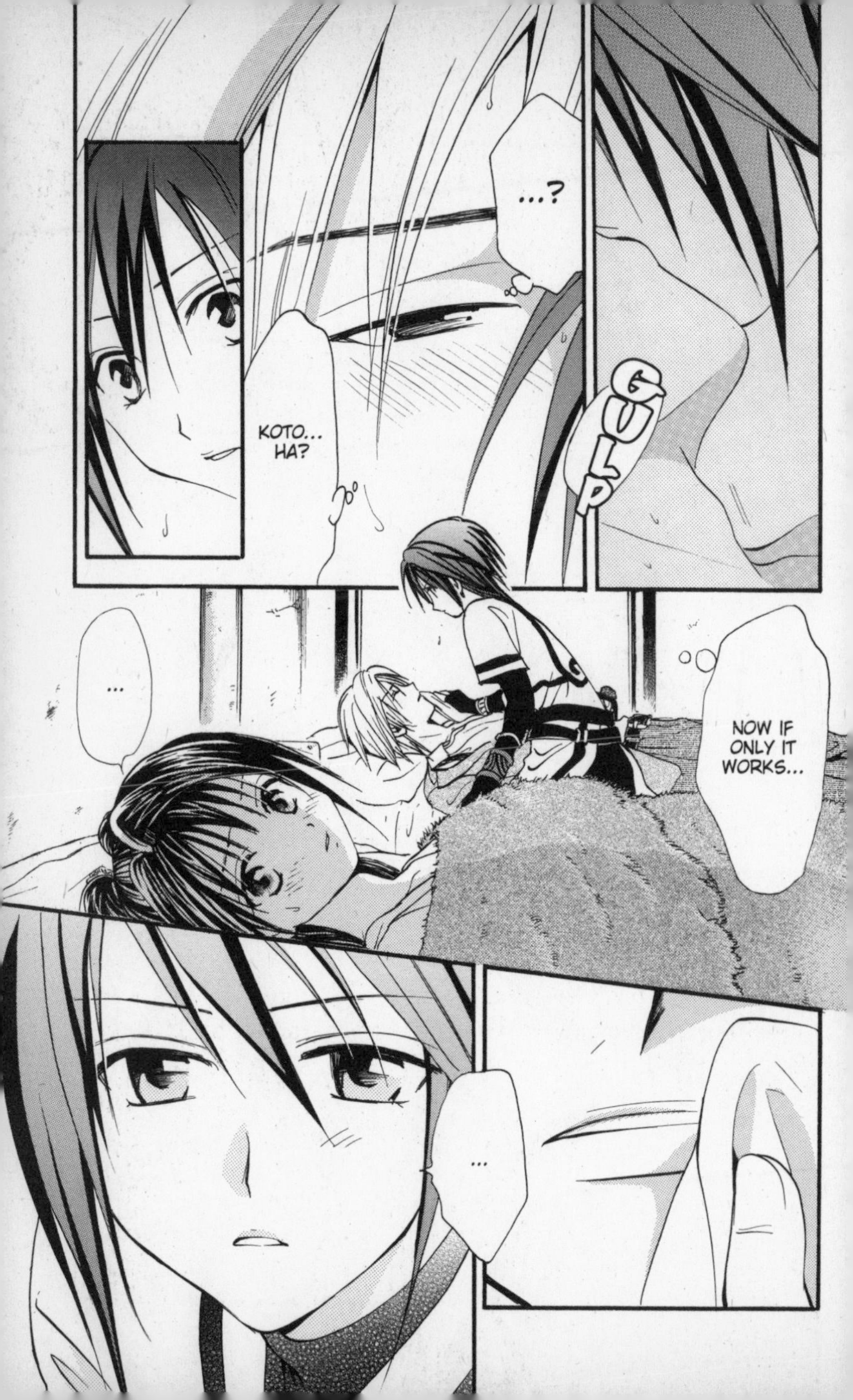
GULP
...?
KOTO... HA?
NOW IF ONLY IT WORKS...
...
...

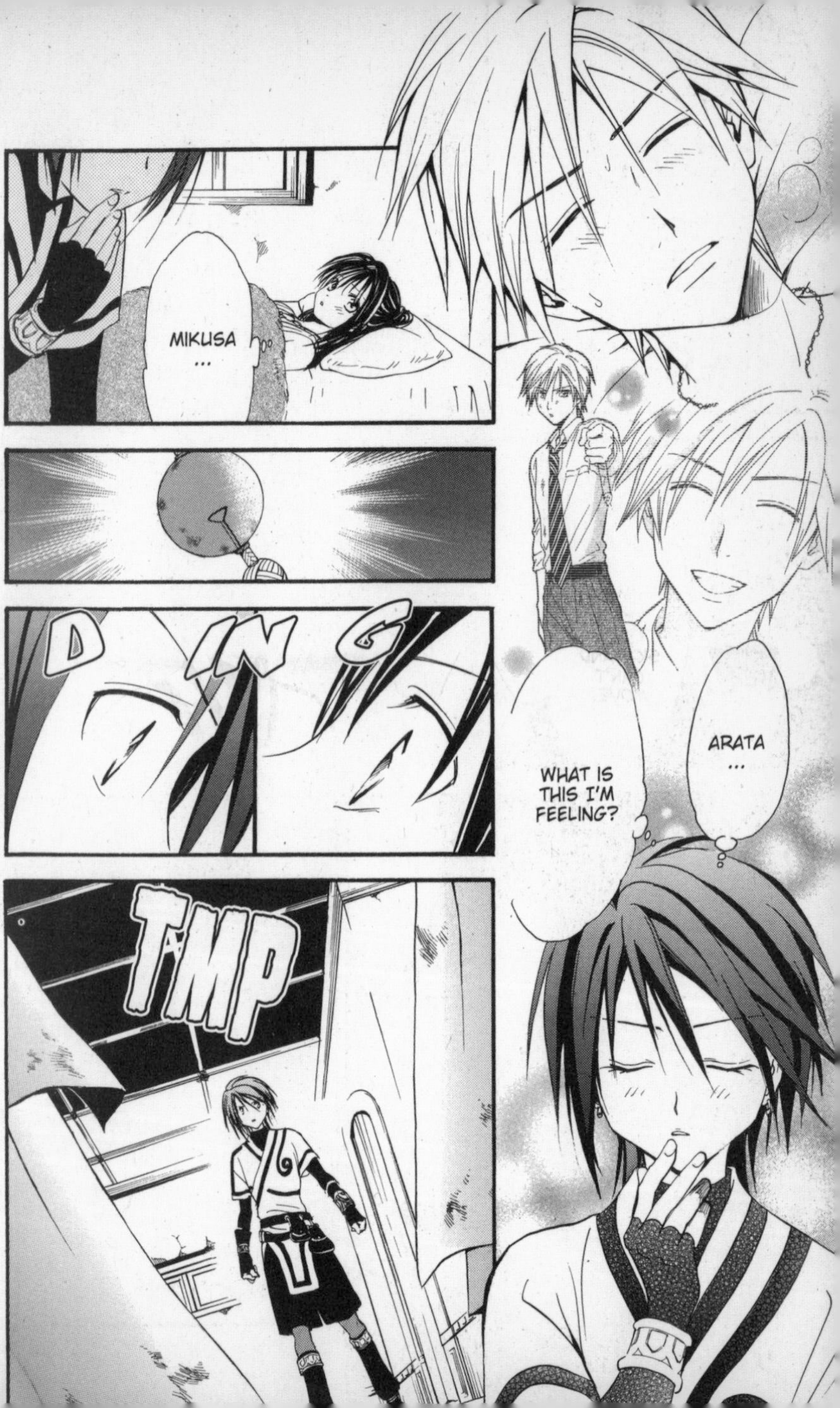
ARATA ...
WHAT IS THIS I'M FEELING?
MIKUSA ...
DING
TMP

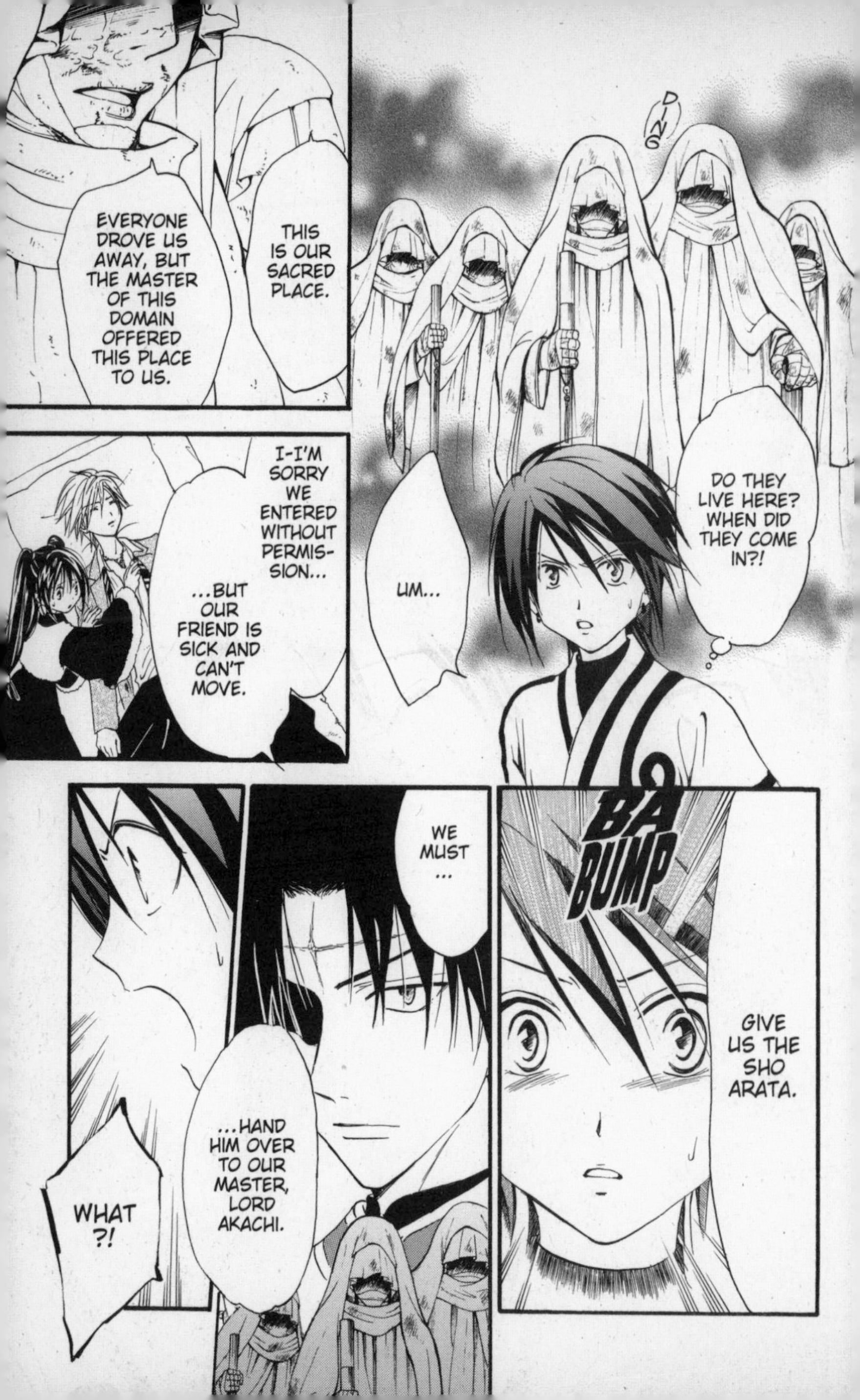

DING
DO THEY LIVE HERE? WHEN DID THEY COME IN?!
UM...
THIS IS OUR SACRED PLACE.
EVERYONE DROVE US AWAY, BUT THE MASTER OF THIS DOMAIN OFFERED THIS PLACE TO US.
I-I'M SORRY WE ENTERED WITHOUT PERMIS-SION...
...BUT OUR FRIEND IS SICK AND CAN'T MOVE.
BA BUMP
GIVE US THE SHO ARATA.
WE MUST ...
...HAND HIM OVER TO OUR MASTER, LORD AKACHI.
WHAT?!

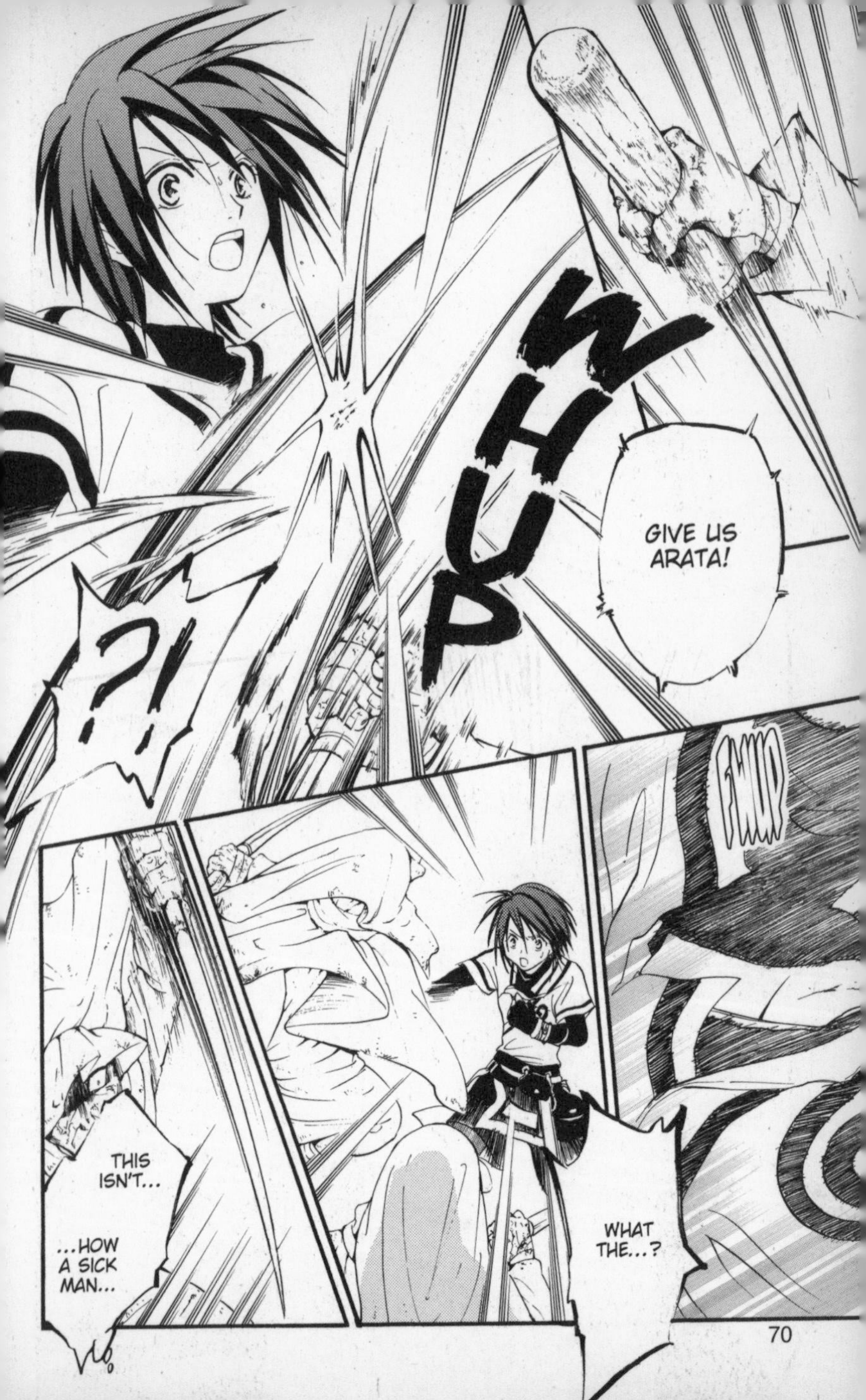
GIVE US ARATA!
WHUP
?!
FWUP
WHAT THE...?
THIS ISN'T...
...HOW A SICK MAN...

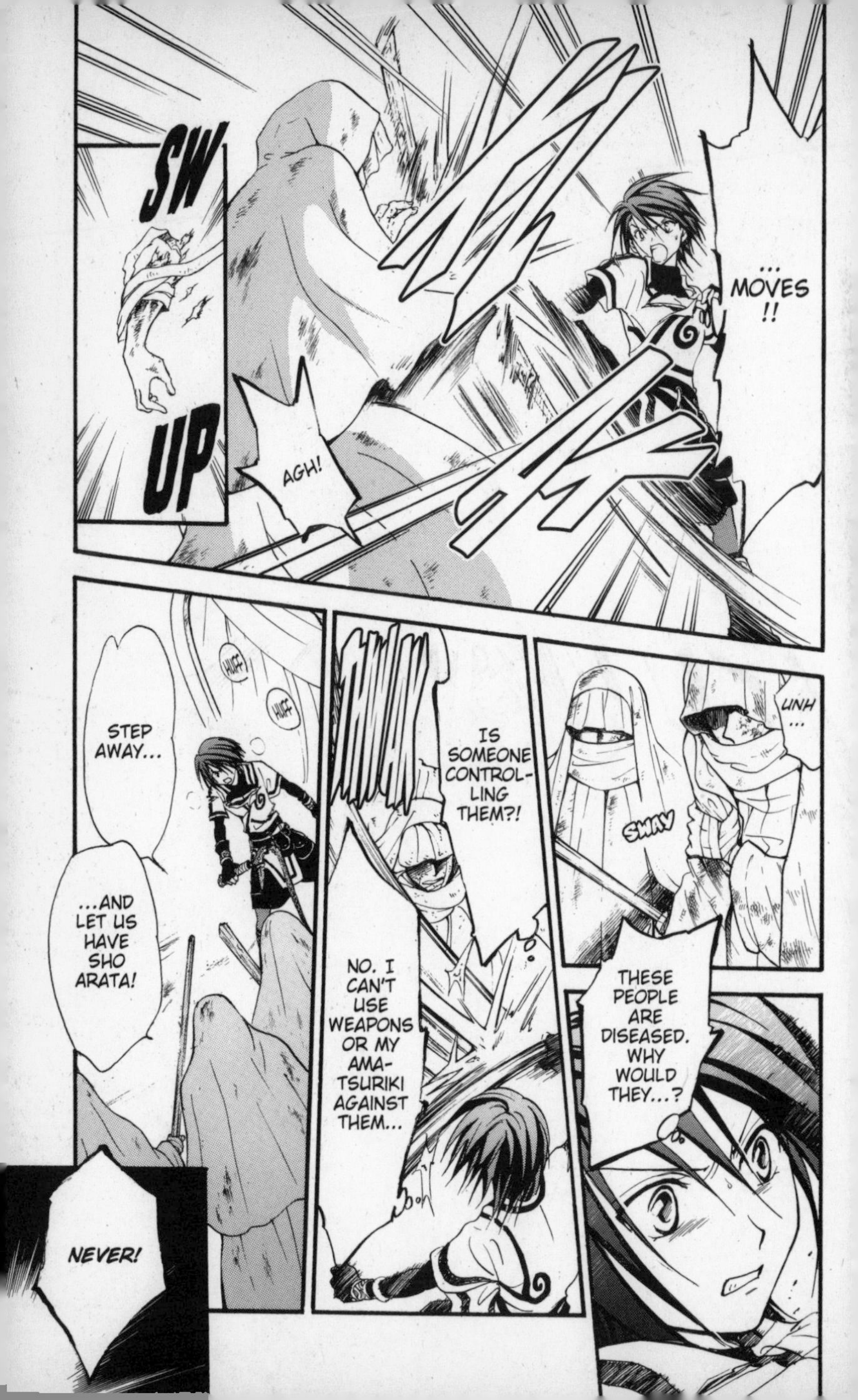
... MOVES !!
SW UP
AGH!
UNH ...
SWAY
THESE PEOPLE ARE DISEASED. WHY WOULD THEY...?
IS SOMEONE CONTROL-LING THEM?!
NO. I CAN'T USE WEAPONS OR MY AMA-TSURIKI AGAINST THEM...
HUFF
HUFF
STEP AWAY...
...AND LET US HAVE SHO ARATA!
NEVER!

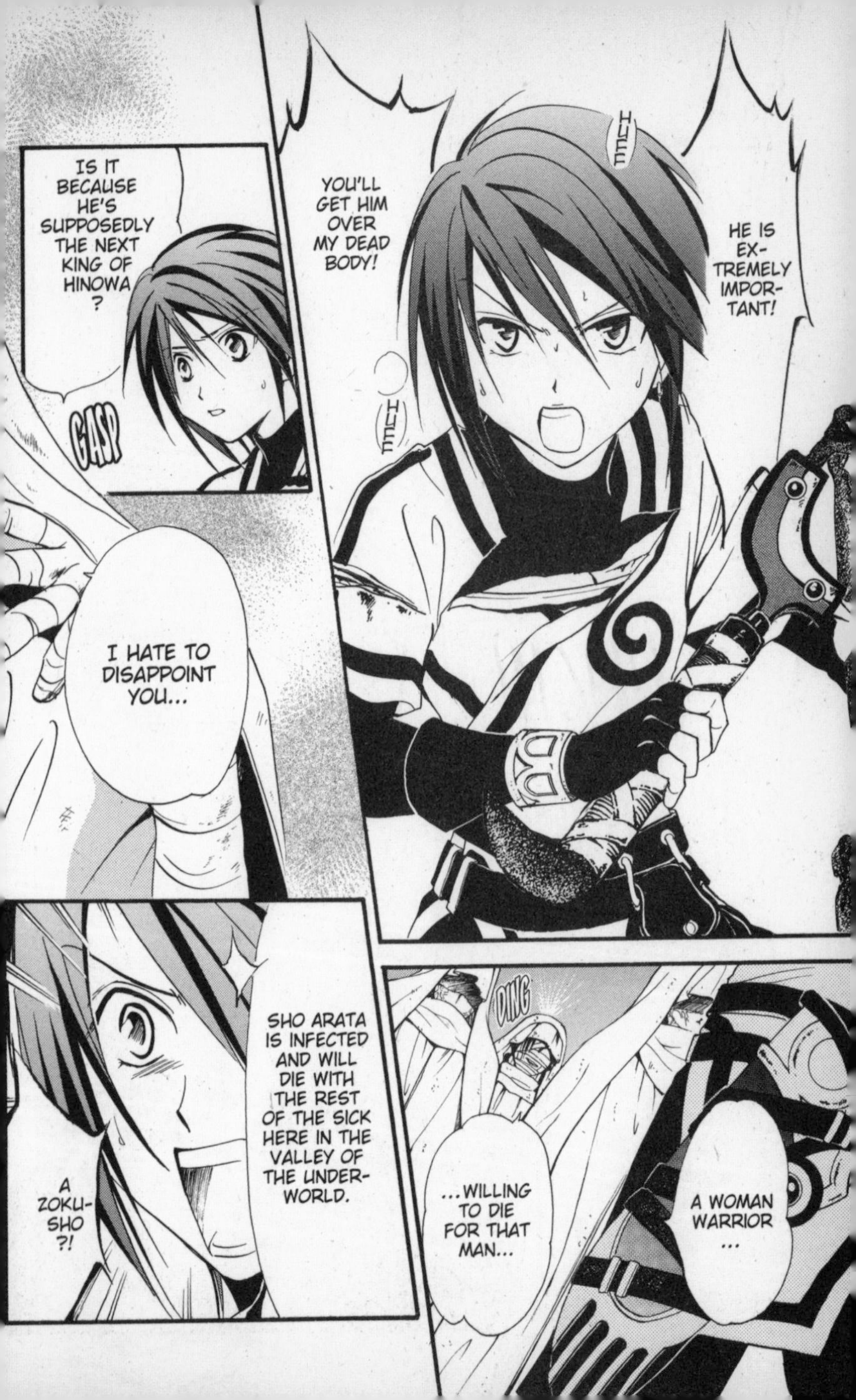
HE IS EX-TREMELY IMPOR-TANT!
HUFF
YOU'LL GET HIM OVER MY DEAD BODY!
HUFF
IS IT BECAUSE HE'S SUPPOSEDLY THE NEXT KING OF HINOWA?
GASP
I HATE TO DISAPPOINT YOU...
DING
A WOMAN WARRIOR...
...WILLING TO DIE FOR THAT MAN...
SHO ARATA IS INFECTED AND WILL DIE WITH THE REST OF THE SICK HERE IN THE VALLEY OF THE UNDER-WORLD.
A ZOKU-SHO?!

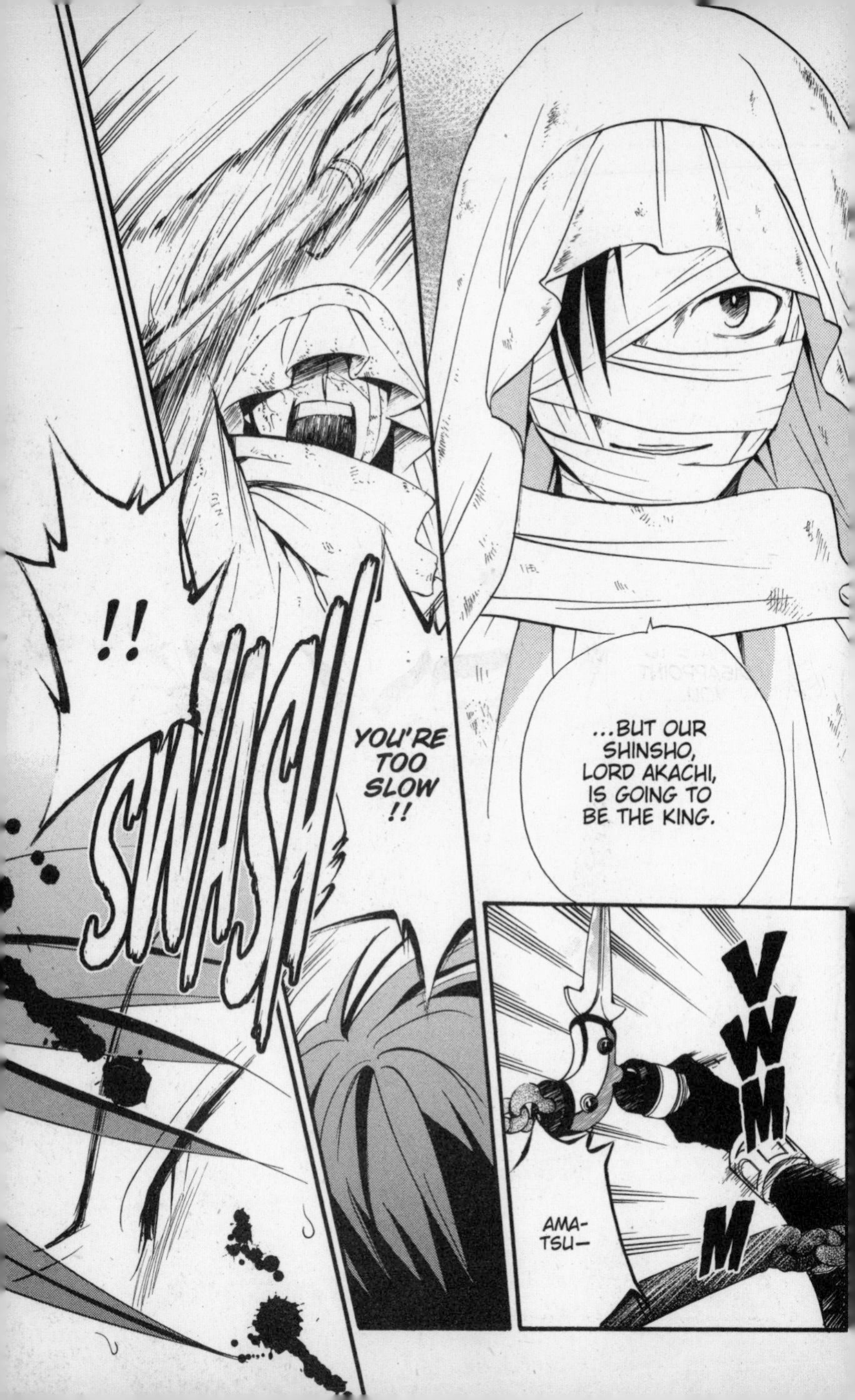
...BUT OUR SHINSHO, LORD AKACHI, IS GOING TO BE THE KING.
VWMM
AMA-TSU—
YOU'RE TOO SLOW!!
!!
SMASH

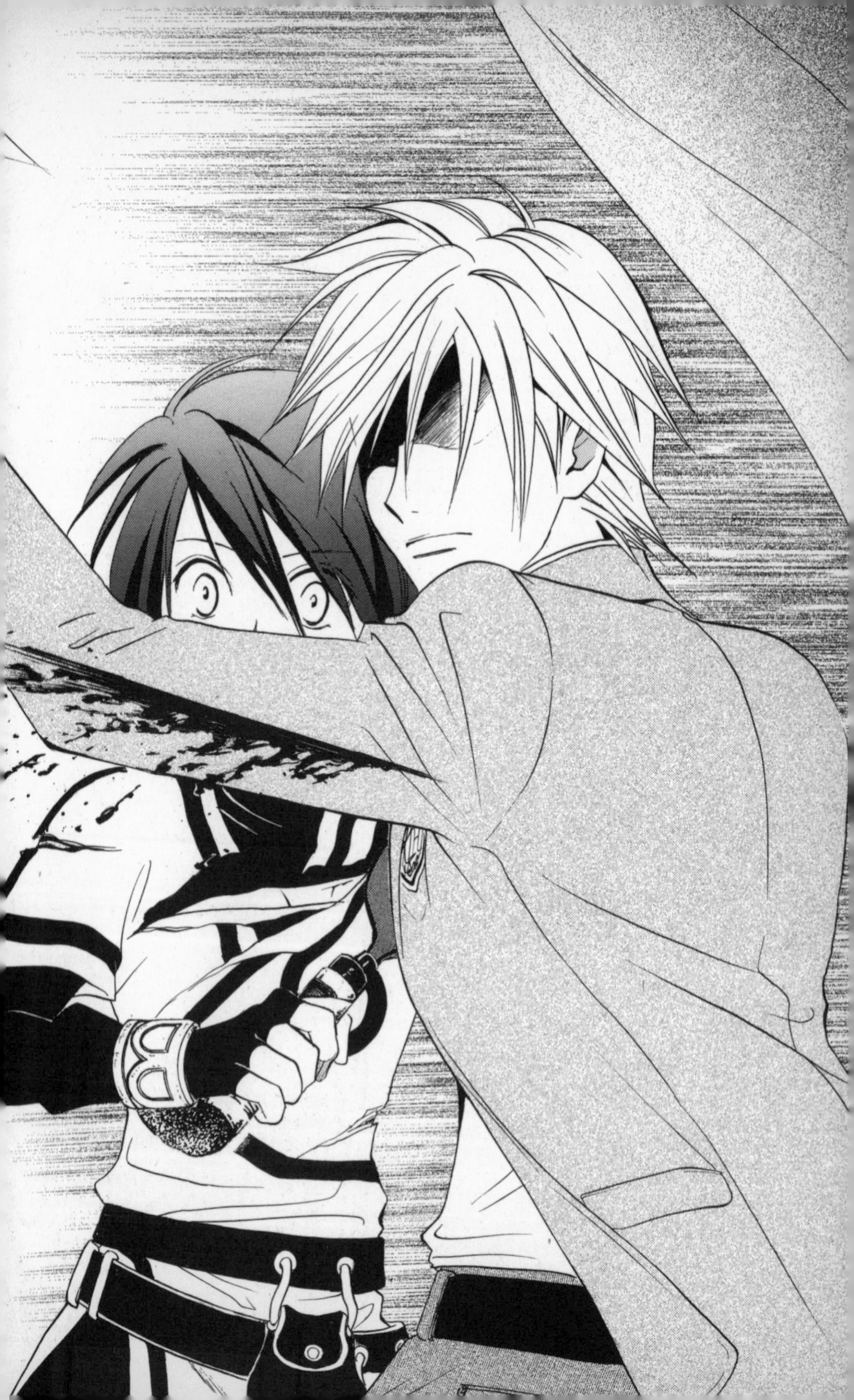

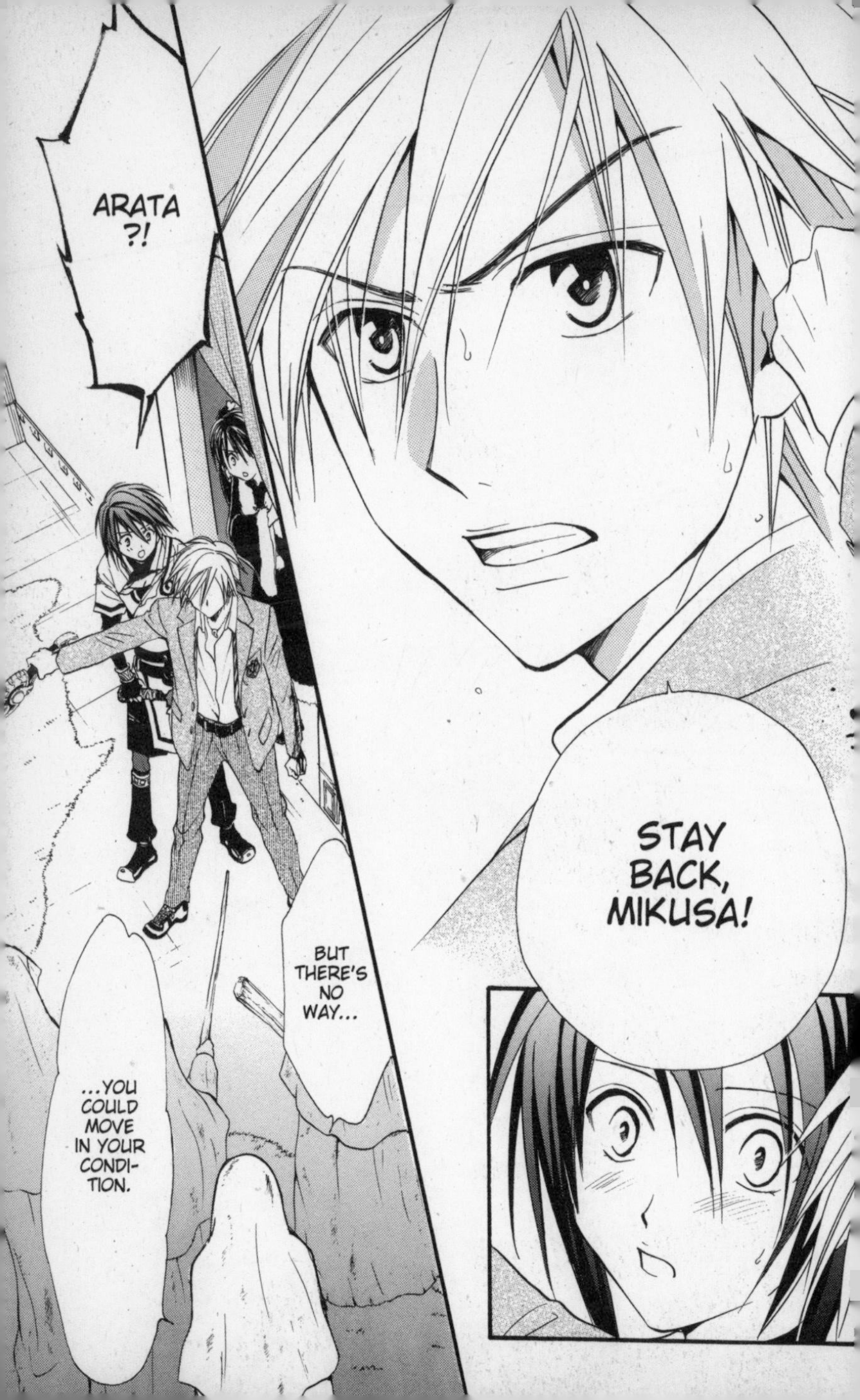
STAY BACK, MIKUSA!
ARATA ?!
BUT THERE'S NO WAY...
...YOU COULD MOVE IN YOUR CONDITION.

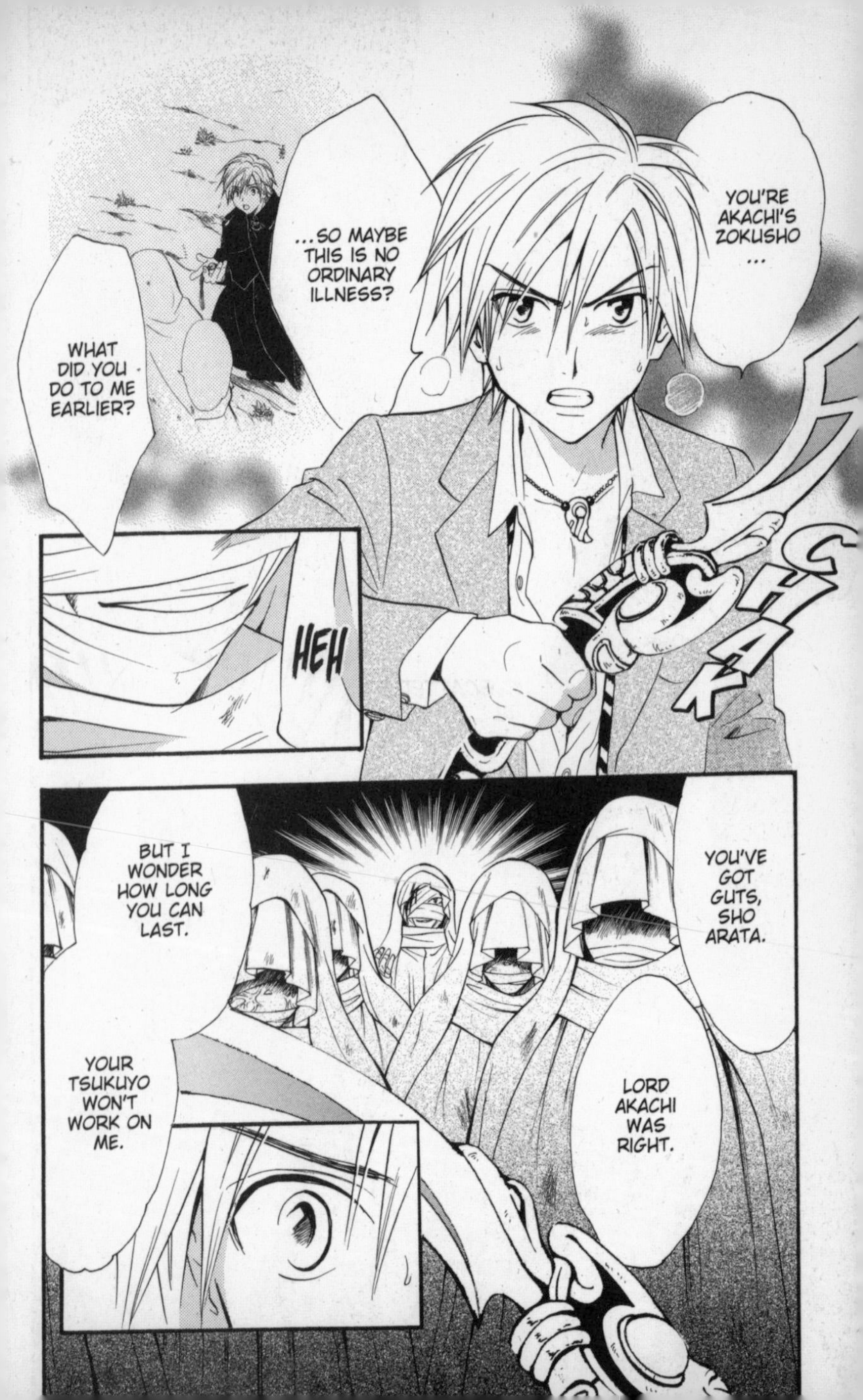
YOU'RE AKACHI'S ZOKUSHO ...
...SO MAYBE THIS IS NO ORDINARY ILLNESS?
WHAT DID YOU DO TO ME EARLIER?
CHAK
HEH
YOU'VE GOT GUTS, SHO ARATA.
LORD AKACHI WAS RIGHT.
BUT I WONDER HOW LONG YOU CAN LAST.
YOUR TSUKUYO WON'T WORK ON ME.

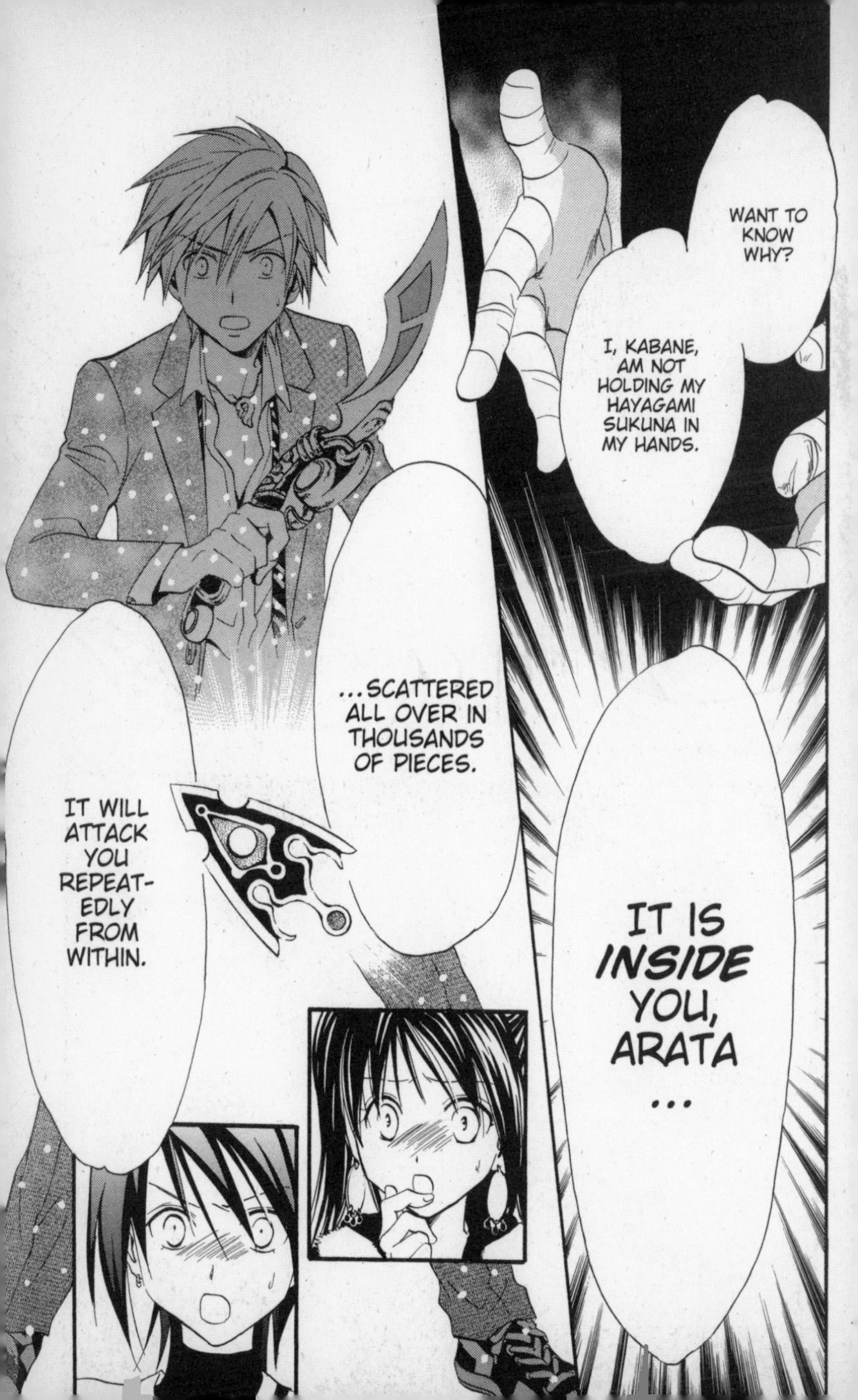
WANT TO KNOW WHY?
I, KABANE, AM NOT HOLDING MY HAYAGAMI SUKUNA IN MY HANDS.
IT IS *INSIDE* YOU, ARATA ...
...SCATTERED ALL OVER IN THOUSANDS OF PIECES.
IT WILL ATTACK YOU REPEAT-EDLY FROM WITHIN.

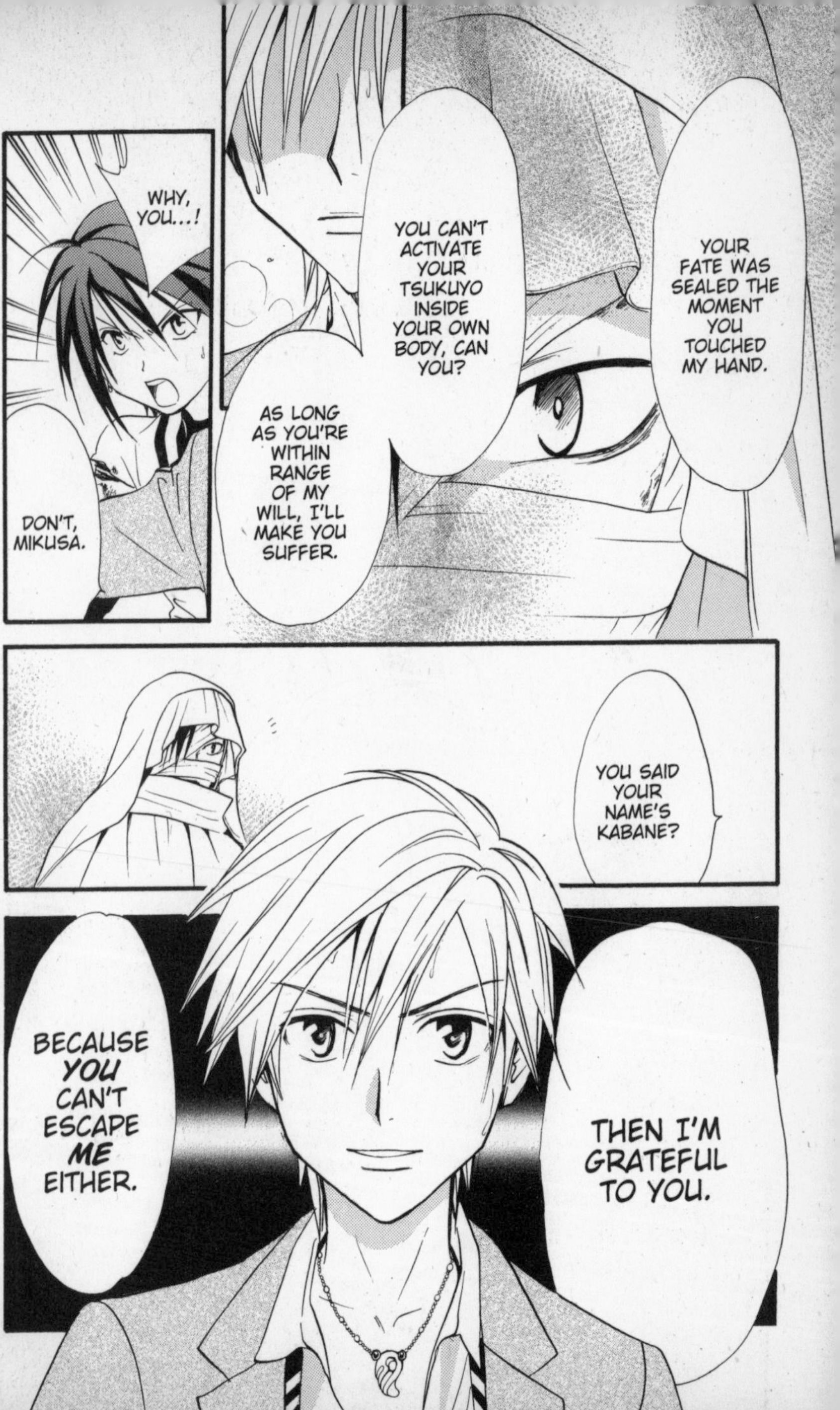
YOUR FATE WAS SEALED THE MOMENT YOU TOUCHED MY HAND.
YOU CAN'T ACTIVATE YOUR TSUKUYO INSIDE YOUR OWN BODY, CAN YOU?
AS LONG AS YOU'RE WITHIN RANGE OF MY WILL, I'LL MAKE YOU SUFFER.
WHY, YOU...!
DON'T, MIKUSA.
YOU SAID YOUR NAME'S KABANE?
THEN I'M GRATEFUL TO YOU.
BECAUSE *YOU* CAN'T ESCAPE *ME* EITHER.

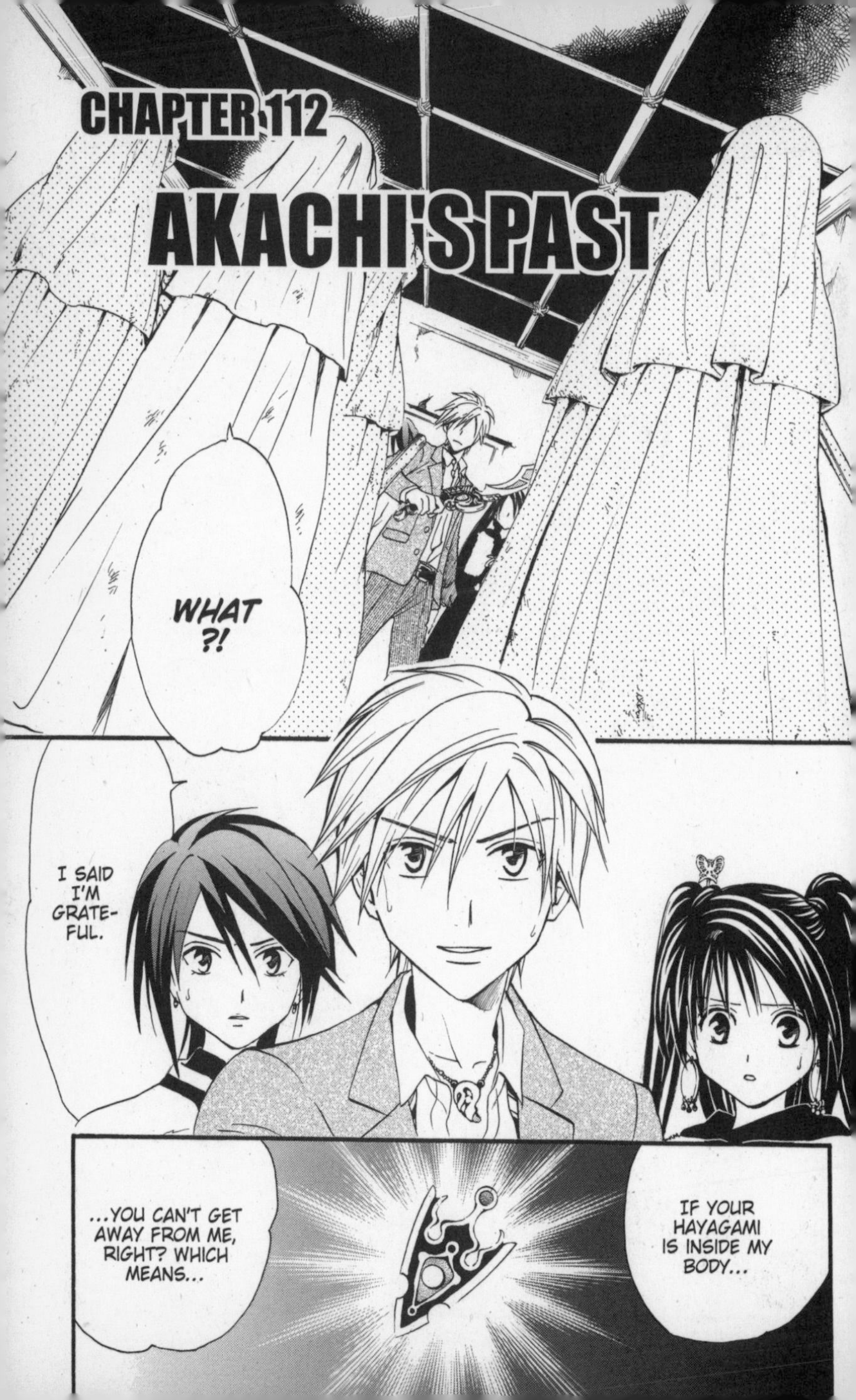
CHAPTER 112
AKACHI'S PAST
WHAT ?!
I SAID I'M GRATE-FUL.
IF YOUR HAYAGAMI IS INSIDE MY BODY...
...YOU CAN'T GET AWAY FROM ME, RIGHT? WHICH MEANS...

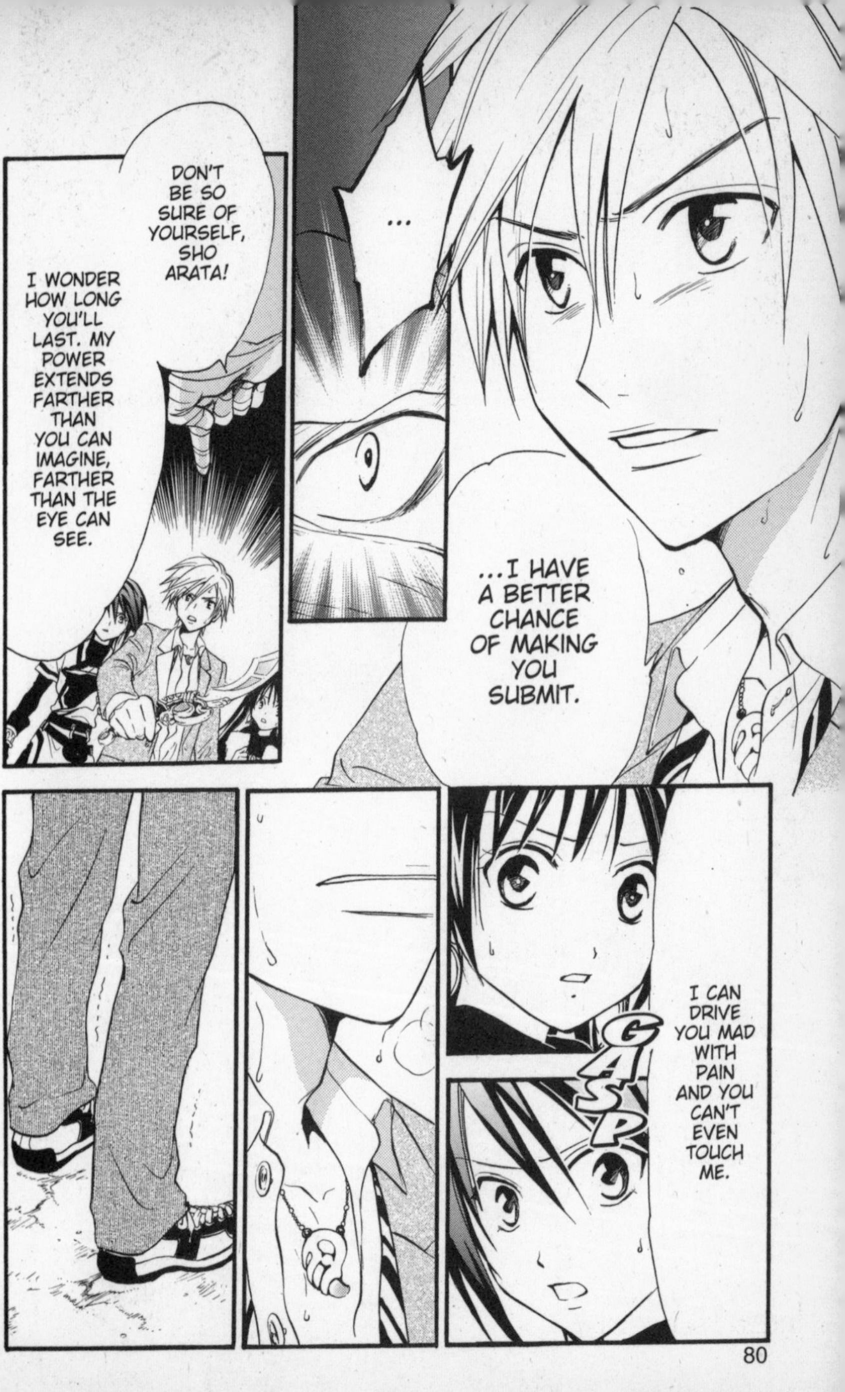
...I HAVE A BETTER CHANCE OF MAKING YOU SUBMIT.
...
DON'T BE SO SURE OF YOURSELF, SHO ARATA!
I WONDER HOW LONG YOU'LL LAST. MY POWER EXTENDS FARTHER THAN YOU CAN IMAGINE, FARTHER THAN THE EYE CAN SEE.
GASP
I CAN DRIVE YOU MAD WITH PAIN AND YOU CAN'T EVEN TOUCH ME.

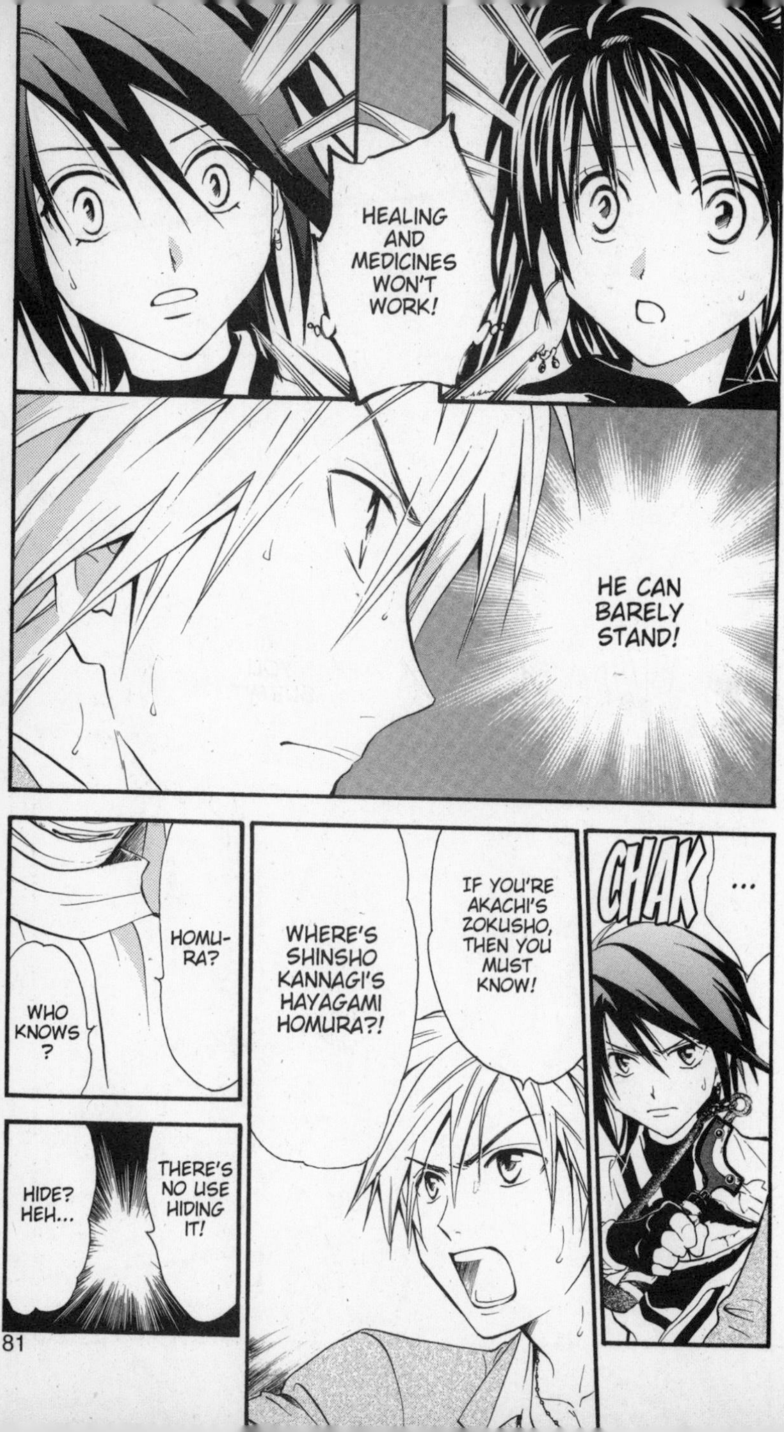

HEALING AND MEDICINES WON'T WORK!
HE CAN BARELY STAND!
CHAK
...
IF YOU'RE AKACHI'S ZOKUSHO, THEN YOU MUST KNOW!
WHERE'S SHINSHO KANNAGI'S HAYAGAMI HOMURA?!
HOMU-RA?
WHO KNOWS?
THERE'S NO USE HIDING IT!
HIDE? HEH...

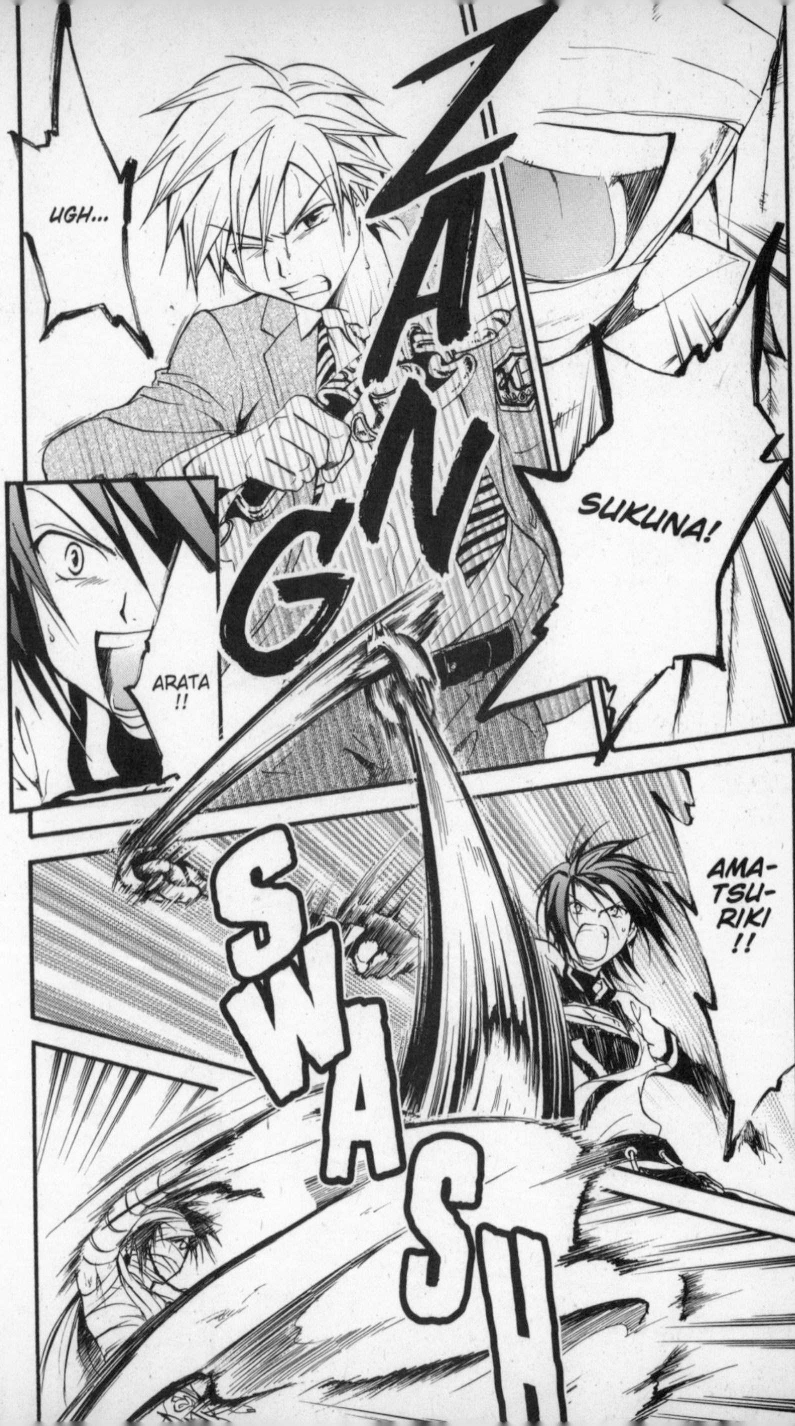
ZANG
UGH...
SUKUNA!
ARATA !!
AMA-TSU-RIKI !!
SWASH

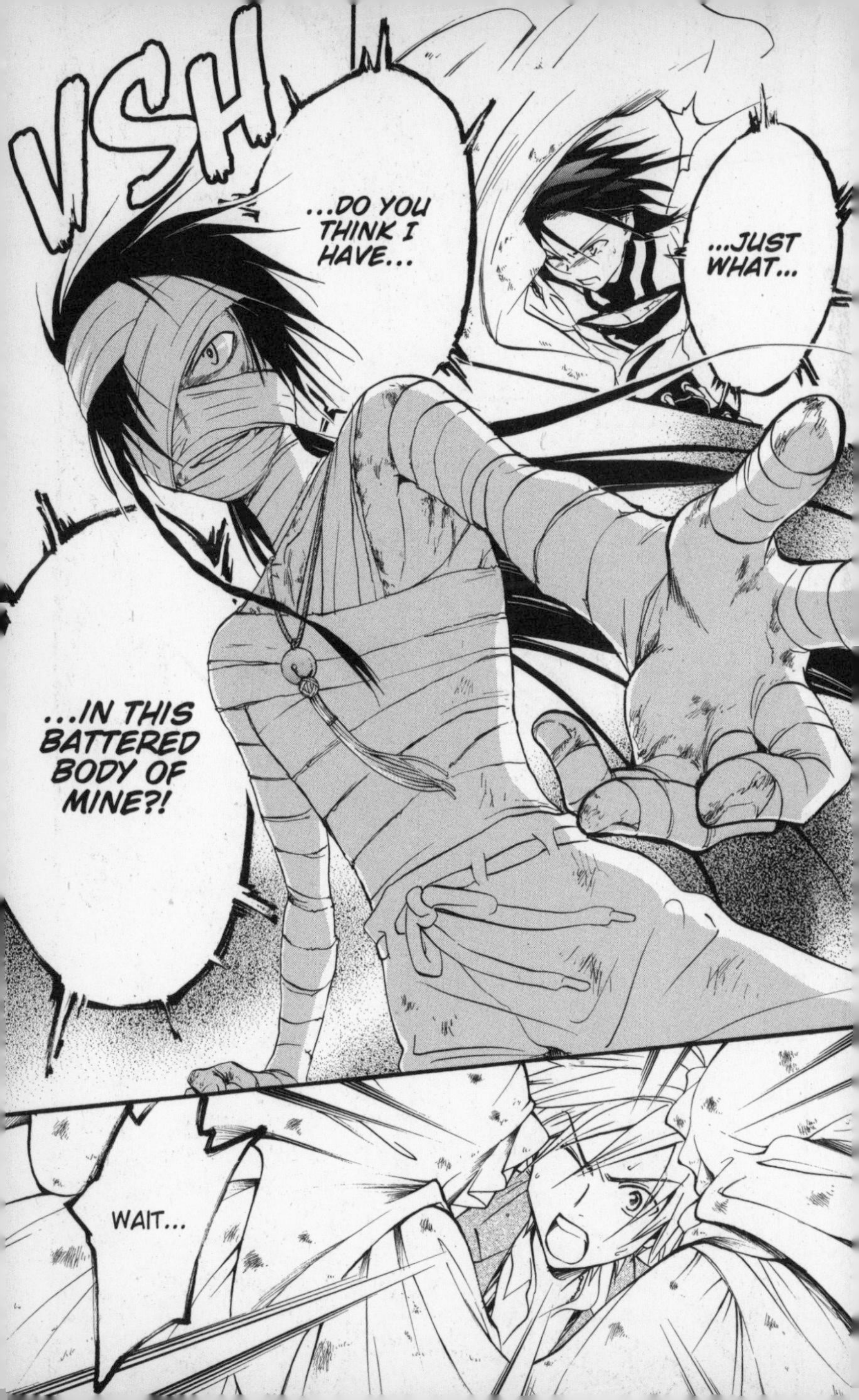
...JUST WHAT...
...DO YOU THINK I HAVE...
VSH
...IN THIS BATTERED BODY OF MINE?!
WAIT...

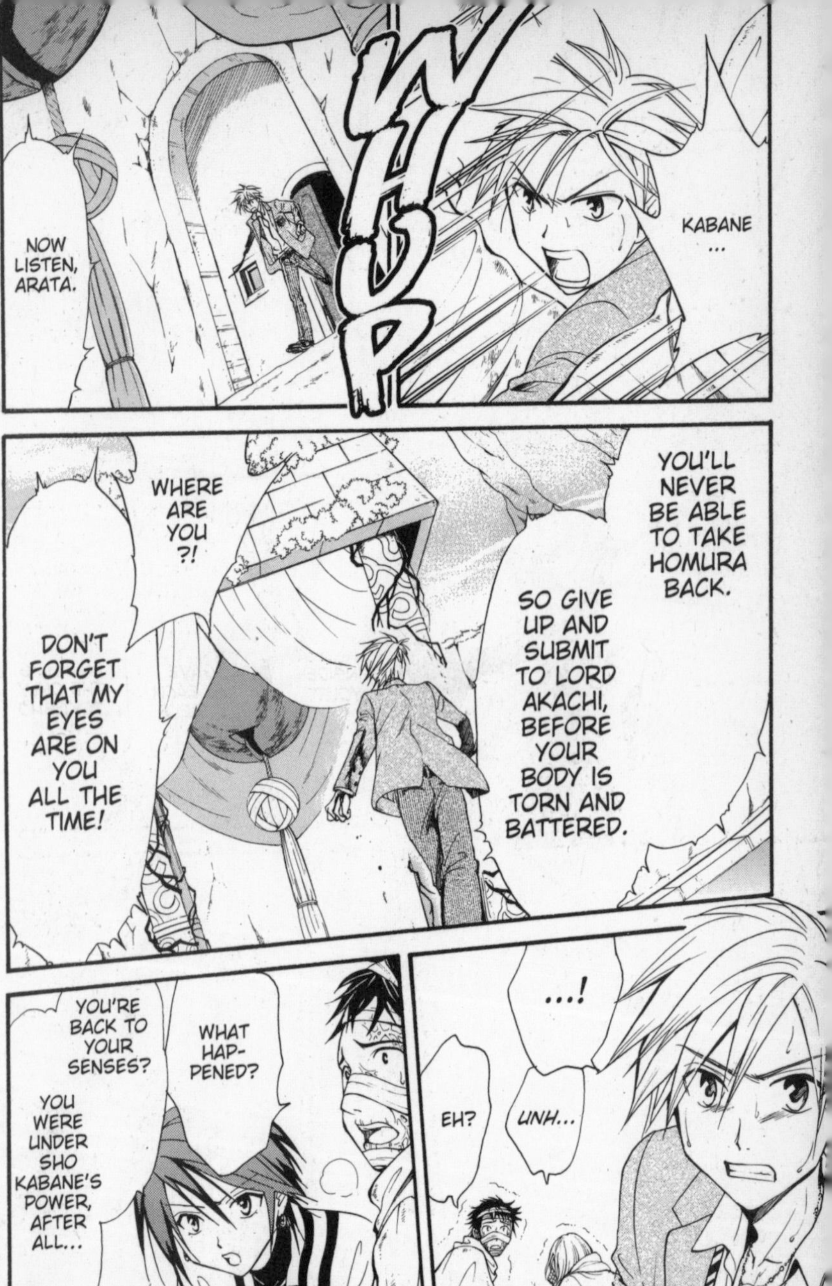
KABANE ...
WHUP
NOW LISTEN, ARATA.
YOU'LL NEVER BE ABLE TO TAKE HOMURA BACK.
SO GIVE UP AND SUBMIT TO LORD AKACHI, BEFORE YOUR BODY IS TORN AND BATTERED.
WHERE ARE YOU ?!
DON'T FORGET THAT MY EYES ARE ON YOU ALL THE TIME!
...!
UNH...
EH?
WHAT HAP-PENED?
YOU'RE BACK TO YOUR SENSES?
YOU WERE UNDER SHO KABANE'S POWER, AFTER ALL...

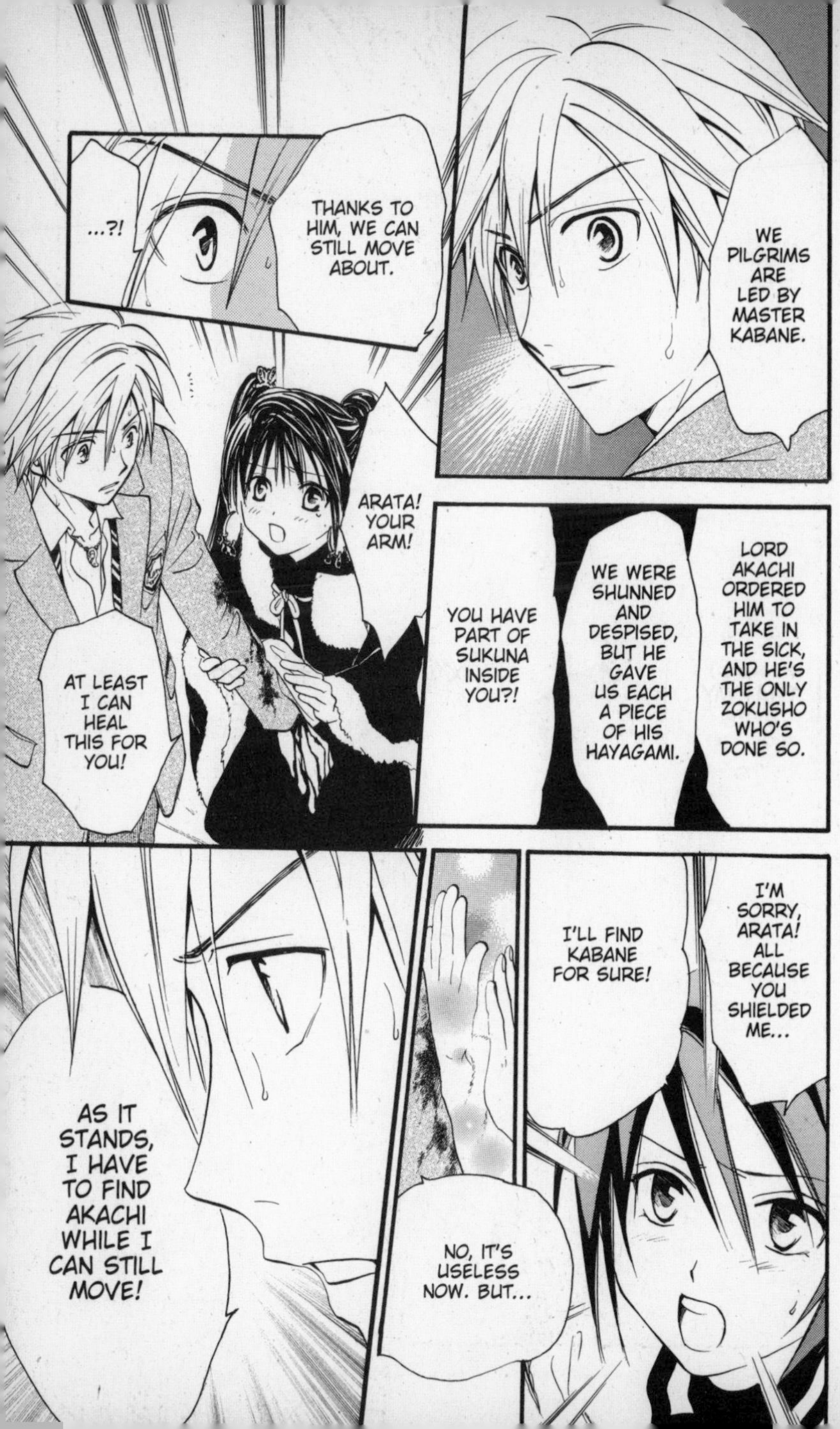

WE PILGRIMS ARE LED BY MASTER KABANE.
THANKS TO HIM, WE CAN STILL MOVE ABOUT.
...?!
LORD AKACHI ORDERED HIM TO TAKE IN THE SICK, AND HE'S THE ONLY ZOKUSHO WHO'S DONE SO.
WE WERE SHUNNED AND DESPISED, BUT HE GAVE US EACH A PIECE OF HIS HAYAGAMI.
YOU HAVE PART OF SUKUNA INSIDE YOU?!
ARATA! YOUR ARM!
AT LEAST I CAN HEAL THIS FOR YOU!
I'M SORRY, ARATA! ALL BECAUSE YOU SHIELDED ME...
I'LL FIND KABANE FOR SURE!
NO, IT'S USELESS NOW. BUT...
AS IT STANDS, I HAVE TO FIND AKACHI WHILE I CAN STILL MOVE!

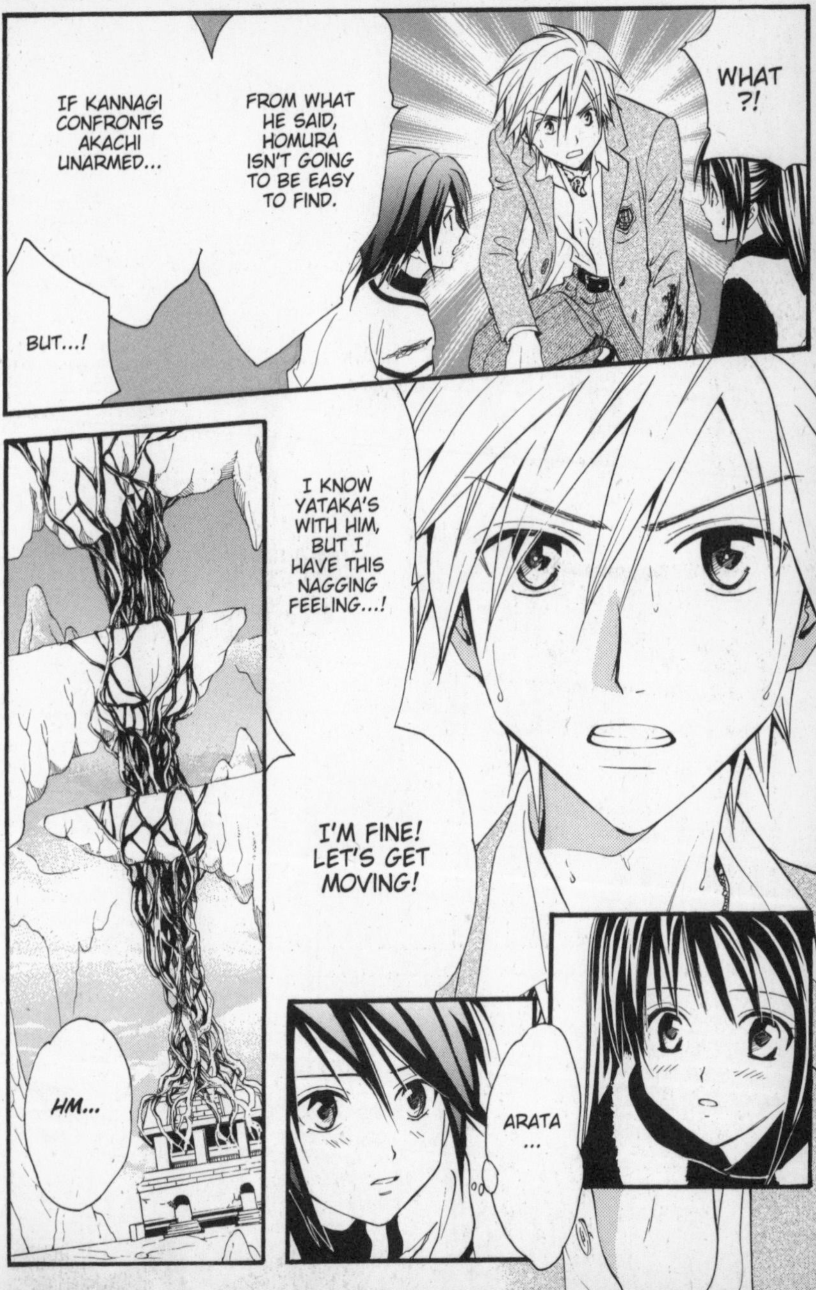
WHAT?!
FROM WHAT HE SAID, HOMURA ISN'T GOING TO BE EASY TO FIND.
IF KANNAGI CONFRONTS AKACHI UNARMED...
BUT...!
I KNOW YATAKA'S WITH HIM, BUT I HAVE THIS NAGGING FEELING...!
I'M FINE! LET'S GET MOVING!
ARATA...
HM...

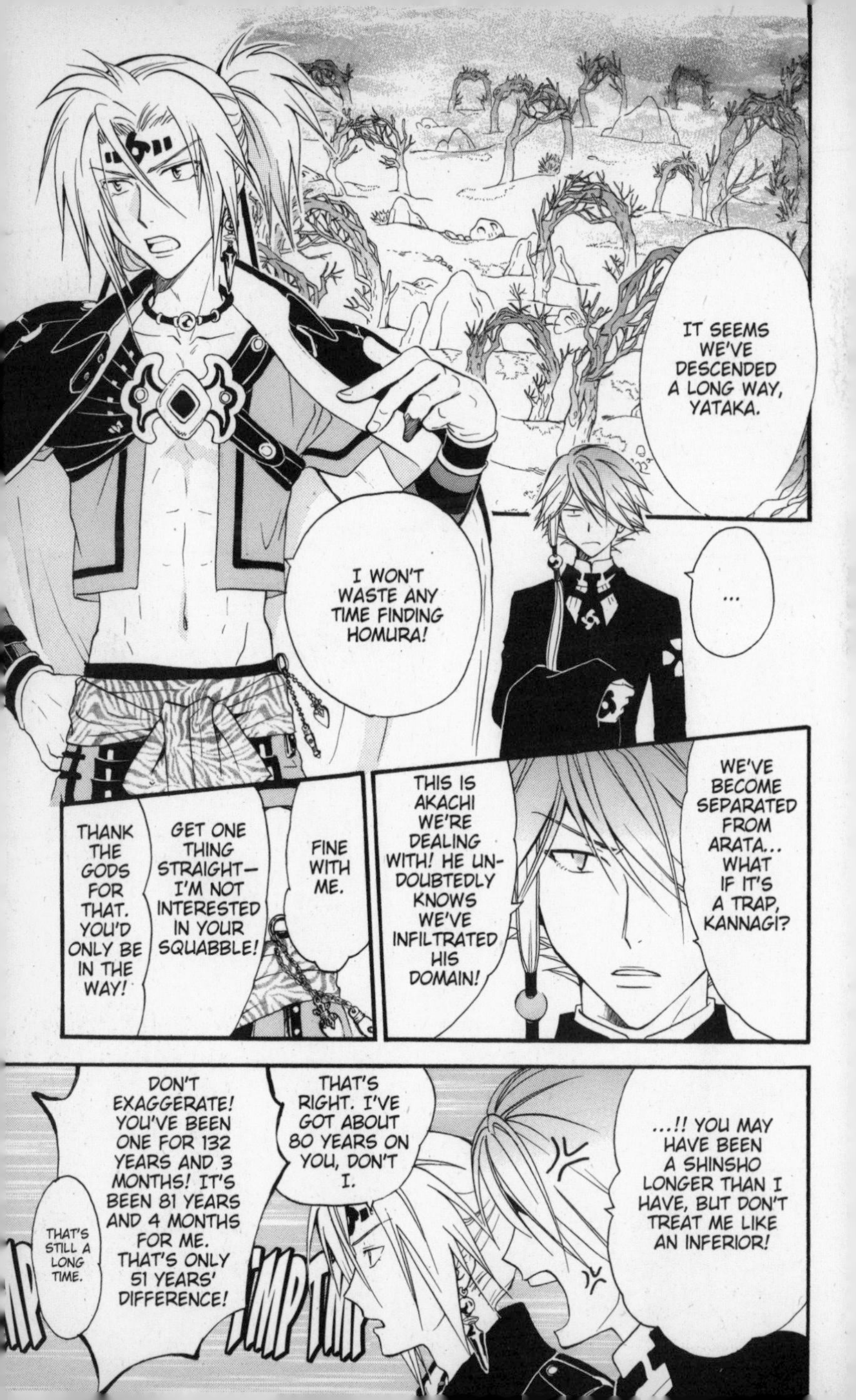
IT SEEMS WE'VE DESCENDED A LONG WAY, YATAKA.
...
I WON'T WASTE ANY TIME FINDING HOMURA!
WE'VE BECOME SEPARATED FROM ARATA... WHAT IF IT'S A TRAP, KANNAGI?
THIS IS AKACHI WE'RE DEALING WITH! HE UNDOUBTEDLY KNOWS WE'VE INFILTRATED HIS DOMAIN!
FINE WITH ME.
GET ONE THING STRAIGHT— I'M NOT INTERESTED IN YOUR SQUABBLE!
THANK THE GODS FOR THAT. YOU'D ONLY BE IN THE WAY!
...!! YOU MAY HAVE BEEN A SHINSHO LONGER THAN I HAVE, BUT DON'T TREAT ME LIKE AN INFERIOR!
THAT'S RIGHT. I'VE GOT ABOUT 80 YEARS ON YOU, DON'T I.
DON'T EXAGGERATE! YOU'VE BEEN ONE FOR 132 YEARS AND 3 MONTHS! IT'S BEEN 81 YEARS AND 4 MONTHS FOR ME. THAT'S ONLY 51 YEARS' DIFFERENCE!
THAT'S STILL A LONG TIME.

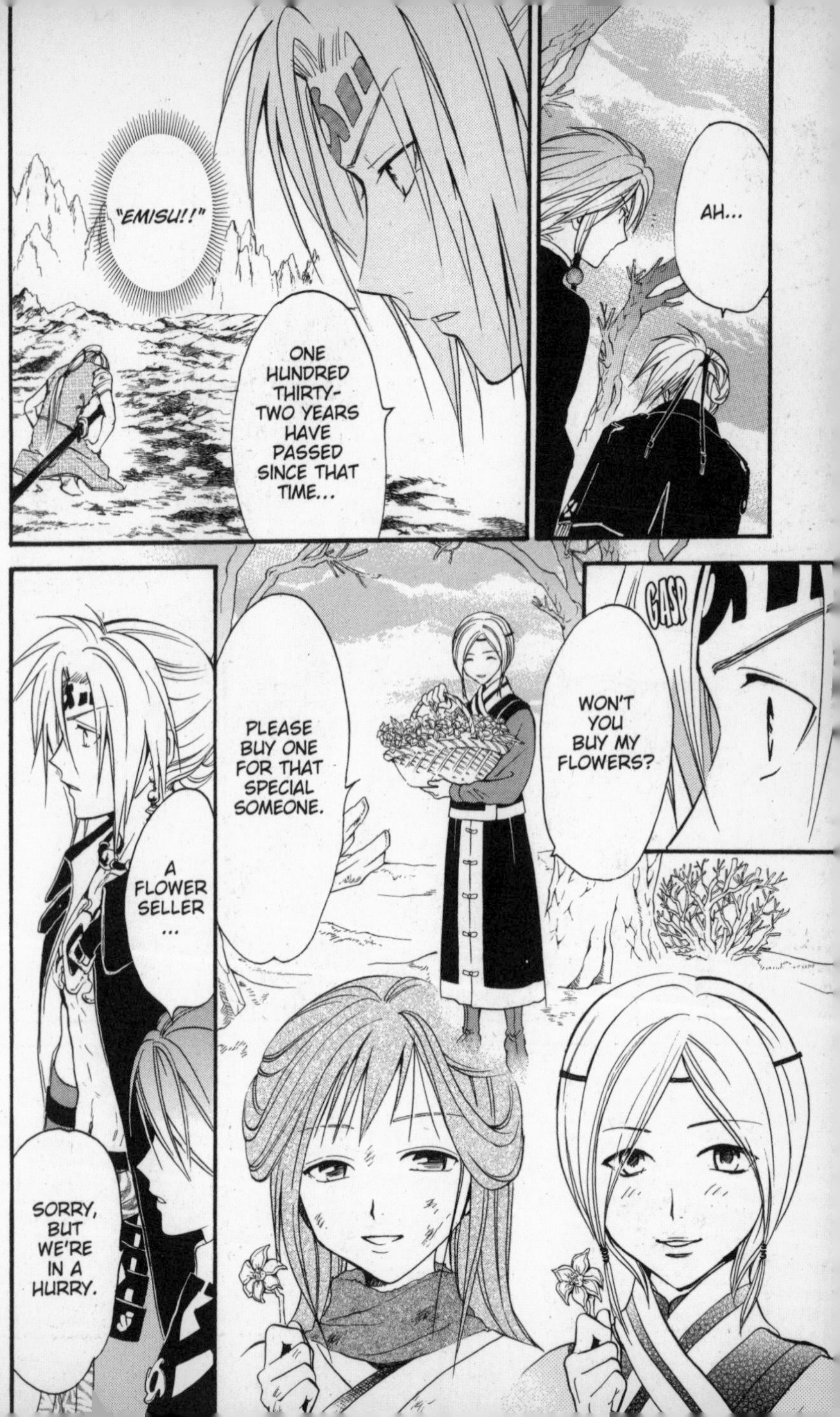
AH...
"EMISU!!"
ONE HUNDRED THIRTY-TWO YEARS HAVE PASSED SINCE THAT TIME...
GASP
WON'T YOU BUY MY FLOWERS?
PLEASE BUY ONE FOR THAT SPECIAL SOMEONE.
A FLOWER SELLER ...
SORRY, BUT WE'RE IN A HURRY.

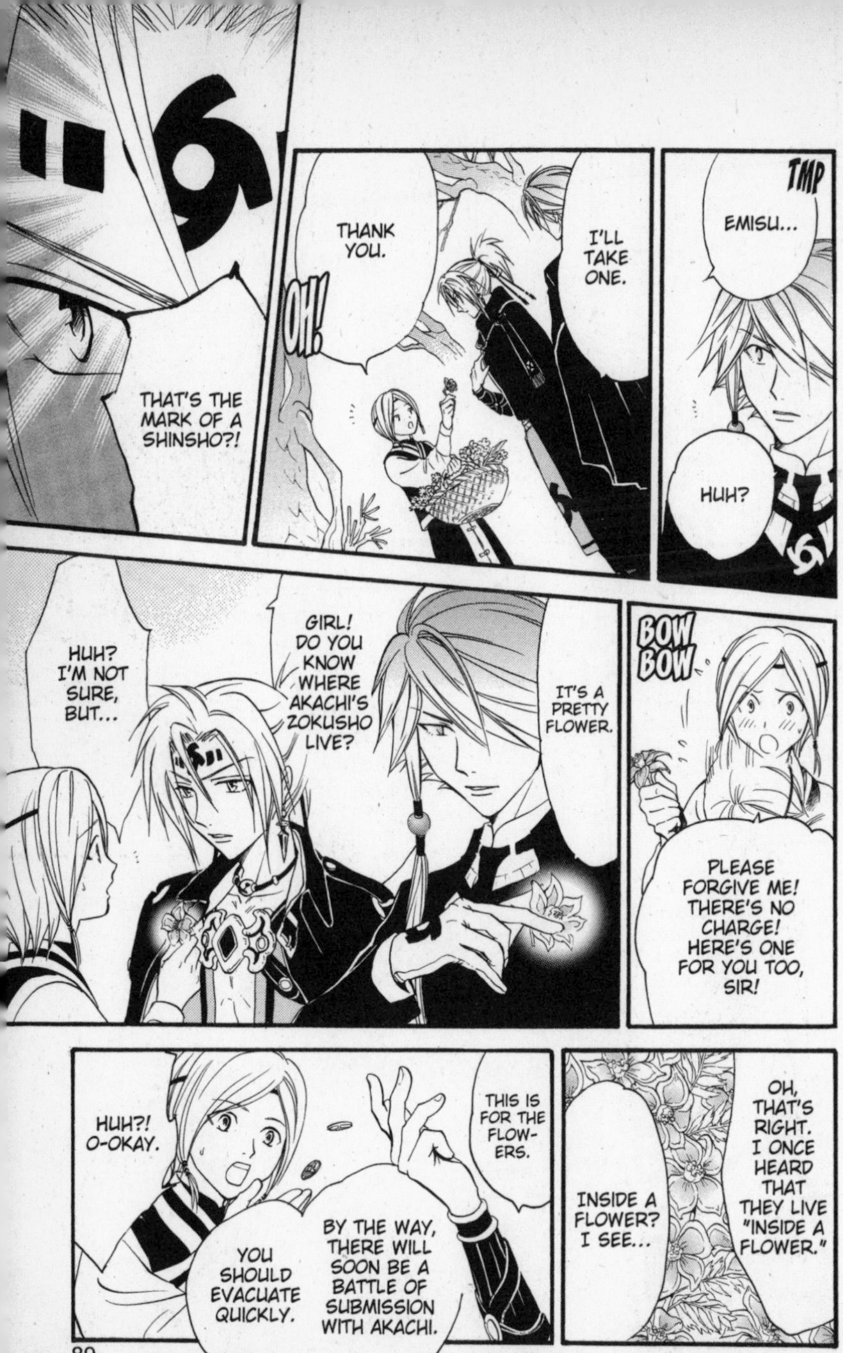
TMP
EMISU...
HUH?
I'LL TAKE ONE.
THANK YOU.
OH!
THAT'S THE MARK OF A SHINSHO?!
BOW BOW
PLEASE FORGIVE ME! THERE'S NO CHARGE! HERE'S ONE FOR YOU TOO, SIR!
IT'S A PRETTY FLOWER.
GIRL! DO YOU KNOW WHERE AKACHI'S ZOKUSHO LIVE?
HUH? I'M NOT SURE, BUT...
OH, THAT'S RIGHT. I ONCE HEARD THAT THEY LIVE "INSIDE A FLOWER."
INSIDE A FLOWER? I SEE...
THIS IS FOR THE FLOWERS.
BY THE WAY, THERE WILL SOON BE A BATTLE OF SUBMISSION WITH AKACHI.
YOU SHOULD EVACUATE QUICKLY.
HUH?! O-OKAY.

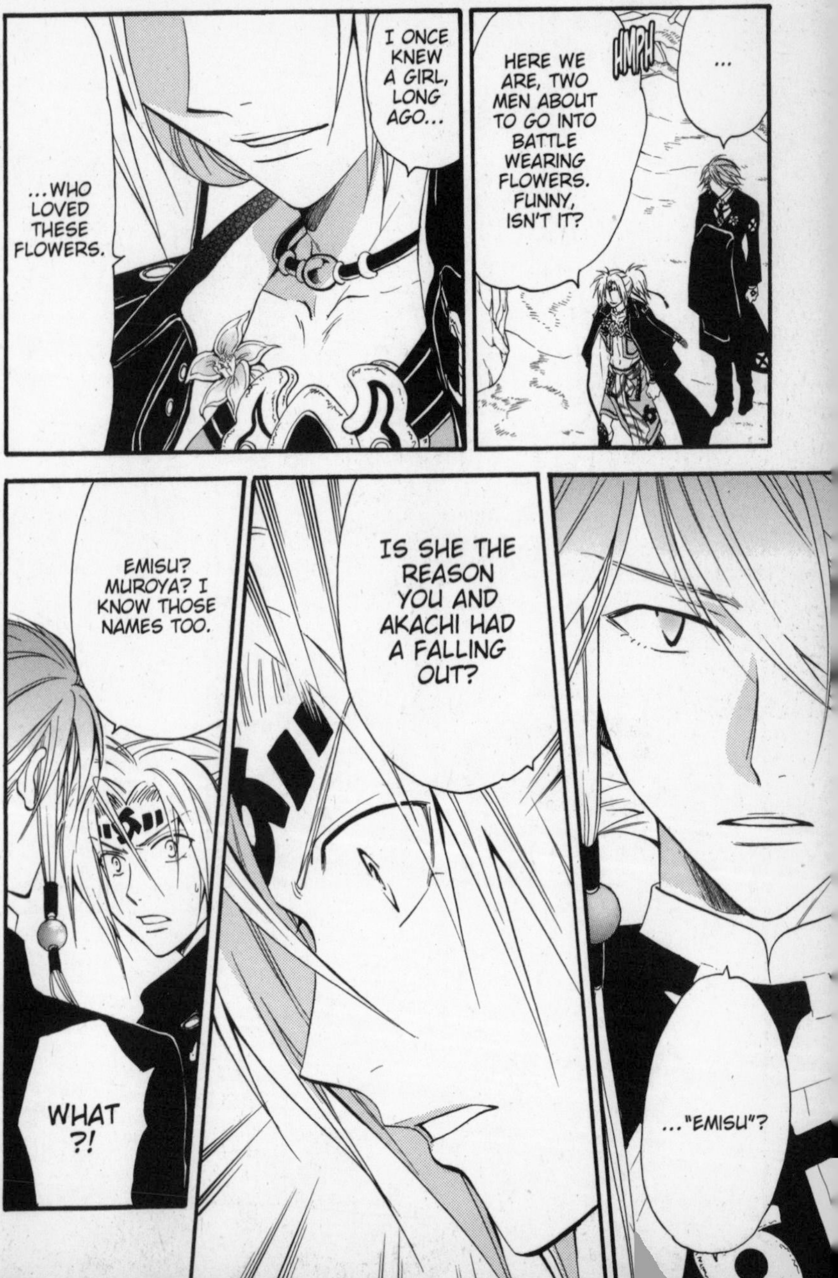
...
HMPH
HERE WE ARE, TWO MEN ABOUT TO GO INTO BATTLE WEARING FLOWERS. FUNNY, ISN'T IT?
I ONCE KNEW A GIRL, LONG AGO...
...WHO LOVED THESE FLOWERS.
..."EMISU"?
IS SHE THE REASON YOU AND AKACHI HAD A FALLING OUT?
EMISU? MUROYA? I KNOW THOSE NAMES TOO.
WHAT?!

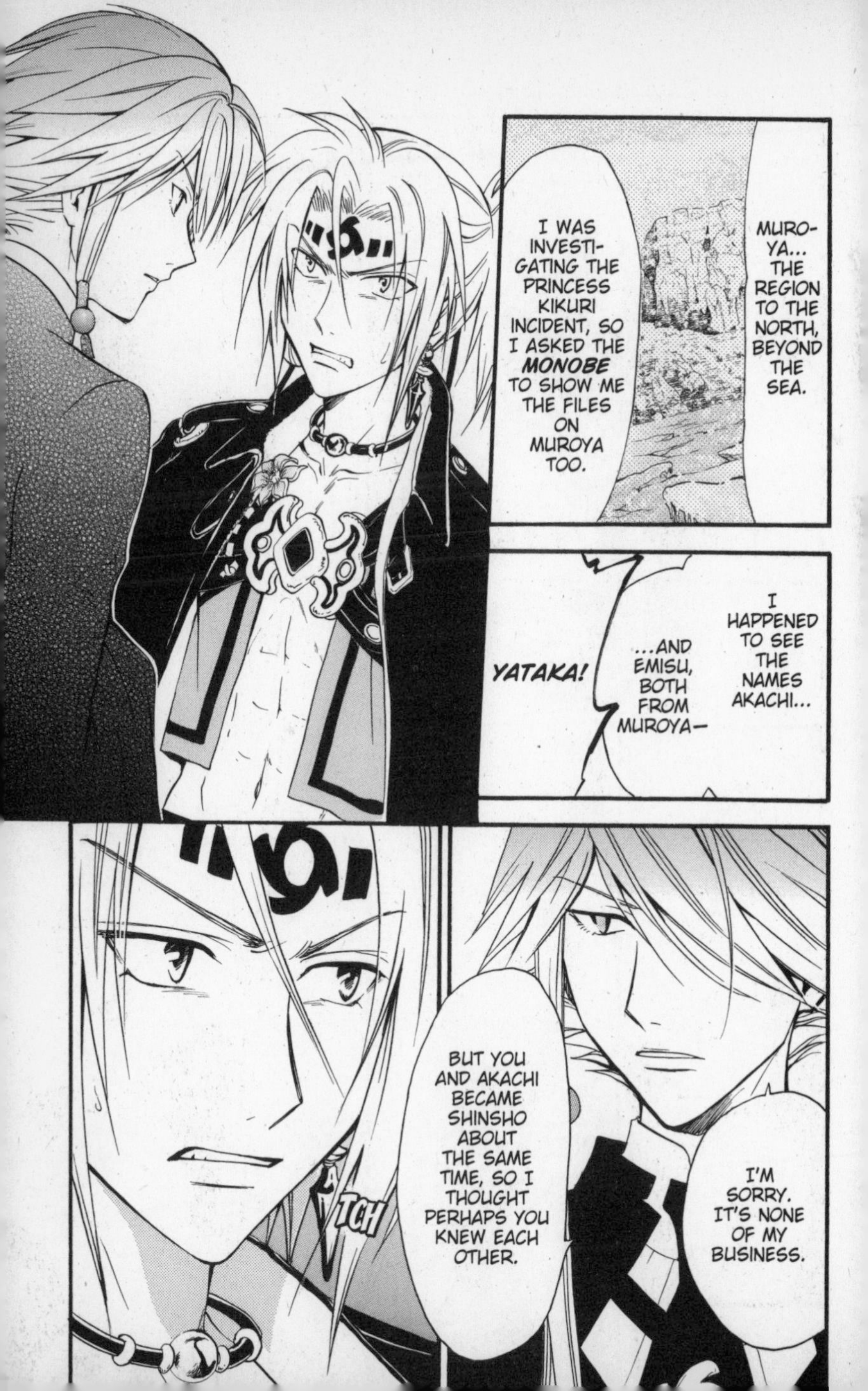
MURO-YA... THE REGION TO THE NORTH, BEYOND THE SEA.
I WAS INVESTIGATING THE PRINCESS KIKURI INCIDENT, SO I ASKED THE ***MONOBE*** TO SHOW ME THE FILES ON MUROYA TOO.
I HAPPENED TO SEE THE NAMES AKACHI...
...AND EMISU, BOTH FROM MUROYA—
YATAKA!
BUT YOU AND AKACHI BECAME SHINSHO ABOUT THE SAME TIME, SO I THOUGHT PERHAPS YOU KNEW EACH OTHER.
I'M SORRY. IT'S NONE OF MY BUSINESS.
TCH

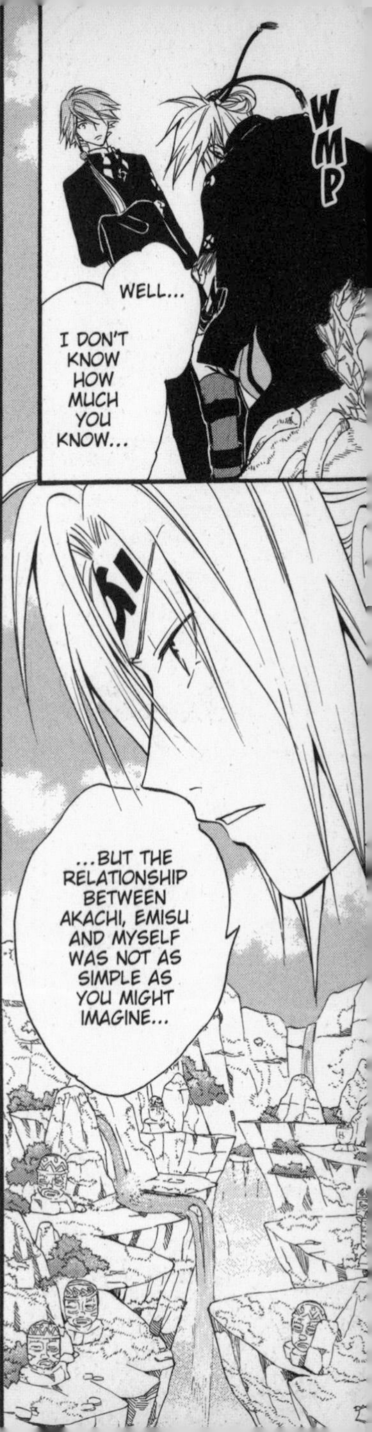
WMP
WELL...
I DON'T KNOW HOW MUCH YOU KNOW...
...BUT THE RELATIONSHIP BETWEEN AKACHI, EMISU AND MYSELF WAS NOT AS SIMPLE AS YOU MIGHT IMAGINE...

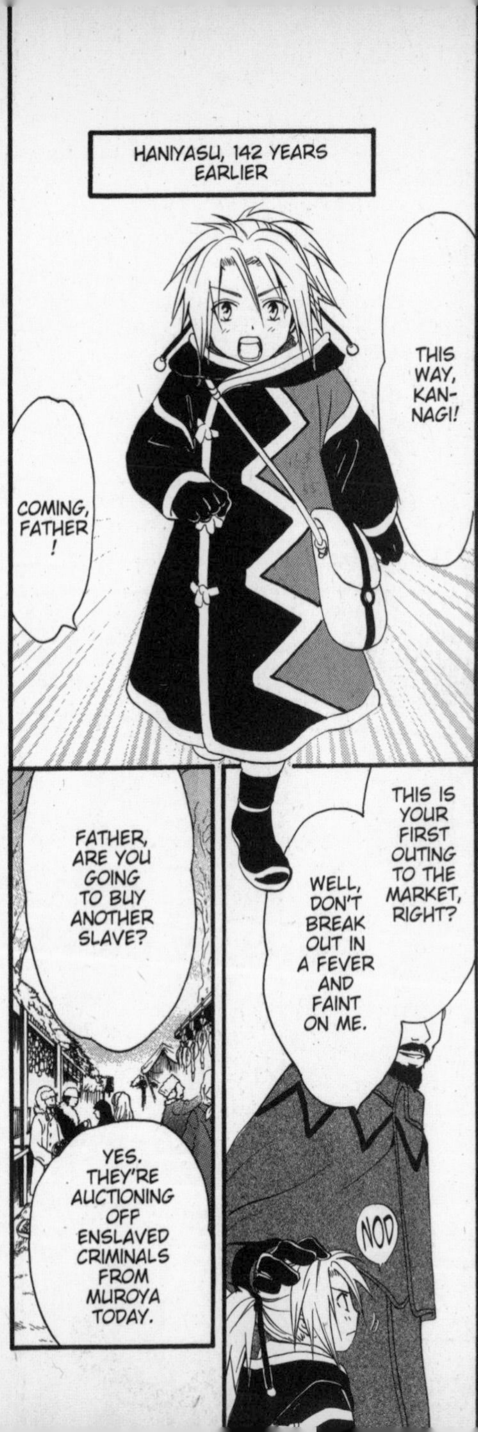
HANIYASU, 142 YEARS EARLIER
THIS WAY, KAN-NAGI!
COMING, FATHER!
THIS IS YOUR FIRST OUTING TO THE MARKET, RIGHT?
WELL, DON'T BREAK OUT IN A FEVER AND FAINT ON ME.
NOD
FATHER, ARE YOU GOING TO BUY ANOTHER SLAVE?
YES. THEY'RE AUCTIONING OFF ENSLAVED CRIMINALS FROM MUROYA TODAY.

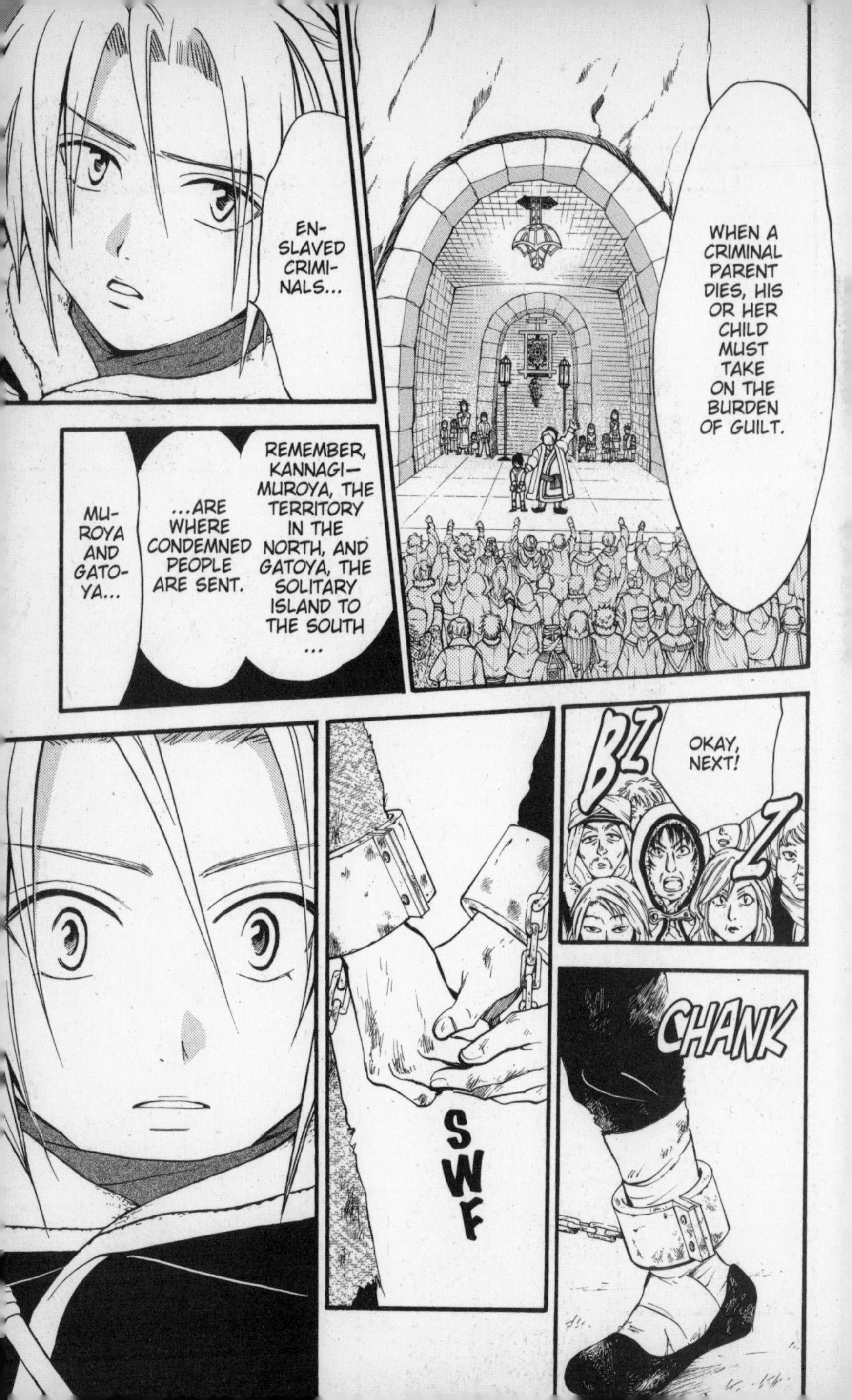

WHEN A CRIMINAL PARENT DIES, HIS OR HER CHILD MUST TAKE ON THE BURDEN OF GUILT.
EN-SLAVED CRIMI-NALS...
REMEMBER, KANNAGI— MUROYA, THE TERRITORY IN THE NORTH, AND GATOYA, THE SOLITARY ISLAND TO THE SOUTH ...
...ARE WHERE CONDEMNED PEOPLE ARE SENT.
MU-ROYA AND GATO-YA...
BZZ
OKAY, NEXT!
CHANK
SWF

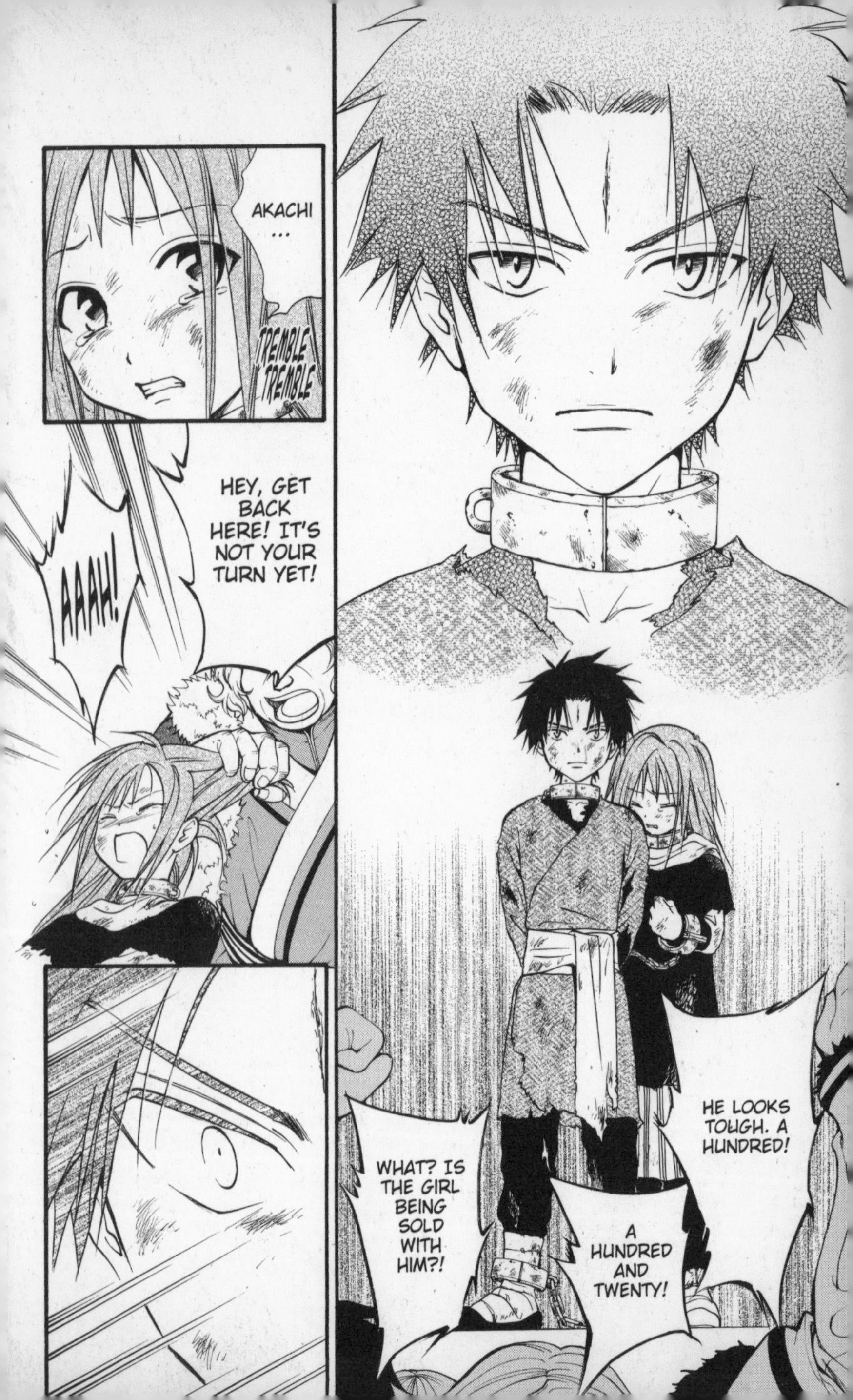
HE LOOKS TOUGH. A HUNDRED!
A HUNDRED AND TWENTY!
WHAT? IS THE GIRL BEING SOLD WITH HIM?!
AKACHI ...
TREMBLE TREMBLE
HEY, GET BACK HERE! IT'S NOT YOUR TURN YET!
AAAH!

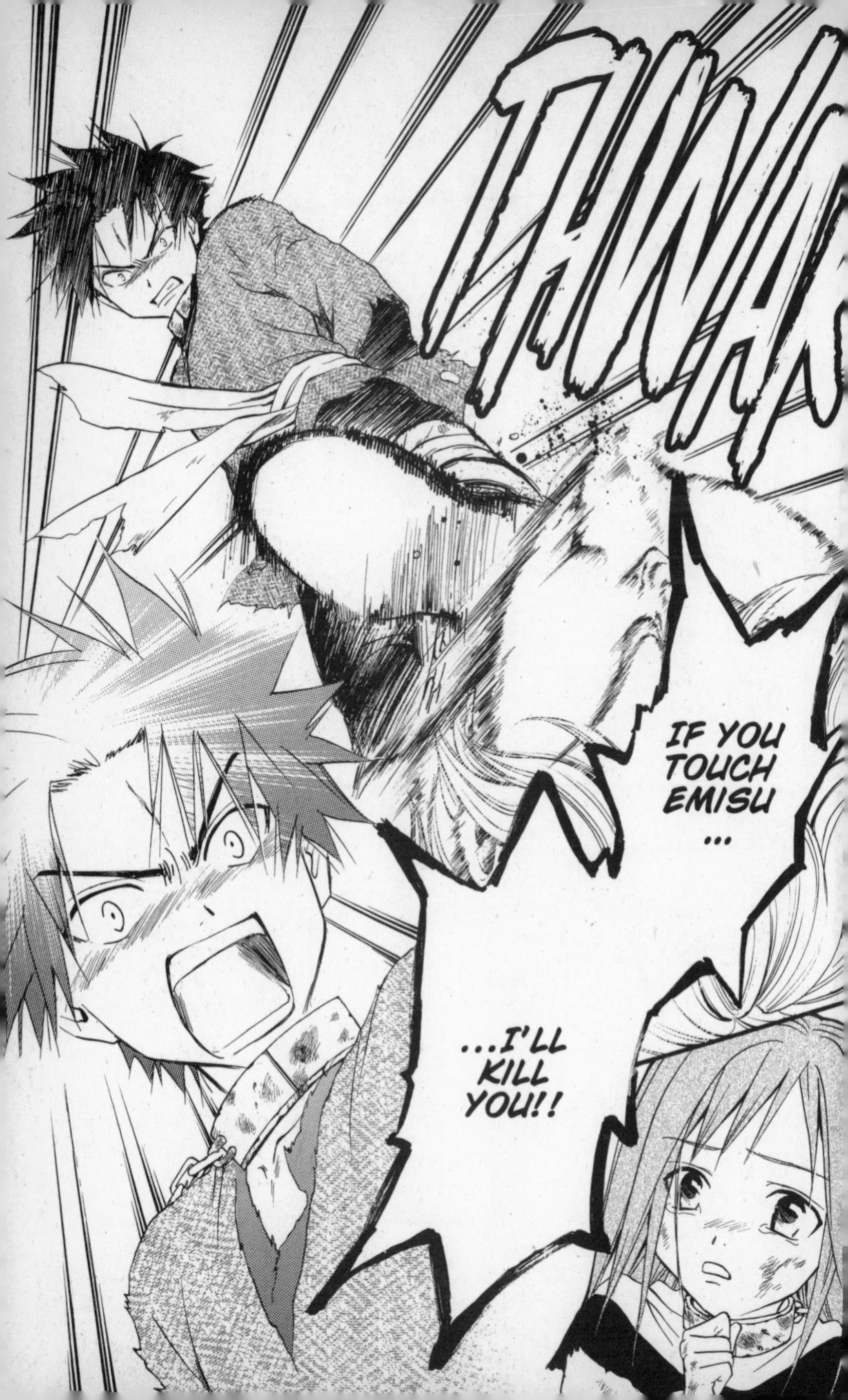
IF YOU TOUCH EMISU ...
...I'LL KILL YOU!!

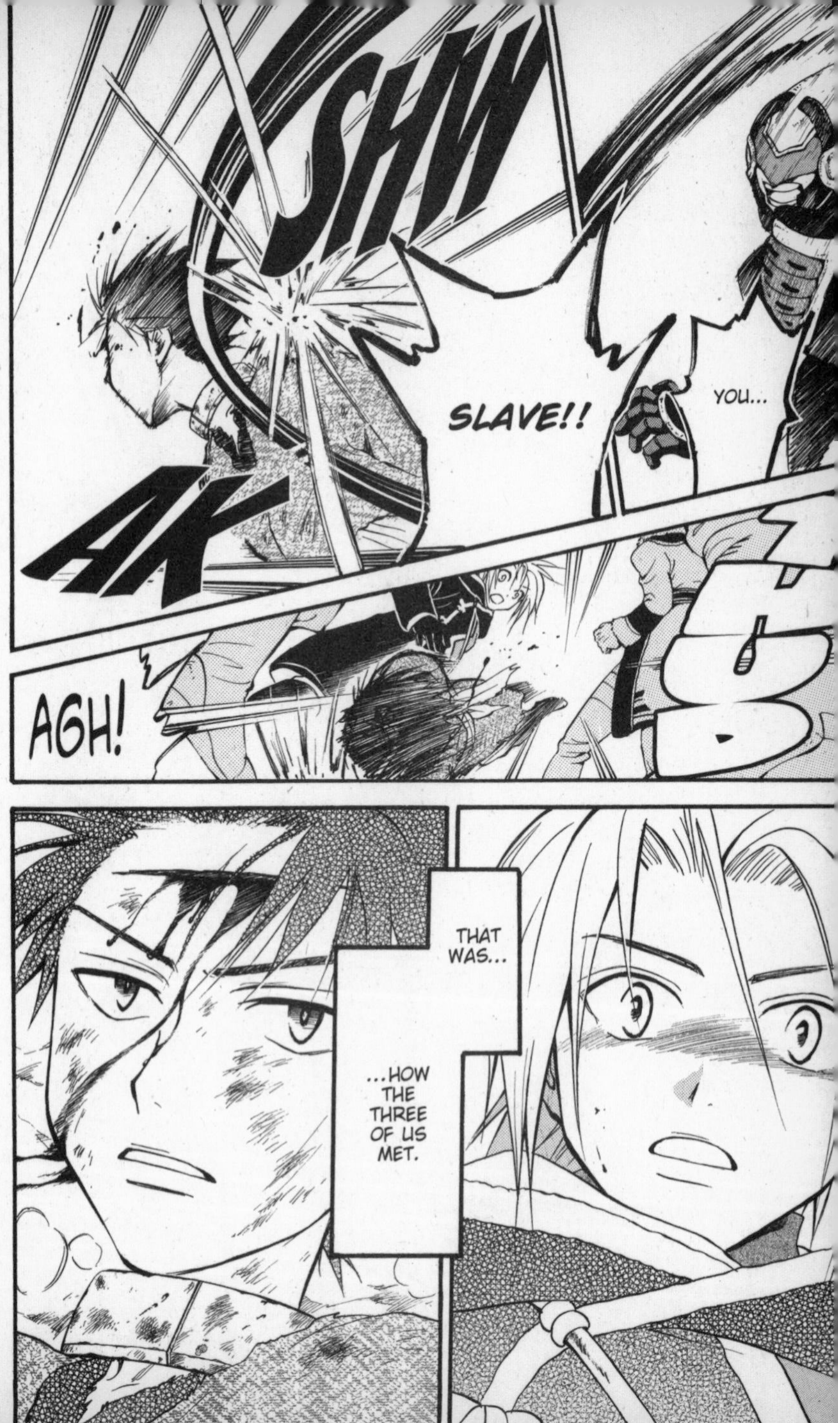
SHN
YOU...
SLAVE!!
AX
AGH!
THAT WAS...
...HOW THE THREE OF US MET.

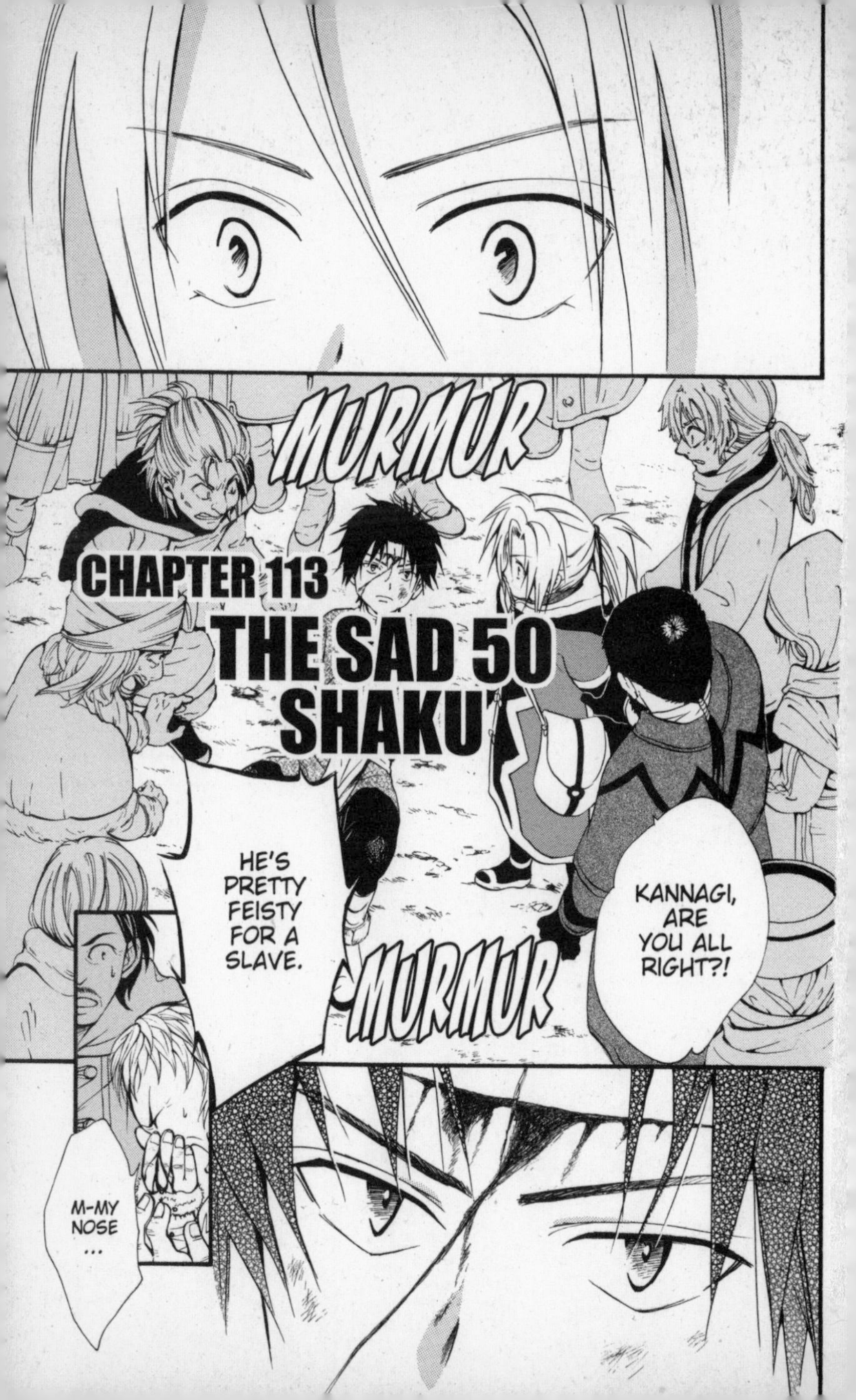
MURMUR
CHAPTER 113
THE SAD 50 SHAKU
KANNAGI, ARE YOU ALL RIGHT?!
HE'S PRETTY FEISTY FOR A SLAVE.
MURMUR
M-MY NOSE ...

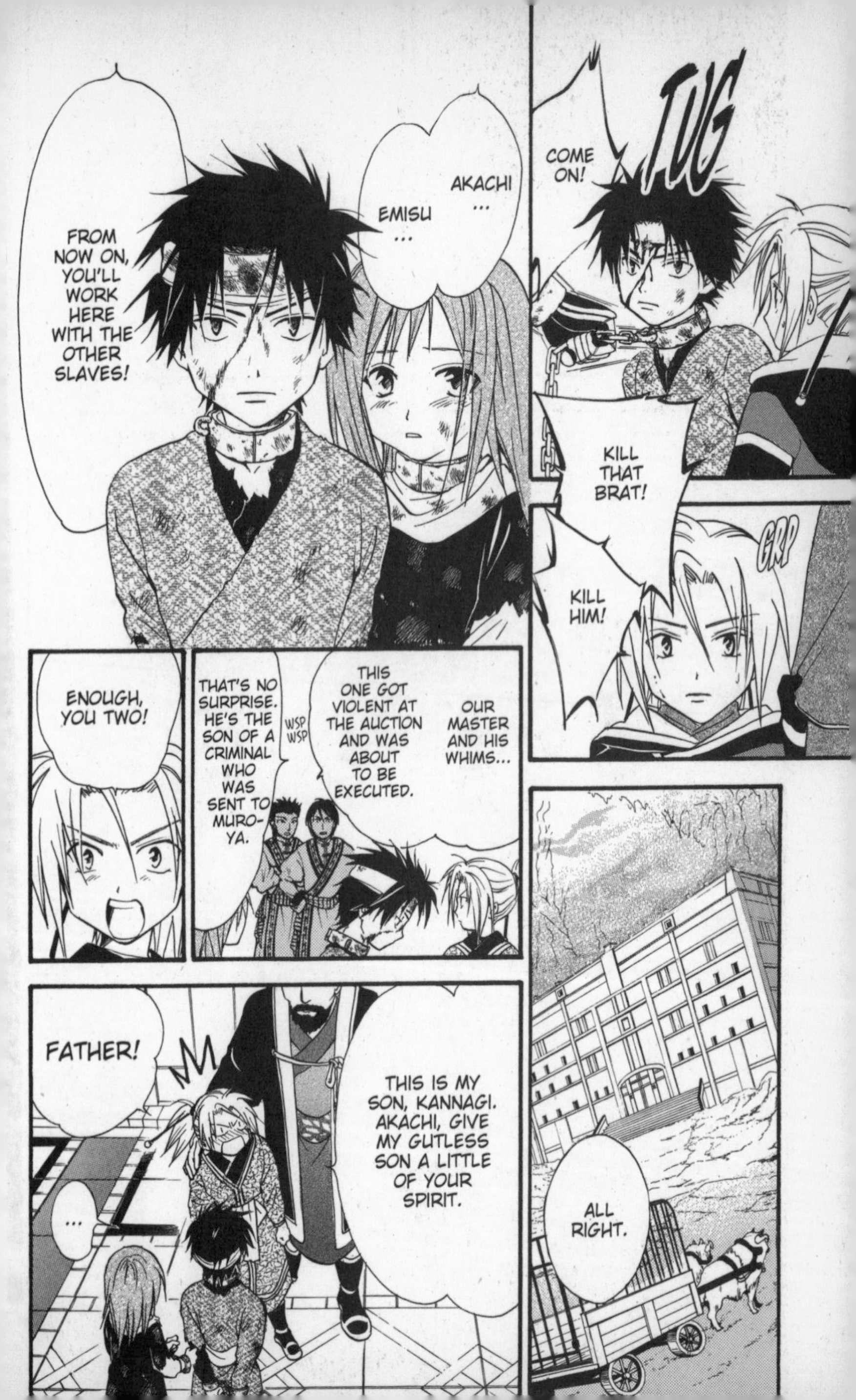
TUG
COME ON!
KILL THAT BRAT!
GRP
KILL HIM!
AKACHI... EMISU...
FROM NOW ON, YOU'LL WORK HERE WITH THE OTHER SLAVES!
ALL RIGHT.
OUR MASTER AND HIS WHIMS...
THIS ONE GOT VIOLENT AT THE AUCTION AND WAS ABOUT TO BE EXECUTED.
WSP WSP
THAT'S NO SURPRISE. HE'S THE SON OF A CRIMINAL WHO WAS SENT TO MURO-YA.
ENOUGH, YOU TWO!
THIS IS MY SON, KANNAGI. AKACHI, GIVE MY GUTLESS SON A LITTLE OF YOUR SPIRIT.
FATHER!
...

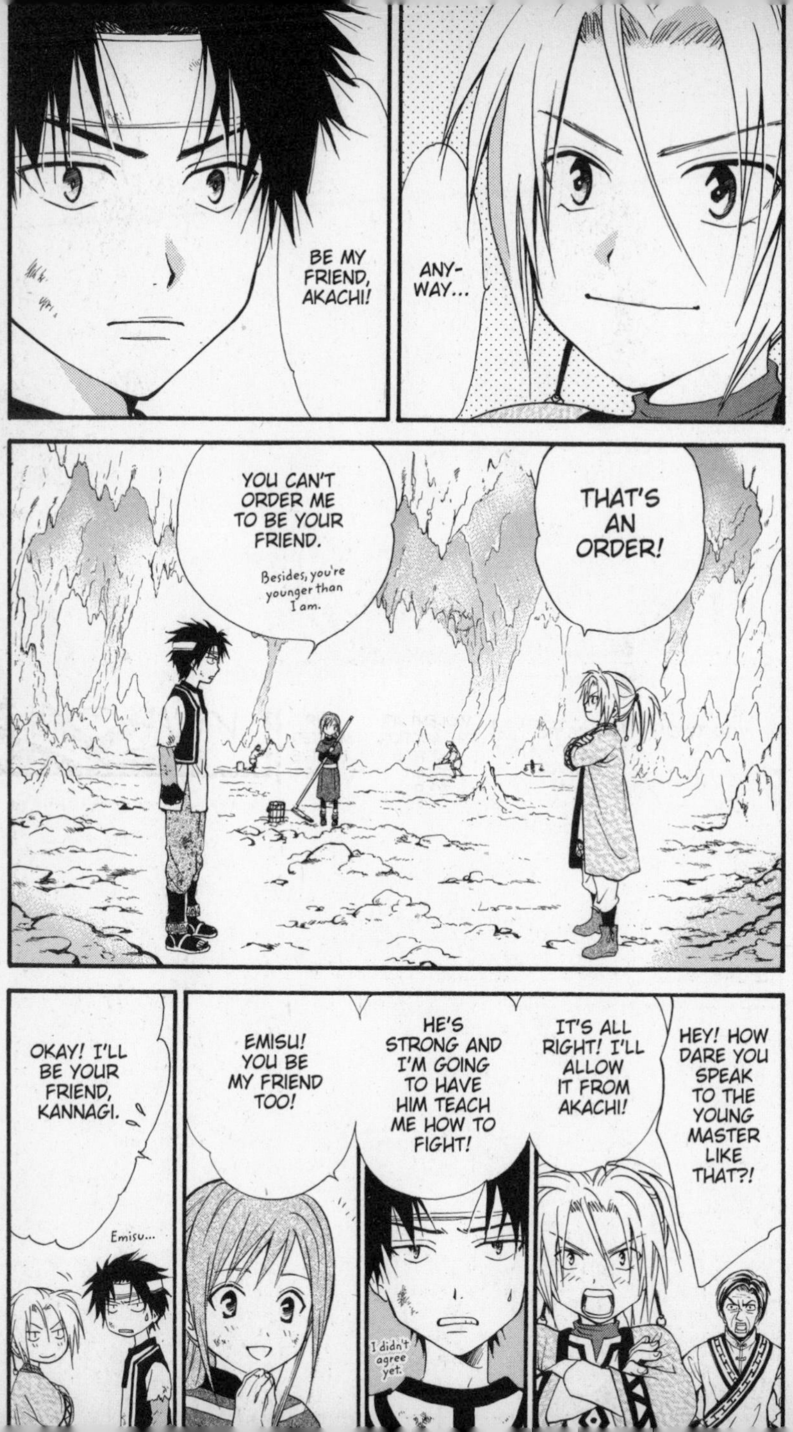
ANY-WAY...
BE MY FRIEND, AKACHI!
THAT'S AN ORDER!
YOU CAN'T ORDER ME TO BE YOUR FRIEND.
Besides, you're younger than I am.
HEY! HOW DARE YOU SPEAK TO THE YOUNG MASTER LIKE THAT?!
IT'S ALL RIGHT! I'LL ALLOW IT FROM AKACHI!
HE'S STRONG AND I'M GOING TO HAVE HIM TEACH ME HOW TO FIGHT!
I didn't agree yet.
EMISU! YOU BE MY FRIEND TOO!
OKAY! I'LL BE YOUR FRIEND, KANNAGI.
Emisu...

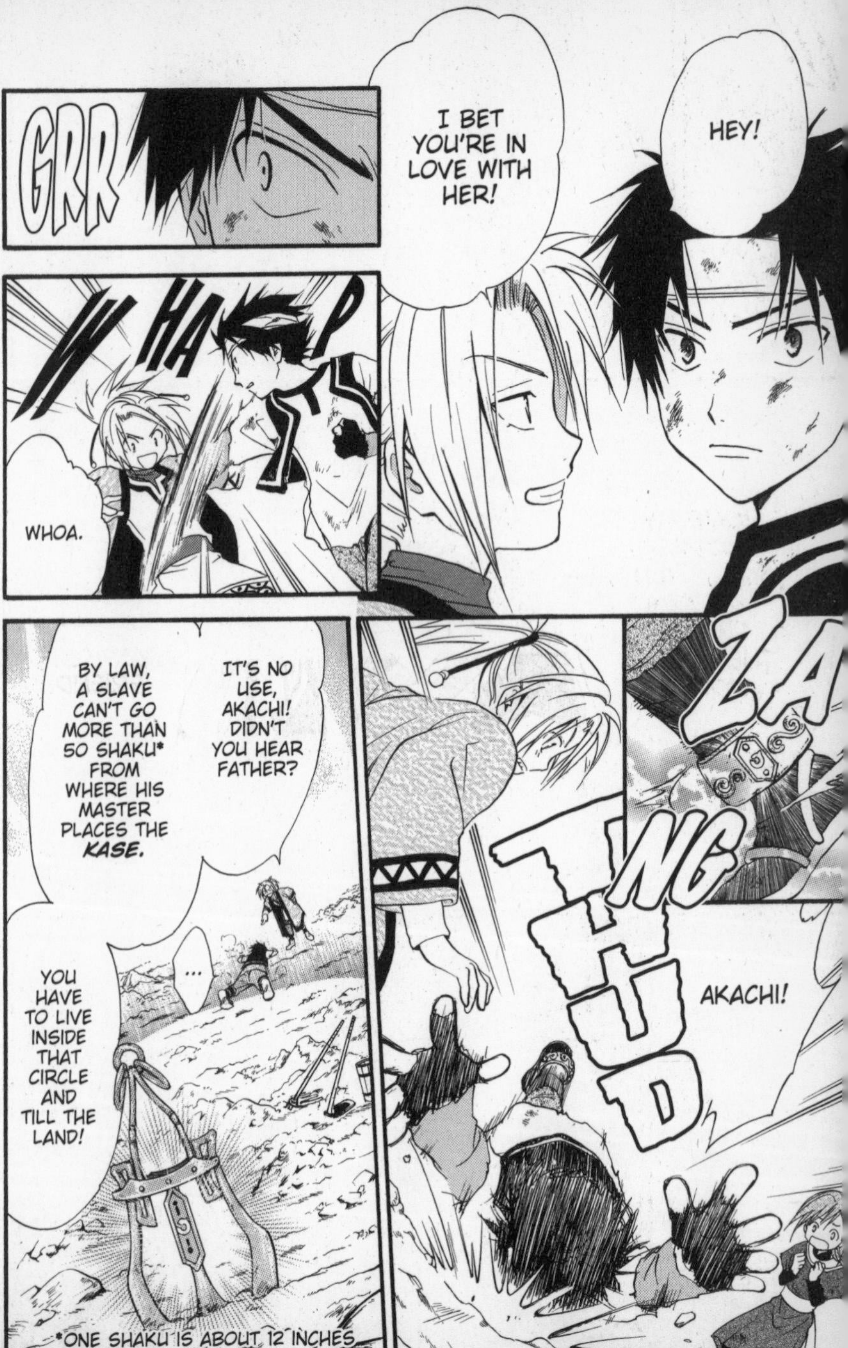
HEY!
I BET YOU'RE IN LOVE WITH HER!
GRR
WHAP
WHOA.
ZANG
THUD
AKACHI!
IT'S NO USE, AKACHI! DIDN'T YOU HEAR FATHER?
BY LAW, A SLAVE CAN'T GO MORE THAN 50 SHAKU* FROM WHERE HIS MASTER PLACES THE ***KASE.***
...
YOU HAVE TO LIVE INSIDE THAT CIRCLE AND TILL THE LAND!
*ONE SHAKU IS ABOUT 12 INCHES

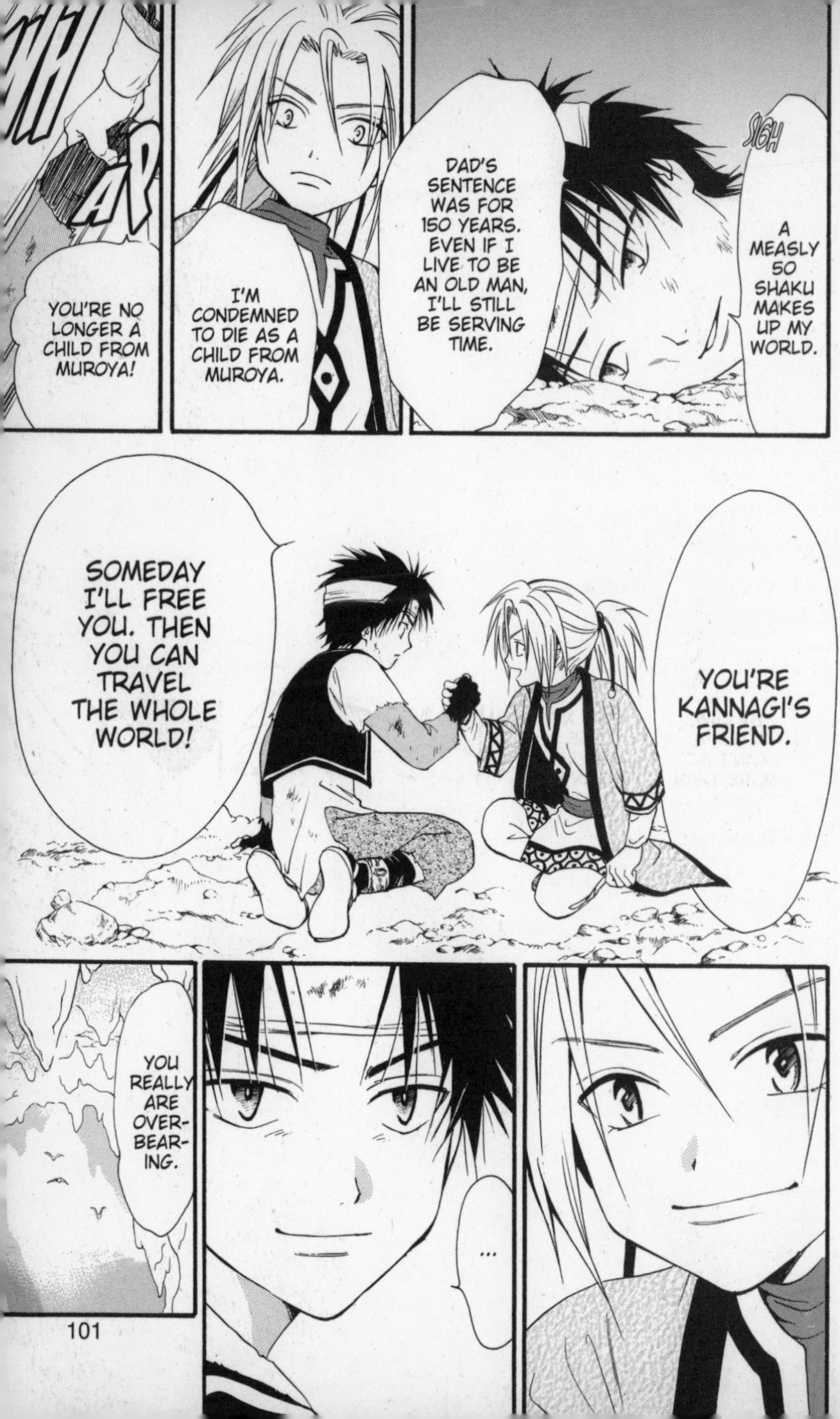
SIGH
A MEASLY 50 SHAKU MAKES UP MY WORLD.
DAD'S SENTENCE WAS FOR 150 YEARS. EVEN IF I LIVE TO BE AN OLD MAN, I'LL STILL BE SERVING TIME.
I'M CONDEMNED TO DIE AS A CHILD FROM MUROYA.
WHAP
YOU'RE NO LONGER A CHILD FROM MUROYA!
YOU'RE KANNAGI'S FRIEND.
SOMEDAY I'LL FREE YOU. THEN YOU CAN TRAVEL THE WHOLE WORLD!
...
YOU REALLY ARE OVER-BEAR-ING.

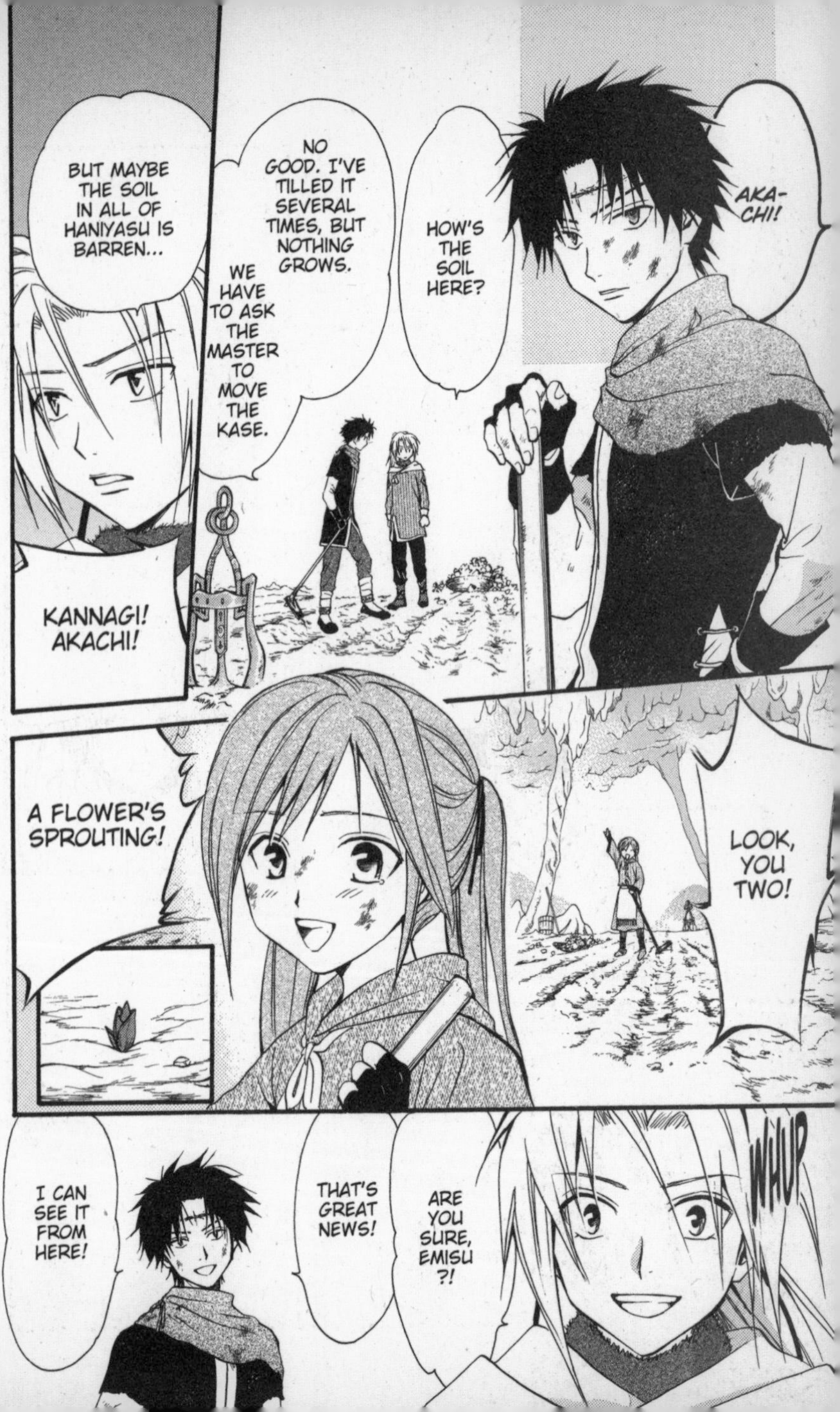
AKA-CHI!
HOW'S THE SOIL HERE?
NO GOOD. I'VE TILLED IT SEVERAL TIMES, BUT NOTHING GROWS.
WE HAVE TO ASK THE MASTER TO MOVE THE KASE.
BUT MAYBE THE SOIL IN ALL OF HANIYASU IS BARREN...
KANNAGI! AKACHI!
LOOK, YOU TWO!
A FLOWER'S SPROUTING!
WHUP
ARE YOU SURE, EMISU?!
THAT'S GREAT NEWS!
I CAN SEE IT FROM HERE!

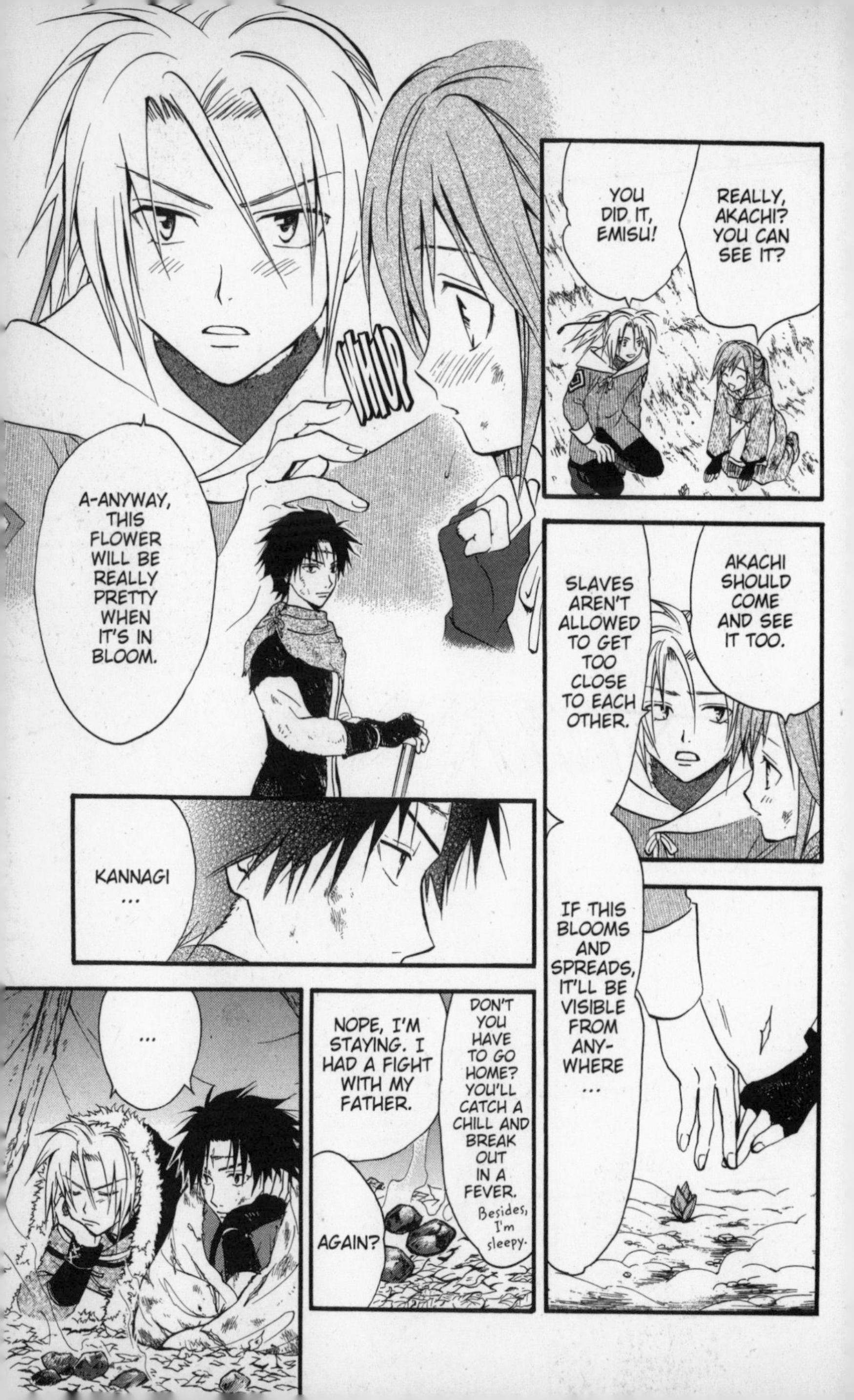
YOU DID IT, EMISU!
REALLY, AKACHI? YOU CAN SEE IT?
AKACHI SHOULD COME AND SEE IT TOO.
SLAVES AREN'T ALLOWED TO GET TOO CLOSE TO EACH OTHER.
IF THIS BLOOMS AND SPREADS, IT'LL BE VISIBLE FROM ANY-WHERE ...
WHIP
A-ANYWAY, THIS FLOWER WILL BE REALLY PRETTY WHEN IT'S IN BLOOM.
KANNAGI ...
DON'T YOU HAVE TO GO HOME? YOU'LL CATCH A CHILL AND BREAK OUT IN A FEVER.
NOPE, I'M STAYING. I HAD A FIGHT WITH MY FATHER.
Besides, I'm sleepy.
AGAIN?
...

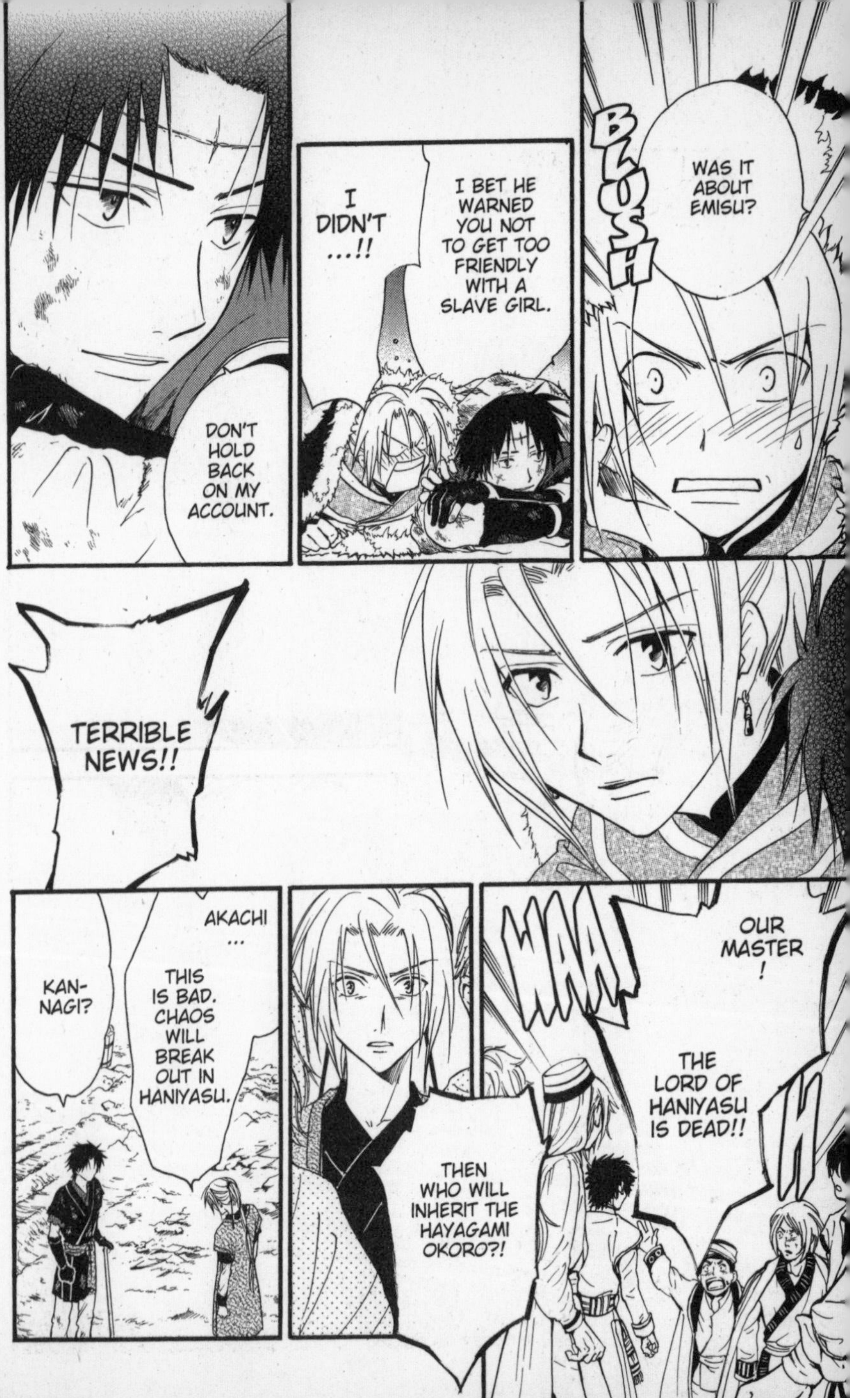

WAS IT ABOUT EMISU?
BLUSH
I BET HE WARNED YOU NOT TO GET TOO FRIENDLY WITH A SLAVE GIRL.
I DIDN'T ...!!
DON'T HOLD BACK ON MY ACCOUNT.
TERRIBLE NEWS!!
WAAH
OUR MASTER!
THE LORD OF HANIYASU IS DEAD!!
THEN WHO WILL INHERIT THE HAYAGAMI OKORO?!
AKACHI...
THIS IS BAD. CHAOS WILL BREAK OUT IN HANIYASU.
KAN-NAGI?

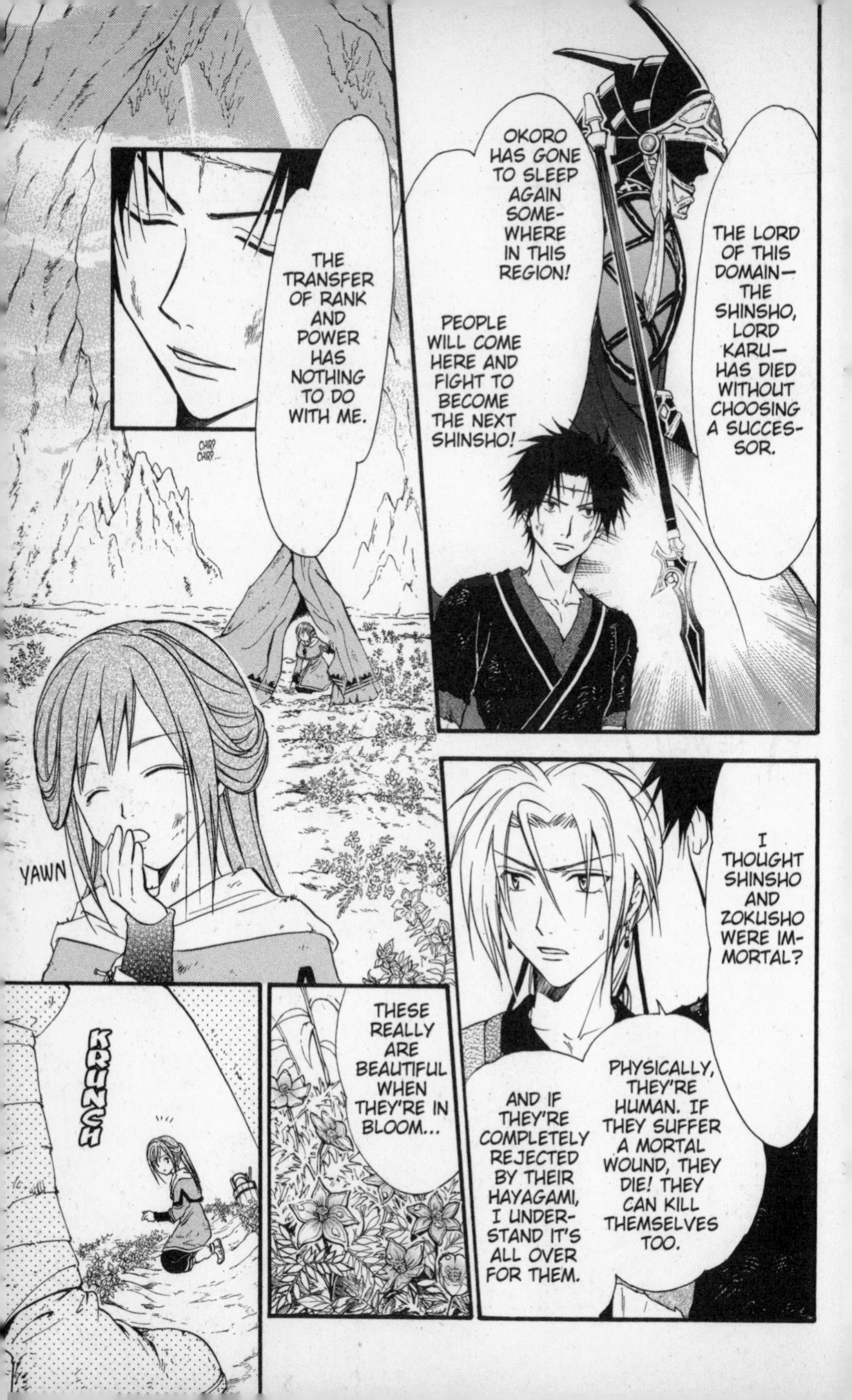
THE LORD OF THIS DOMAIN—THE SHINSHO, LORD KARU—HAS DIED WITHOUT CHOOSING A SUCCES-SOR.
OKORO HAS GONE TO SLEEP AGAIN SOME-WHERE IN THIS REGION!
PEOPLE WILL COME HERE AND FIGHT TO BECOME THE NEXT SHINSHO!
THE TRANSFER OF RANK AND POWER HAS NOTHING TO DO WITH ME.
CHIRP CHIRP...
YAWN
I THOUGHT SHINSHO AND ZOKUSHO WERE IM-MORTAL?
PHYSICALLY, THEY'RE HUMAN. IF THEY SUFFER A MORTAL WOUND, THEY DIE! THEY CAN KILL THEMSELVES TOO.
AND IF THEY'RE COMPLETELY REJECTED BY THEIR HAYAGAMI, I UNDER-STAND IT'S ALL OVER FOR THEM.
THESE REALLY ARE BEAUTIFUL WHEN THEY'RE IN BLOOM...
KRUNCH

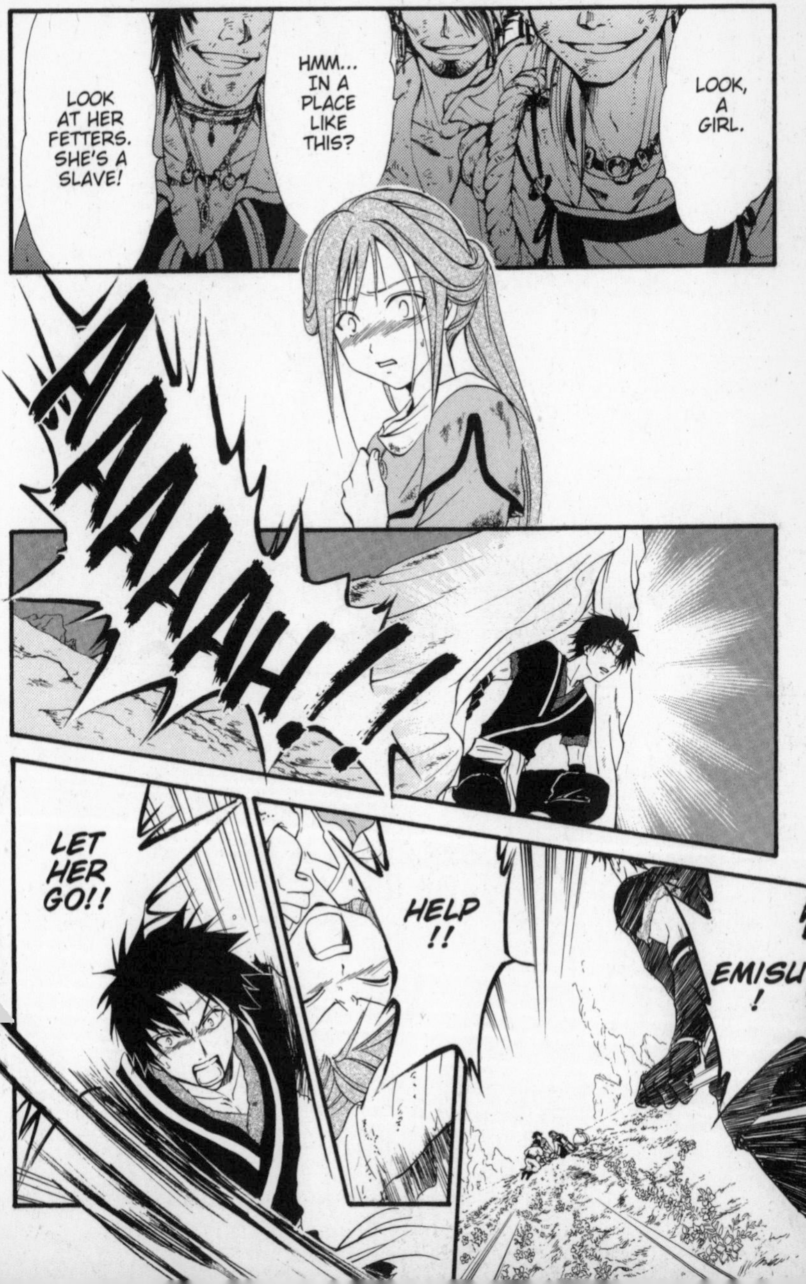
LOOK, A GIRL.
HMM... IN A PLACE LIKE THIS?
LOOK AT HER FETTERS. SHE'S A SLAVE!
AAAAAH!!
EMISU!
HELP!!
LET HER GO!!

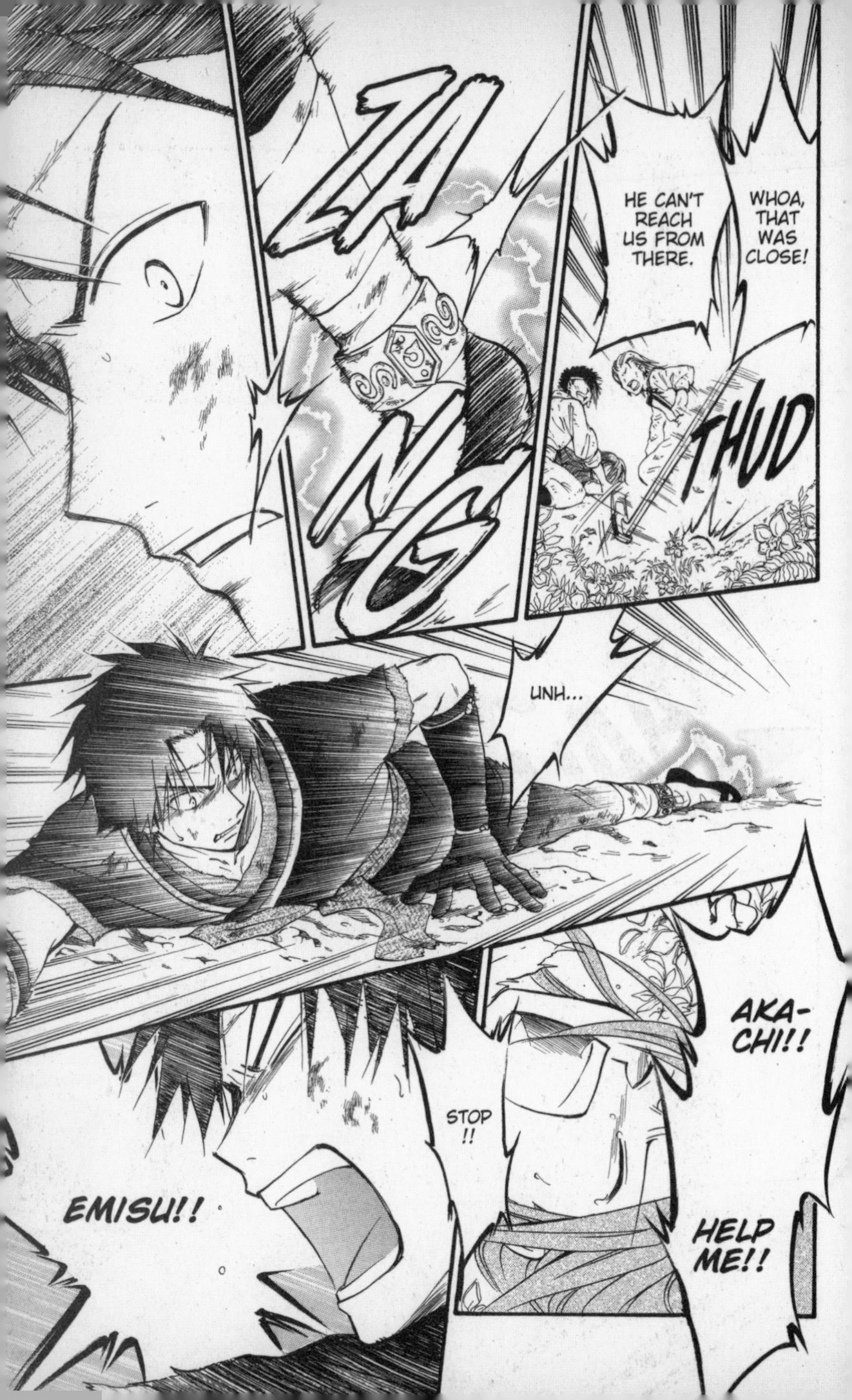
WHOA, THAT WAS CLOSE!
HE CAN'T REACH US FROM THERE.
THUD
ZANG
UNH...
AKA-CHI!!
STOP !!
HELP ME!!
EMISU!!

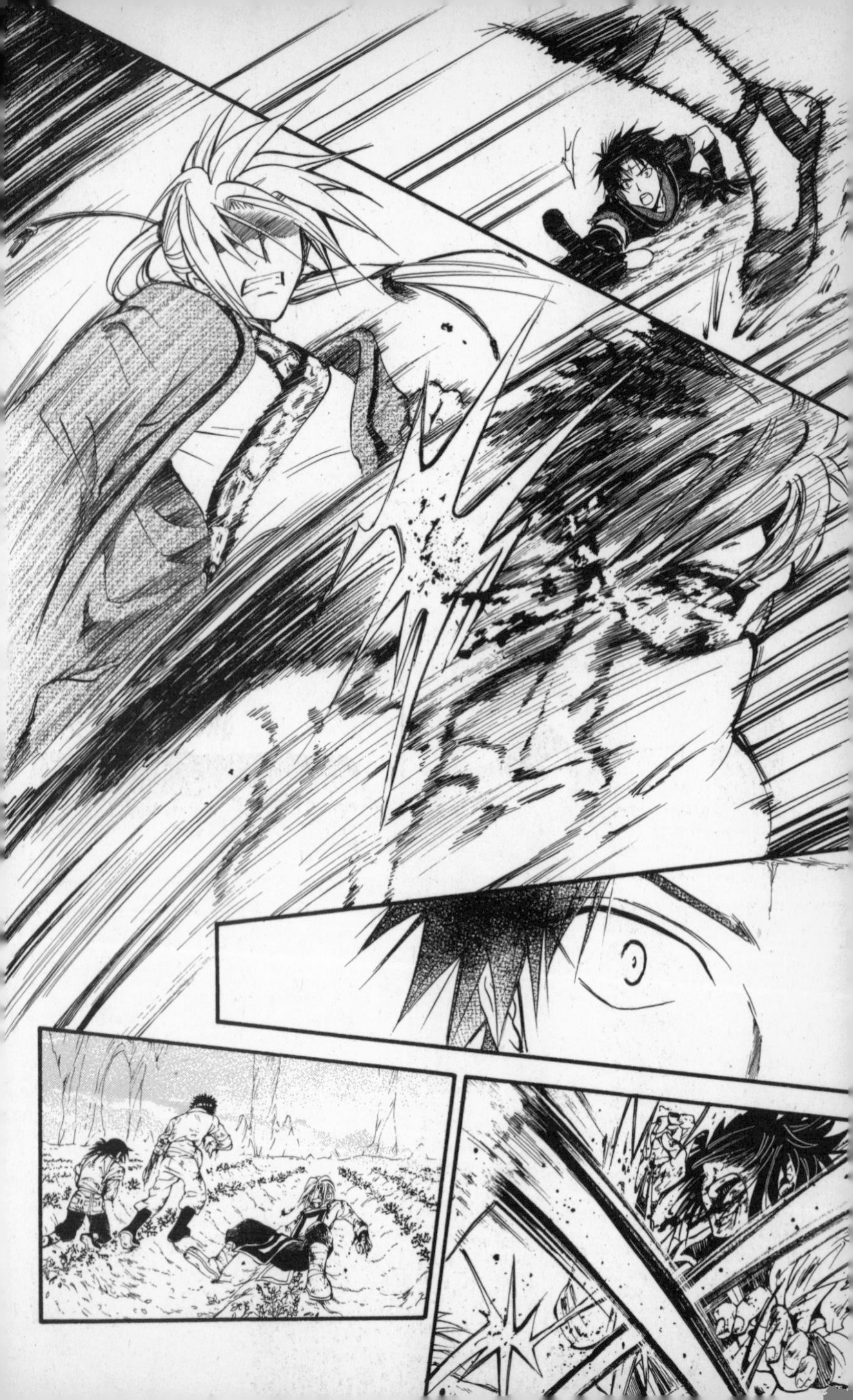

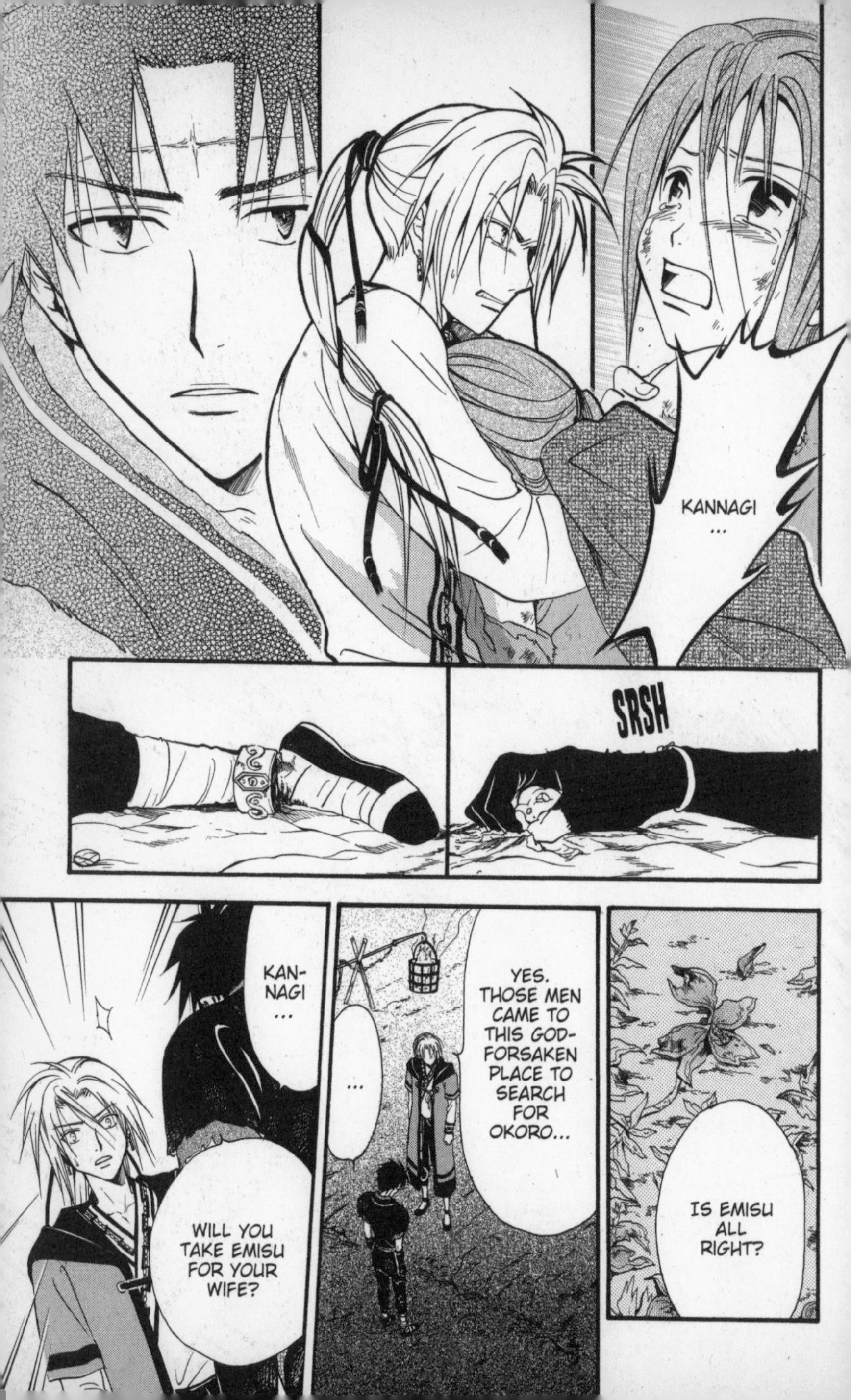
KANNAGI ...
SRSH
IS EMISU ALL RIGHT?
YES. THOSE MEN CAME TO THIS GOD-FORSAKEN PLACE TO SEARCH FOR OKORO...
...
KAN-NAGI ...
WILL YOU TAKE EMISU FOR YOUR WIFE?

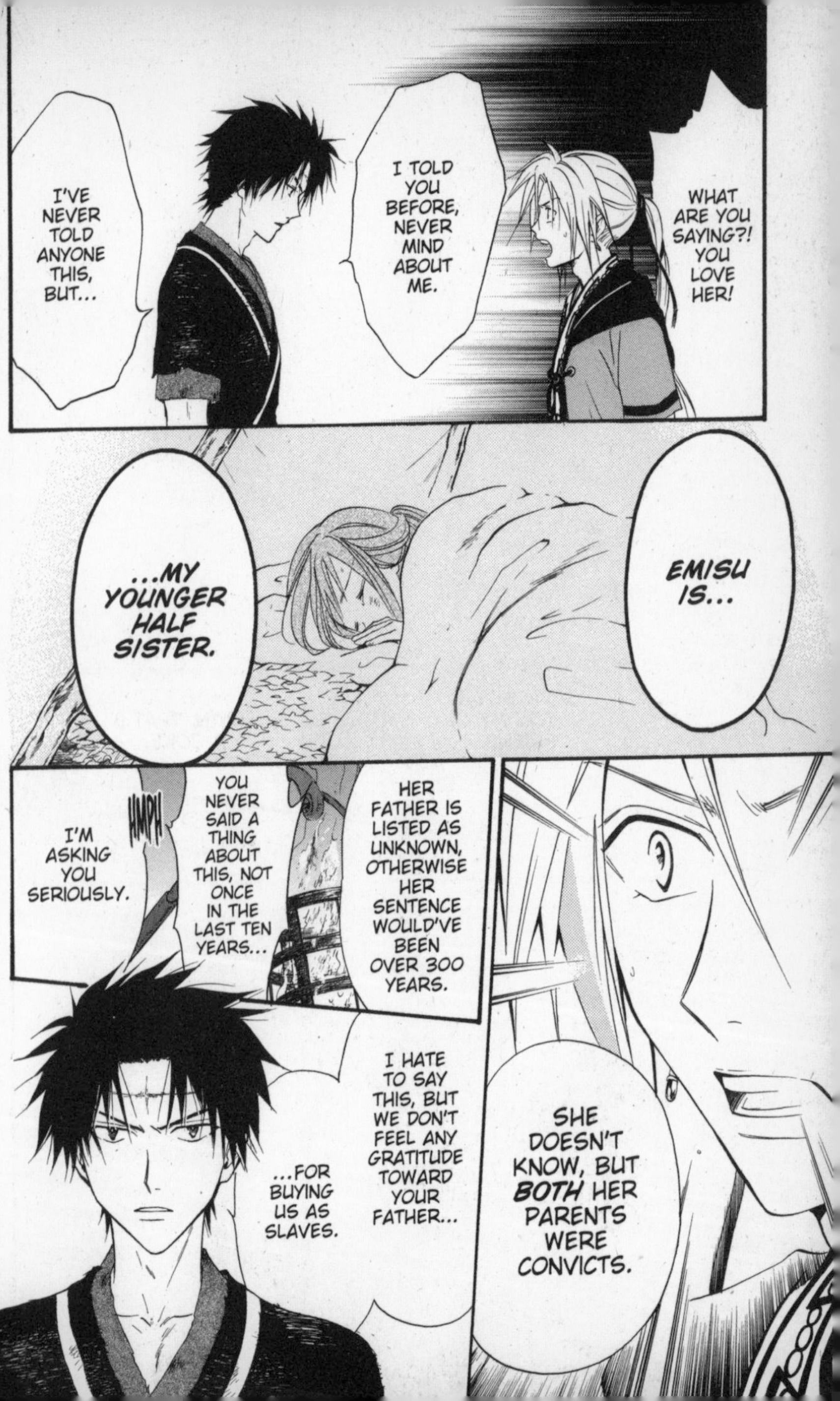
WHAT ARE YOU SAYING?! YOU LOVE HER!
I TOLD YOU BEFORE, NEVER MIND ABOUT ME.
I'VE NEVER TOLD ANYONE THIS, BUT...
EMISU IS...
...MY YOUNGER HALF SISTER.
SHE DOESN'T KNOW, BUT BOTH HER PARENTS WERE CONVICTS.
HER FATHER IS LISTED AS UNKNOWN, OTHERWISE HER SENTENCE WOULD'VE BEEN OVER 300 YEARS.
YOU NEVER SAID A THING ABOUT THIS, NOT ONCE IN THE LAST TEN YEARS...
HMPH
I'M ASKING YOU SERIOUSLY.
I HATE TO SAY THIS, BUT WE DON'T FEEL ANY GRATITUDE TOWARD YOUR FATHER...
...FOR BUYING US AS SLAVES.

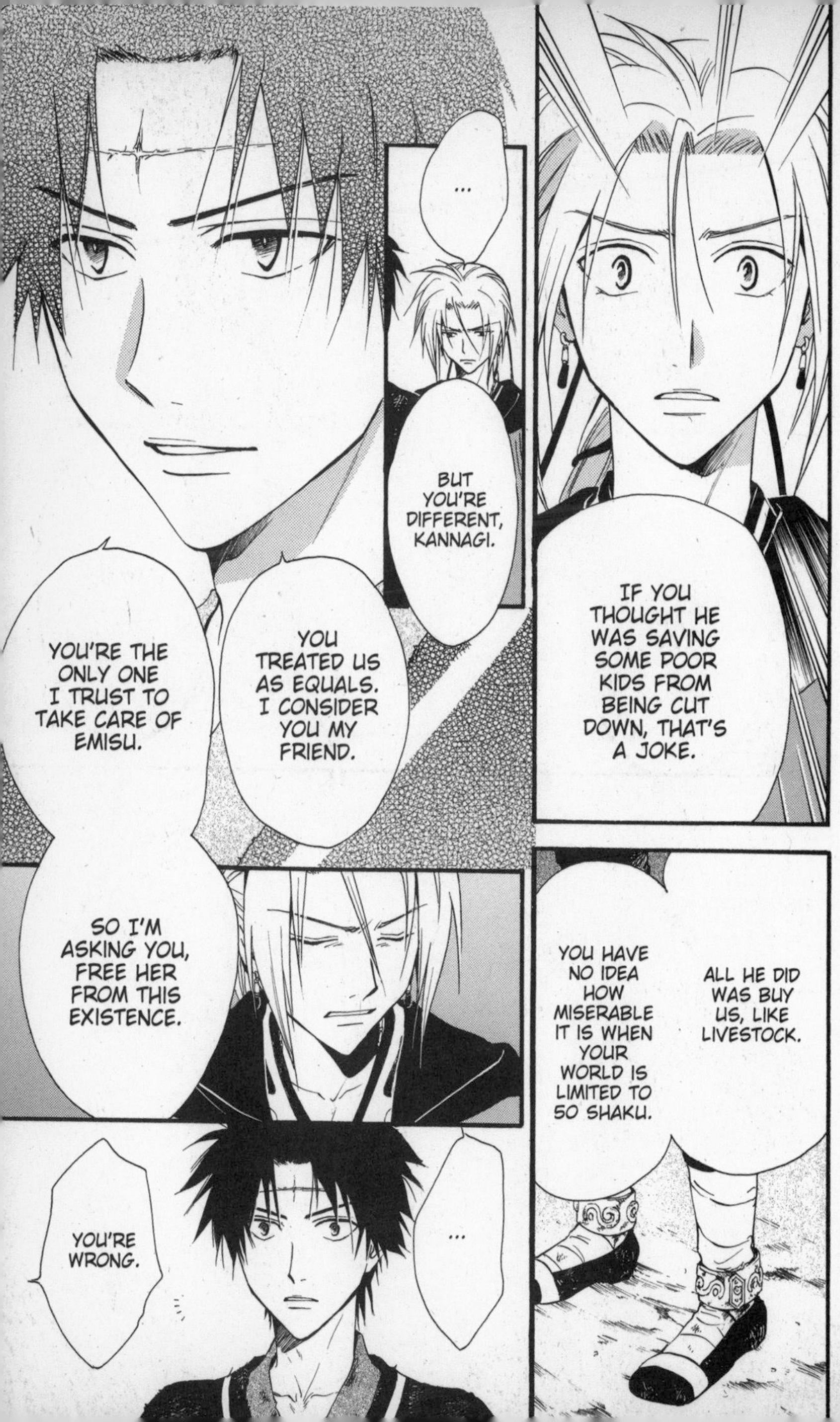
IF YOU THOUGHT HE WAS SAVING SOME POOR KIDS FROM BEING CUT DOWN, THAT'S A JOKE.
ALL HE DID WAS BUY US, LIKE LIVESTOCK.
YOU HAVE NO IDEA HOW MISERABLE IT IS WHEN YOUR WORLD IS LIMITED TO 50 SHAKU.
...
BUT YOU'RE DIFFERENT, KANNAGI.
YOU TREATED US AS EQUALS. I CONSIDER YOU MY FRIEND.
YOU'RE THE ONLY ONE I TRUST TO TAKE CARE OF EMISU.
SO I'M ASKING YOU, FREE HER FROM THIS EXISTENCE.
...
YOU'RE WRONG.

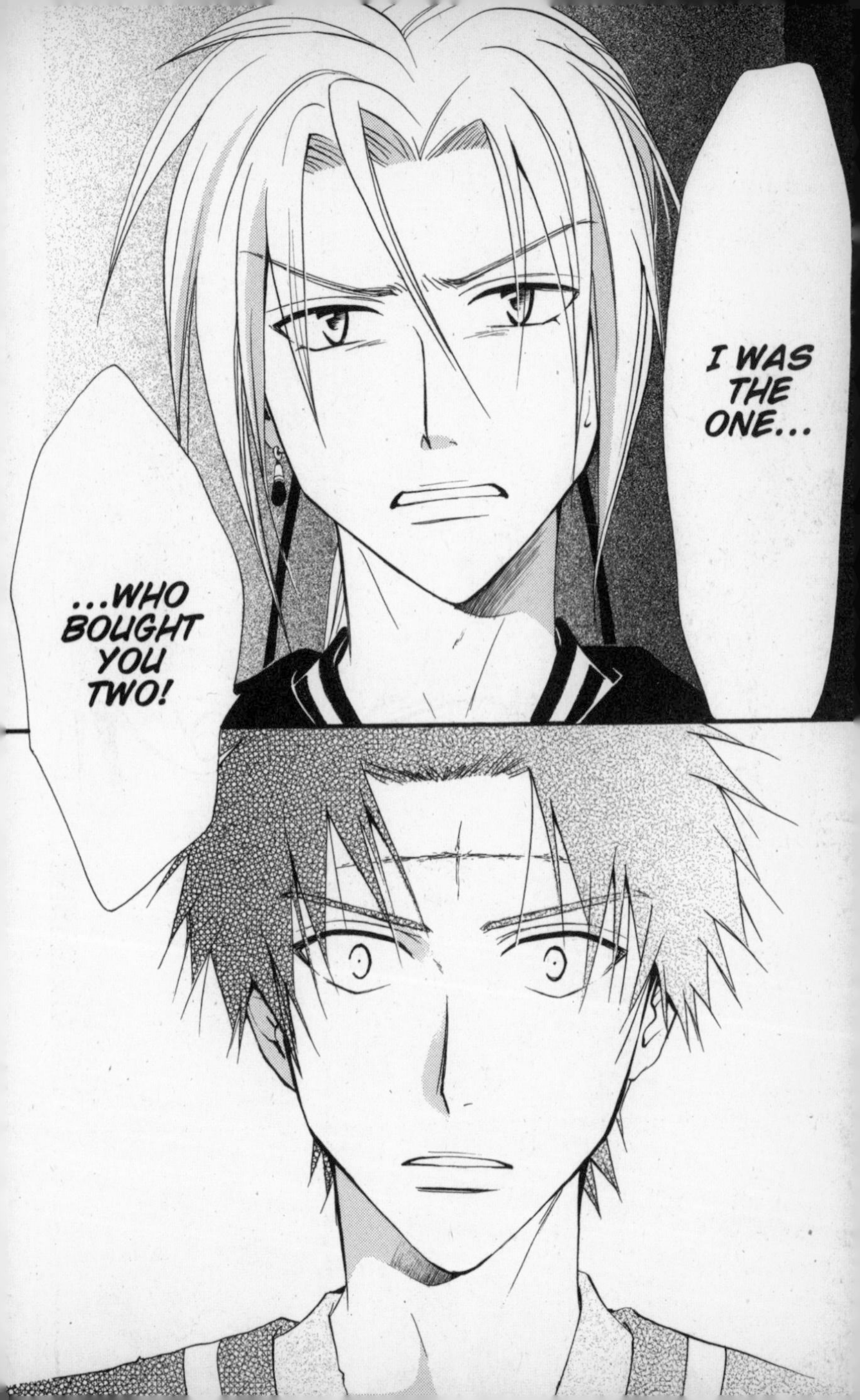
I WAS THE ONE...
...WHO BOUGHT YOU TWO!

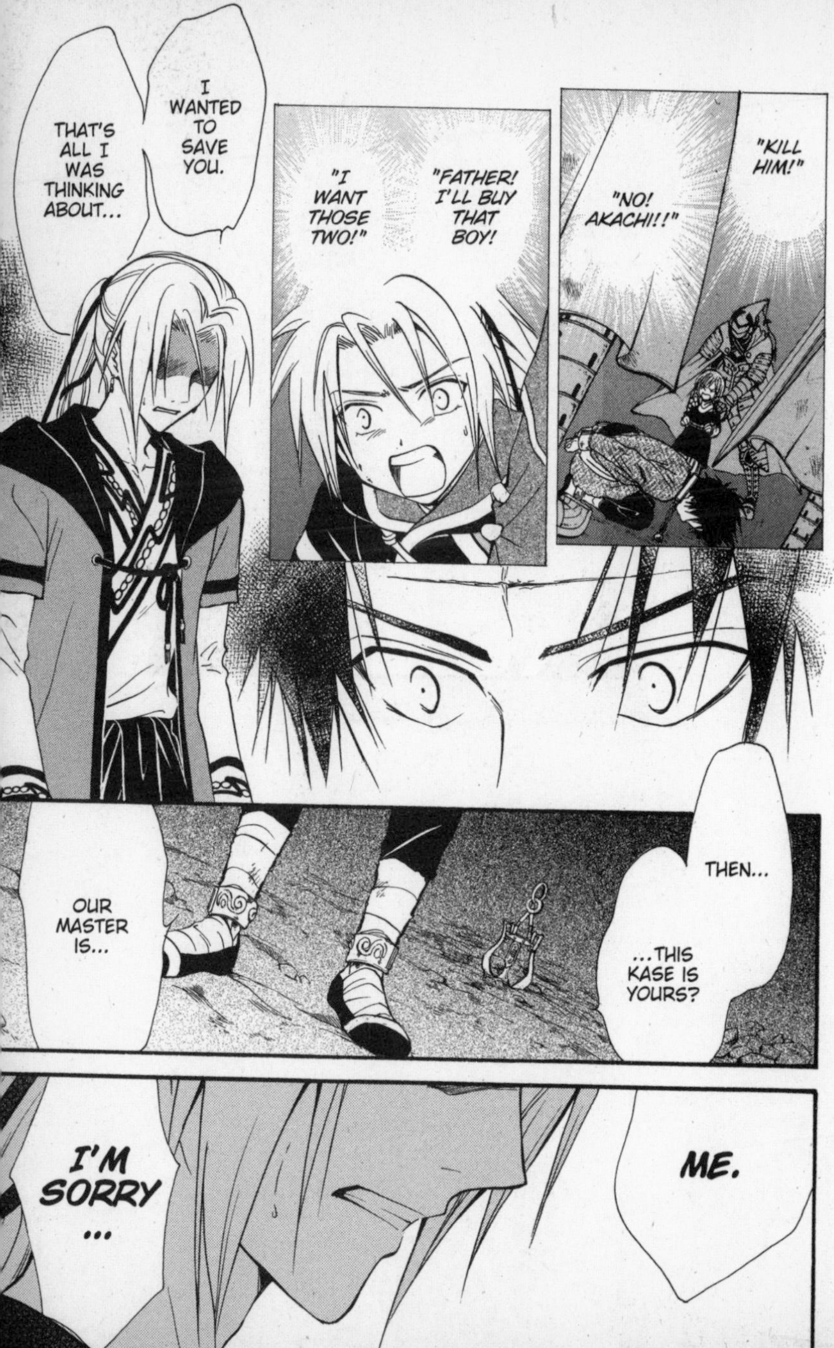
"KILL HIM!"
"NO! AKACHI!!"
"FATHER! I'LL BUY THAT BOY!
"I WANT THOSE TWO!"
I WANTED TO SAVE YOU.
THAT'S ALL I WAS THINKING ABOUT...
THEN...
...THIS KASE IS YOURS?
OUR MASTER IS...
ME.
I'M SORRY...

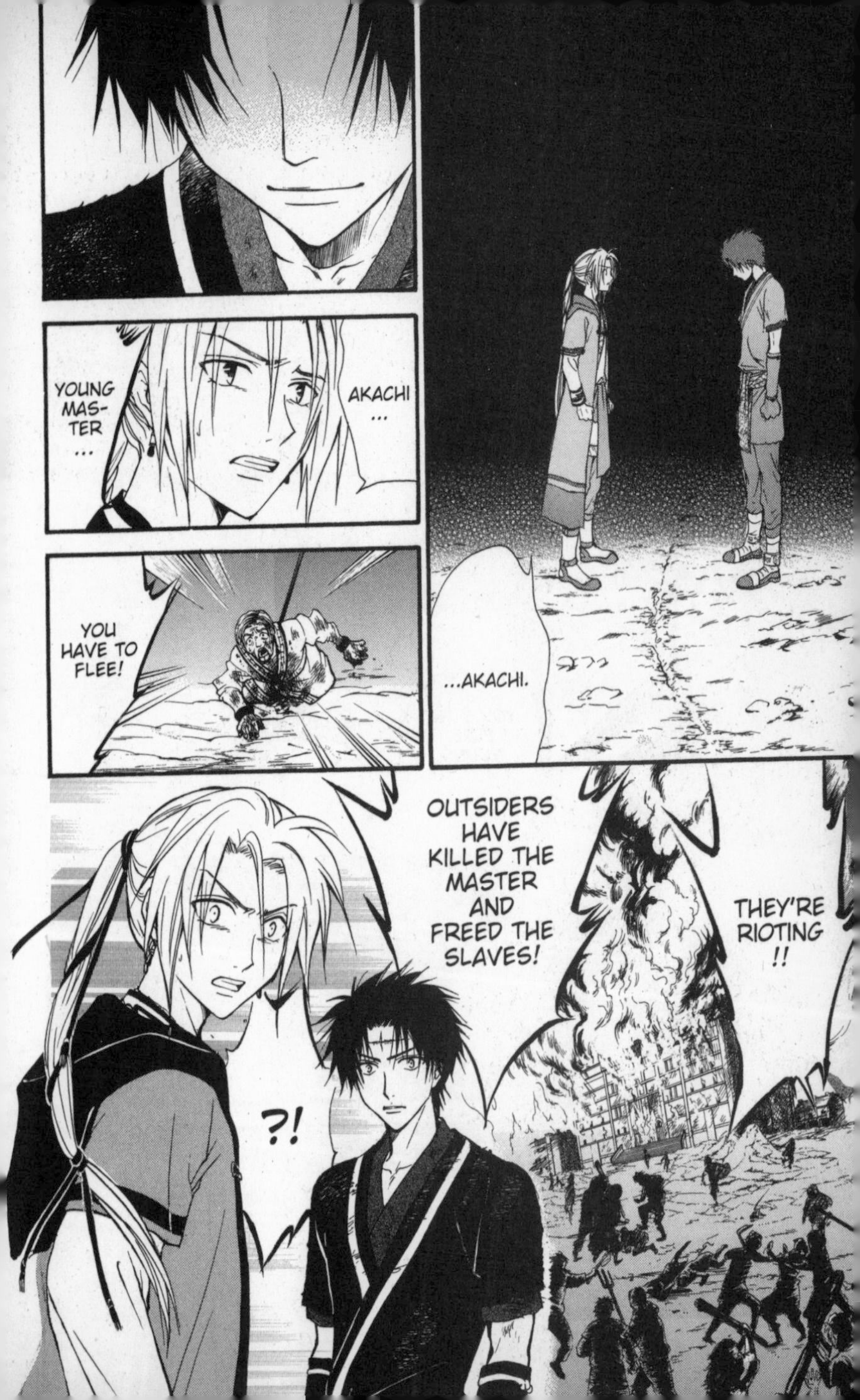
...AKACHI.
AKACHI ...
YOUNG MAS- TER ...
YOU HAVE TO FLEE!
THEY'RE RIOTING !!
OUTSIDERS HAVE KILLED THE MASTER AND FREED THE SLAVES!
?!

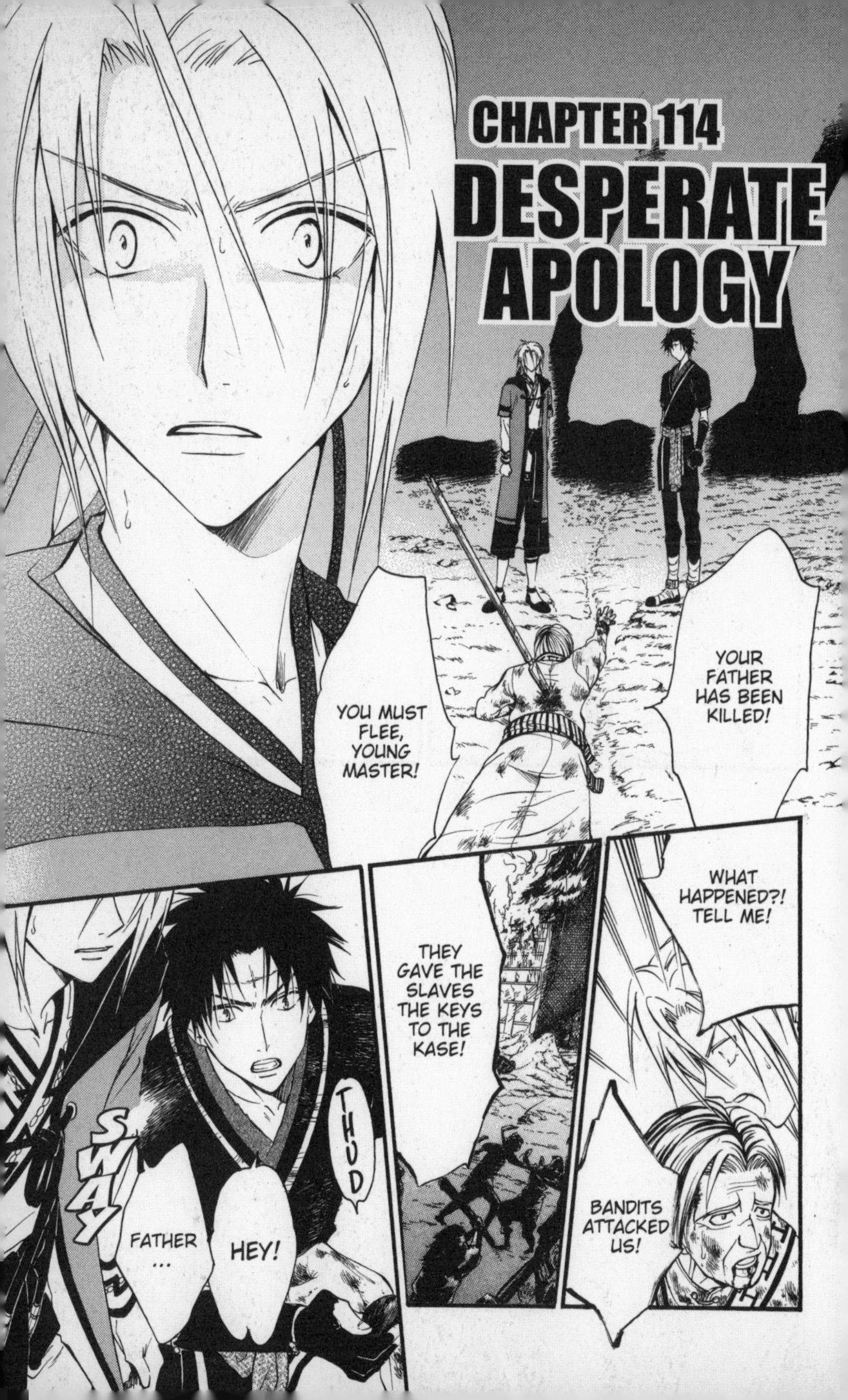
CHAPTER 114
DESPERATE APOLOGY
YOUR FATHER HAS BEEN KILLED!
YOU MUST FLEE, YOUNG MASTER!
WHAT HAPPENED?! TELL ME!
BANDITS ATTACKED US!
THEY GAVE THE SLAVES THE KEYS TO THE KASE!
THUD
HEY!
SWAY
FATHER ...

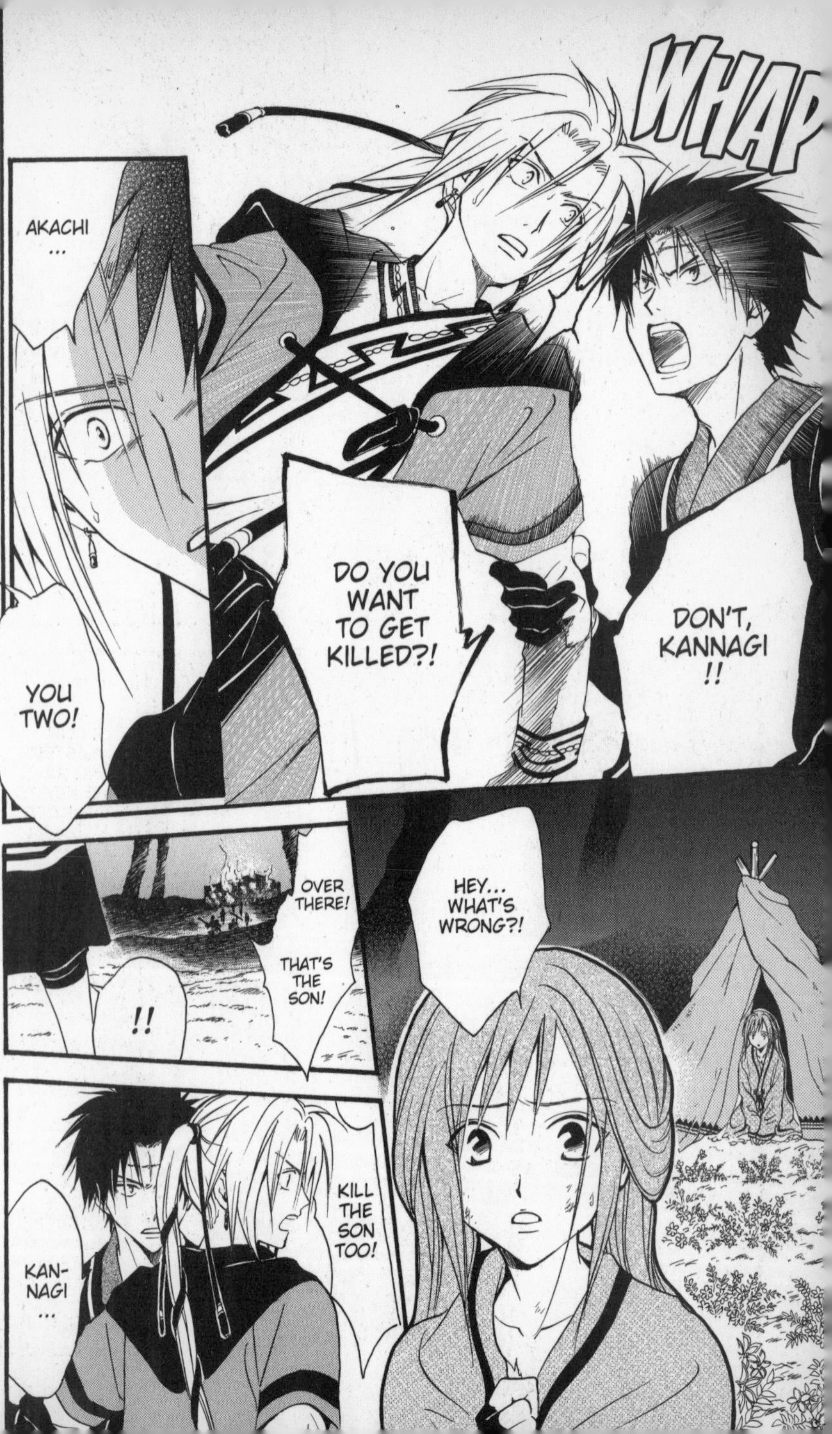
WHAP
DON'T, KANNAGI !!
DO YOU WANT TO GET KILLED?!
AKACHI ...
YOU TWO!
HEY... WHAT'S WRONG?!
OVER THERE!
THAT'S THE SON!
!!
KILL THE SON TOO!
KAN-NAGI ...

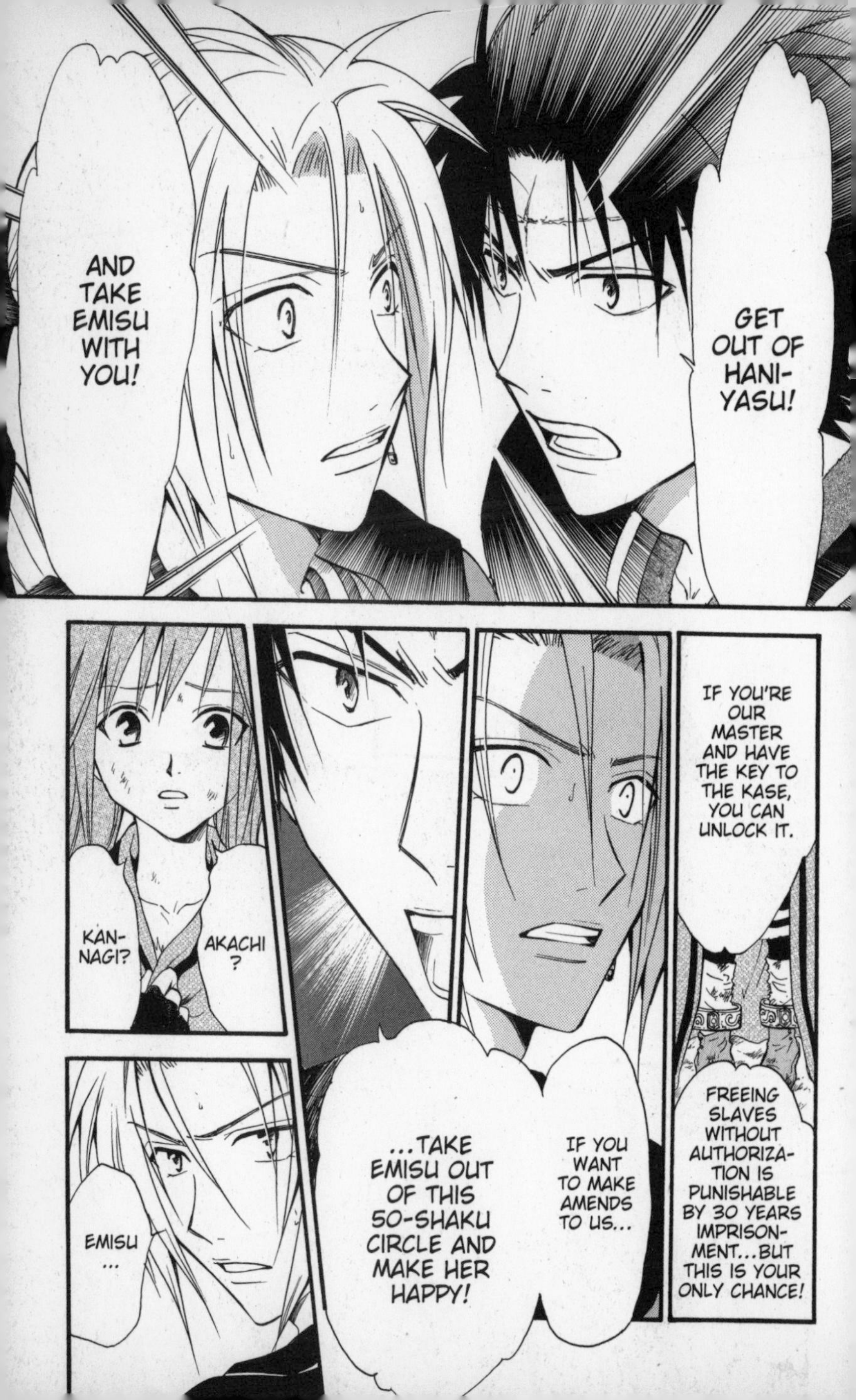
GET OUT OF HANI-YASU!
AND TAKE EMISU WITH YOU!
IF YOU'RE OUR MASTER AND HAVE THE KEY TO THE KASE, YOU CAN UNLOCK IT.
FREEING SLAVES WITHOUT AUTHORIZA-TION IS PUNISHABLE BY 30 YEARS IMPRISON-MENT...BUT THIS IS YOUR ONLY CHANCE!
IF YOU WANT TO MAKE AMENDS TO US...
...TAKE EMISU OUT OF THIS 50-SHAKU CIRCLE AND MAKE HER HAPPY!
AKACHI ?
KAN-NAGI?
EMISU ...

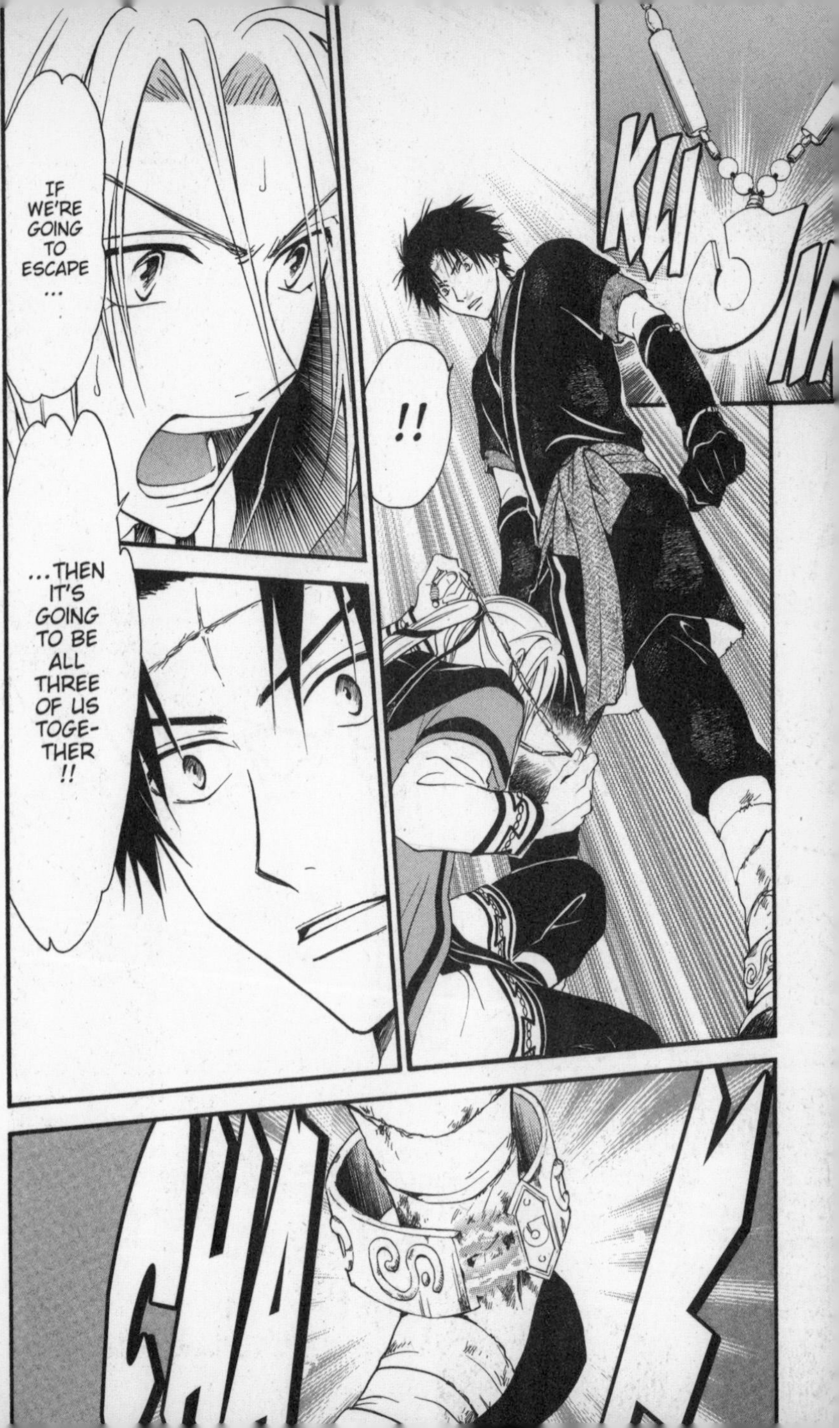
KLI
N
!!
IF WE'RE GOING TO ESCAPE ...
...THEN IT'S GOING TO BE ALL THREE OF US TOGE-THER!!
CHA
K

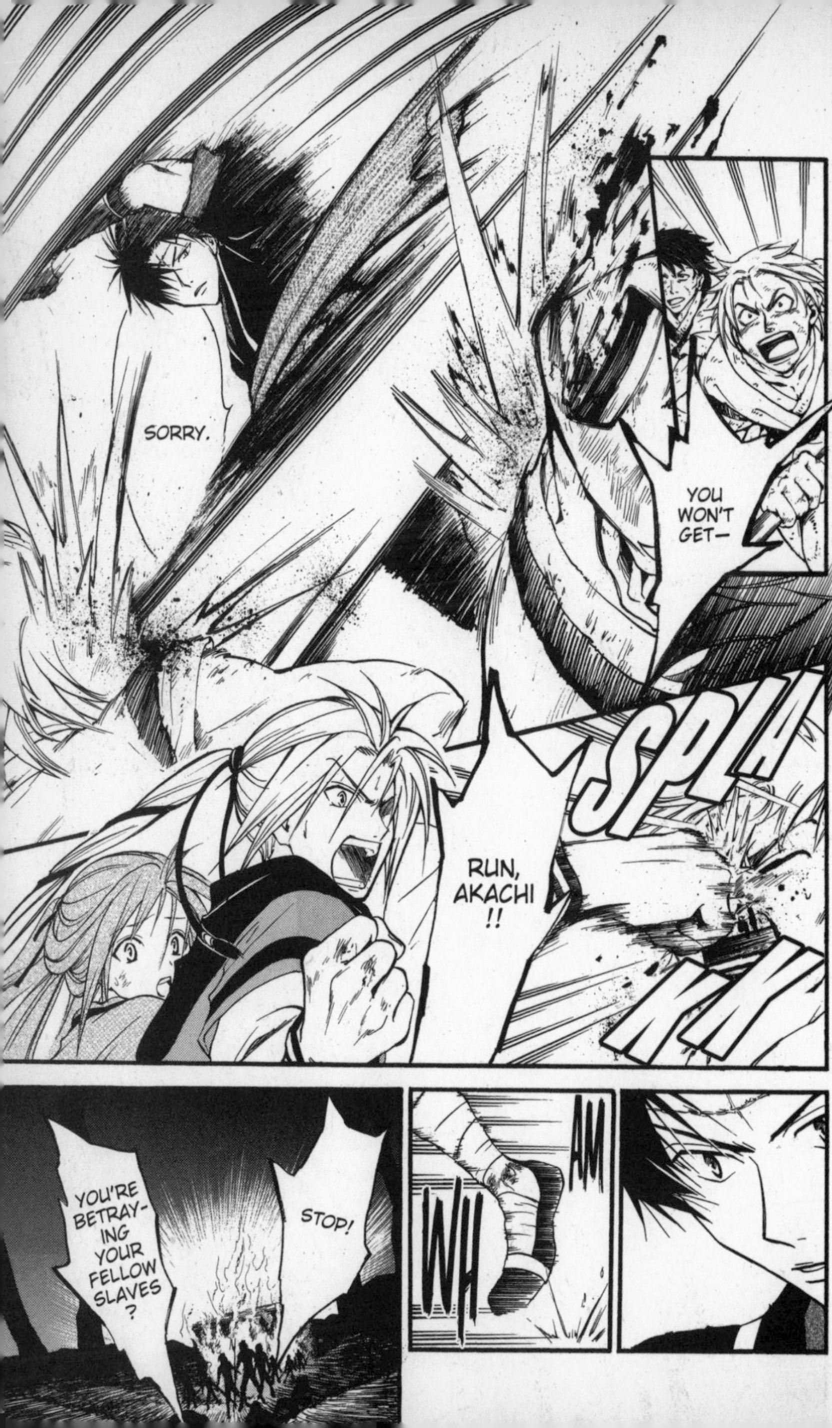
YOU WON'T GET—
SORRY.
SPLA
RUN, AKACHI!!
WHAM
STOP!
YOU'RE BETRAY-ING YOUR FELLOW SLAVES?

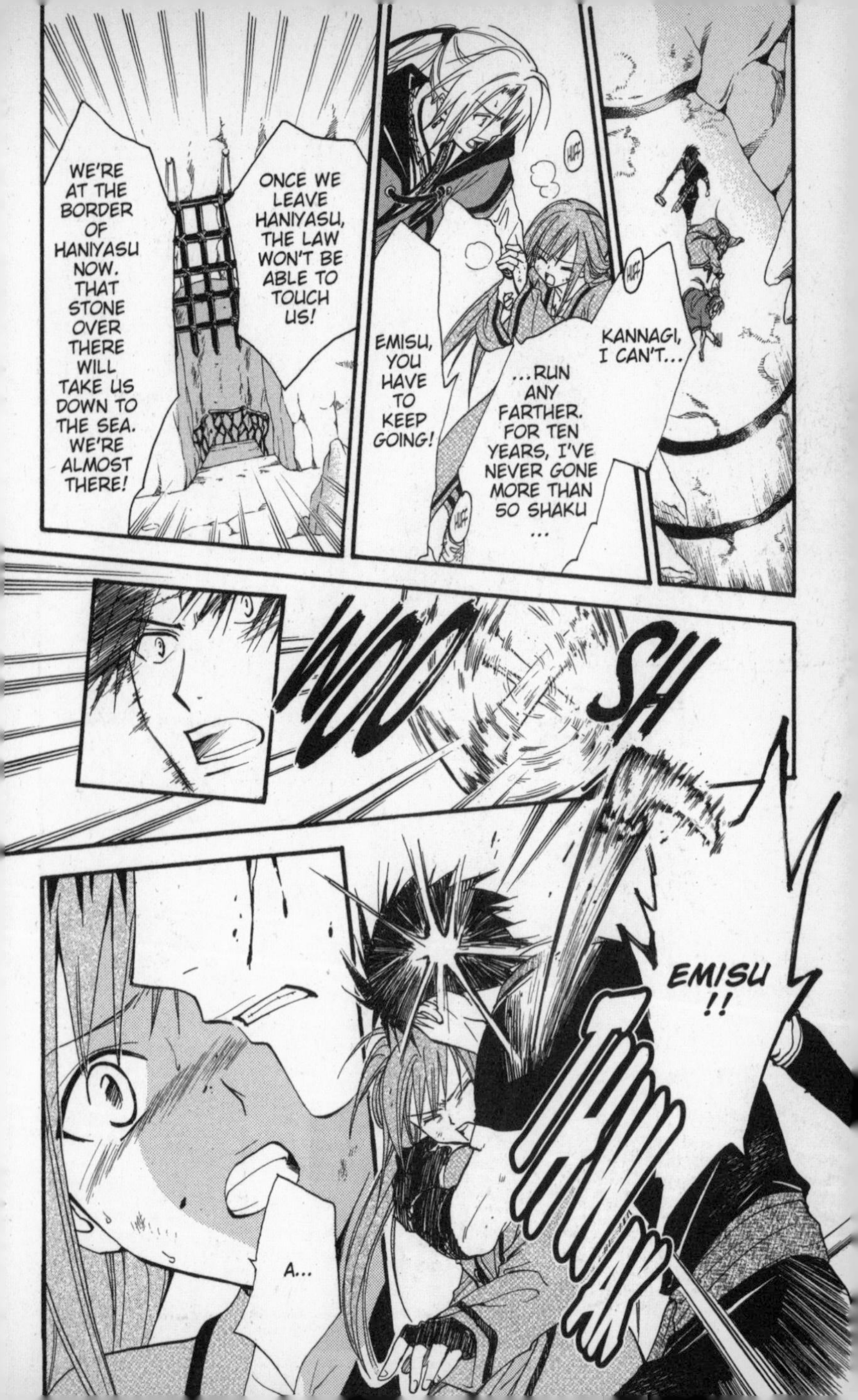
HUFF
KANNAGI, I CAN'T...
...RUN ANY FARTHER. FOR TEN YEARS, I'VE NEVER GONE MORE THAN 50 SHAKU ...
HUFF
EMISU, YOU HAVE TO KEEP GOING!
HUFF
ONCE WE LEAVE HANIYASU, THE LAW WON'T BE ABLE TO TOUCH US!
WE'RE AT THE BORDER OF HANIYASU NOW. THAT STONE OVER THERE WILL TAKE US DOWN TO THE SEA. WE'RE ALMOST THERE!
WOOOSH
EMISU !!
A...

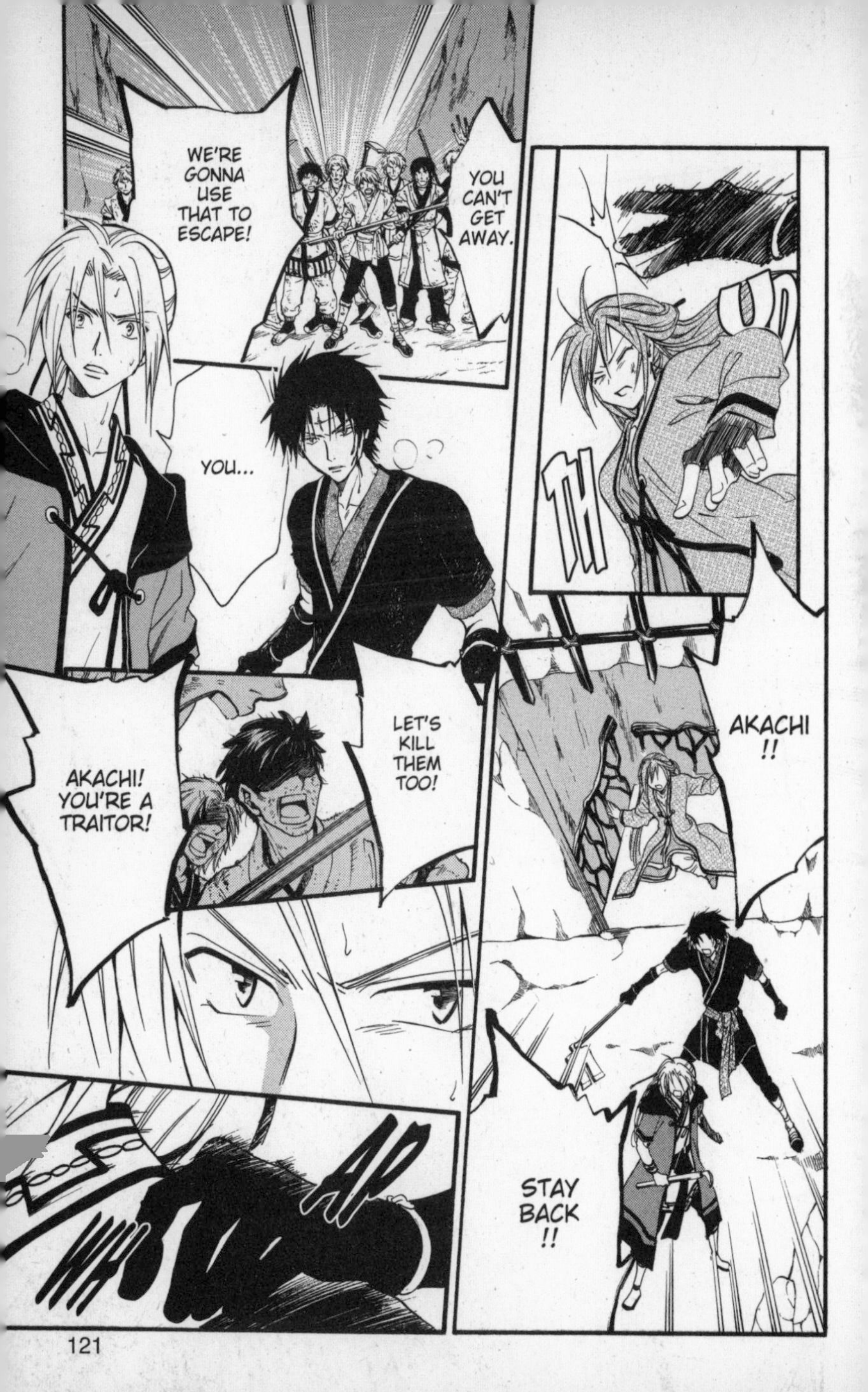
WE'RE GONNA USE THAT TO ESCAPE!
YOU CAN'T GET AWAY.
THUD
YOU...
AKACHI!!
LET'S KILL THEM TOO!
AKACHI! YOU'RE A TRAITOR!
STAY BACK!!
WHAP

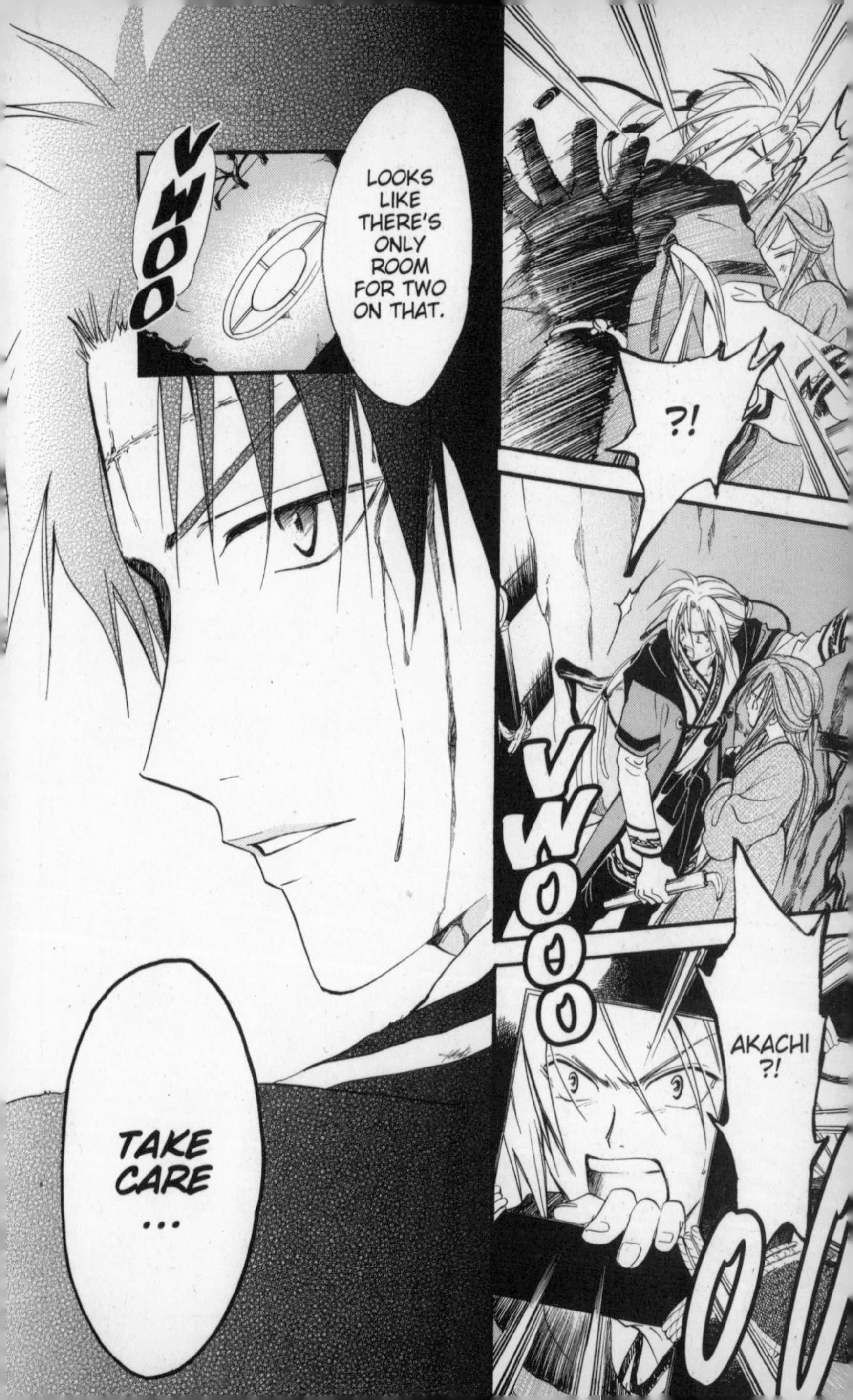
?!
VWOOO
AKACHI ?!
VWOO
LOOKS LIKE THERE'S ONLY ROOM FOR TWO ON THAT.
TAKE CARE ...

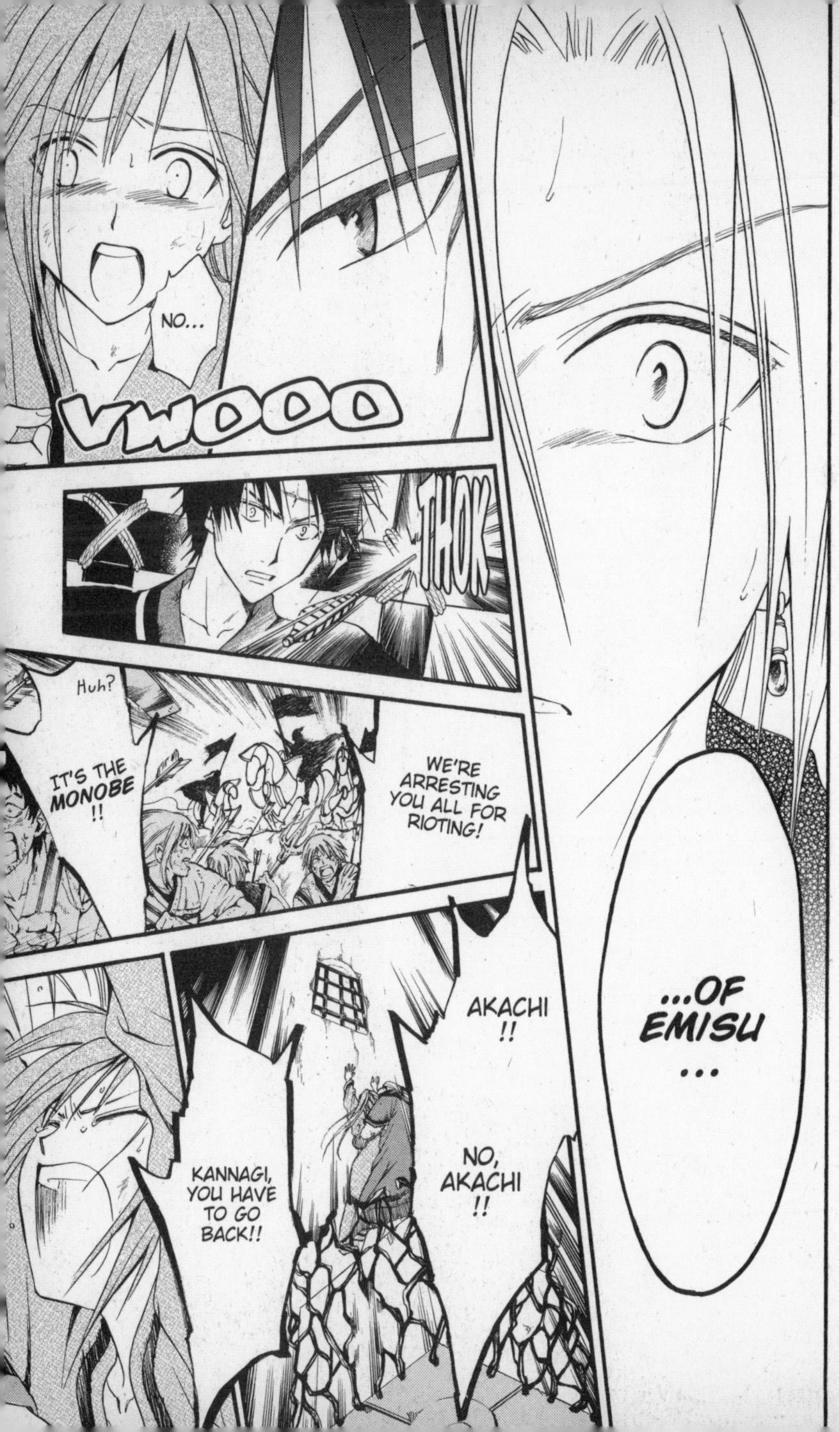
...OF EMISU ...
NO...
VWOOO
THOK
Huh?
WE'RE ARRESTING YOU ALL FOR RIOTING!
IT'S THE MONOBE !!
AKACHI !!
NO, AKACHI !!
KANNAGI, YOU HAVE TO GO BACK!!

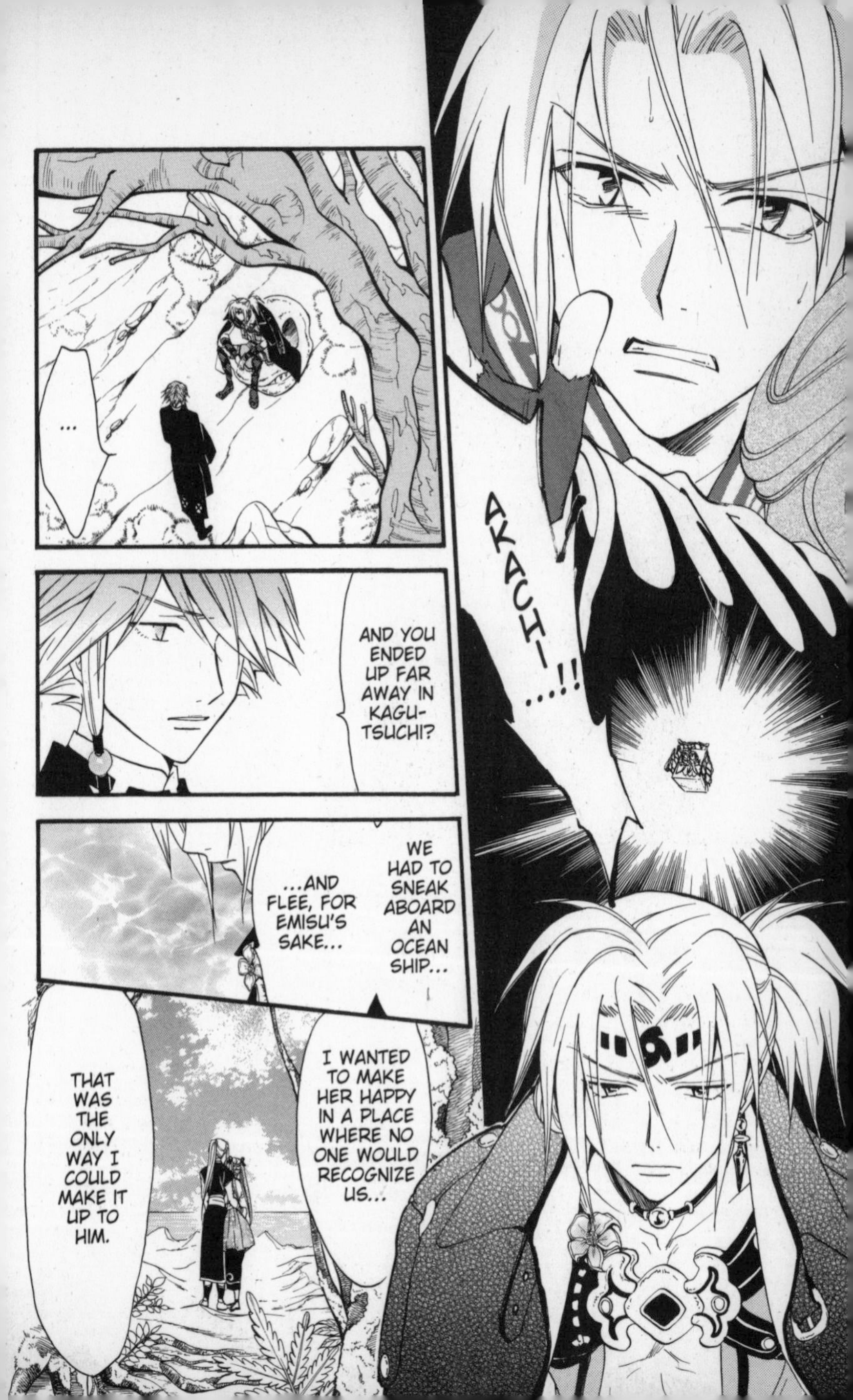
AKACHI...!!
...
AND YOU ENDED UP FAR AWAY IN KAGUTSUCHI?
WE HAD TO SNEAK ABOARD AN OCEAN SHIP...
...AND FLEE, FOR EMISU'S SAKE...
I WANTED TO MAKE HER HAPPY IN A PLACE WHERE NO ONE WOULD RECOGNIZE US...
THAT WAS THE ONLY WAY I COULD MAKE IT UP TO HIM.

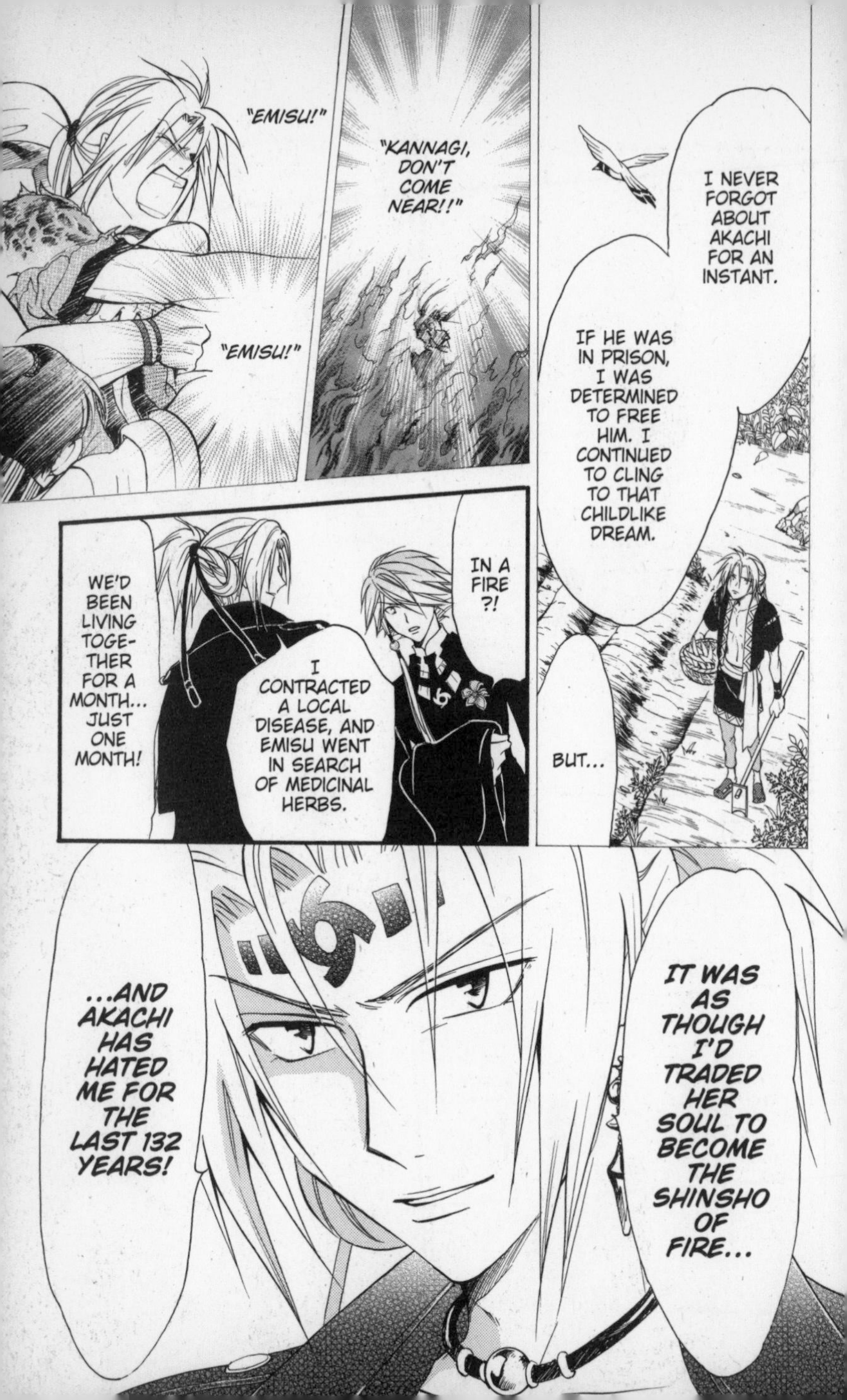
I NEVER FORGOT ABOUT AKACHI FOR AN INSTANT.
IF HE WAS IN PRISON, I WAS DETERMINED TO FREE HIM. I CONTINUED TO CLING TO THAT CHILDLIKE DREAM.
BUT...
"KANNAGI, DON'T COME NEAR!!"
"EMISU!"
"EMISU!"
IN A FIRE?!
I CONTRACTED A LOCAL DISEASE, AND EMISU WENT IN SEARCH OF MEDICINAL HERBS.
WE'D BEEN LIVING TOGE-THER FOR A MONTH... JUST ONE MONTH!
IT WAS AS THOUGH I'D TRADED HER SOUL TO BECOME THE SHINSHO OF FIRE...
...AND AKACHI HAS HATED ME FOR THE LAST 132 YEARS!

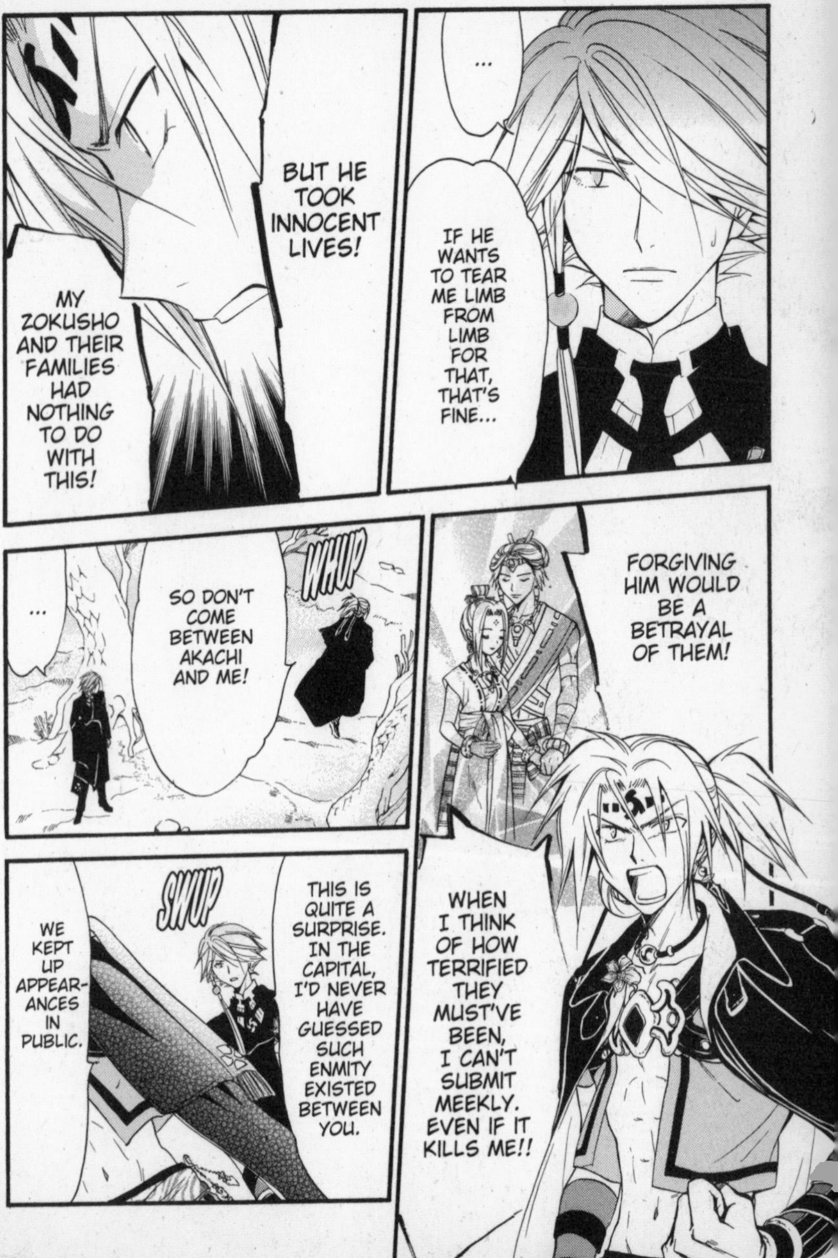
...
IF HE WANTS TO TEAR ME LIMB FROM LIMB FOR THAT, THAT'S FINE...
BUT HE TOOK INNOCENT LIVES!
MY ZOKUSHO AND THEIR FAMILIES HAD NOTHING TO DO WITH THIS!
FORGIVING HIM WOULD BE A BETRAYAL OF THEM!
WHEN I THINK OF HOW TERRIFIED THEY MUST'VE BEEN, I CAN'T SUBMIT MEEKLY. EVEN IF IT KILLS ME!!
WHUP
SO DON'T COME BETWEEN AKACHI AND ME!
...
SWUP
THIS IS QUITE A SURPRISE. IN THE CAPITAL, I'D NEVER HAVE GUESSED SUCH ENMITY EXISTED BETWEEN YOU.
WE KEPT UP APPEARANCES IN PUBLIC.

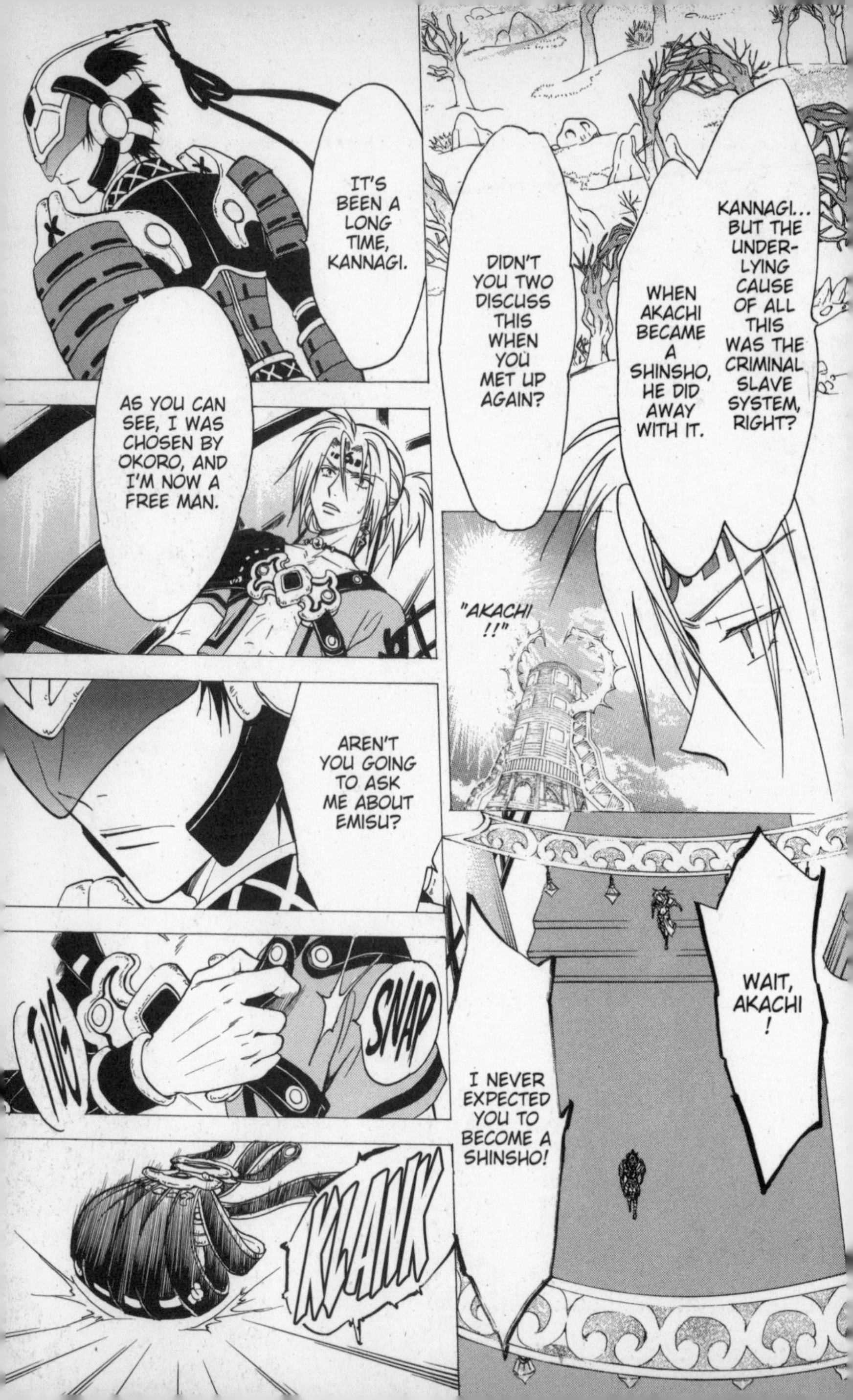
KANNAGI... BUT THE UNDER-LYING CAUSE OF ALL THIS WAS THE CRIMINAL SLAVE SYSTEM, RIGHT?
WHEN AKACHI BECAME A SHINSHO, HE DID AWAY WITH IT.
DIDN'T YOU TWO DISCUSS THIS WHEN YOU MET UP AGAIN?
"AKACHI !!"
WAIT, AKACHI!
I NEVER EXPECTED YOU TO BECOME A SHINSHO!
IT'S BEEN A LONG TIME, KANNAGI.
AS YOU CAN SEE, I WAS CHOSEN BY OKORO, AND I'M NOW A FREE MAN.
AREN'T YOU GOING TO ASK ME ABOUT EMISU?
SNAP
TUG
KLANK

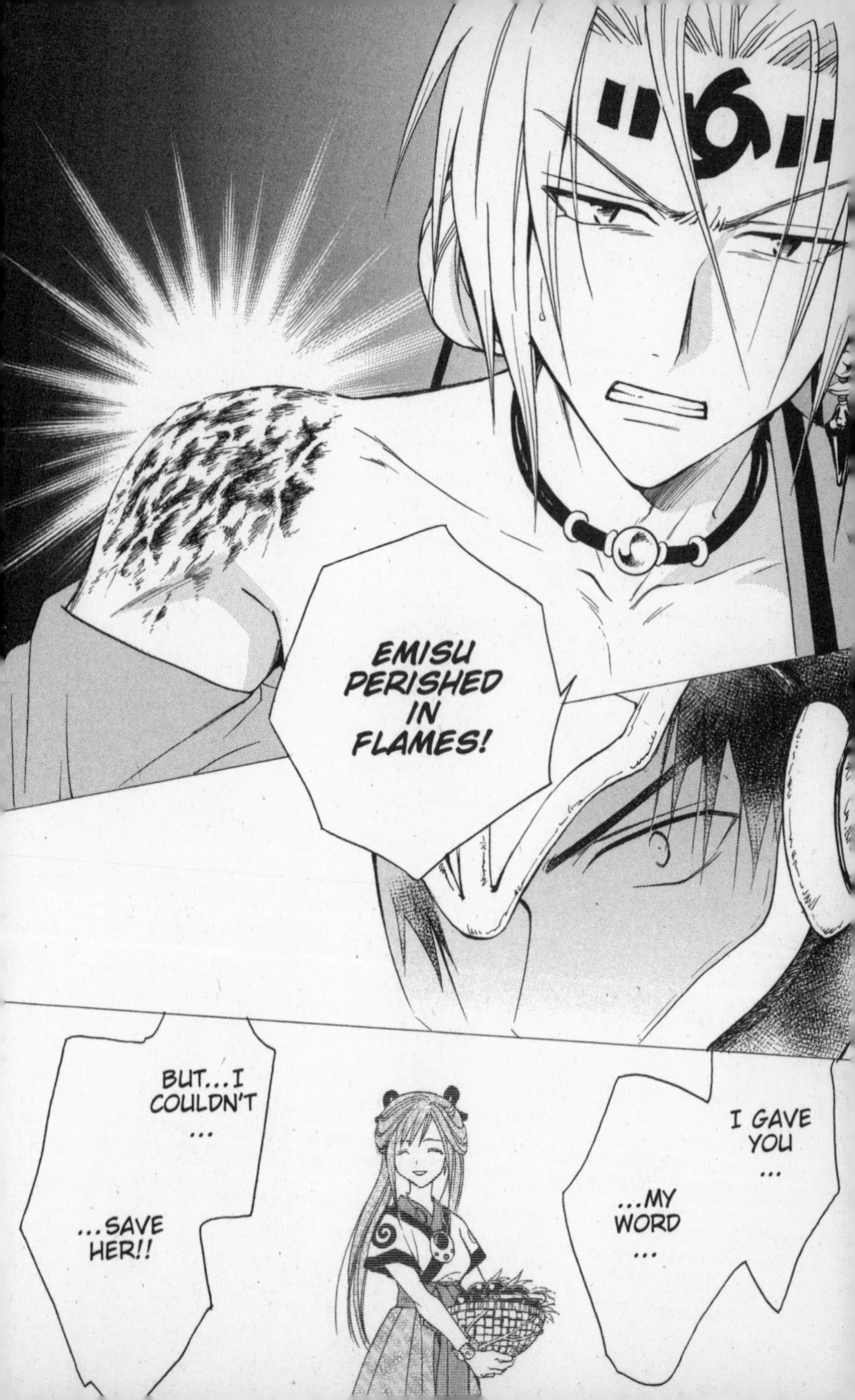
EMISU PERISHED IN FLAMES!
I GAVE YOU ...
...MY WORD ...
BUT...I COULDN'T ...
...SAVE HER!!

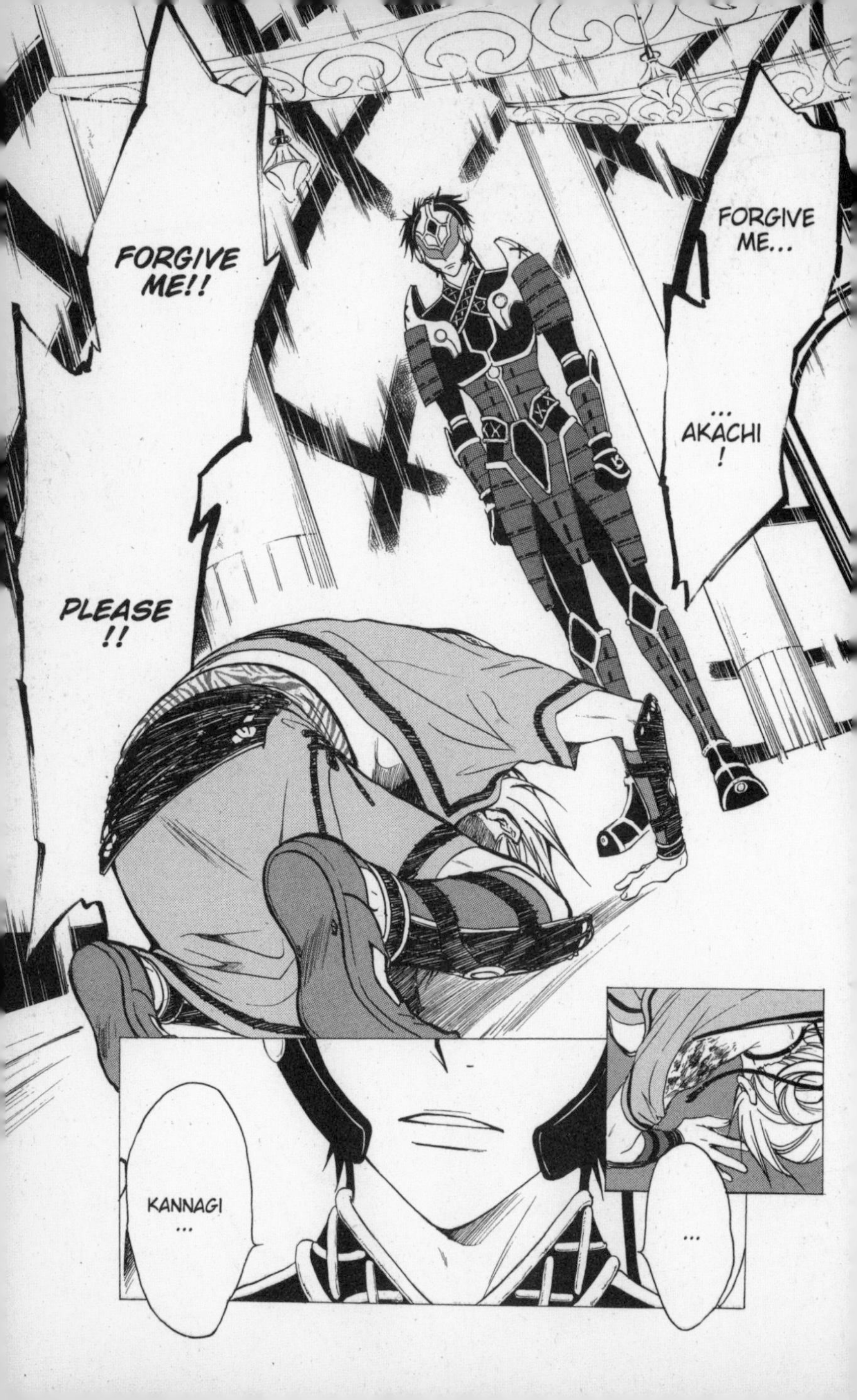
FORGIVE ME...
...AKACHI!
FORGIVE ME!!
PLEASE!!
...
KANNAGI ...

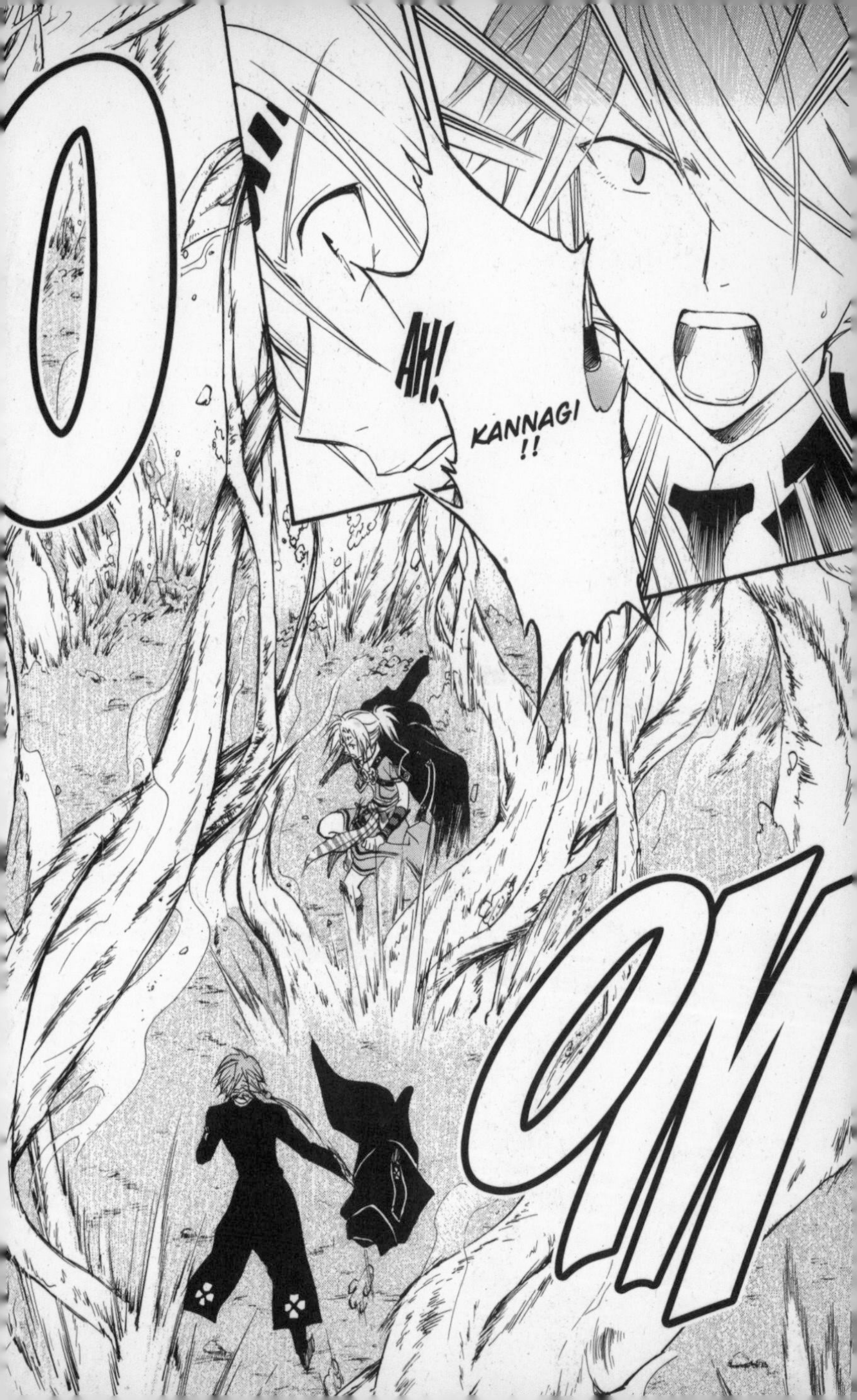
KANNAGI!!
AH!

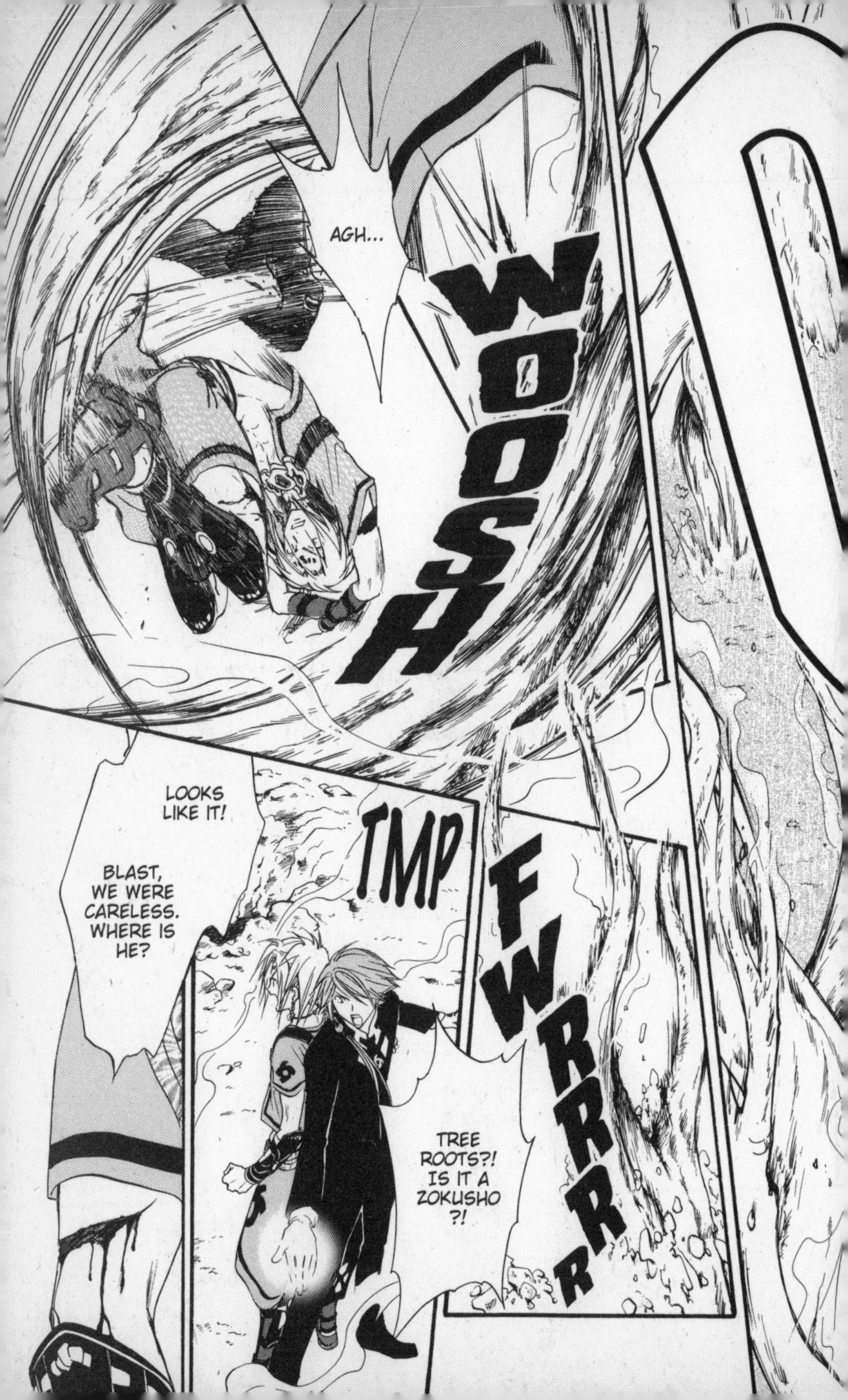
AGH...
WOOSH
FWRRRRR
TMP
TREE ROOTS?! IS IT A ZOKUSHO ?!
LOOKS LIKE IT!
BLAST, WE WERE CARELESS. WHERE IS HE?

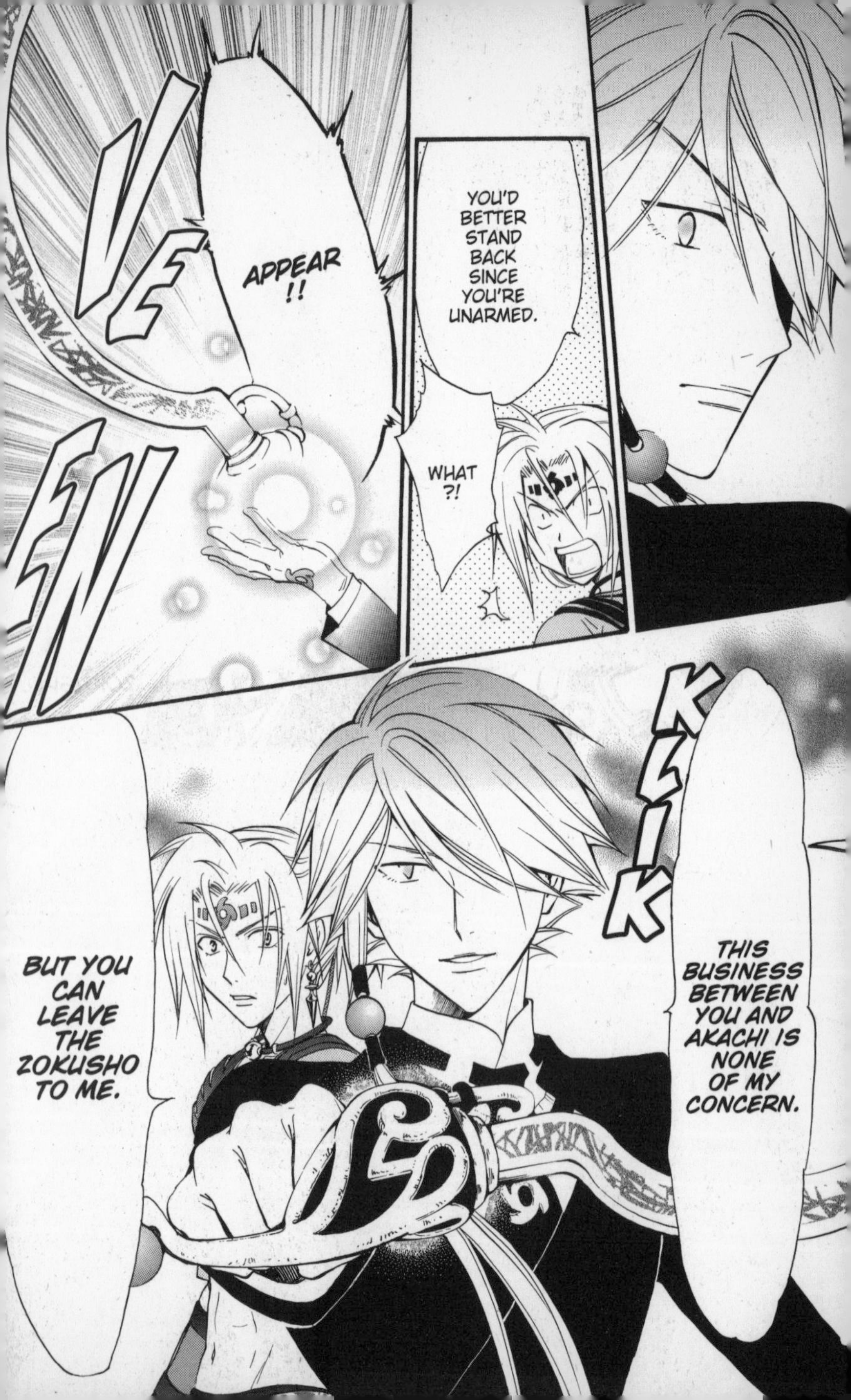
YOU'D BETTER STAND BACK SINCE YOU'RE UNARMED.
WHAT ?!
APPEAR !!
VEEN
KLIK
THIS BUSINESS BETWEEN YOU AND AKACHI IS NONE OF MY CONCERN.
BUT YOU CAN LEAVE THE ZOKUSHO TO ME.

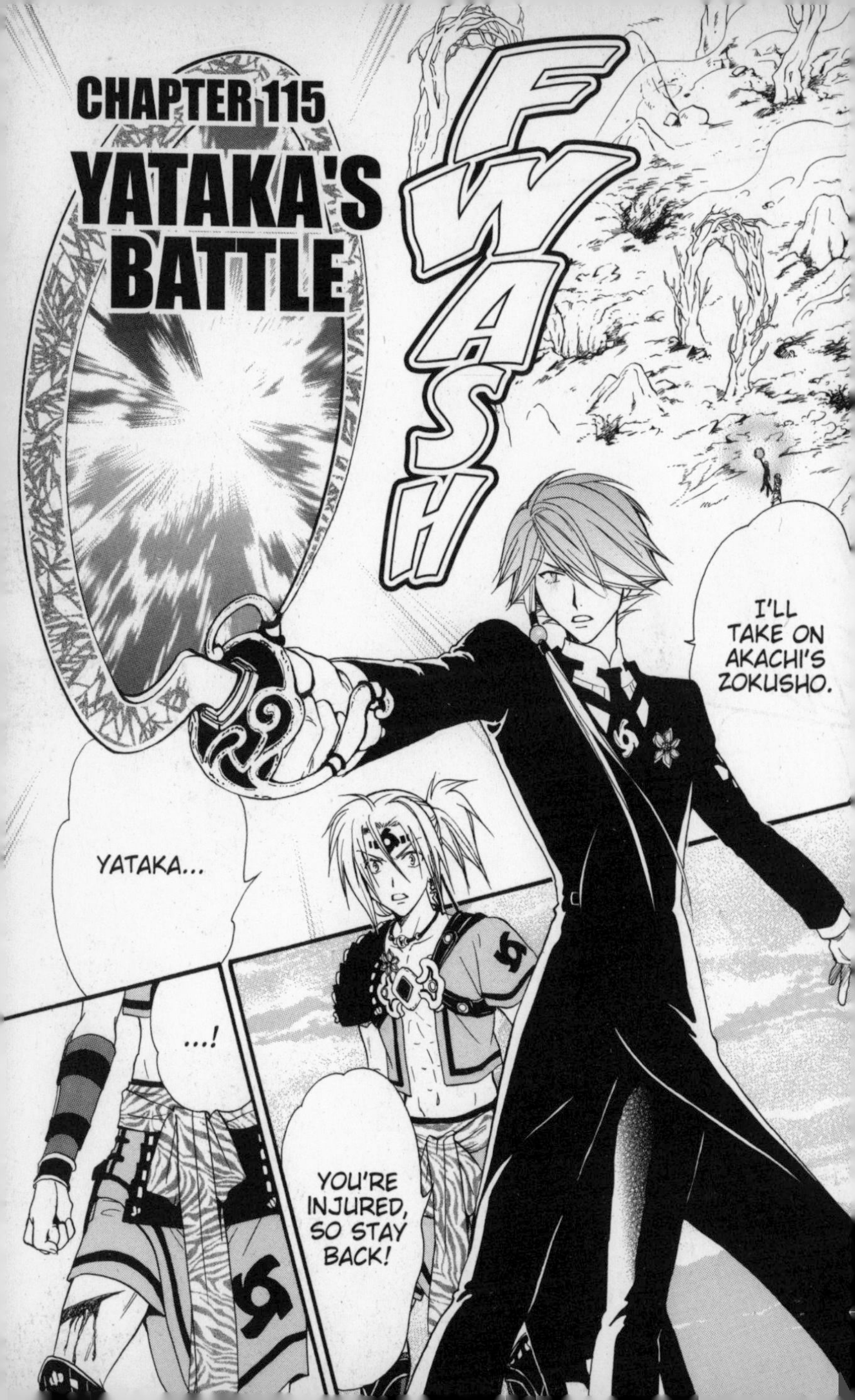
CHAPTER 115
YATAKA'S BATTLE
FWASH
I'LL TAKE ON AKACHI'S ZOKUSHO.
YATAKA...
...!
YOU'RE INJURED, SO STAY BACK!

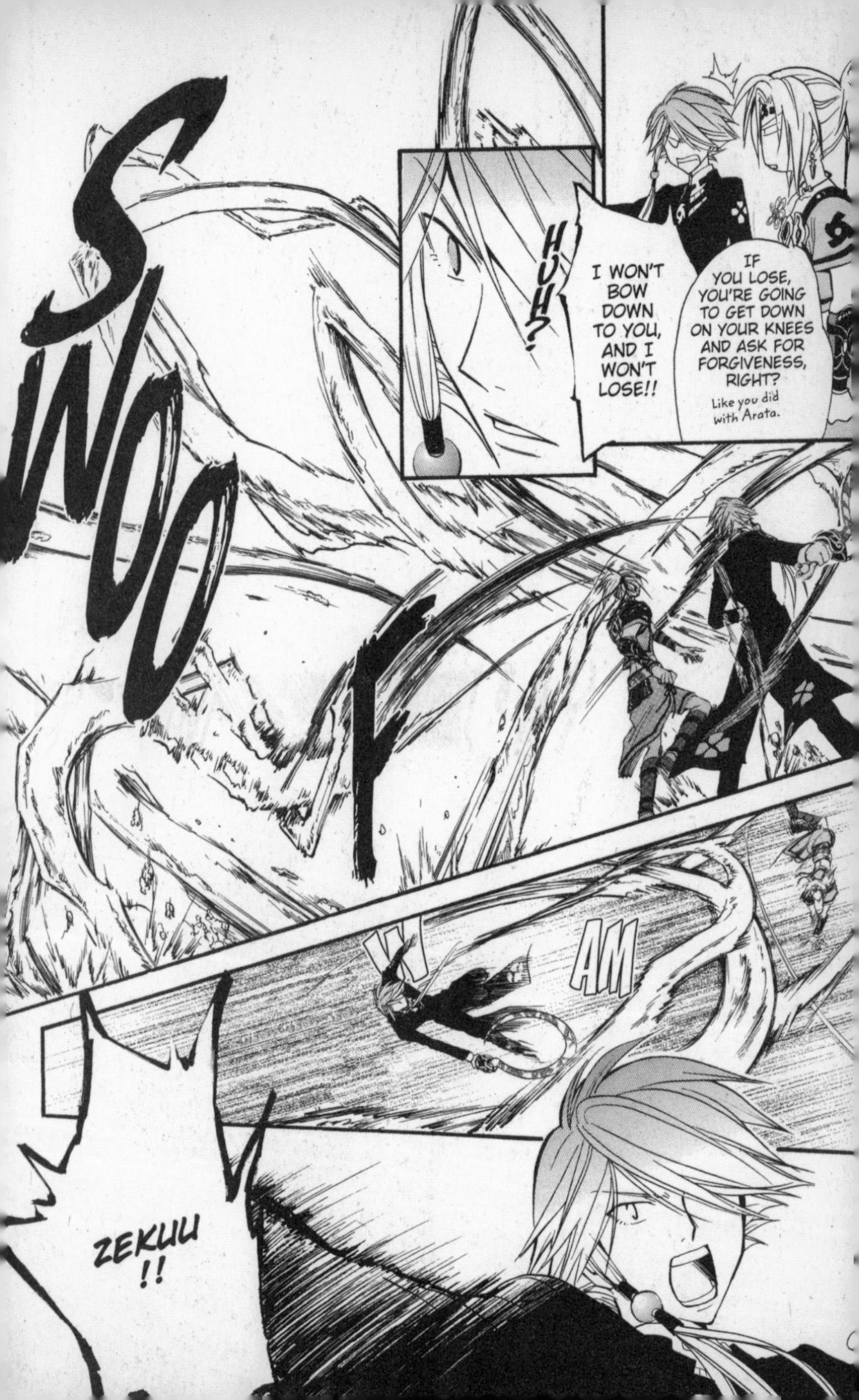
IF YOU LOSE, YOU'RE GOING TO GET DOWN ON YOUR KNEES AND ASK FOR FORGIVENESS, RIGHT?
Like you did with Arata.
HUH?
I WON'T BOW DOWN TO YOU, AND I WON'T LOSE!!
SWOOF
AM
ZEKUU!!

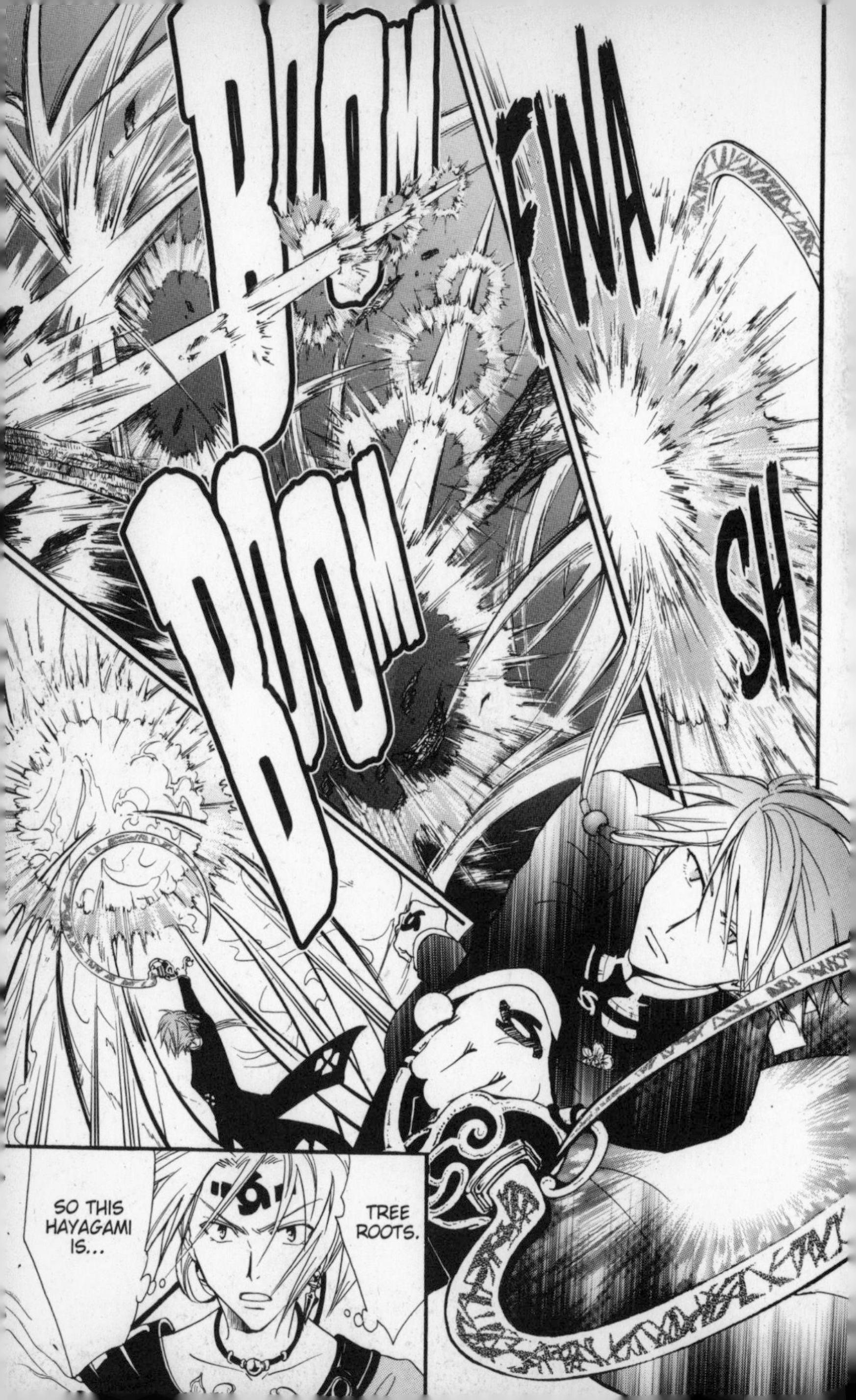
FWA
BOOM
SH
BOOM
SO THIS HAYAGAMI IS...
TREE ROOTS.

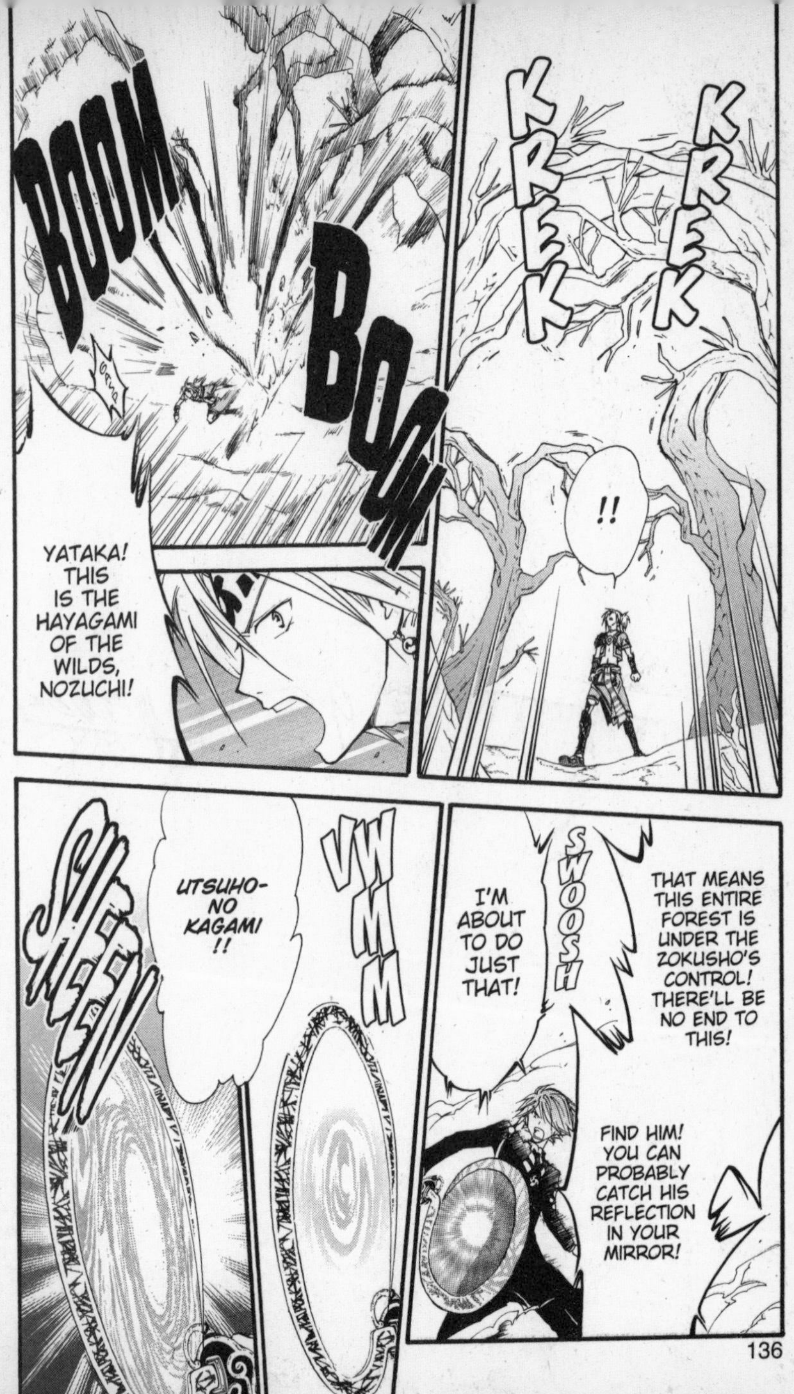
KREK
KREK
!!
BOOM
BOOM
YATAKA! THIS IS THE HAYAGAMI OF THE WILDS, NOZUCHI!
THAT MEANS THIS ENTIRE FOREST IS UNDER THE ZOKUSHO'S CONTROL! THERE'LL BE NO END TO THIS!
FIND HIM! YOU CAN PROBABLY CATCH HIS REFLECTION IN YOUR MIRROR!
SWOOSH
I'M ABOUT TO DO JUST THAT!
VWMMM
UTSUHO-NO KAGAMI !!

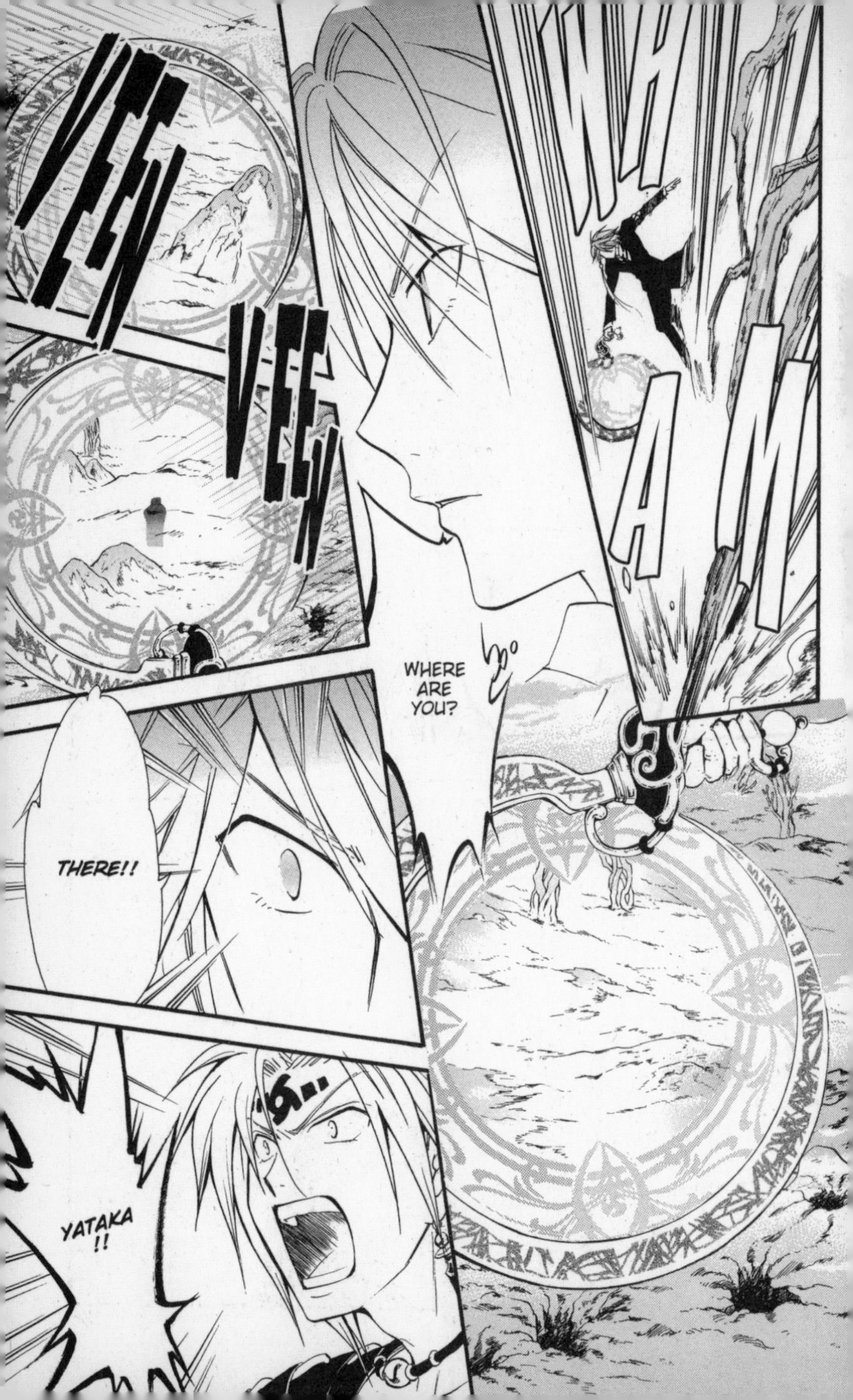
WHERE ARE YOU?
VEEN
VEEN
THERE!!
YATAKA !!

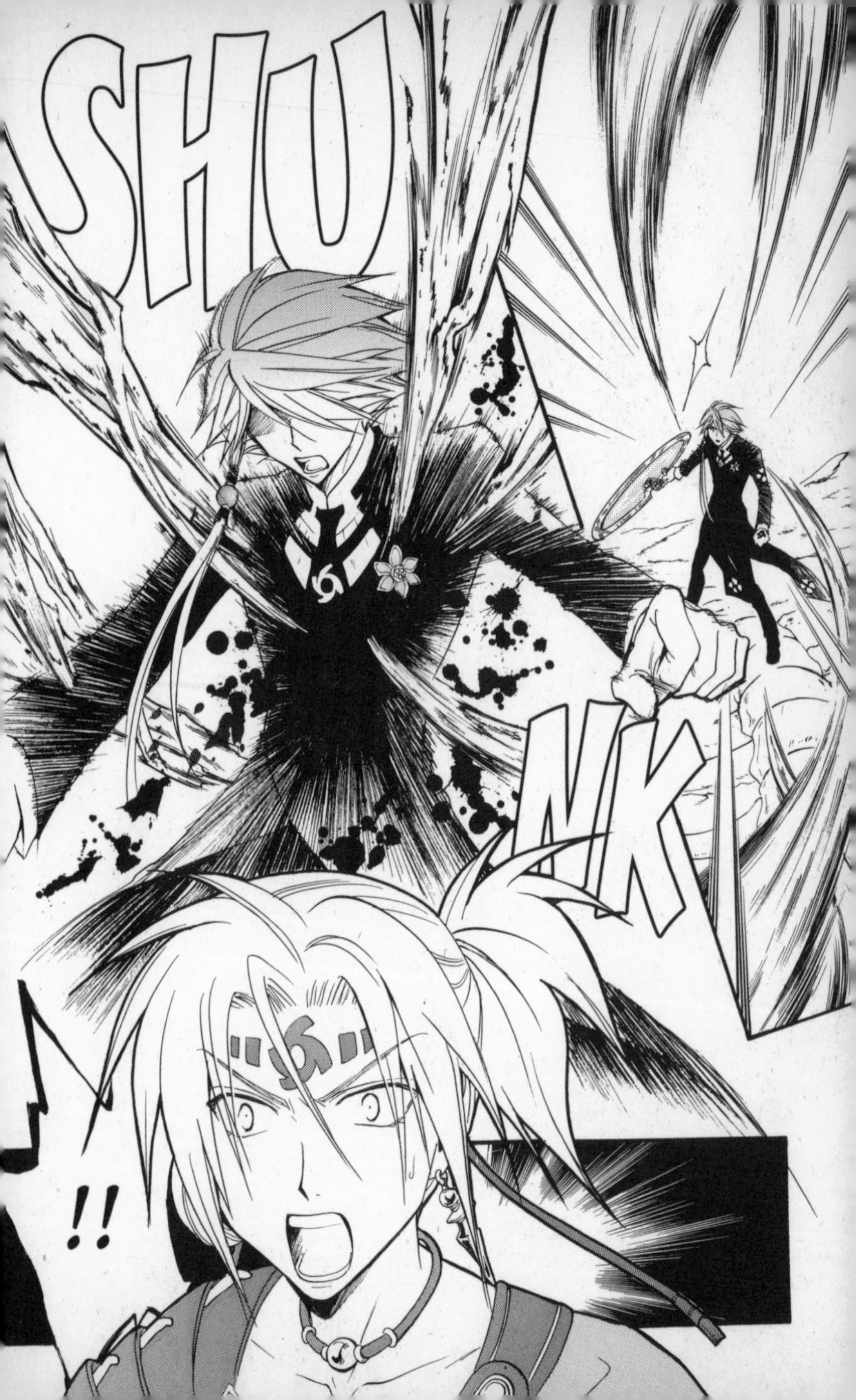
SHUNK
!!

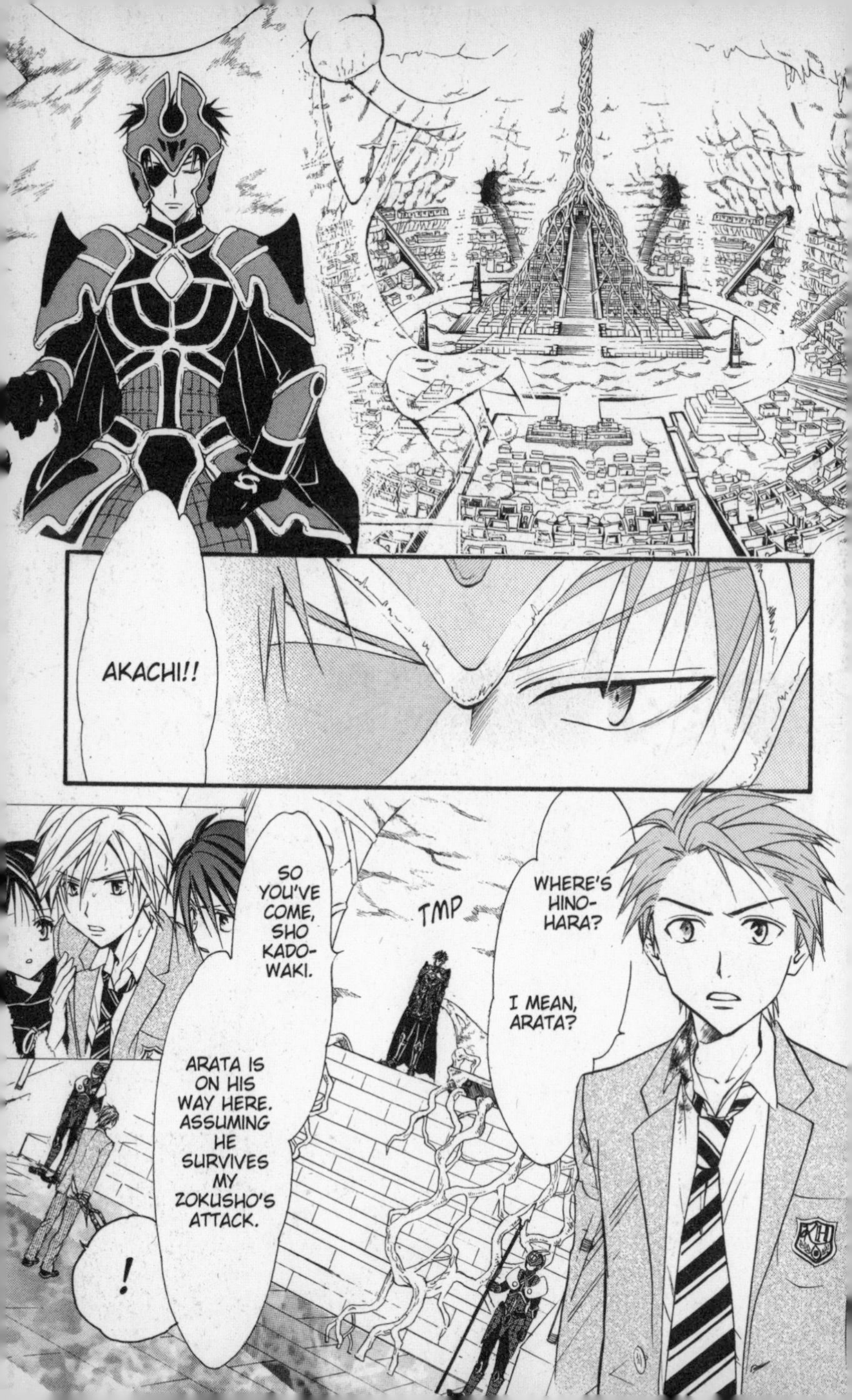
AKACHI!!
WHERE'S HINO-HARA?
I MEAN, ARATA?
TMP
SO YOU'VE COME, SHO KADO-WAKI.
ARATA IS ON HIS WAY HERE. ASSUMING HE SURVIVES MY ZOKUSHO'S ATTACK.
!

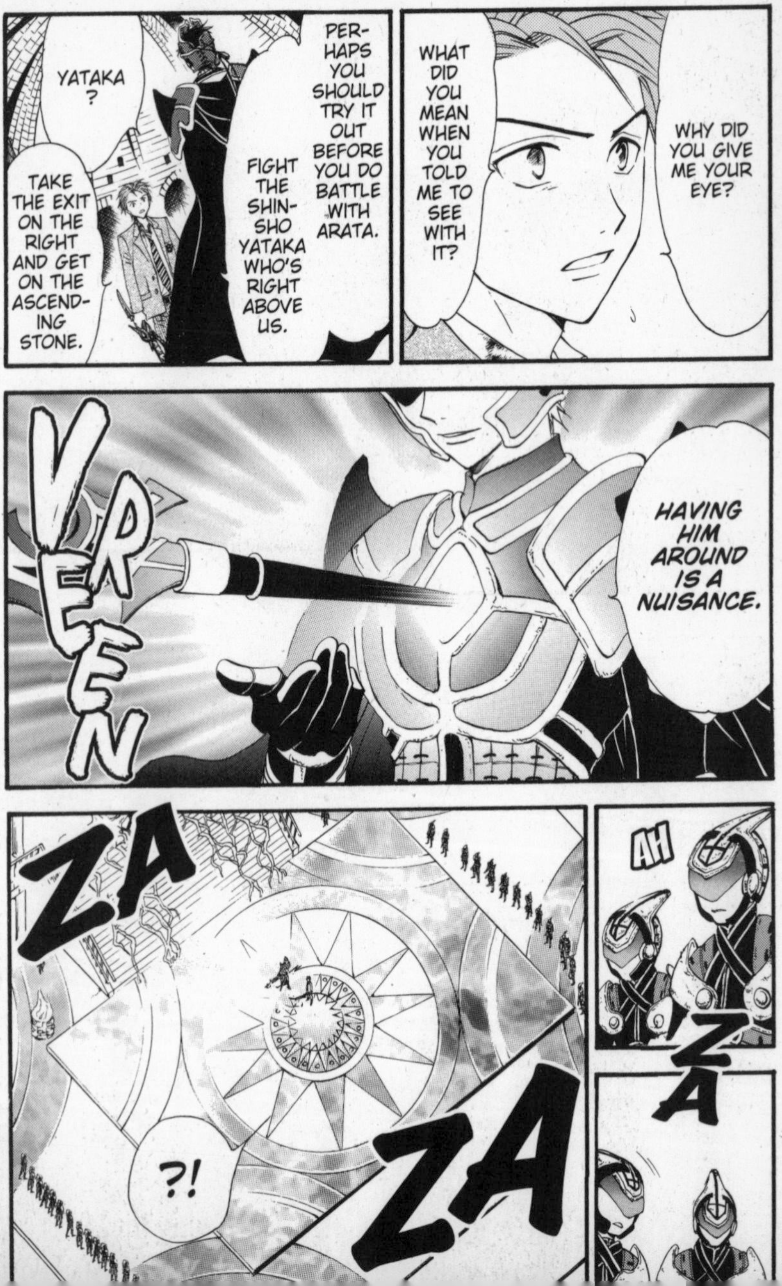
WHY DID YOU GIVE ME YOUR EYE?
WHAT DID YOU MEAN WHEN YOU TOLD ME TO SEE WITH IT?
PER-HAPS YOU SHOULD TRY IT OUT BEFORE YOU DO BATTLE WITH ARATA.
FIGHT THE SHIN-SHO YATAKA WHO'S RIGHT ABOVE US.
YATAKA?
TAKE THE EXIT ON THE RIGHT AND GET ON THE ASCEND-ING STONE.
HAVING HIM AROUND IS A NUISANCE.
VREEN
AH
ZA
ZA
?!
ZA

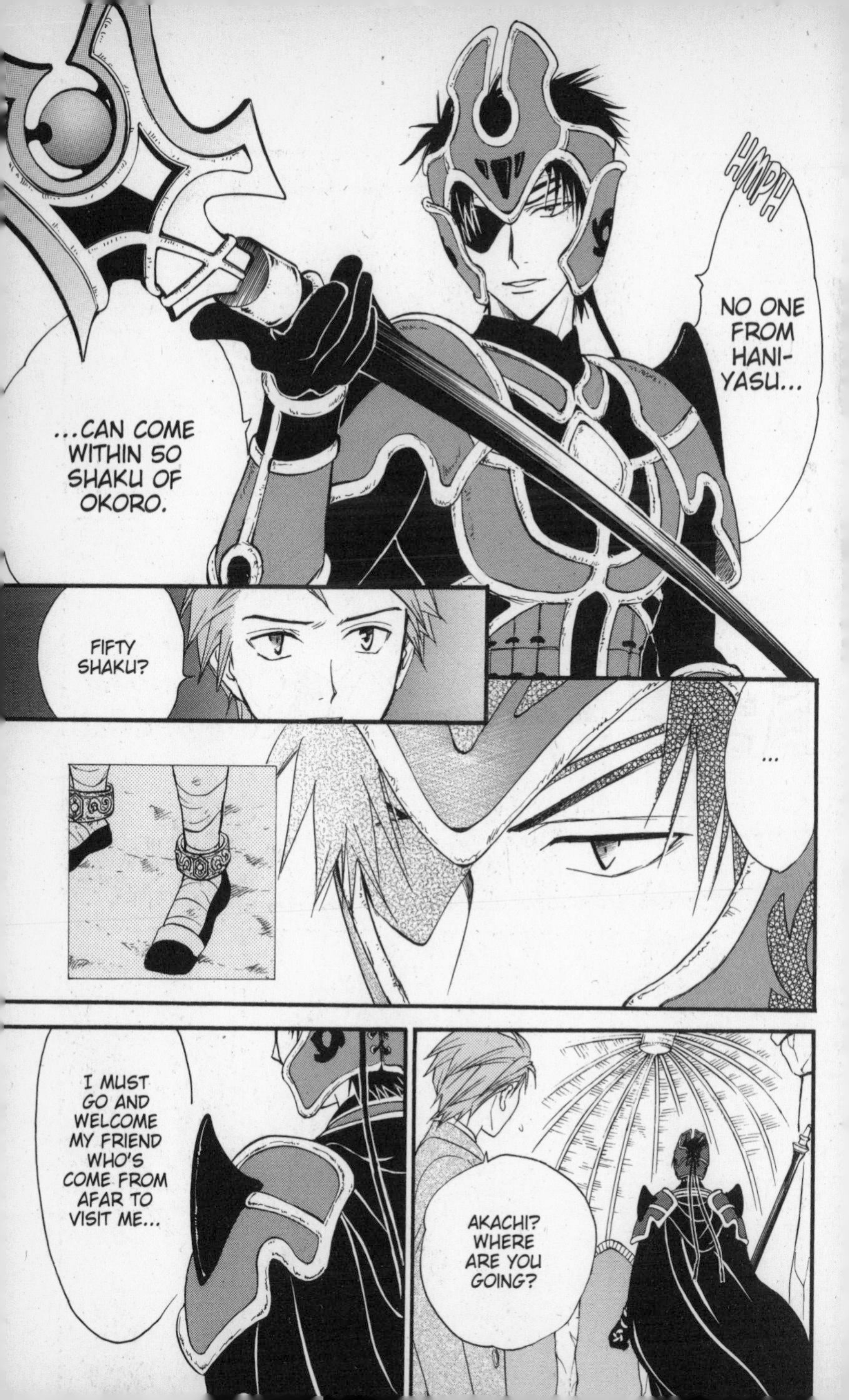
HMPH
NO ONE FROM HANI-YASU...
...CAN COME WITHIN 50 SHAKU OF OKORO.
FIFTY SHAKU?
...
AKACHI? WHERE ARE YOU GOING?
I MUST GO AND WELCOME MY FRIEND WHO'S COME FROM AFAR TO VISIT ME...

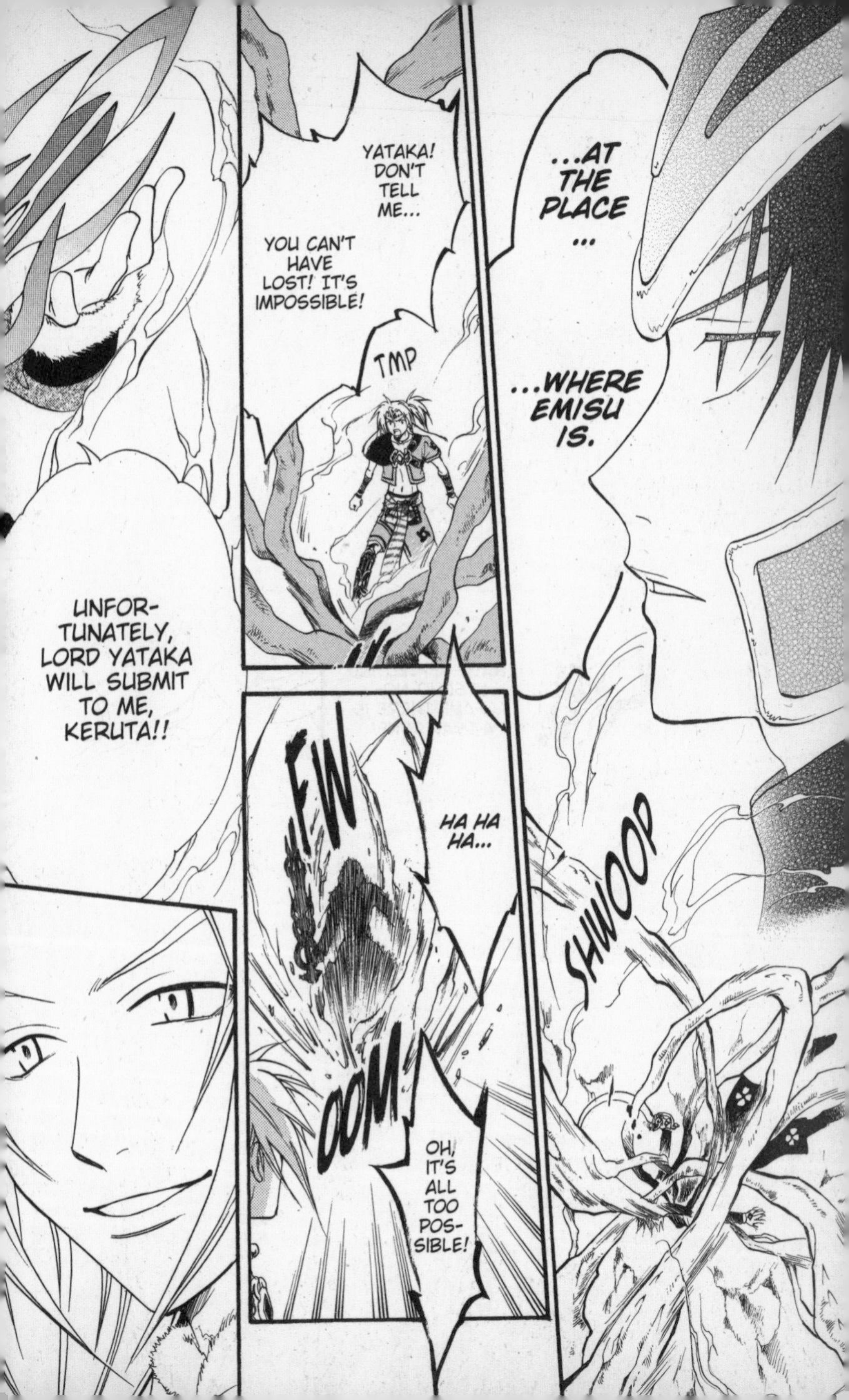
...AT THE PLACE ...
...WHERE EMISU IS.
SHWOOP
YATAKA! DON'T TELL ME...
YOU CAN'T HAVE LOST! IT'S IMPOSSIBLE!
TMP
FWOOM
HA HA HA...
OH, IT'S ALL TOO POS-SIBLE!
UNFOR-TUNATELY, LORD YATAKA WILL SUBMIT TO ME, KERUTA!!

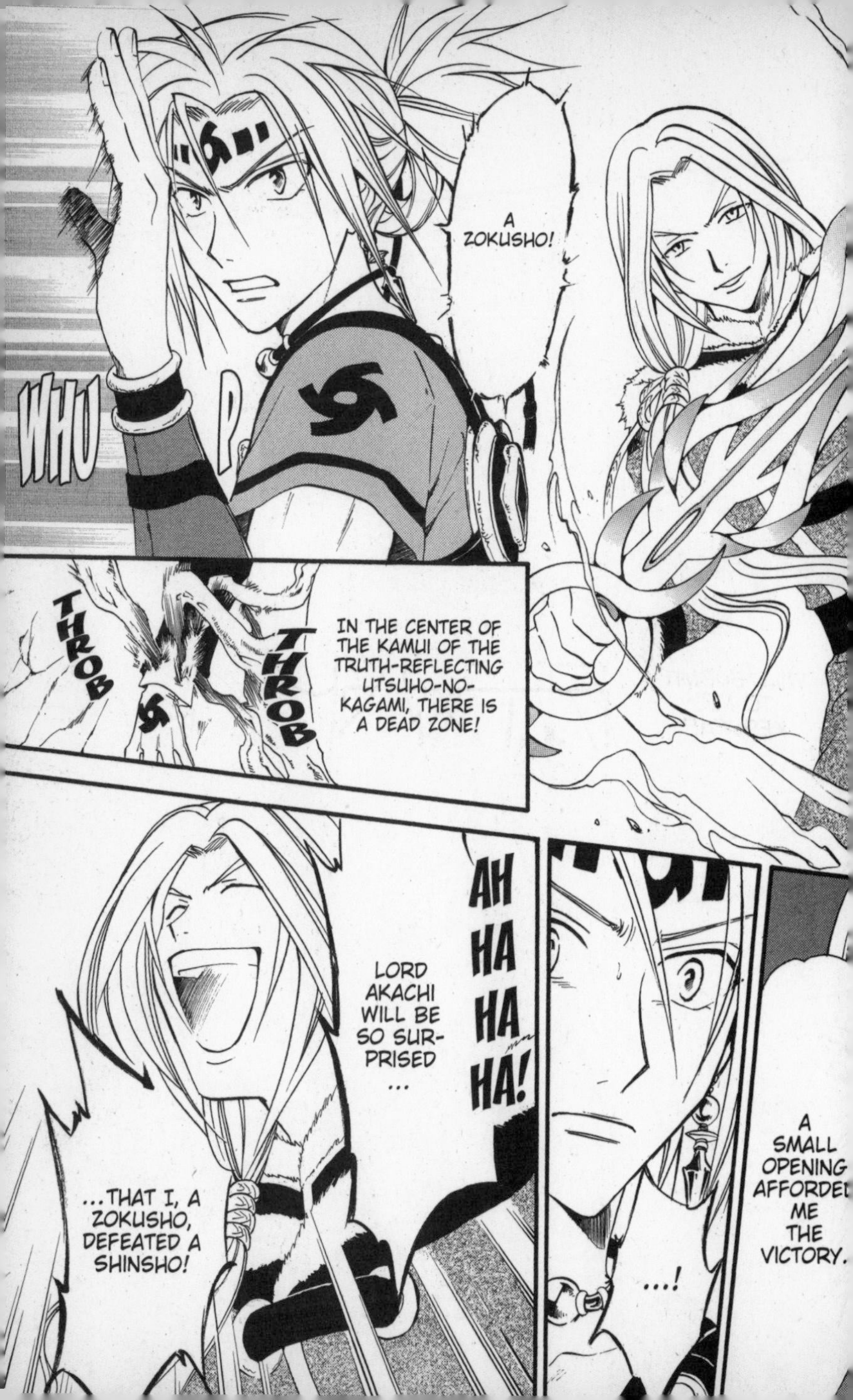
A ZOKUSHO!
WHUP
IN THE CENTER OF THE KAMUI OF THE TRUTH-REFLECTING UTSUHO-NO-KAGAMI, THERE IS A DEAD ZONE!
THROB THROB
A SMALL OPENING AFFORDED ME THE VICTORY.
...!
LORD AKACHI WILL BE SO SUR-PRISED ...
AH HA HA HA HA!
...THAT I, A ZOKUSHO, DEFEATED A SHINSHO!

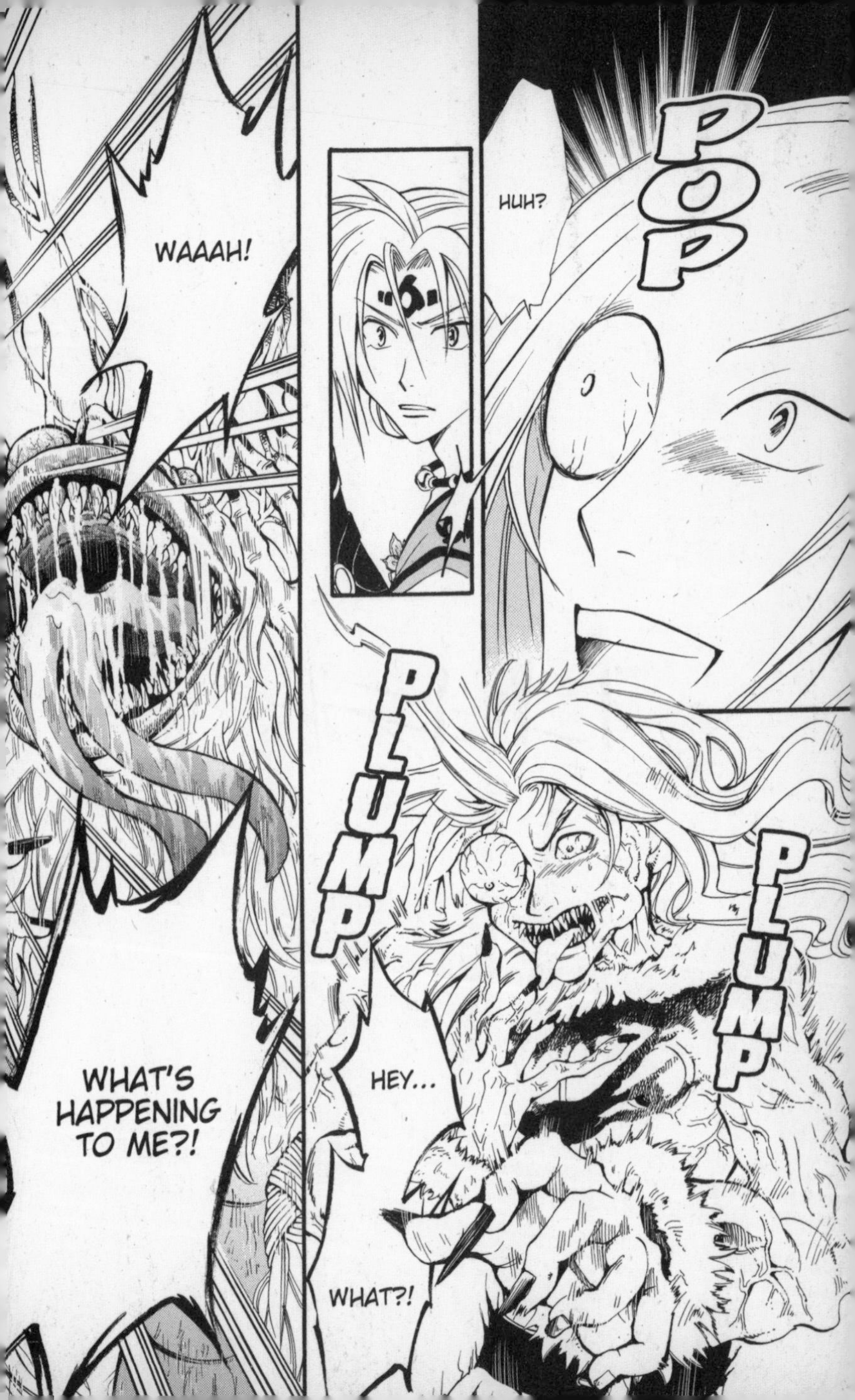
POP
HUH?
PLUMP
PLUMP
HEY...
WHAT?!
WAAAH!
WHAT'S HAPPENING TO ME?!

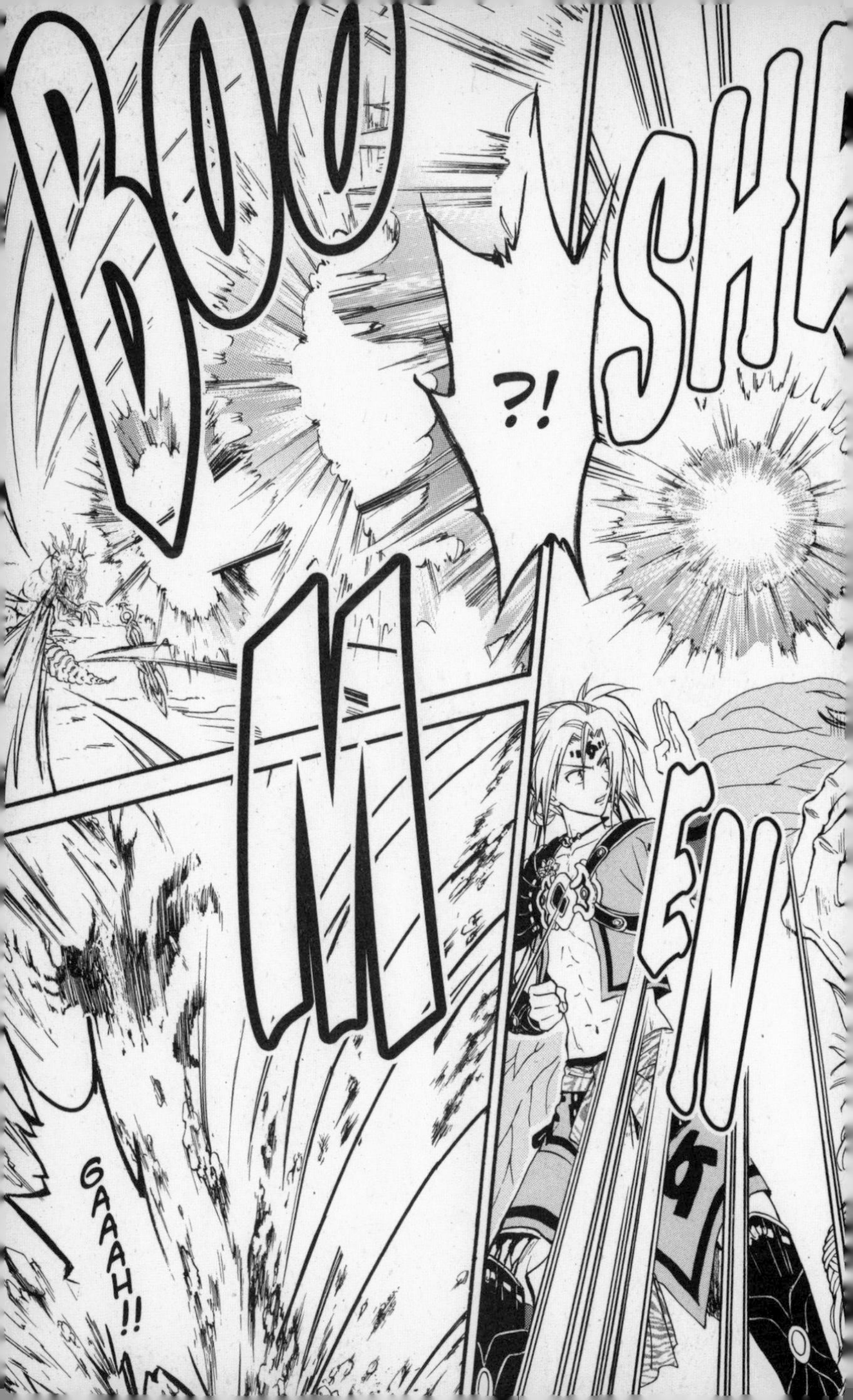
SH
EN
?!
BOOOM
GAAAH!!

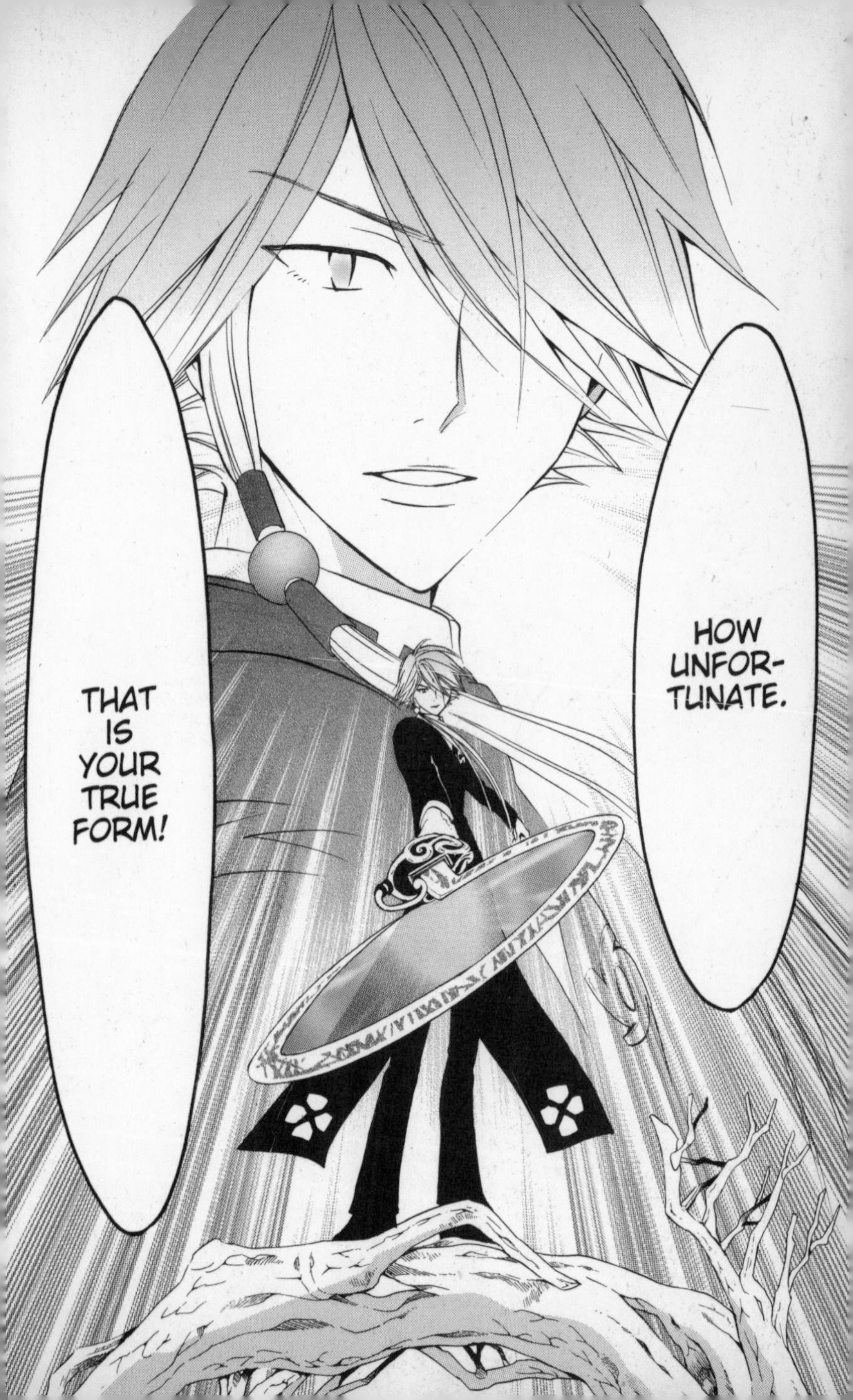
HOW UNFOR-TUNATE.
THAT IS YOUR TRUE FORM!

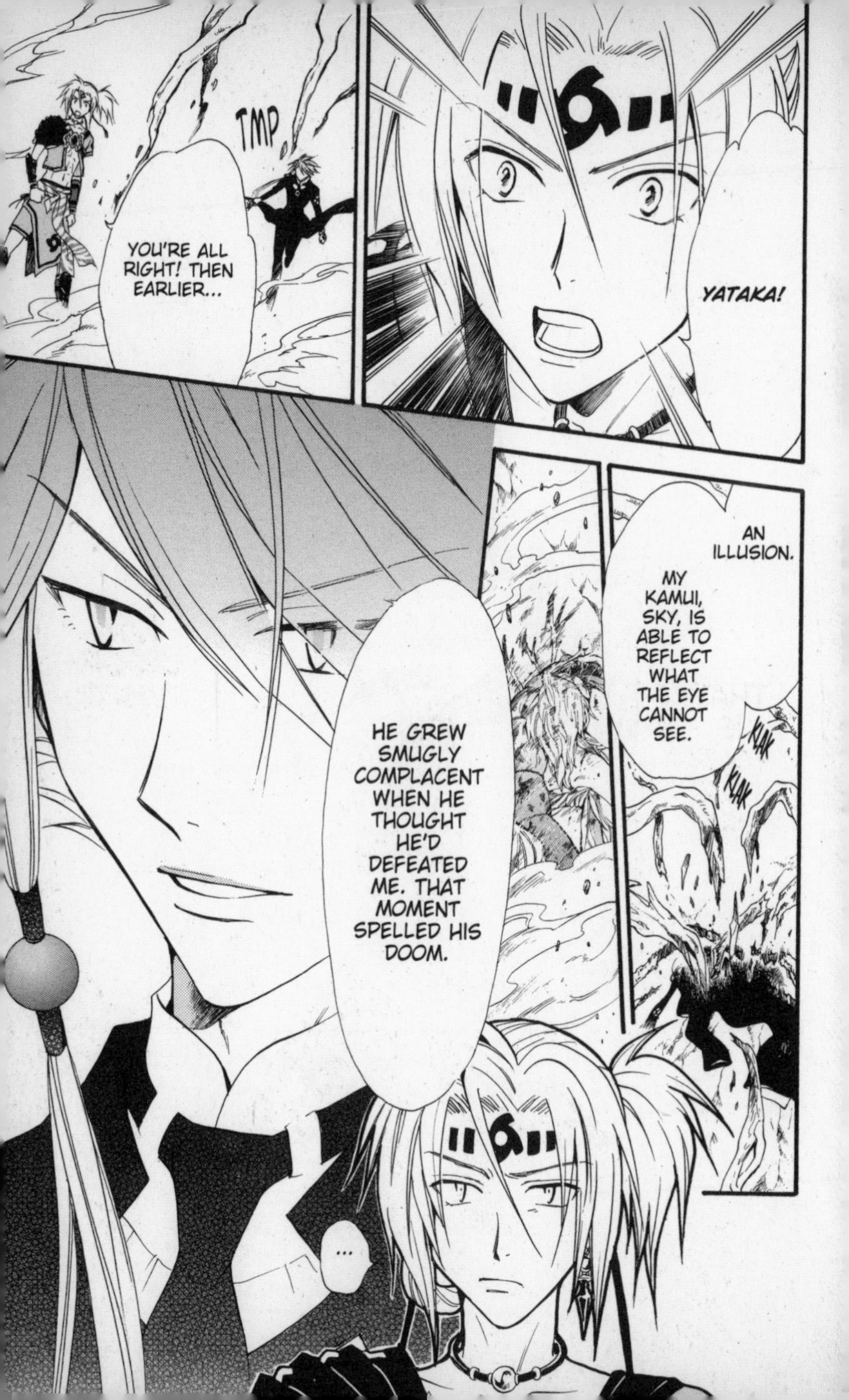
YATAKA!
TMP
YOU'RE ALL RIGHT! THEN EARLIER...
AN ILLUSION.
MY KAMUI, SKY, IS ABLE TO REFLECT WHAT THE EYE CANNOT SEE.
KLAK
KLAK
HE GREW SMUGLY COMPLACENT WHEN HE THOUGHT HE'D DEFEATED ME. THAT MOMENT SPELLED HIS DOOM.
...

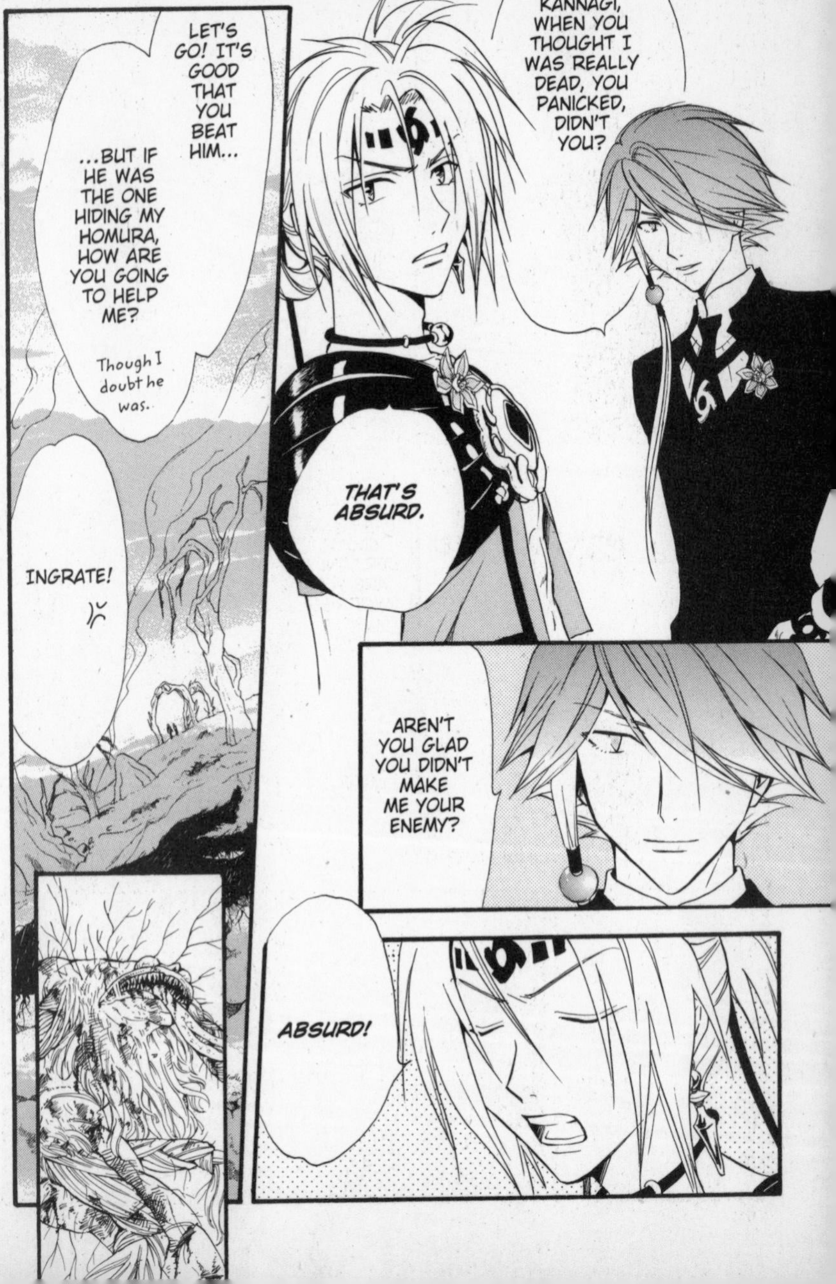
KANNAGI, WHEN YOU THOUGHT I WAS REALLY DEAD, YOU PANICKED, DIDN'T YOU?
THAT'S ABSURD.
AREN'T YOU GLAD YOU DIDN'T MAKE ME YOUR ENEMY?
ABSURD!
LET'S GO! IT'S GOOD THAT YOU BEAT HIM...
...BUT IF HE WAS THE ONE HIDING MY HOMURA, HOW ARE YOU GOING TO HELP ME?
Though I doubt he was..
INGRATE!

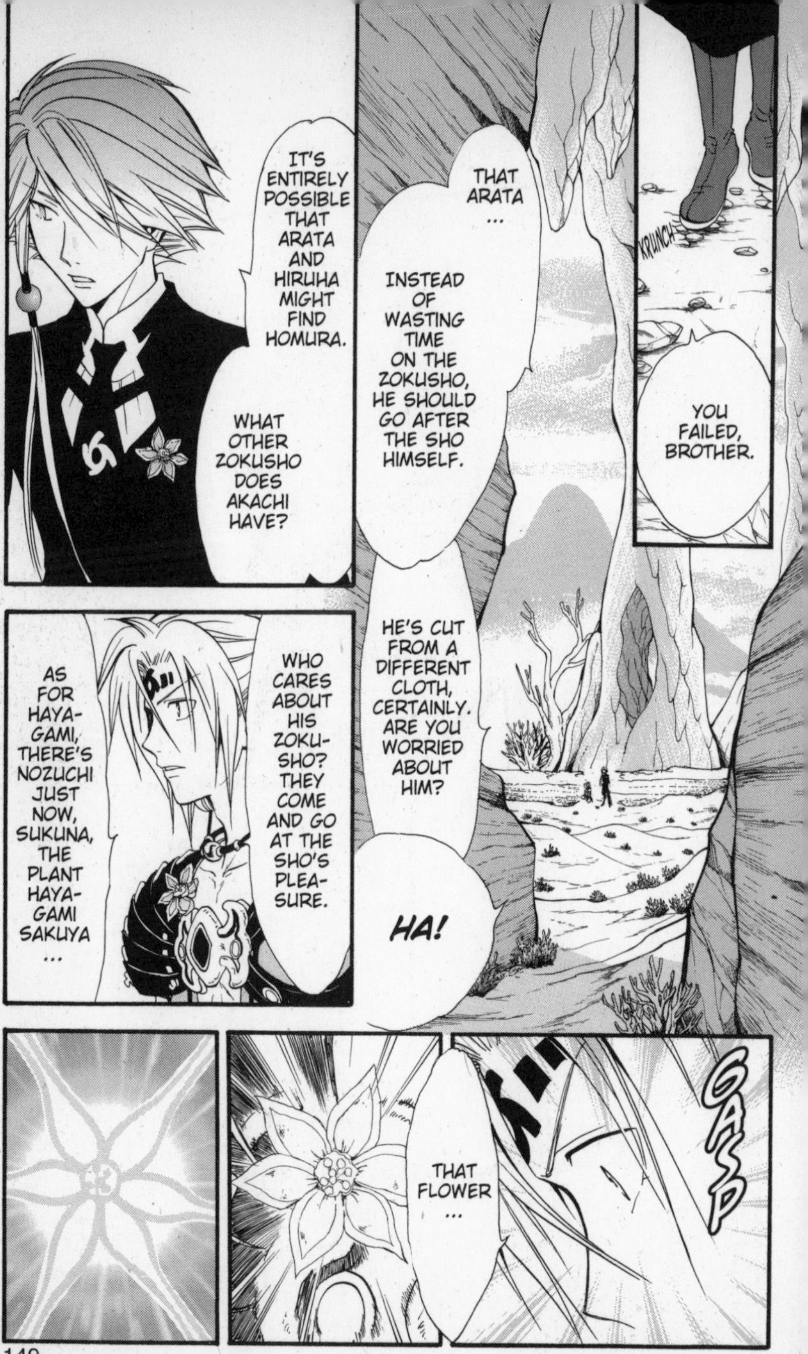
KRUNCH
YOU FAILED, BROTHER.
THAT ARATA ...
INSTEAD OF WASTING TIME ON THE ZOKUSHO, HE SHOULD GO AFTER THE SHO HIMSELF.
HE'S CUT FROM A DIFFERENT CLOTH, CERTAINLY. ARE YOU WORRIED ABOUT HIM?
HA!
IT'S ENTIRELY POSSIBLE THAT ARATA AND HIRUHA MIGHT FIND HOMURA.
WHAT OTHER ZOKUSHO DOES AKACHI HAVE?
WHO CARES ABOUT HIS ZOKU-SHO? THEY COME AND GO AT THE SHO'S PLEA-SURE.
AS FOR HAYA-GAMI, THERE'S NOZUCHI JUST NOW, SUKUNA, THE PLANT HAYA-GAMI SAKUYA ...
GASP
THAT FLOWER ...

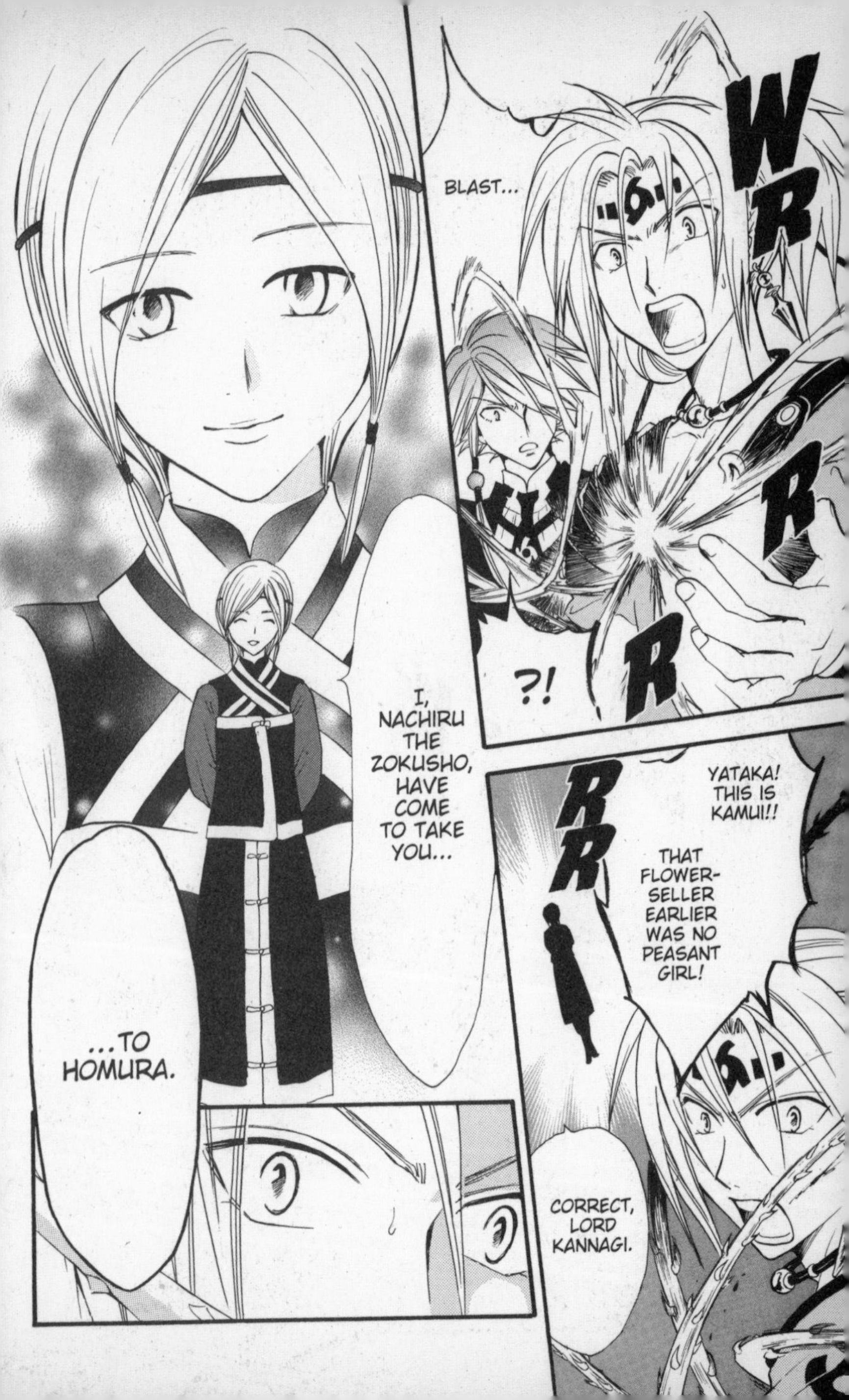
BLAST...
WRRR
?!
RR
YATAKA! THIS IS KAMUI!!
THAT FLOWER-SELLER EARLIER WAS NO PEASANT GIRL!
CORRECT, LORD KANNAGI.
I, NACHIRU THE ZOKUSHO, HAVE COME TO TAKE YOU...
...TO HOMURA.

CHAPTER 116
MY ANGUISH

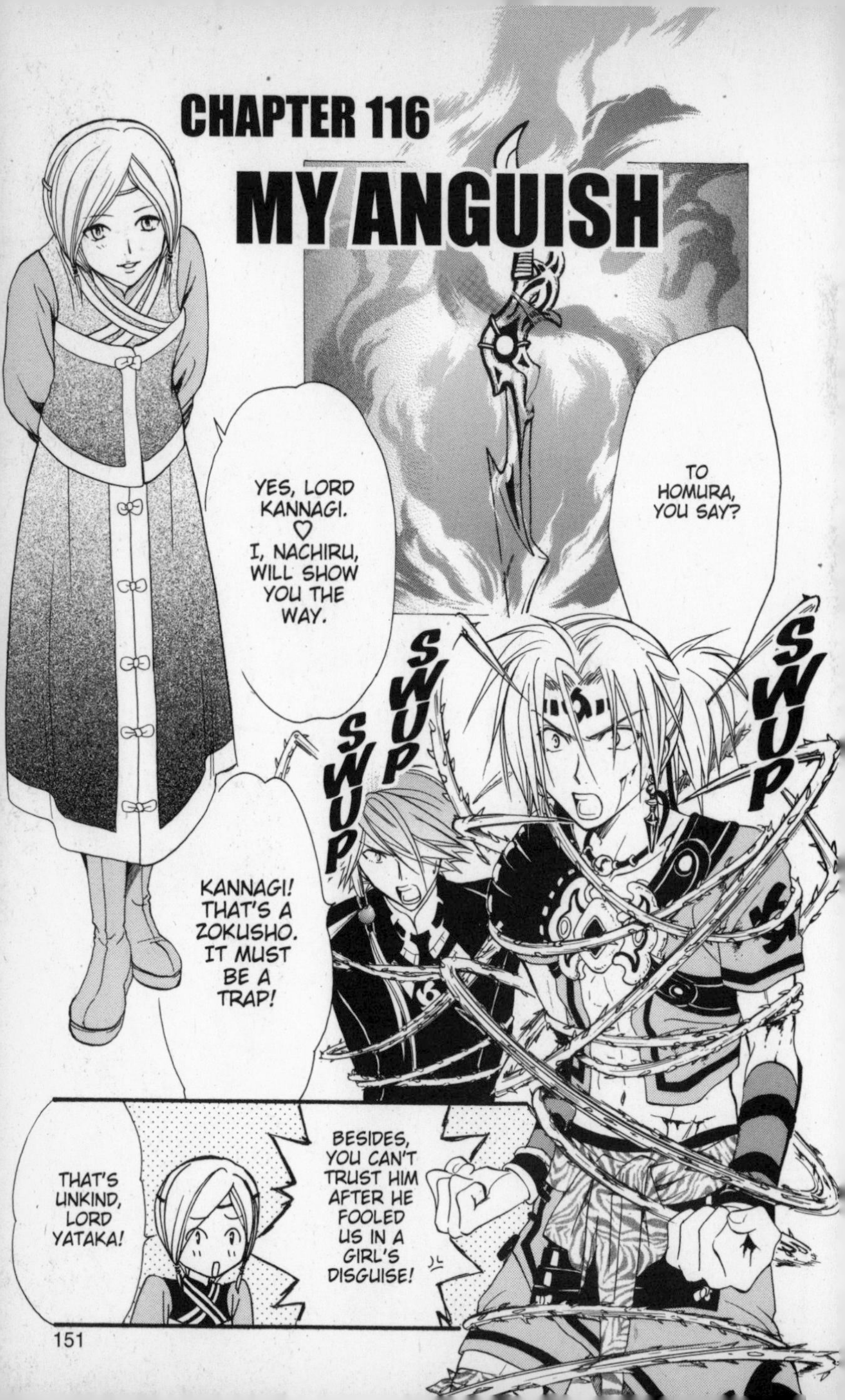
TO HOMURA, YOU SAY?
YES, LORD KANNAGI. ♡ I, NACHIRU, WILL SHOW YOU THE WAY.
SWUP
SWUP
SWUP
SWUP
KANNAGI! THAT'S A ZOKUSHO. IT MUST BE A TRAP!
BESIDES, YOU CAN'T TRUST HIM AFTER HE FOOLED US IN A GIRL'S DISGUISE!
THAT'S UNKIND, LORD YATAKA!

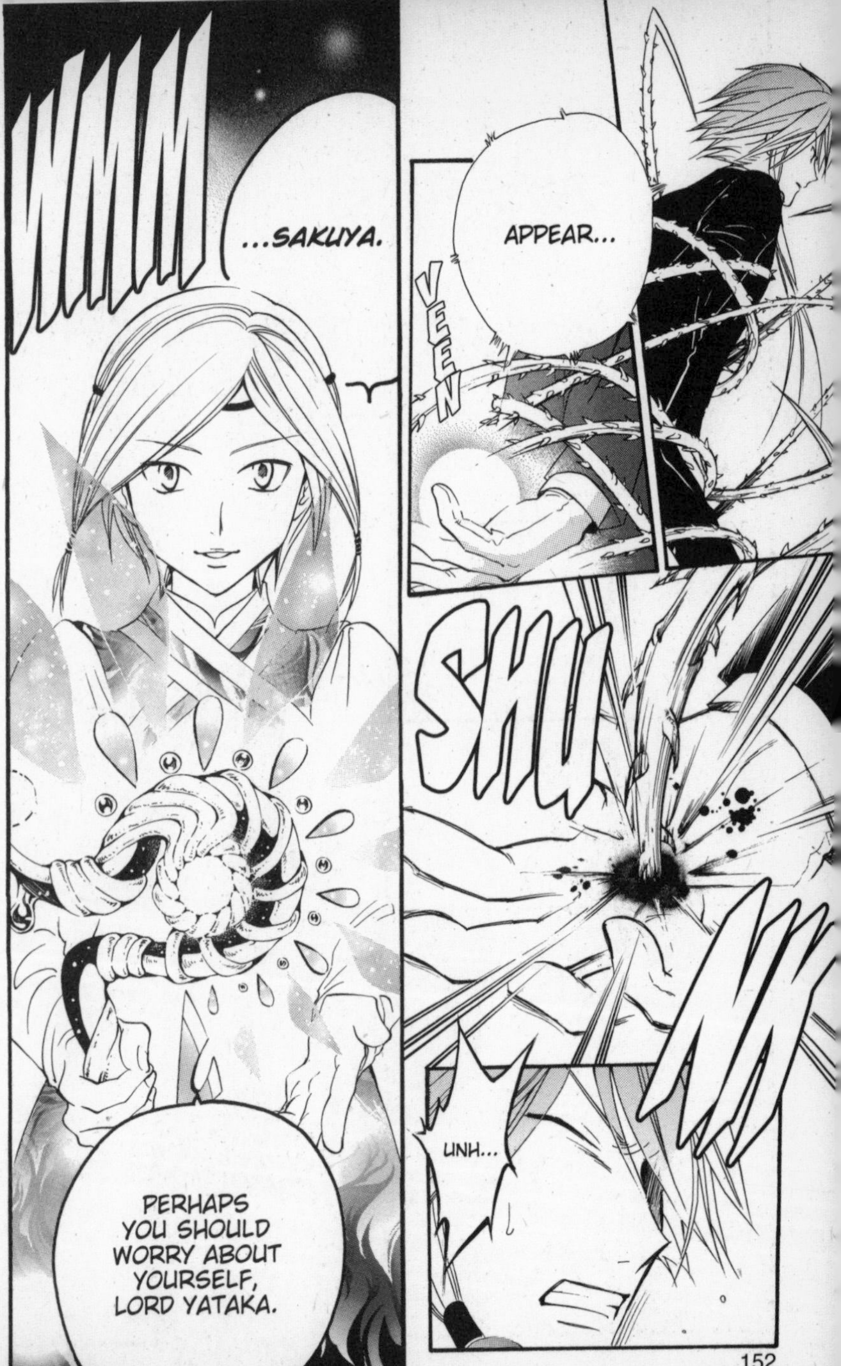
APPEAR...
VEEN
SHU
NN
UNH...
WMMM
...SAKUYA.
PERHAPS YOU SHOULD WORRY ABOUT YOURSELF, LORD YATAKA.

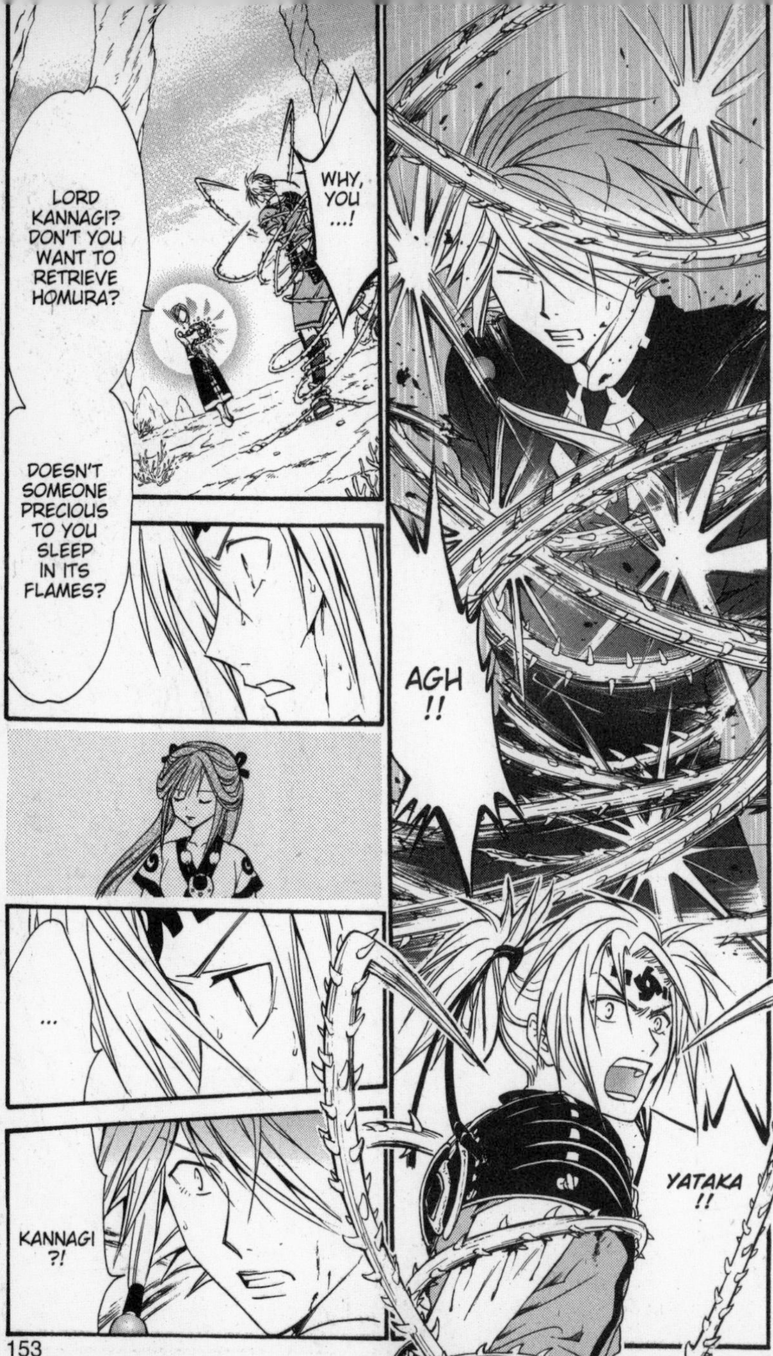
AGH!!
YATAKA!!
WHY, YOU ...!
LORD KANNAGI? DON'T YOU WANT TO RETRIEVE HOMURA?
DOESN'T SOMEONE PRECIOUS TO YOU SLEEP IN ITS FLAMES?
...
KANNAGI?!

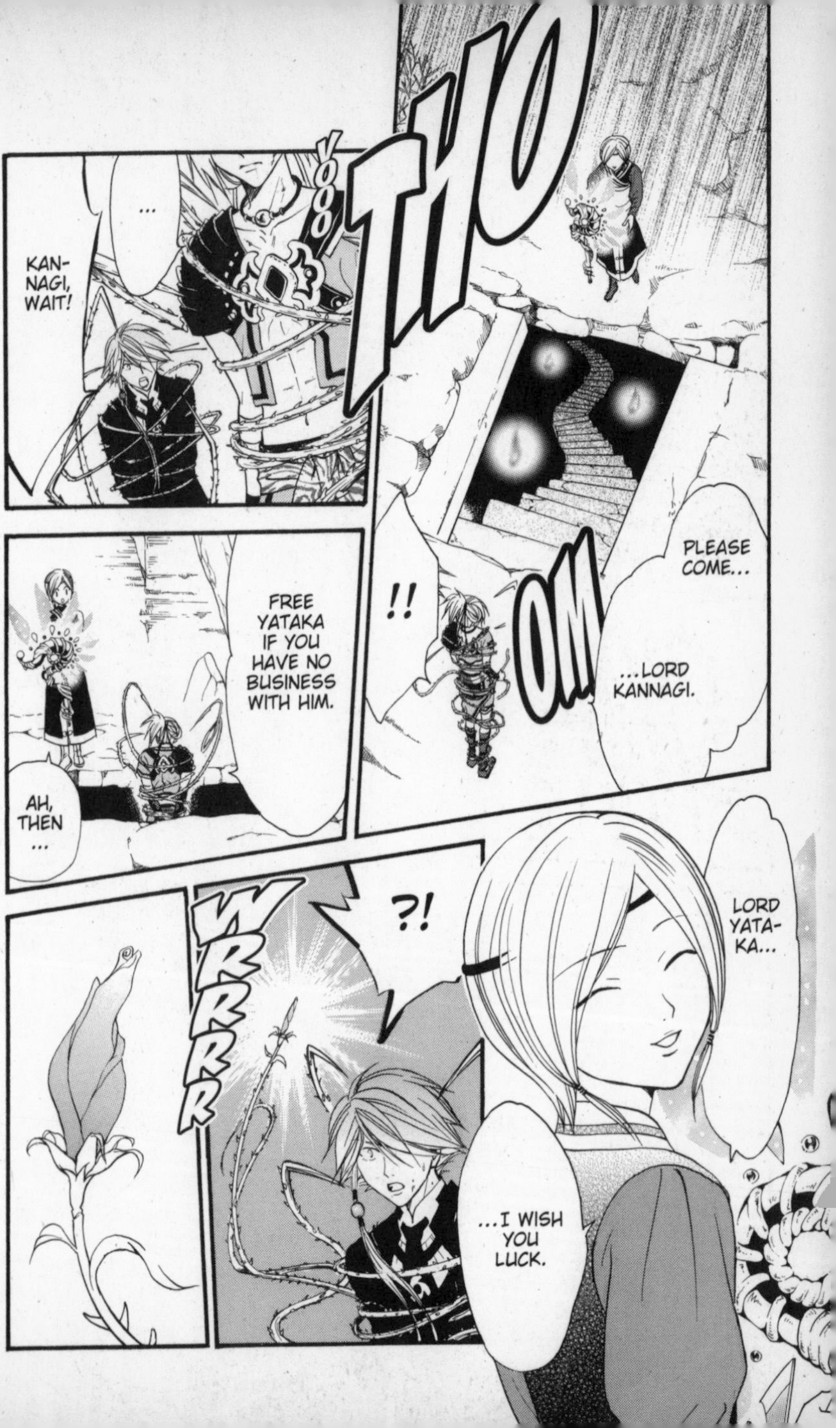
THO
PLEASE COME...
...LORD KANNAGI.
!!
OM
VOOO
...
KAN-NAGI, WAIT!
FREE YATAKA IF YOU HAVE NO BUSINESS WITH HIM.
AH, THEN ...
LORD YATA-KA...
...I WISH YOU LUCK.
?!
WRRRR

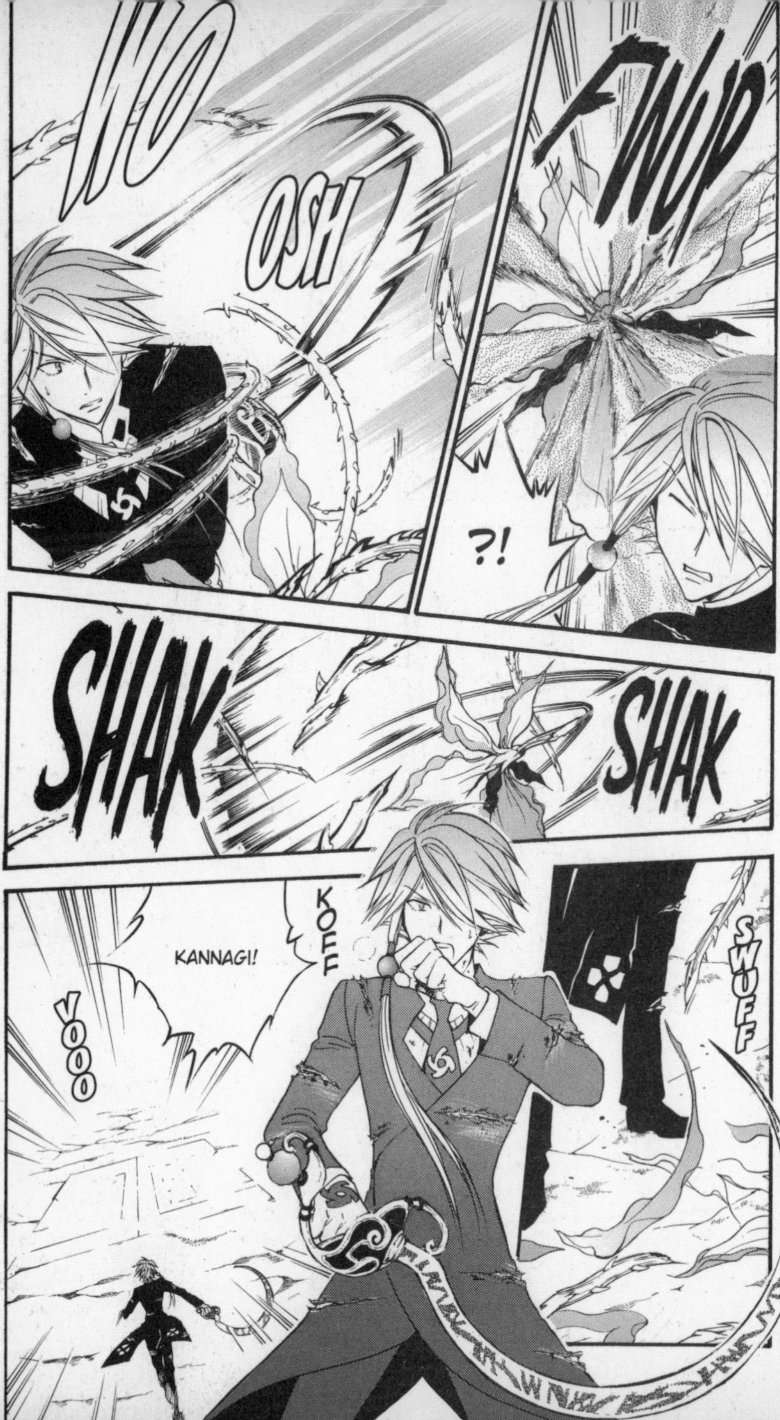
FWUP
?!
WHO
OSH
SHAK
SHAK
SWUFF
KOFF
KANNAGI!
VOOO

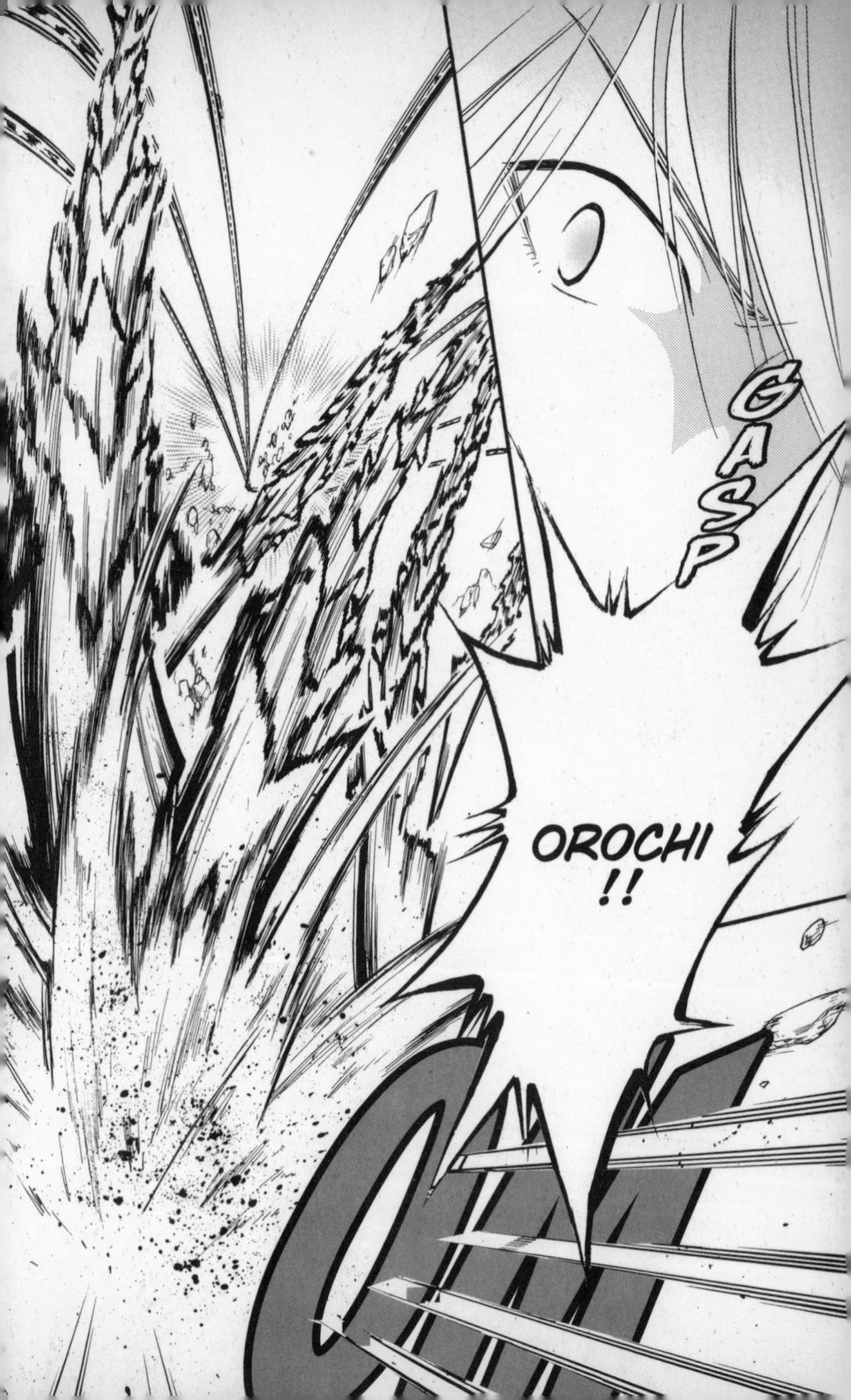
GASP
OROCHI !!

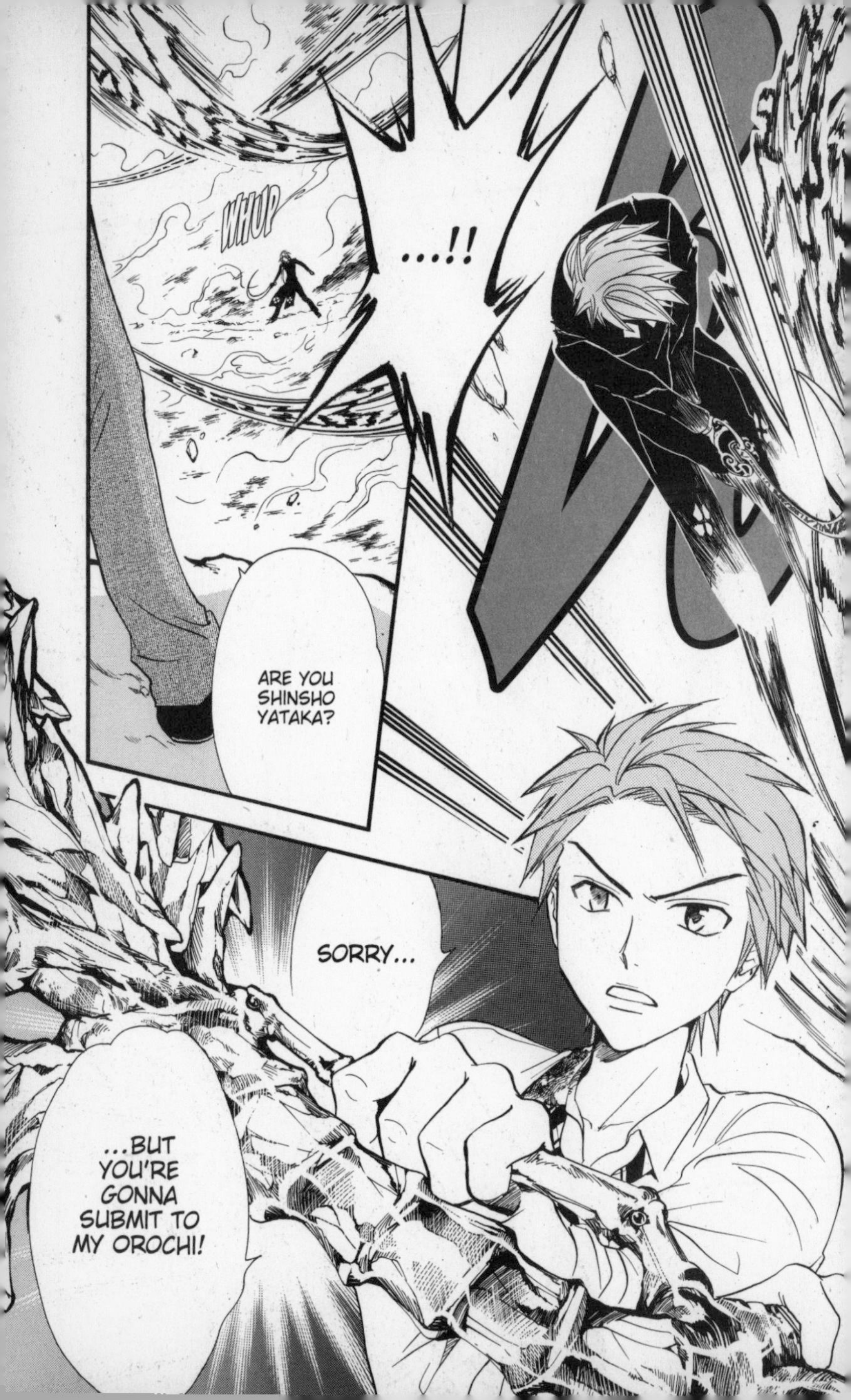
...!!
WHUP
ARE YOU SHINSHO YATAKA?
SORRY...
...BUT YOU'RE GONNA SUBMIT TO MY OROCHI!

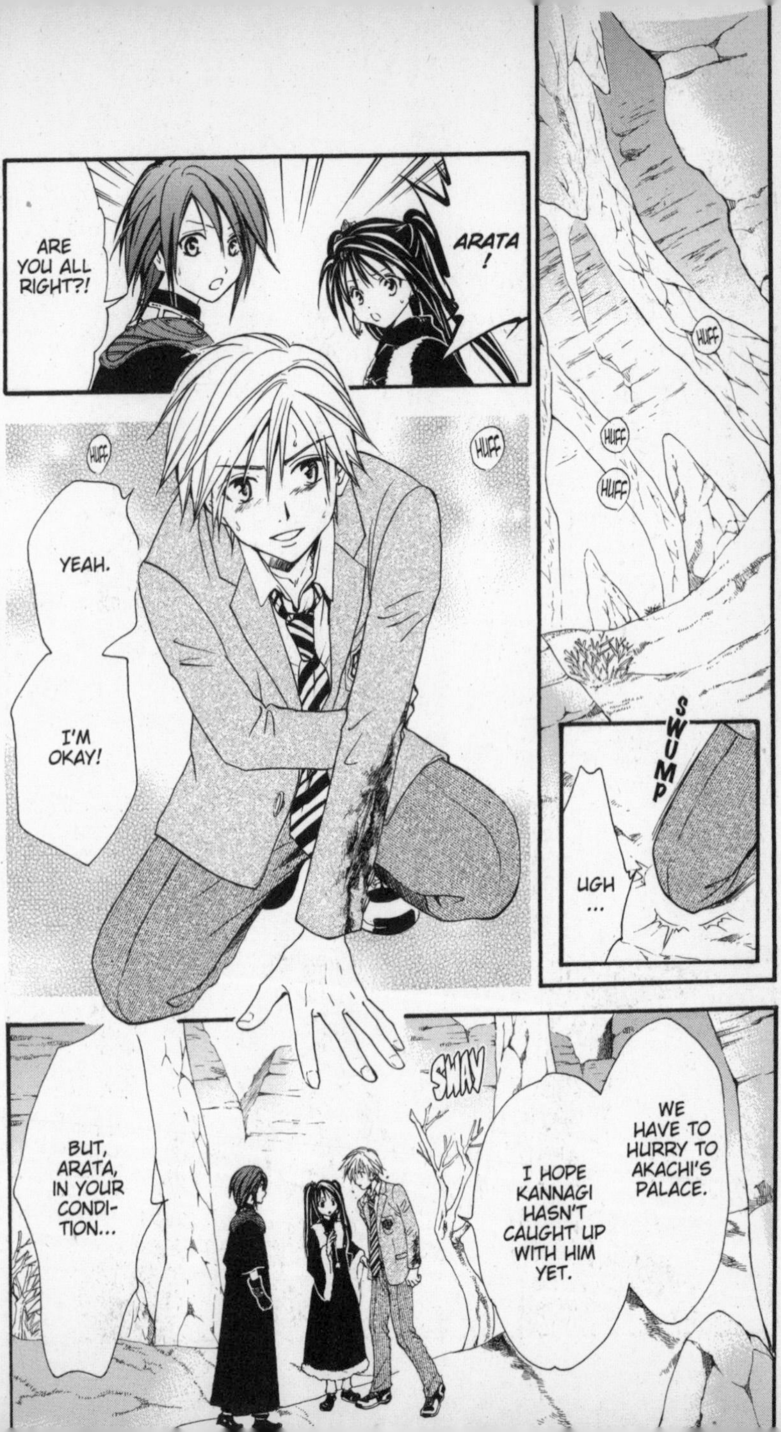
HUFF
HUFF
HUFF
SWUMP
UGH ...
ARATA !
ARE YOU ALL RIGHT?!
HUFF
HUFF
YEAH.
I'M OKAY!
SWAY
WE HAVE TO HURRY TO AKACHI'S PALACE.
I HOPE KANNAGI HASN'T CAUGHT UP WITH HIM YET.
BUT, ARATA, IN YOUR CONDI-TION...

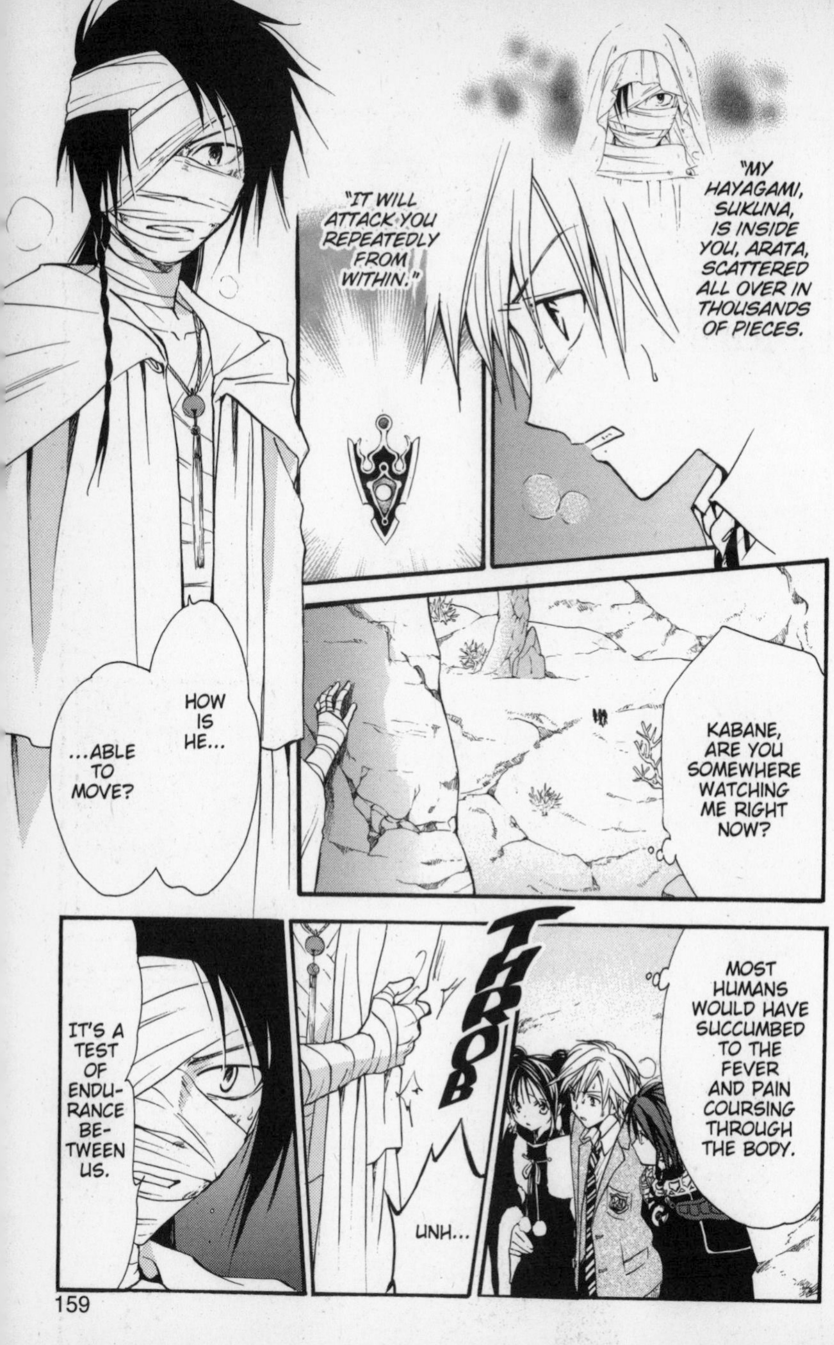
"MY HAYAGAMI, SUKUNA, IS INSIDE YOU, ARATA, SCATTERED ALL OVER IN THOUSANDS OF PIECES.
"IT WILL ATTACK YOU REPEATEDLY FROM WITHIN."
KABANE, ARE YOU SOMEWHERE WATCHING ME RIGHT NOW?
HOW IS HE...
...ABLE TO MOVE?
MOST HUMANS WOULD HAVE SUCCUMBED TO THE FEVER AND PAIN COURSING THROUGH THE BODY.
THROB
UNH...
IT'S A TEST OF ENDU-RANCE BE-TWEEN US.

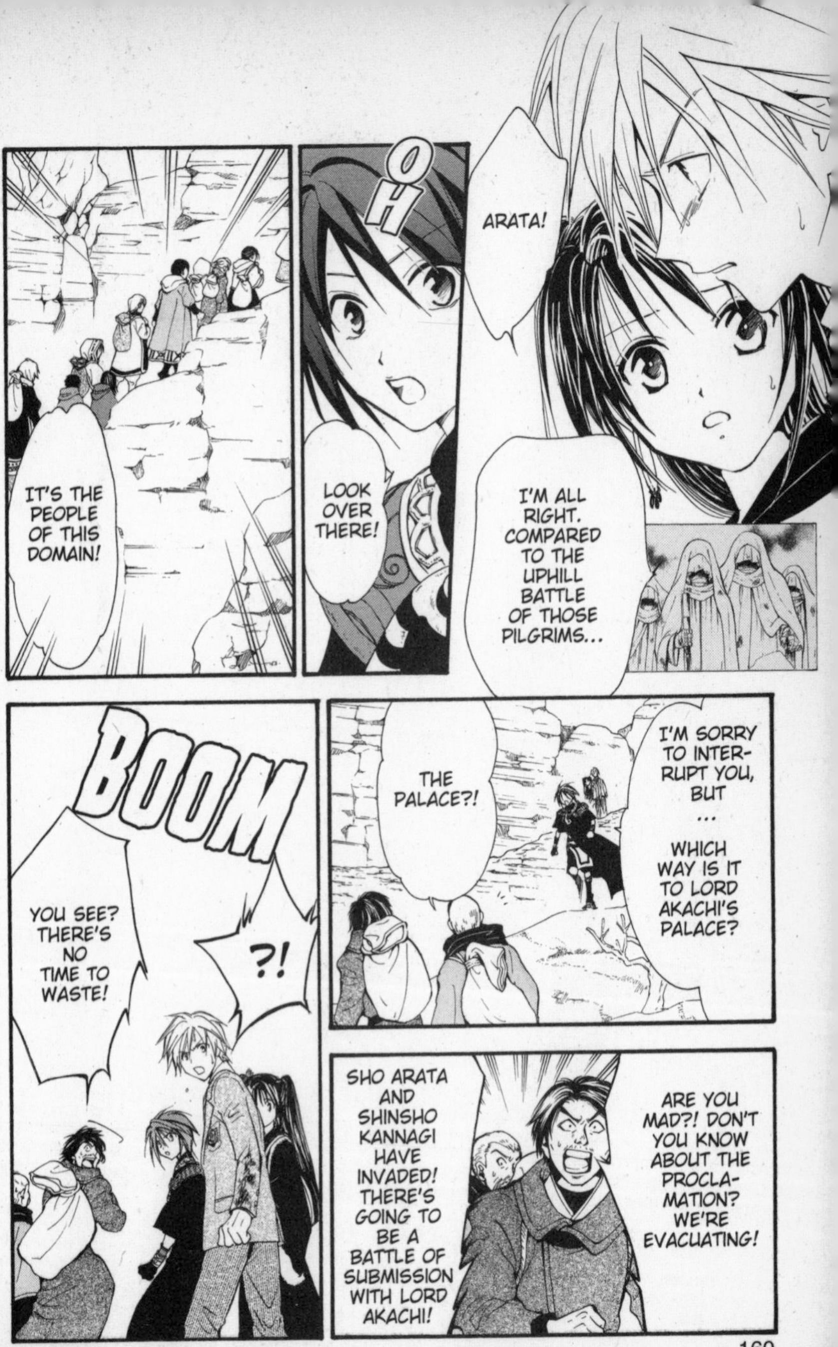
ARATA!
I'M ALL RIGHT. COMPARED TO THE UPHILL BATTLE OF THOSE PILGRIMS...
OH
LOOK OVER THERE!
IT'S THE PEOPLE OF THIS DOMAIN!
I'M SORRY TO INTERRUPT YOU, BUT ... WHICH WAY IS IT TO LORD AKACHI'S PALACE?
THE PALACE?!
ARE YOU MAD?! DON'T YOU KNOW ABOUT THE PROCLAMATION? WE'RE EVACUATING!
SHO ARATA AND SHINSHO KANNAGI HAVE INVADED! THERE'S GOING TO BE A BATTLE OF SUBMISSION WITH LORD AKACHI!
BOOM
?!
YOU SEE? THERE'S NO TIME TO WASTE!

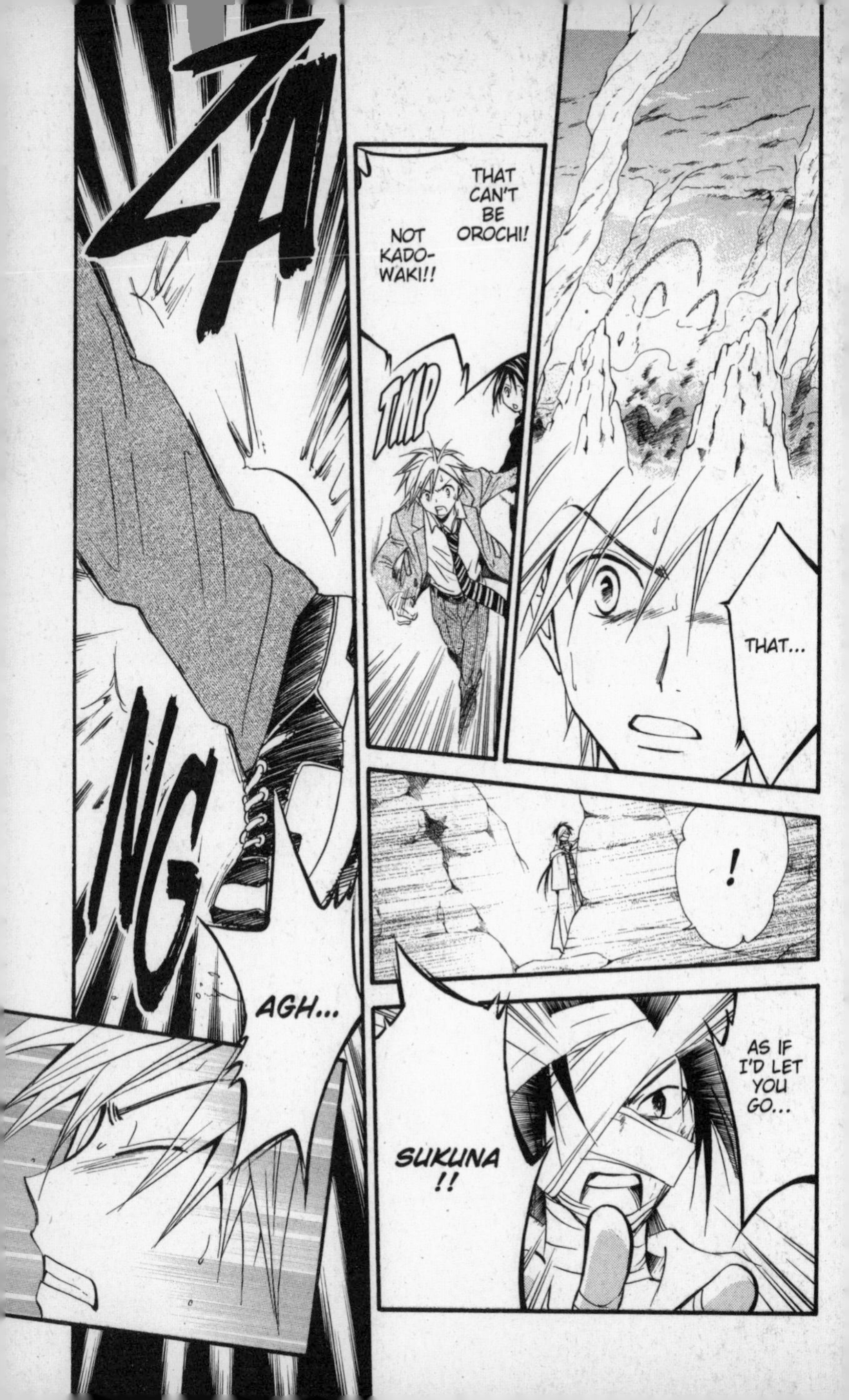
THAT...
THAT CAN'T BE OROCHI!
NOT KADOWAKI!!
TMP
!
AS IF I'D LET YOU GO...
SUKUNA!!
ZA
NG
AGH...

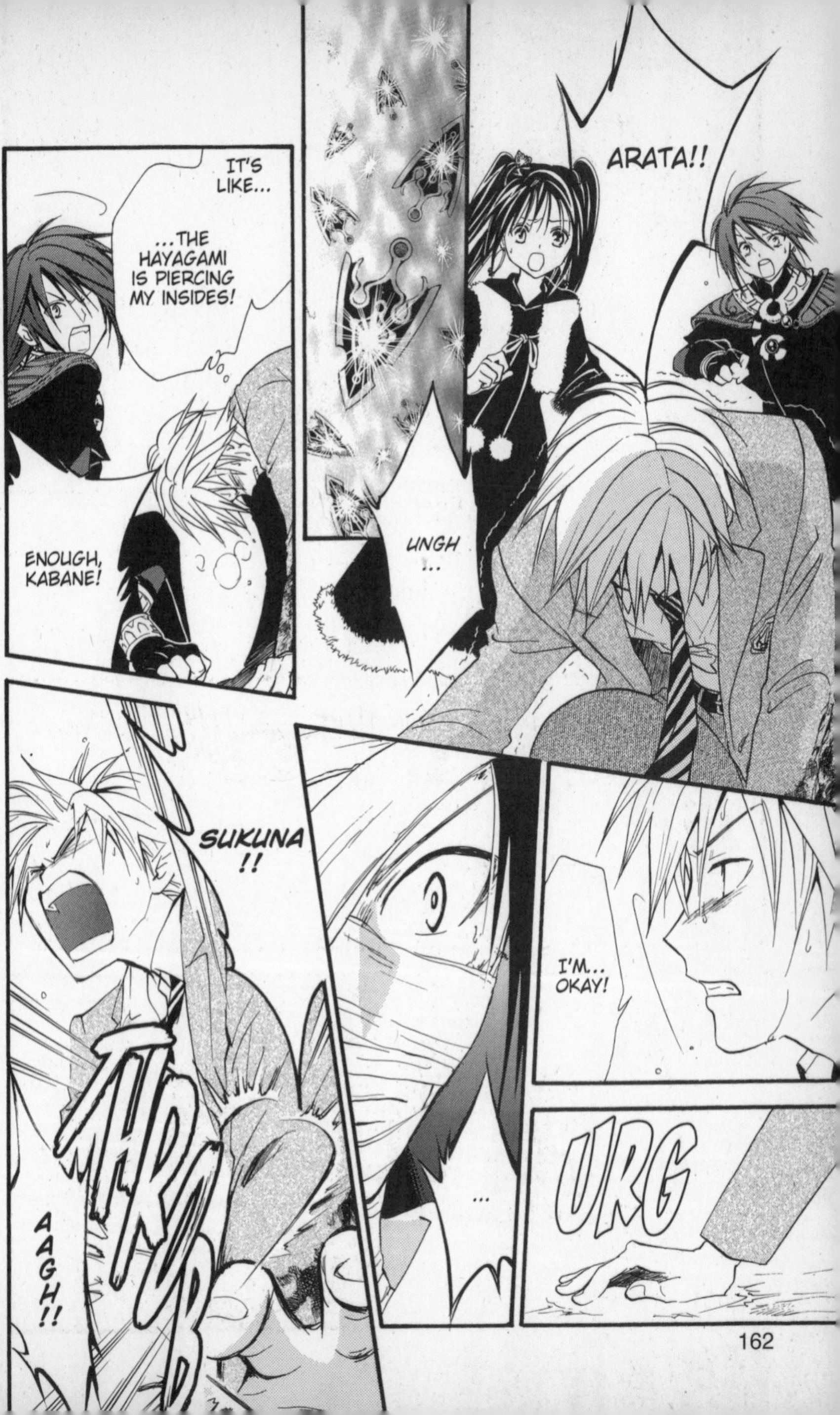
ARATA!!
UNGH...
IT'S LIKE...
...THE HAYAGAMI IS PIERCING MY INSIDES!
ENOUGH, KABANE!
I'M... OKAY!
URG
...
SUKUNA!!
AAGH!!

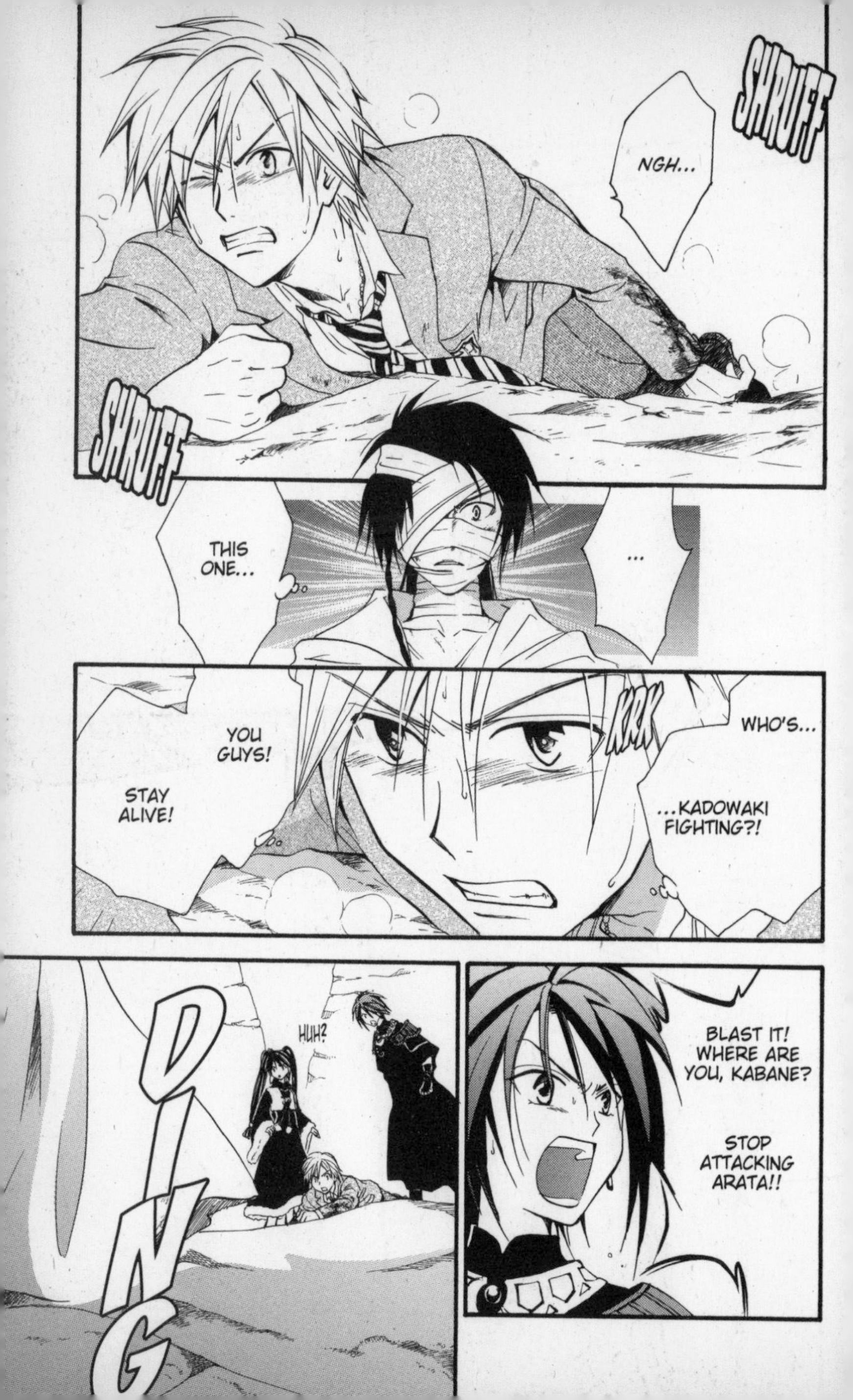
SHRUFF
NGH...
SHRUFF
...
THIS ONE...
WHO'S...
...KADOWAKI FIGHTING?!
KRK
YOU GUYS!
STAY ALIVE!
BLAST IT! WHERE ARE YOU, KABANE?
STOP ATTACKING ARATA!!
HUH?
DING

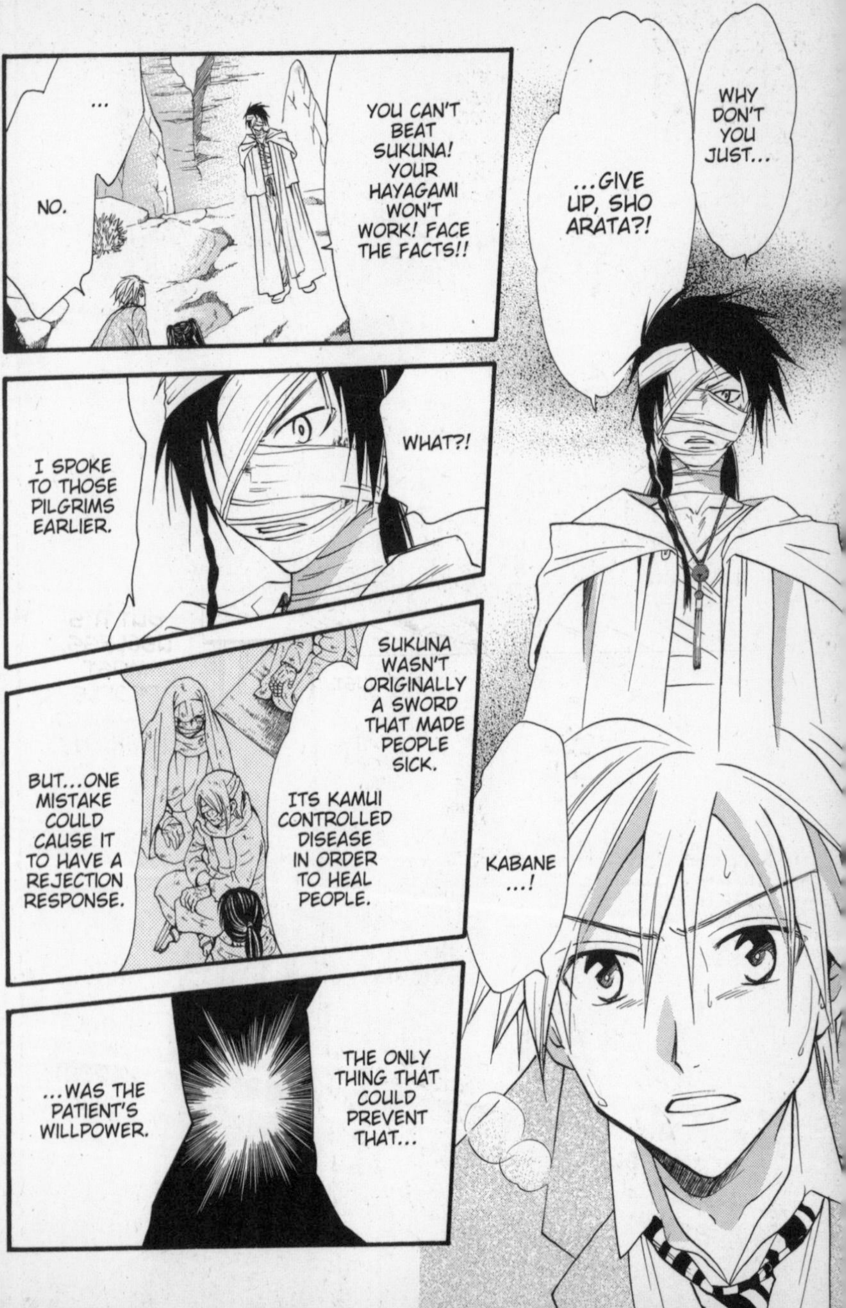
WHY DON'T YOU JUST...
...GIVE UP, SHO ARATA?!
KABANE ...!
YOU CAN'T BEAT SUKUNA! YOUR HAYAGAMI WON'T WORK! FACE THE FACTS!!
...
NO.
WHAT?!
I SPOKE TO THOSE PILGRIMS EARLIER.
SUKUNA WASN'T ORIGINALLY A SWORD THAT MADE PEOPLE SICK.
ITS KAMUI CONTROLLED DISEASE IN ORDER TO HEAL PEOPLE.
BUT...ONE MISTAKE COULD CAUSE IT TO HAVE A REJECTION RESPONSE.
THE ONLY THING THAT COULD PREVENT THAT...
...WAS THE PATIENT'S WILLPOWER.

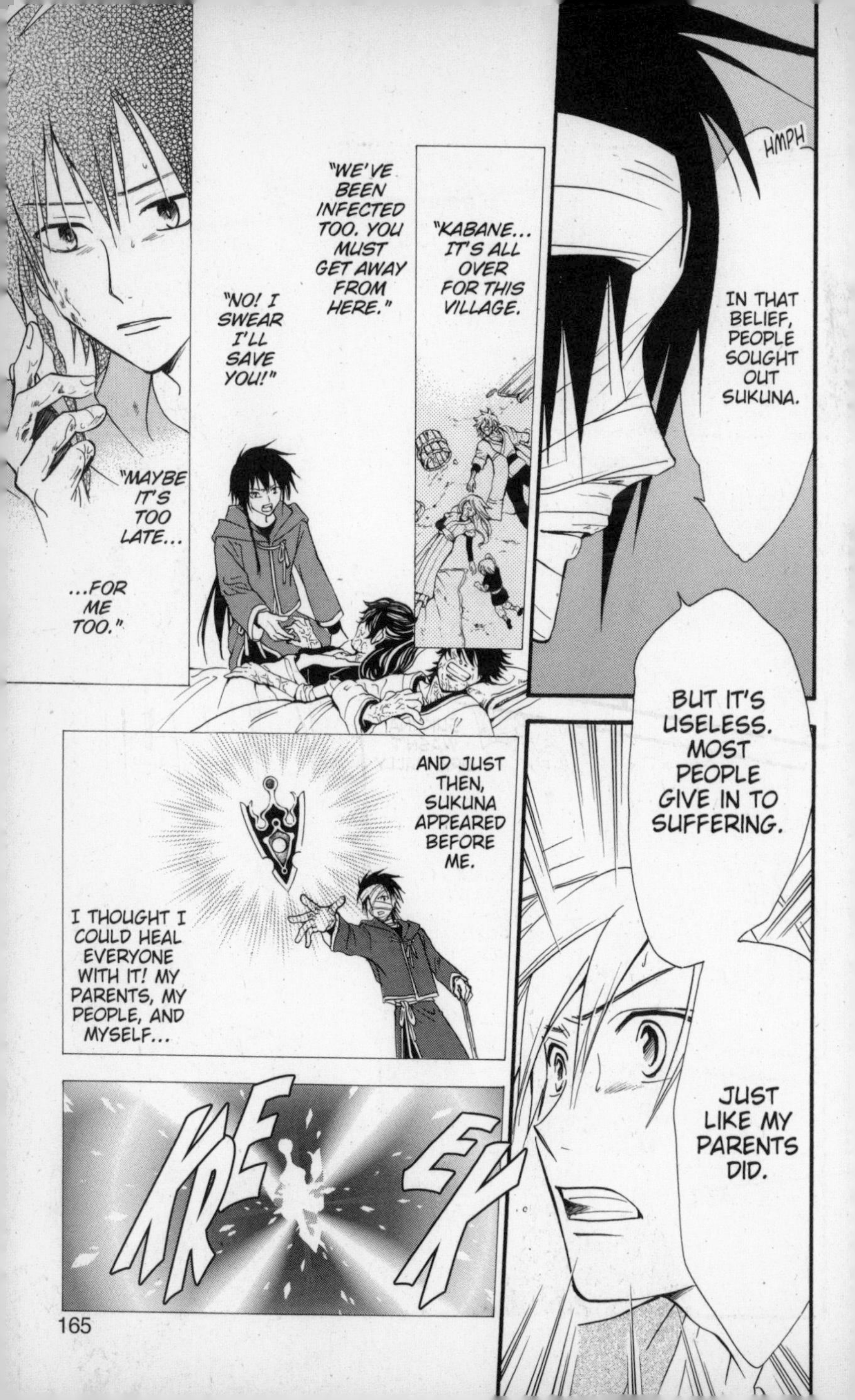
HMPH
IN THAT BELIEF, PEOPLE SOUGHT OUT SUKUNA.
"KABANE... IT'S ALL OVER FOR THIS VILLAGE.
"WE'VE BEEN INFECTED TOO. YOU MUST GET AWAY FROM HERE."
"NO! I SWEAR I'LL SAVE YOU!"
"MAYBE IT'S TOO LATE...
...FOR ME TOO."
AND JUST THEN, SUKUNA APPEARED BEFORE ME.
I THOUGHT I COULD HEAL EVERYONE WITH IT! MY PARENTS, MY PEOPLE, AND MYSELF...
KREEK
BUT IT'S USELESS. MOST PEOPLE GIVE IN TO SUFFERING.
JUST LIKE MY PARENTS DID.

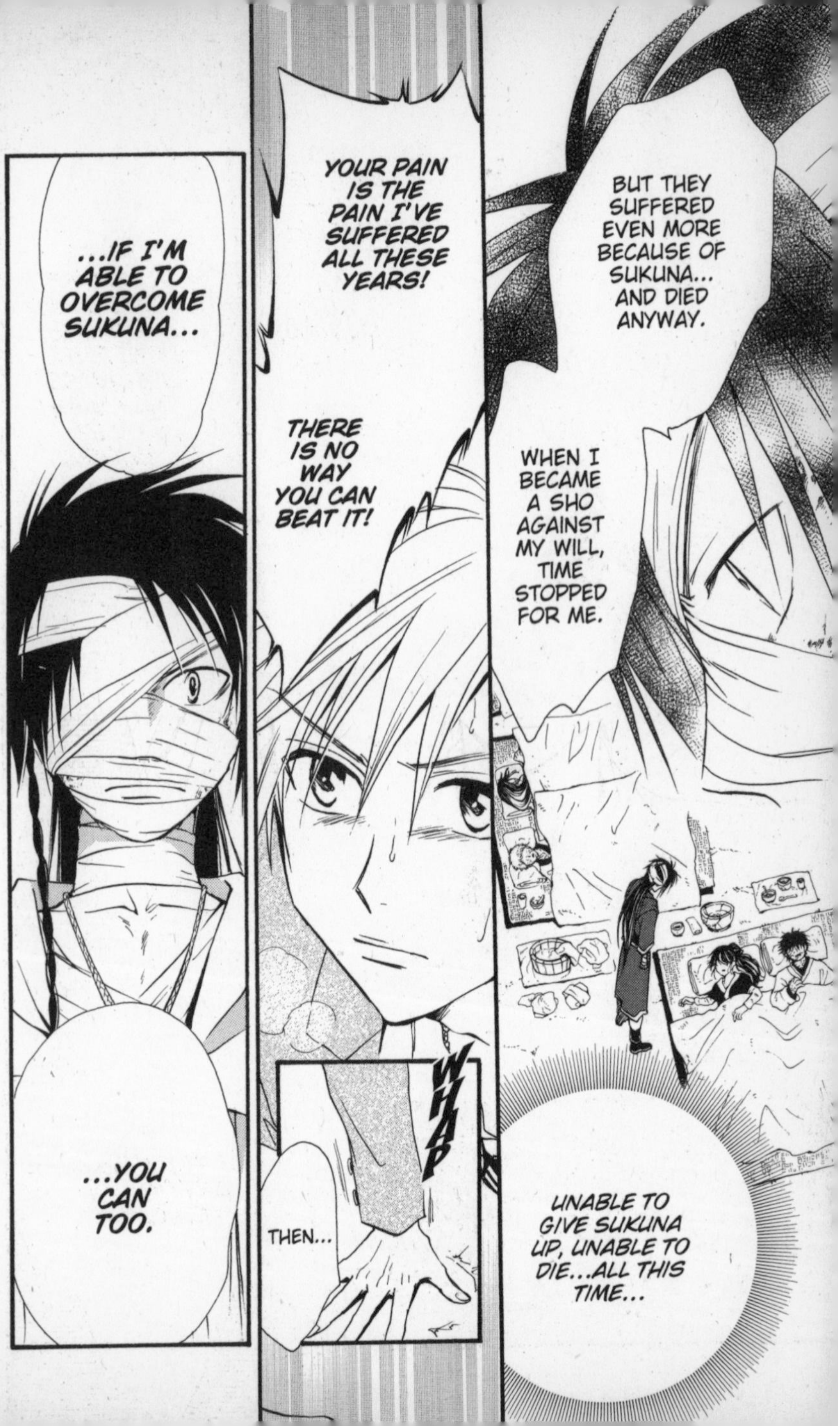

BUT THEY SUFFERED EVEN MORE BECAUSE OF SUKUNA... AND DIED ANYWAY.
WHEN I BECAME A SHO AGAINST MY WILL, TIME STOPPED FOR ME.
UNABLE TO GIVE SUKUNA UP, UNABLE TO DIE...ALL THIS TIME...
YOUR PAIN IS THE PAIN I'VE SUFFERED ALL THESE YEARS!
THERE IS NO WAY YOU CAN BEAT IT!
WHAP
THEN...
...IF I'M ABLE TO OVERCOME SUKUNA...
...YOU CAN TOO.

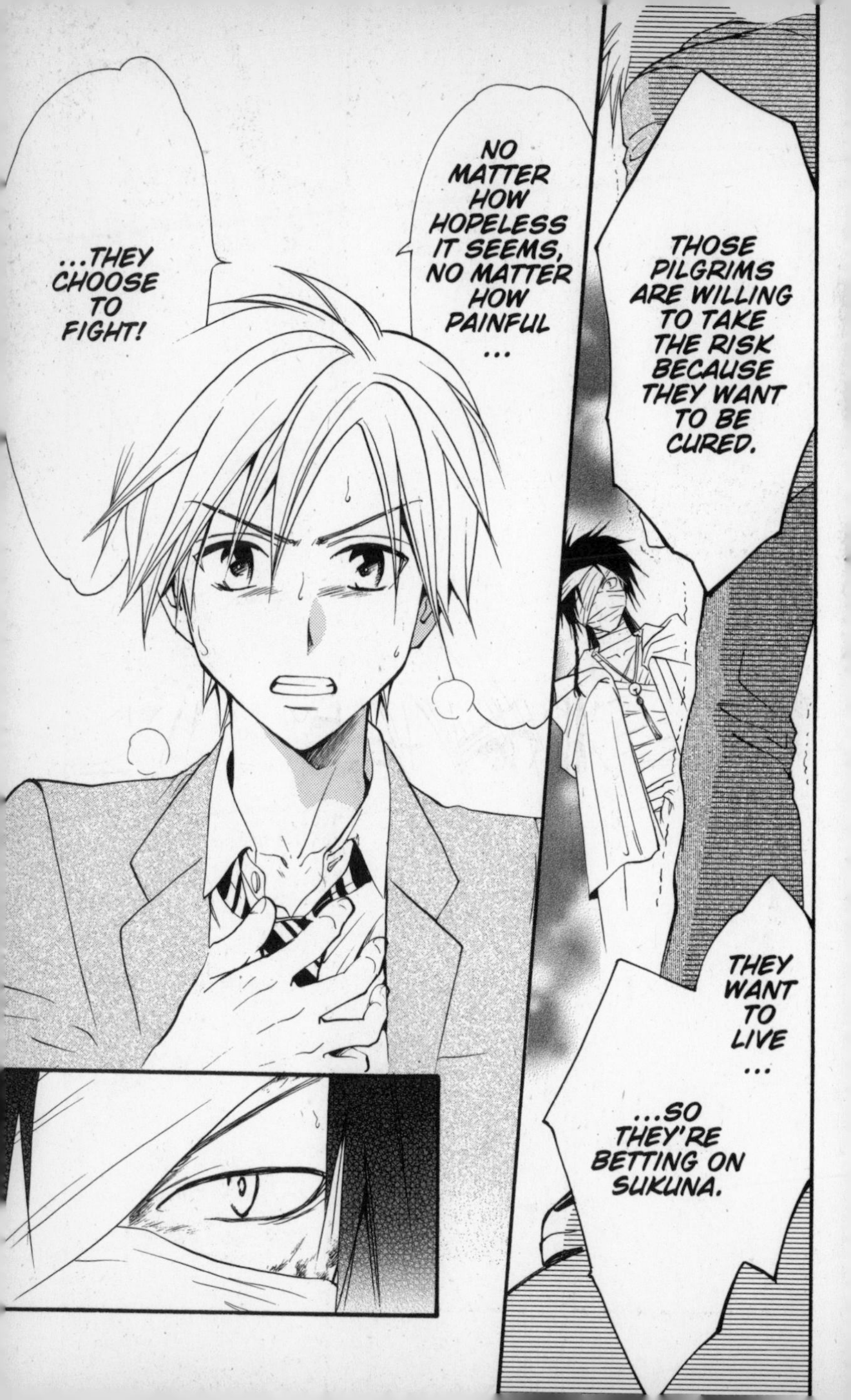
THOSE PILGRIMS ARE WILLING TO TAKE THE RISK BECAUSE THEY WANT TO BE CURED.
THEY WANT TO LIVE...
...SO THEY'RE BETTING ON SUKUNA.
NO MATTER HOW HOPELESS IT SEEMS, NO MATTER HOW PAINFUL...
...THEY CHOOSE TO FIGHT!

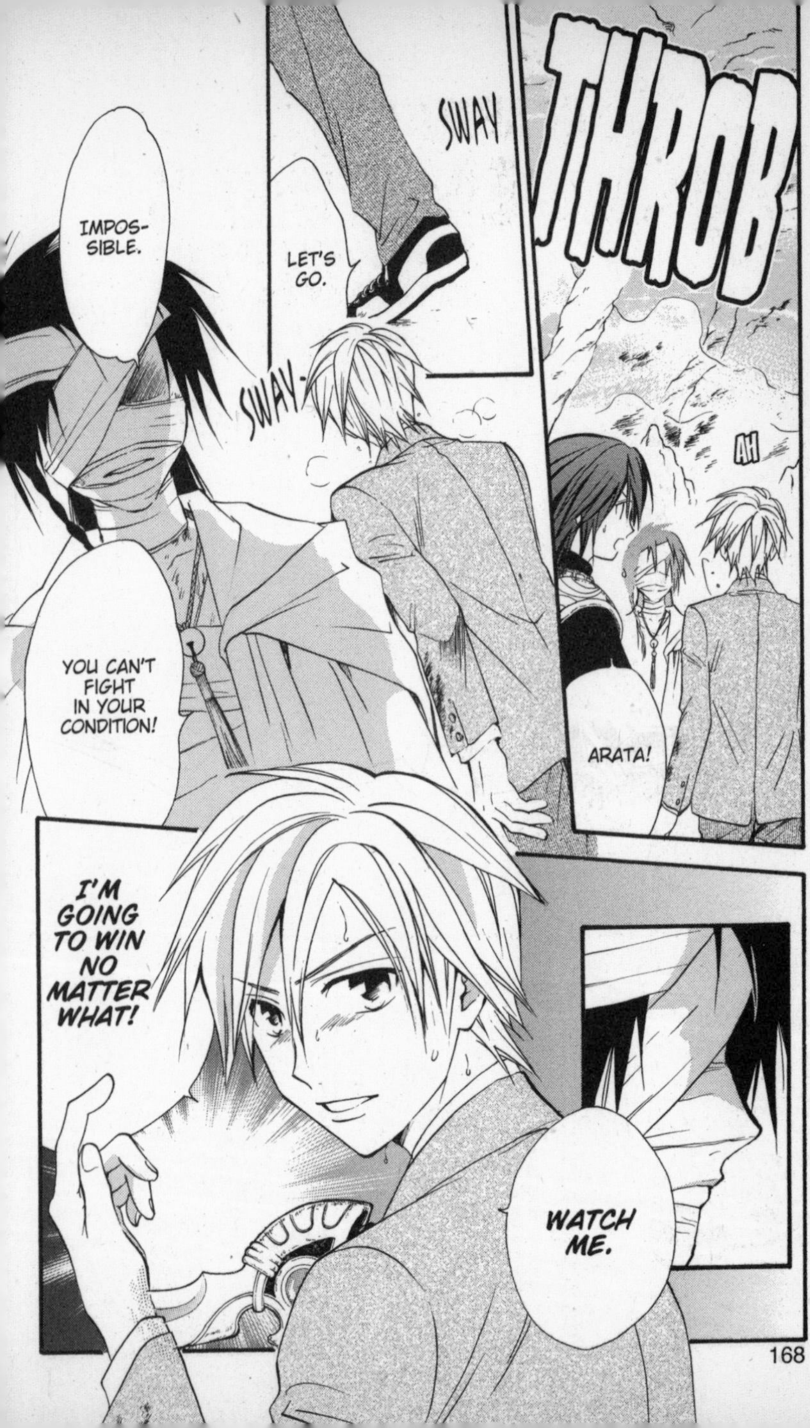
THROB
AH
ARATA!
SWAY
LET'S GO.
IMPOS-SIBLE.
SWAY-
YOU CAN'T FIGHT IN YOUR CONDITION!
I'M GOING TO WIN NO MATTER WHAT!
WATCH ME.

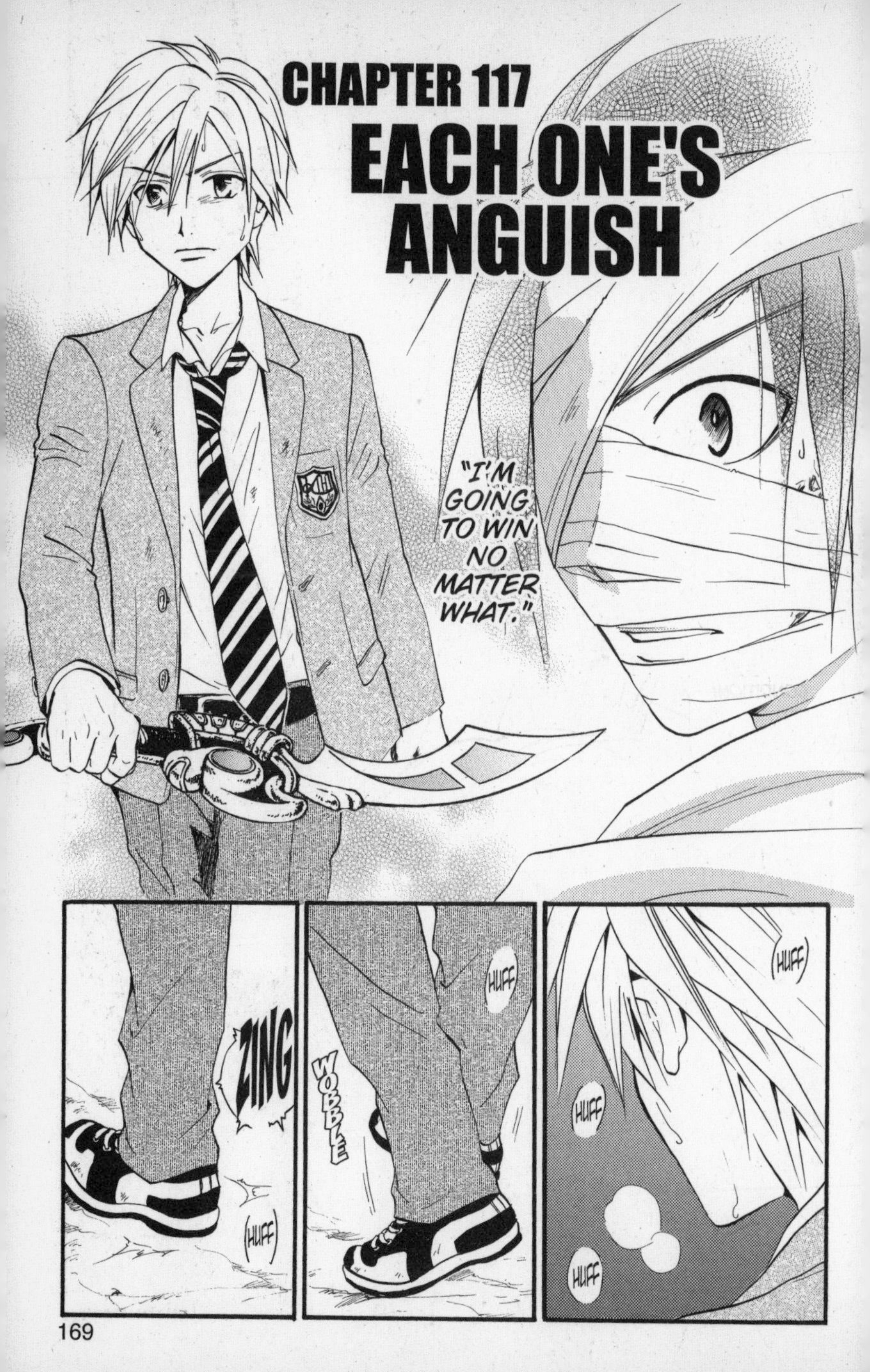
CHAPTER 117
EACH ONE'S ANGUISH
"I'M GOING TO WIN NO MATTER WHAT."
(HUFF)
HUFF
HUFF
HUFF
WOBBLE
ZING
(HUFF)

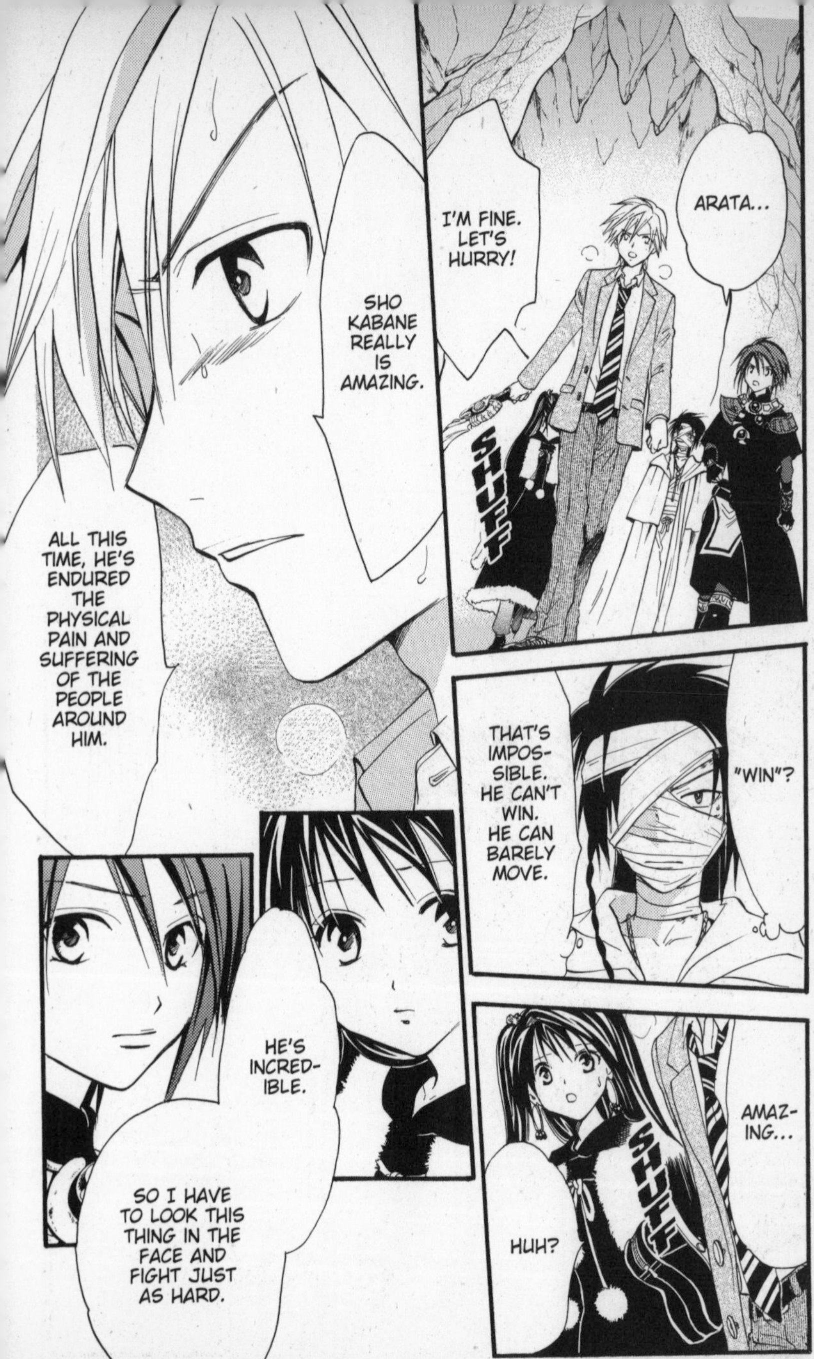
ARATA...
I'M FINE. LET'S HURRY!
SHUFF
SHO KABANE REALLY IS AMAZING.
ALL THIS TIME, HE'S ENDURED THE PHYSICAL PAIN AND SUFFERING OF THE PEOPLE AROUND HIM.
"WIN"?
THAT'S IMPOSSIBLE. HE CAN'T WIN. HE CAN BARELY MOVE.
AMAZING...
HUH?
SHUFF
HE'S INCREDIBLE.
SO I HAVE TO LOOK THIS THING IN THE FACE AND FIGHT JUST AS HARD.

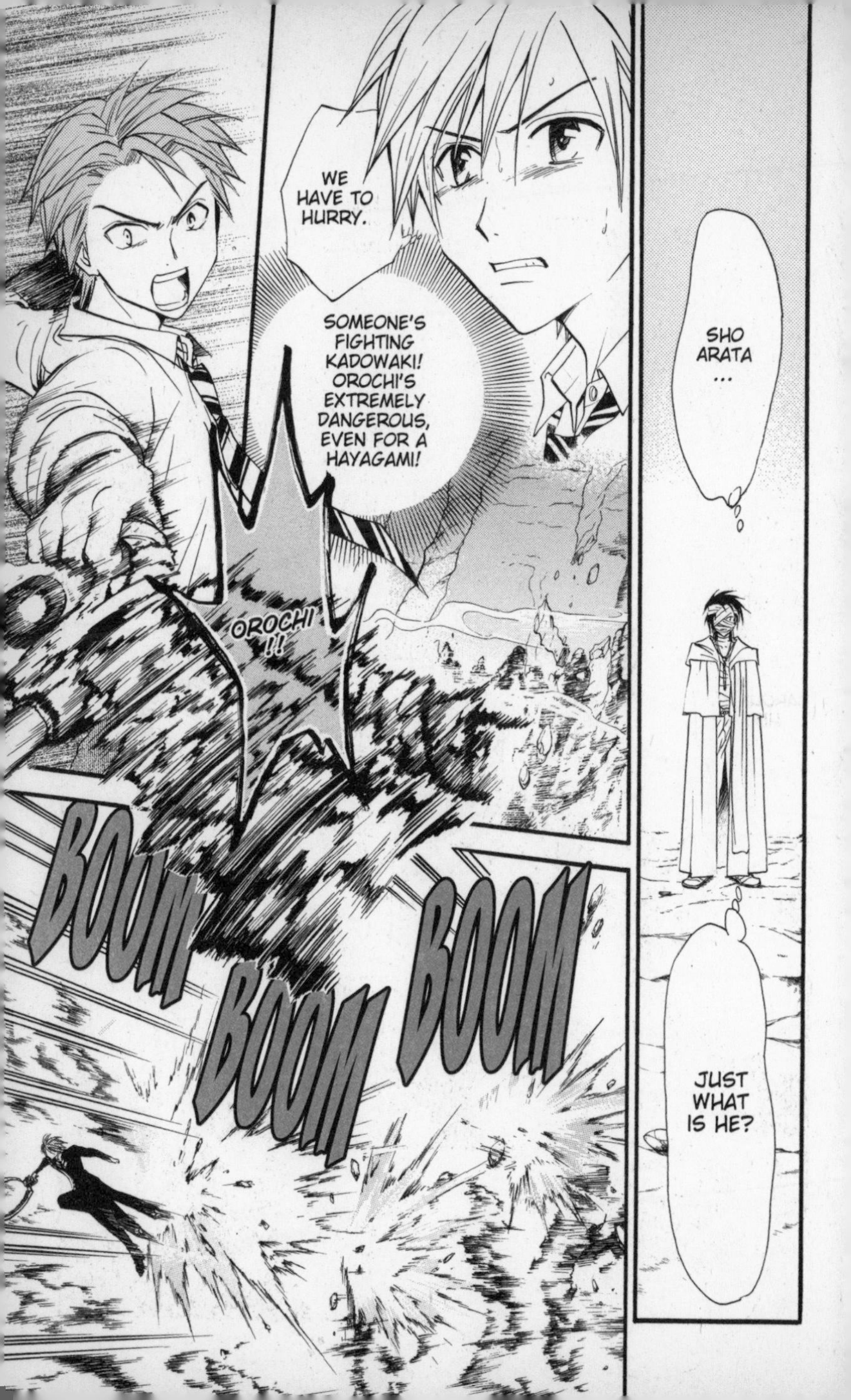
SHO ARATA ...
JUST WHAT IS HE?
WE HAVE TO HURRY.
SOMEONE'S FIGHTING KADOWAKI! OROCHI'S EXTREMELY DANGEROUS, EVEN FOR A HAYAGAMI!
OROCHI!!
BOOM
BOOM
BOOM

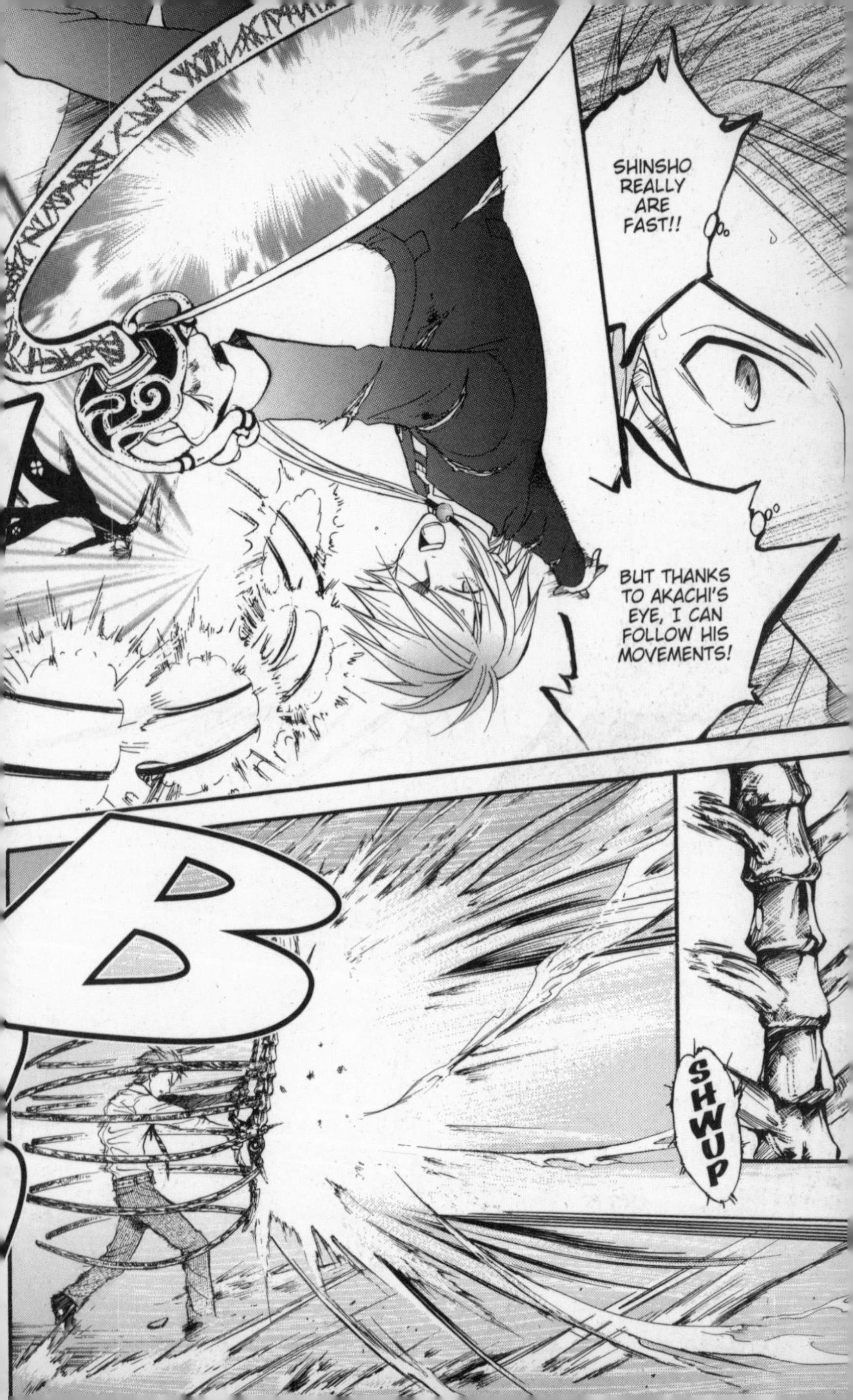
SHINSHO REALLY ARE FAST!!
BUT THANKS TO AKACHI'S EYE, I CAN FOLLOW HIS MOVEMENTS!
SHWUP
B

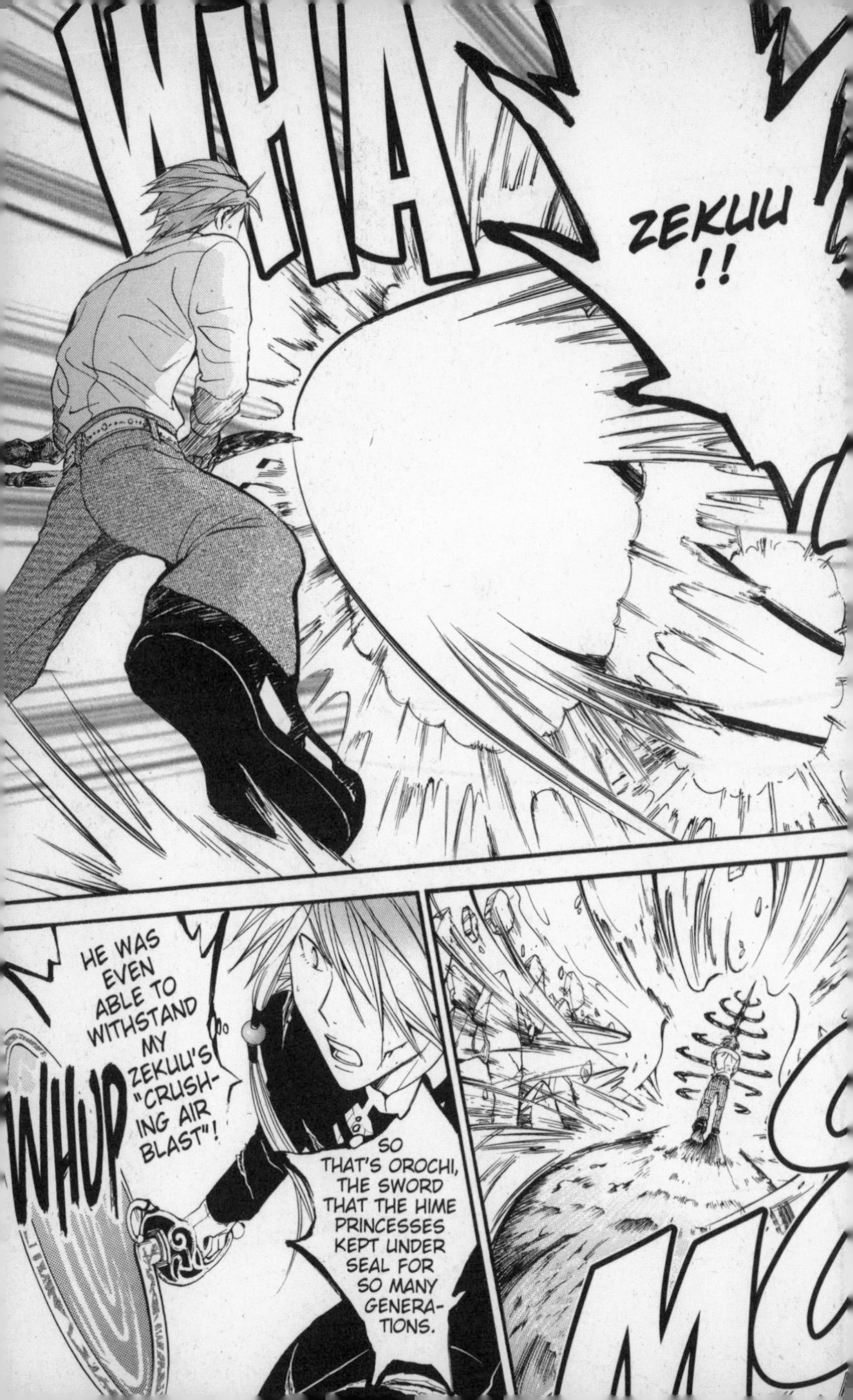
WHA
ZEKUU !!
HE WAS EVEN ABLE TO WITHSTAND MY ZEKUU'S "CRUSHING AIR BLAST"!
WHUP
SO THAT'S OROCHI, THE SWORD THAT THE HIME PRINCESSES KEPT UNDER SEAL FOR SO MANY GENERATIONS.

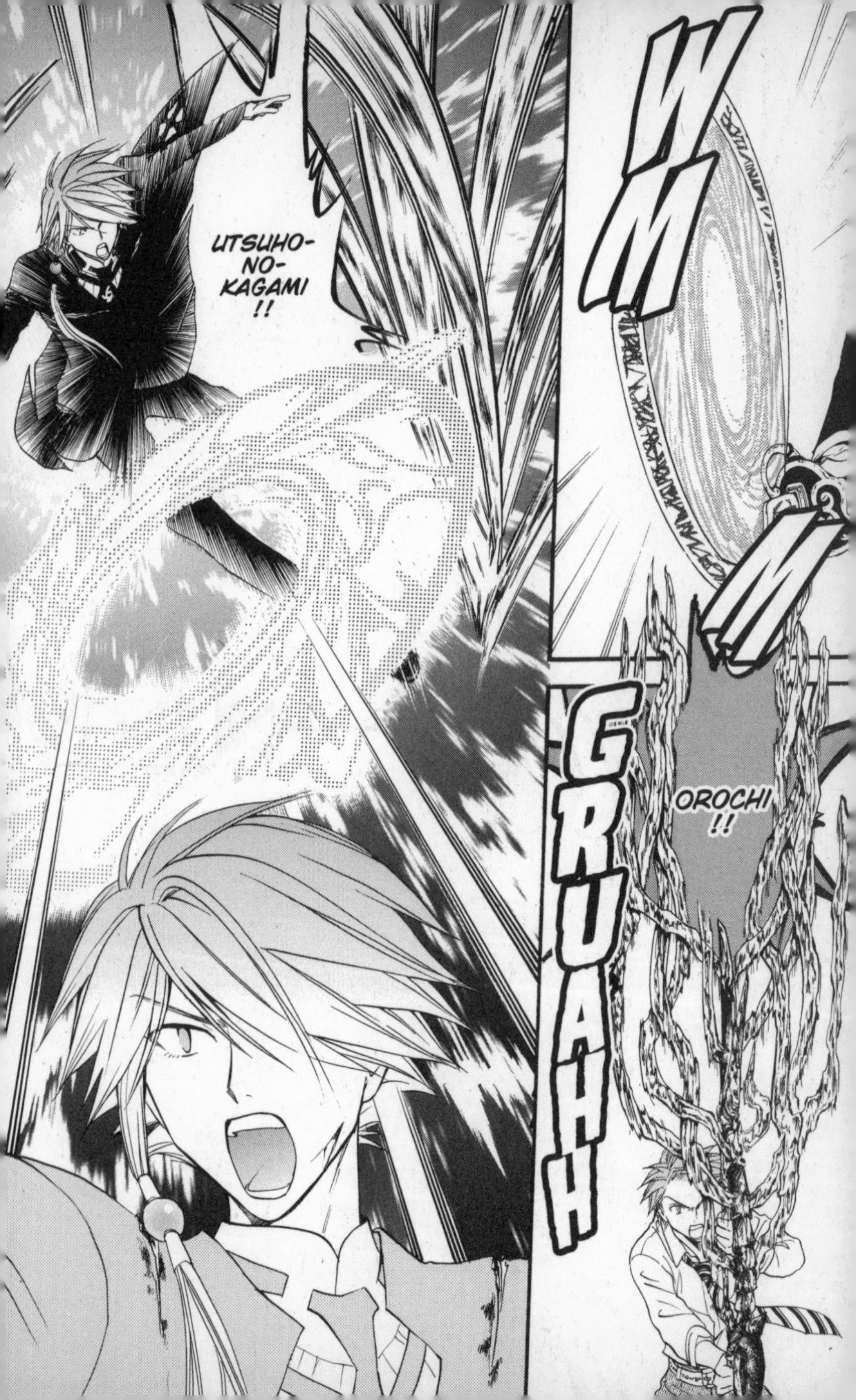
WMM
GRUAHH
OROCHI!!
UTSUHO-NO-KAGAMI!!

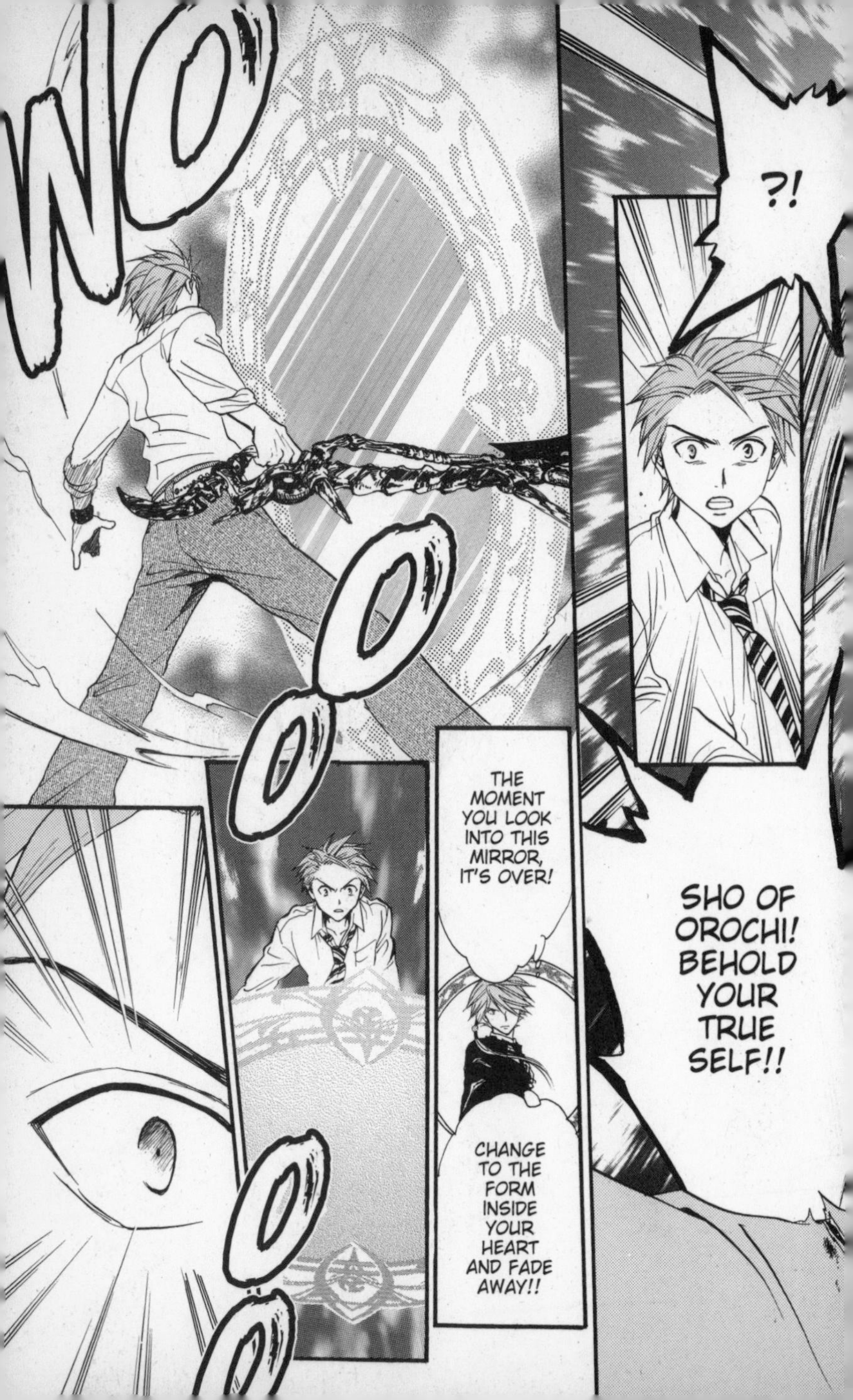
?!
WOOOOOOO
SHO OF OROCHI! BEHOLD YOUR TRUE SELF!!
THE MOMENT YOU LOOK INTO THIS MIRROR, IT'S OVER!
CHANGE TO THE FORM INSIDE YOUR HEART AND FADE AWAY!!

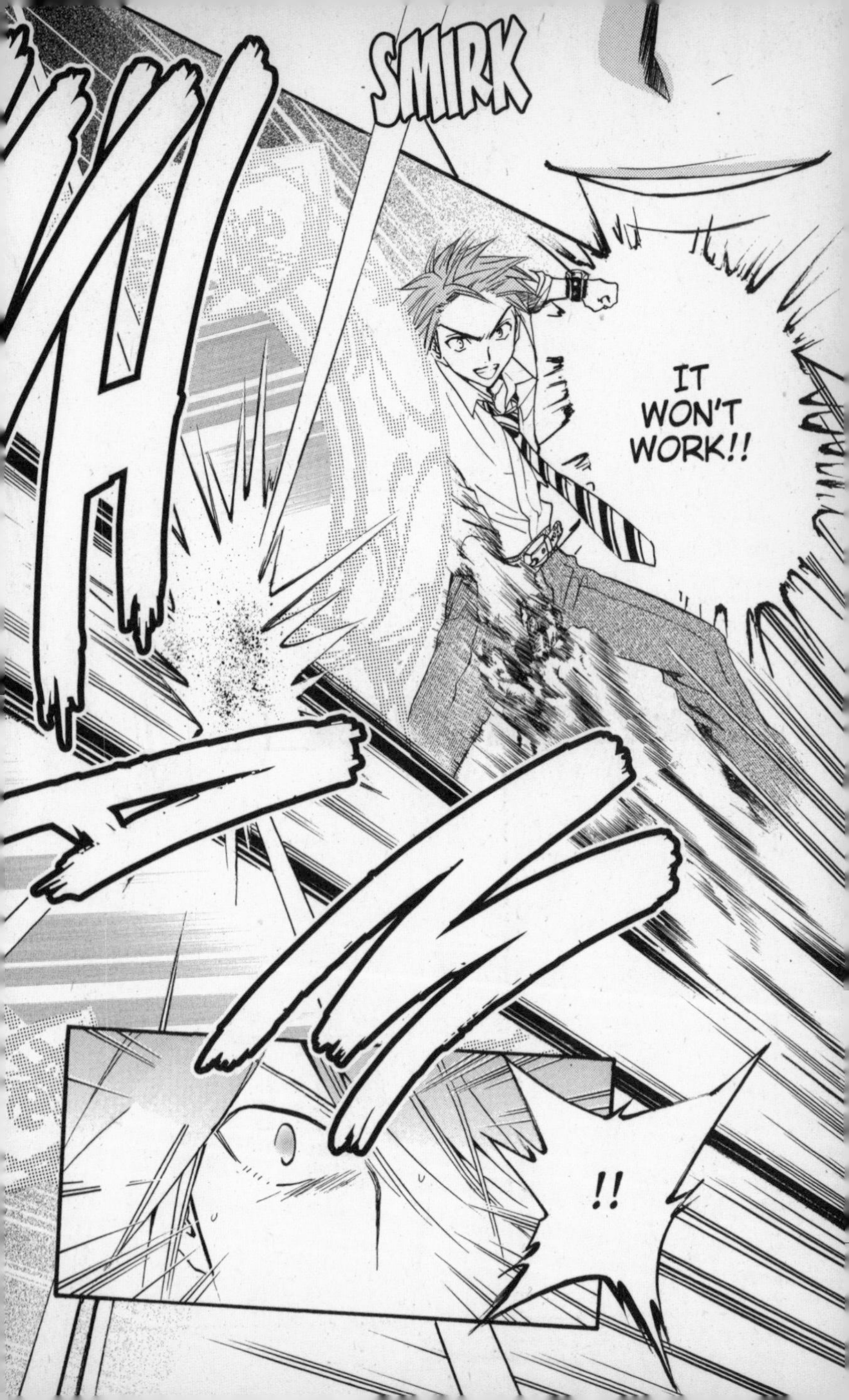
SMIRK
IT WON'T WORK!!
!!

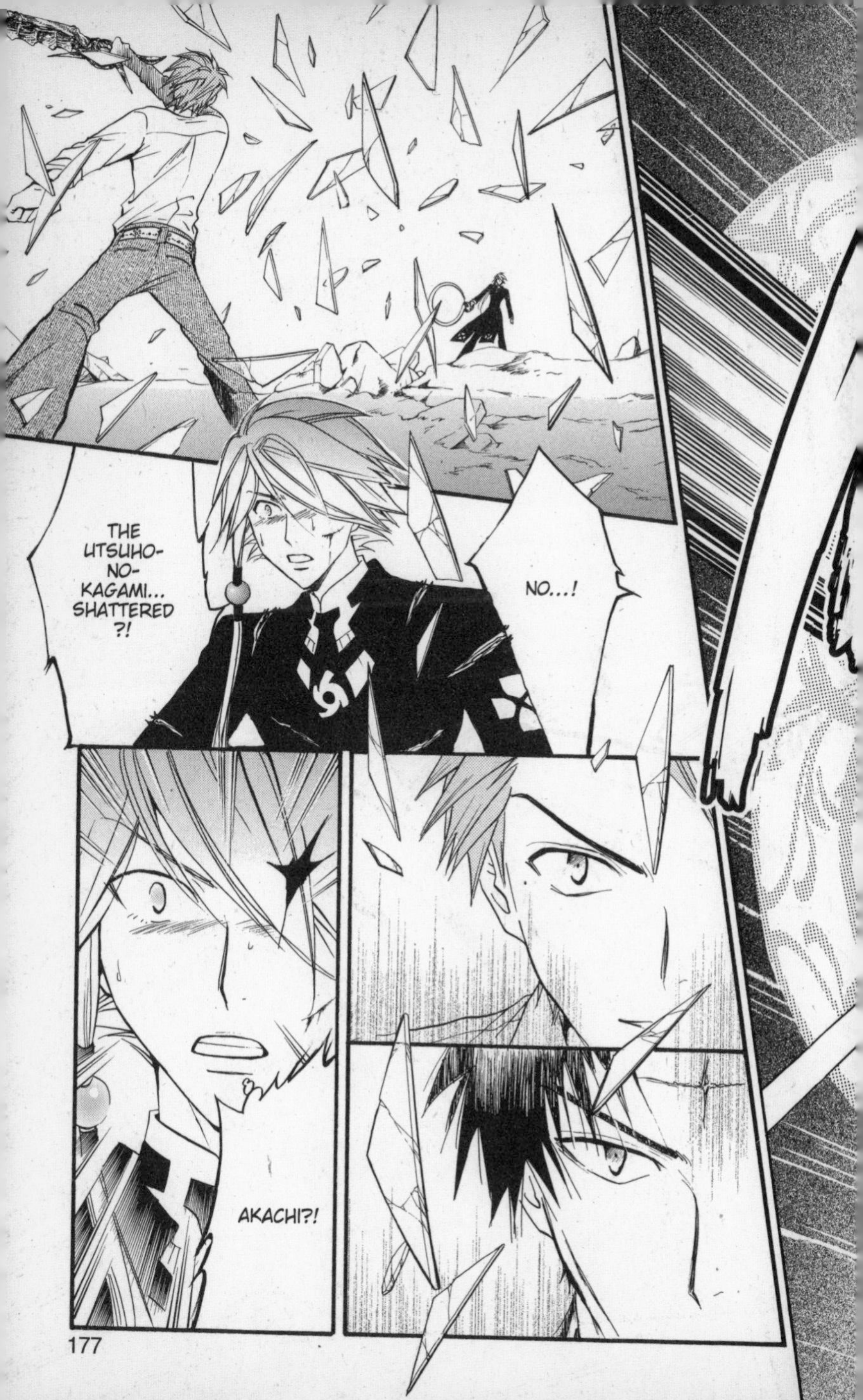
THE UTSUHO-NO-KAGAMI... SHATTERED?!
NO...!
AKACHI?!

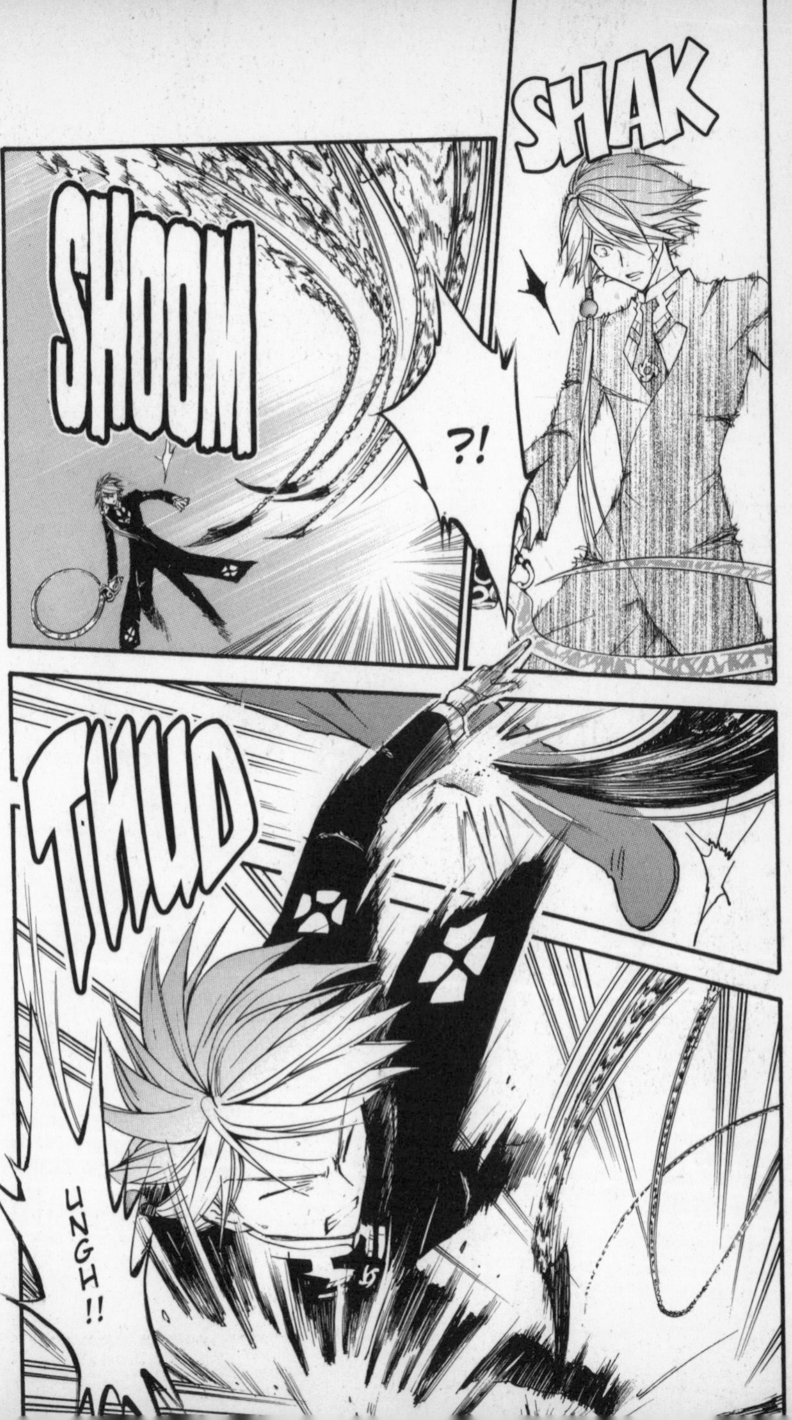
SHAK
?!
SHOOM
THUD
UNGH!!

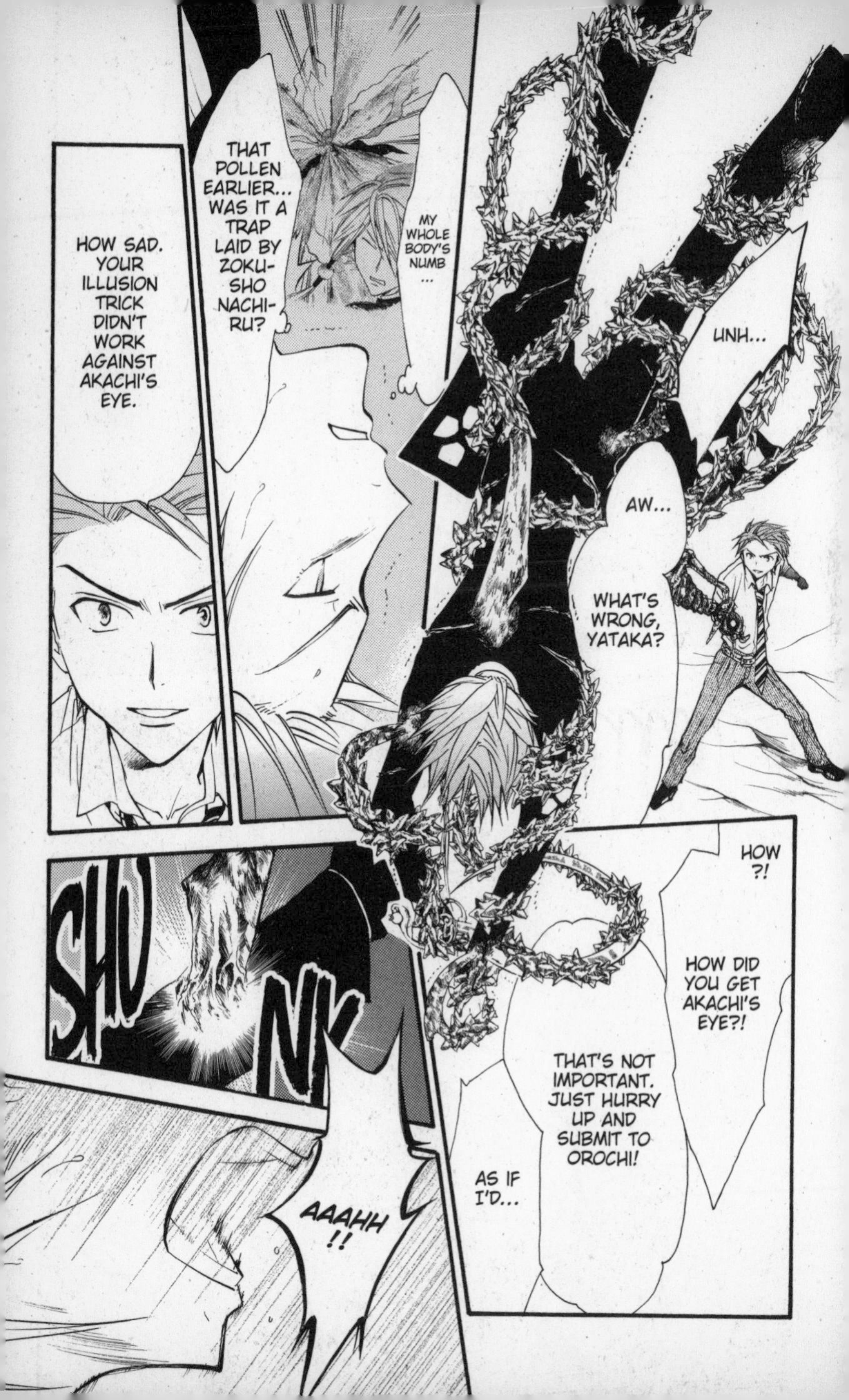
UNH...
AW...
WHAT'S WRONG, YATAKA?
MY WHOLE BODY'S NUMB...
THAT POLLEN EARLIER... WAS IT A TRAP LAID BY ZOKU-SHO NACHI-RU?
HOW SAD. YOUR ILLUSION TRICK DIDN'T WORK AGAINST AKACHI'S EYE.
HOW?!
HOW DID YOU GET AKACHI'S EYE?!
THAT'S NOT IMPORTANT. JUST HURRY UP AND SUBMIT TO OROCHI!
AS IF I'D...
SHUNK
AAAHH!!

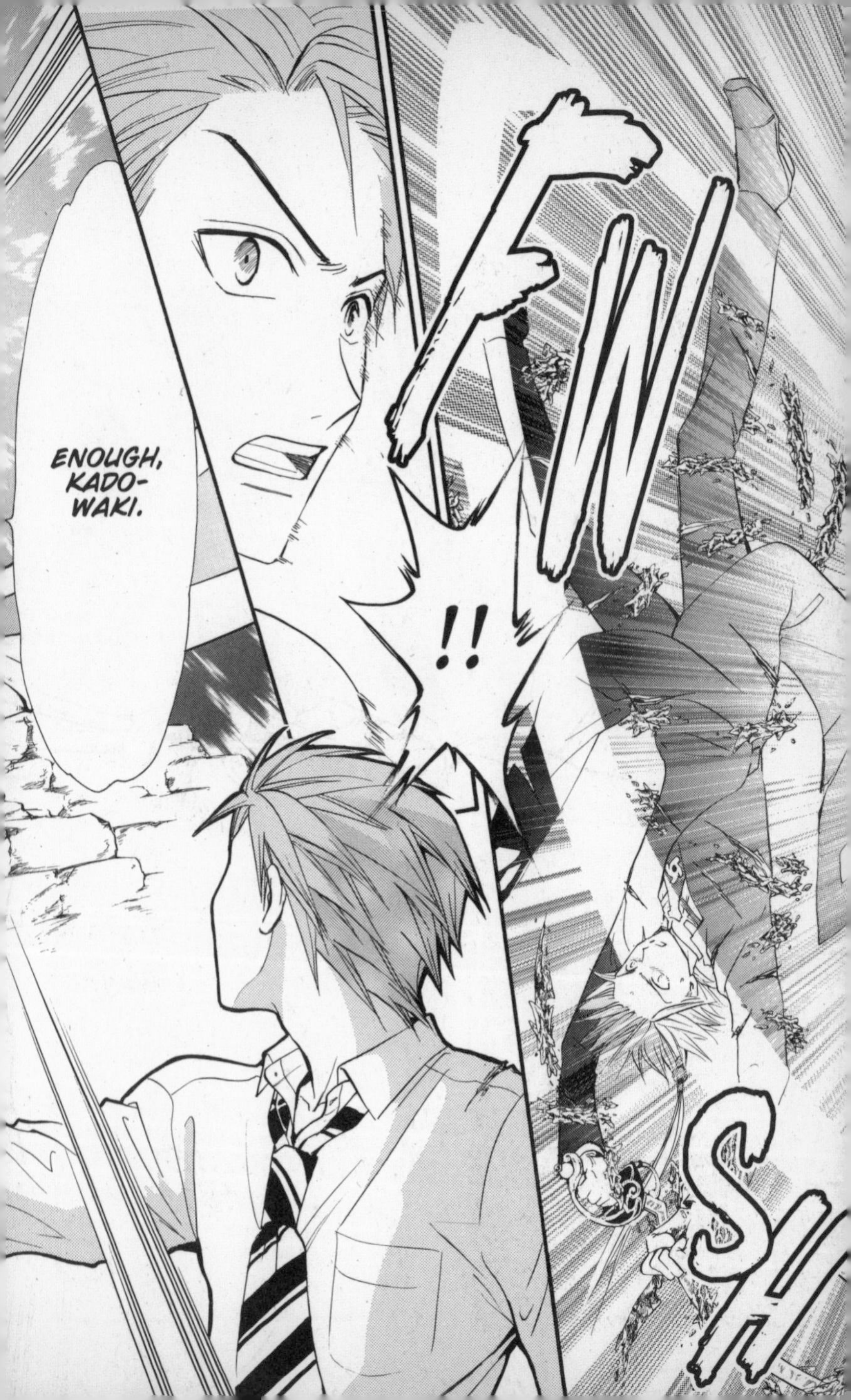

ENOUGH, KADO-WAKI.
!!
SH

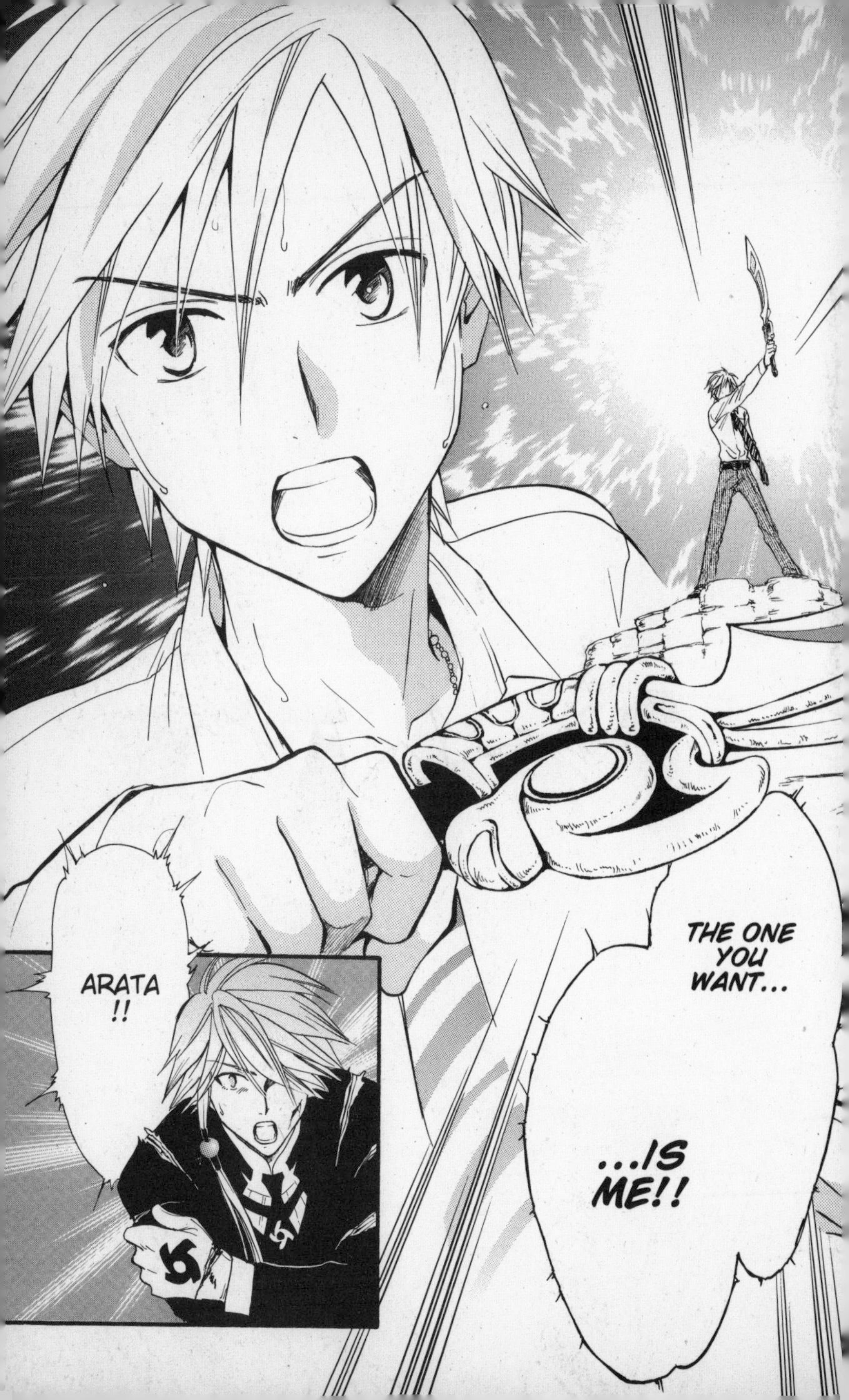
THE ONE YOU WANT...
...IS ME!!
ARATA !!

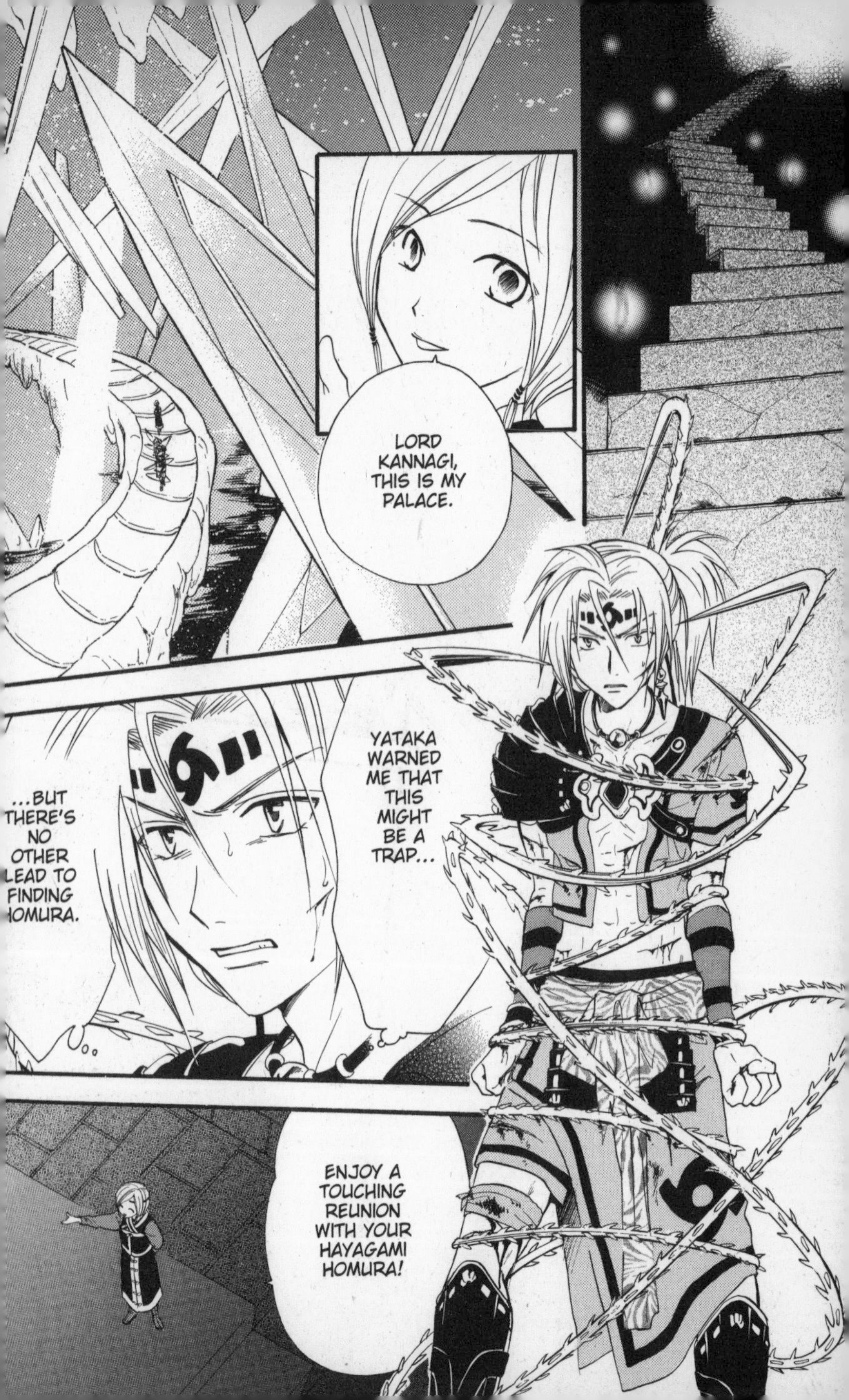
LORD KANNAGI, THIS IS MY PALACE.
YATAKA WARNED ME THAT THIS MIGHT BE A TRAP...
...BUT THERE'S NO OTHER LEAD TO FINDING HOMURA.
ENJOY A TOUCHING REUNION WITH YOUR HAYAGAMI HOMURA!

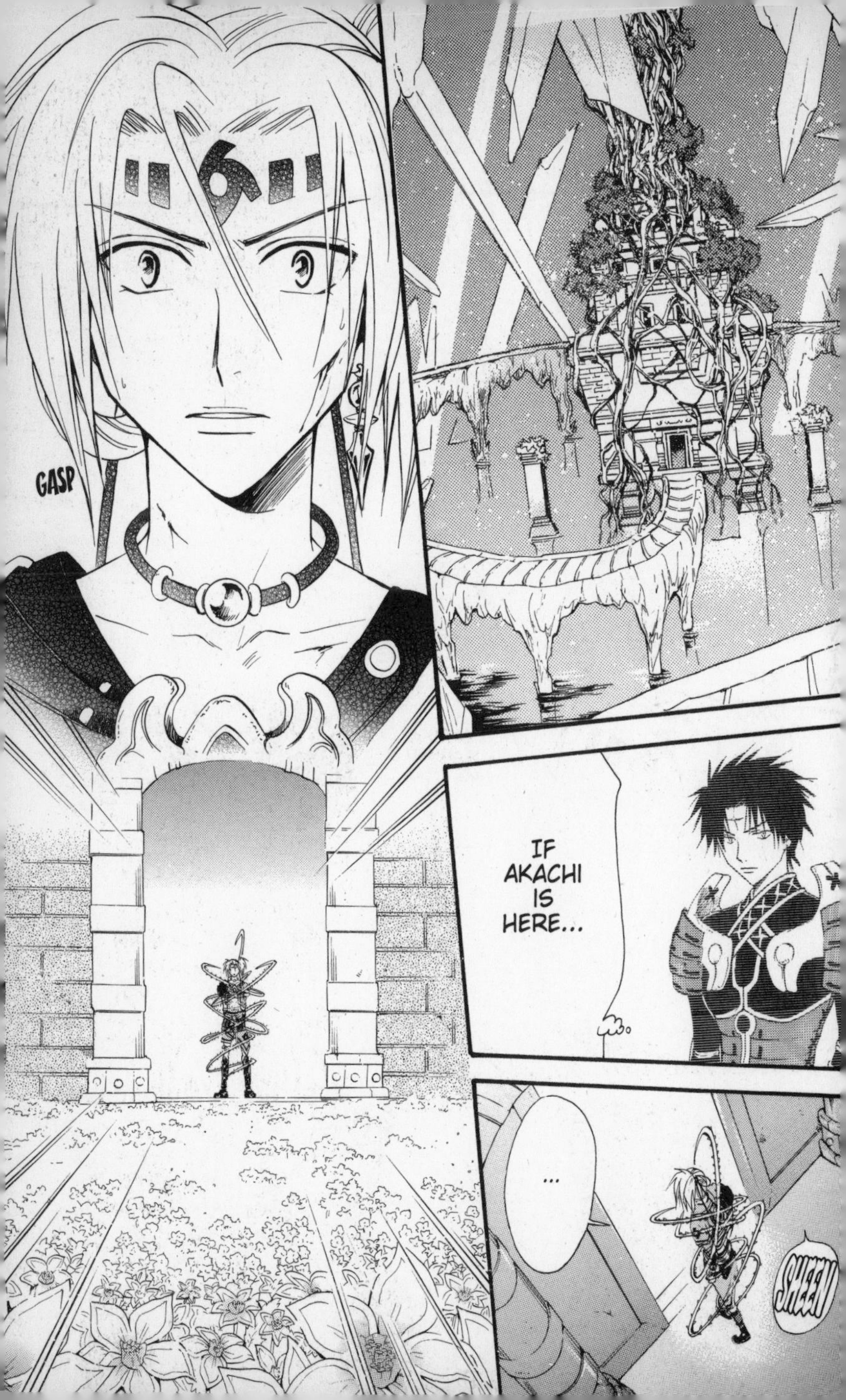
IF AKACHI IS HERE...
...
SHEEN
GASP

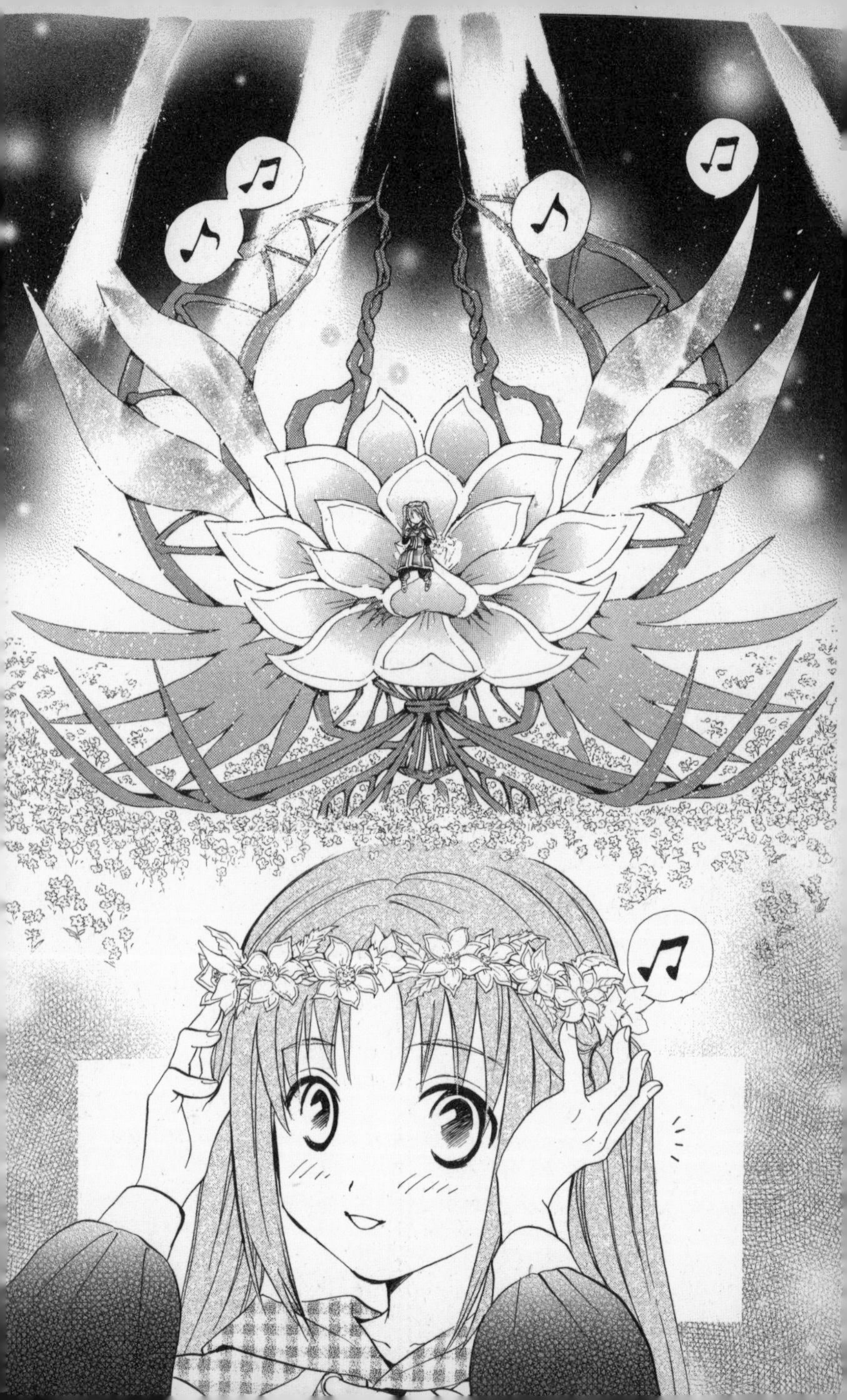

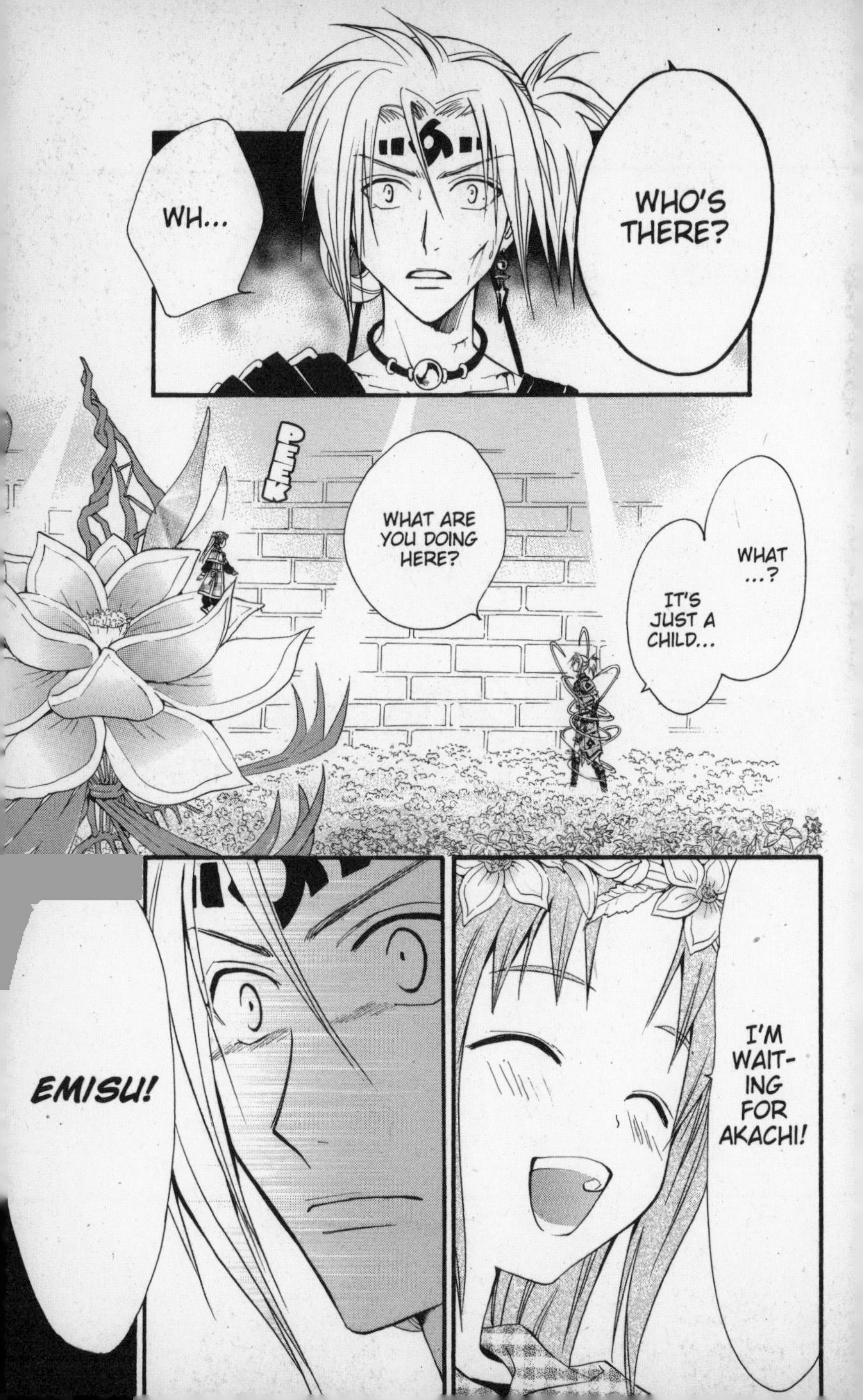
WHO'S THERE?
WH...
WHAT ...?
IT'S JUST A CHILD...
PEEK
WHAT ARE YOU DOING HERE?
I'M WAIT-ING FOR AKACHI!
EMISU!

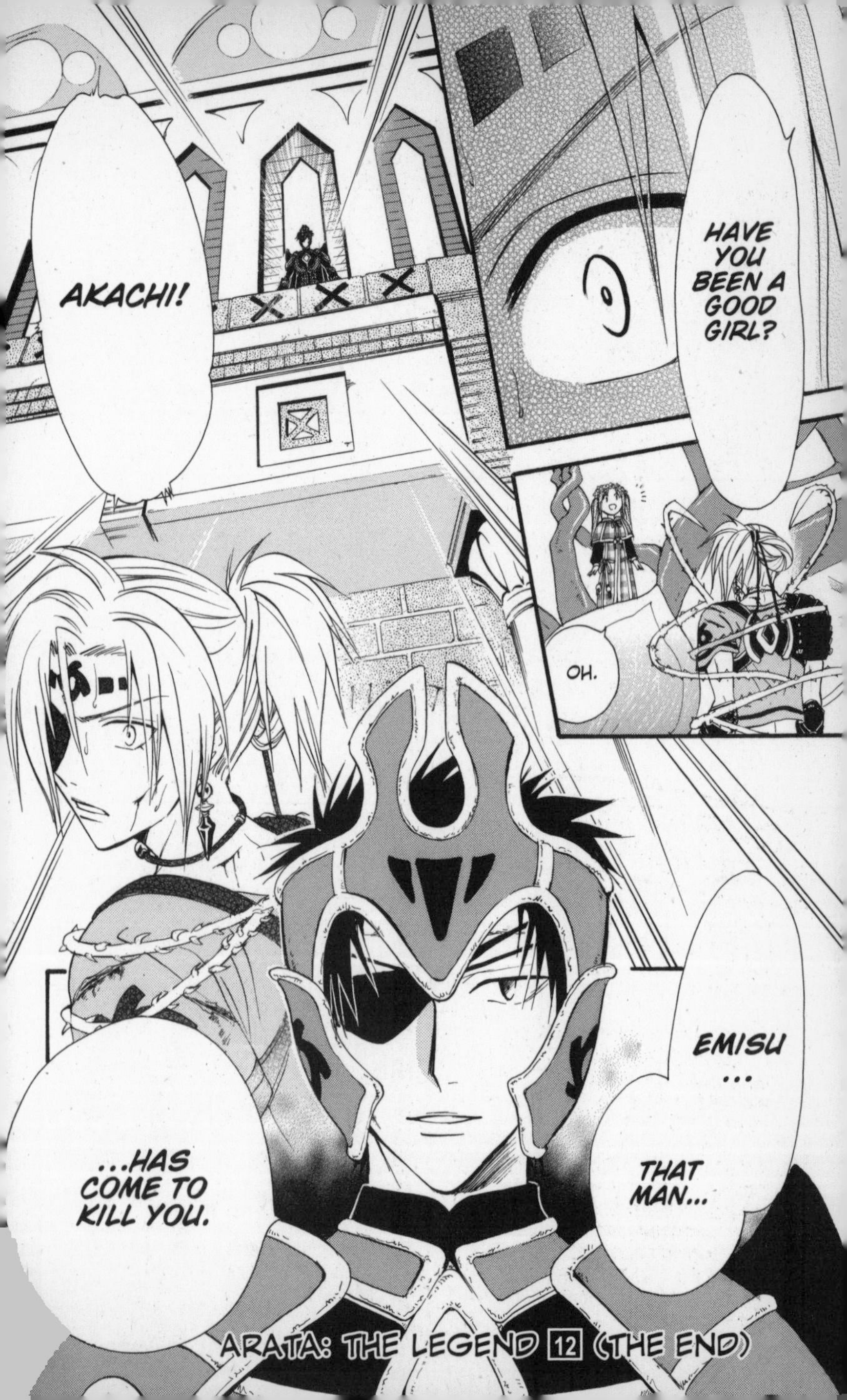
HAVE YOU BEEN A GOOD GIRL?
OH.
AKACHI!
EMISU...
THAT MAN...
...HAS COME TO KILL YOU.
ARATA: THE LEGEND 12 (THE END)

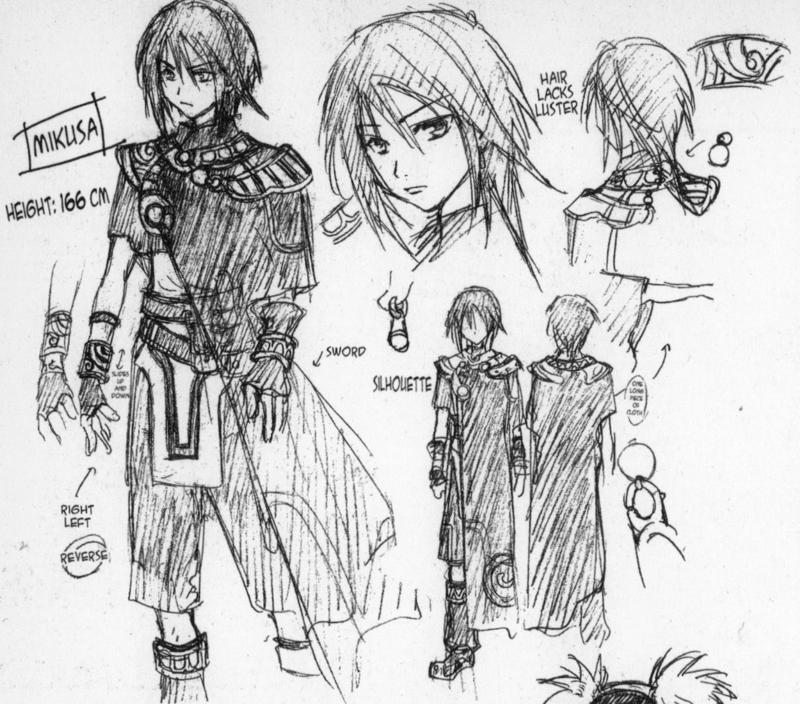
MIKUSA
HEIGHT: 166 CM
HAIR LACKS LUSTER
SWORD
SLIDES UP AND DOWN
SILHOUETTE
ONE LONG PIECE OF CLOTH
RIGHT
LEFT
REVERSE

CHARACTER DESIGNS

THIS TIME EVERYTHING IS PRETTY NORMAL. (HA!) THERE WAS A LOT OF TENSION IN VOLUME 11...

MIKUSA AND RAMI ARE BOTH 15 YEARS OLD. MIKUSA ACTS COOL, BUT ONCE IN A WHILE SHE'LL SHOW HER FEMININE SIDE, WHICH IS THE KEY TO HER CHARACTER.

I GUESS I HAD MORE TIME TO DESIGN THESE TWO CHARACTERS. I ESPECIALLY LIKE RAMI THOUGH. JUST ENTERING ADOLESCENCE, SHE'S QUITE PRECOCIOUS (HEE) AND BOLD (TENDS TO HAVE A ONE-TRACK MIND) BUT CHARMING, DON'T YOU THINK?

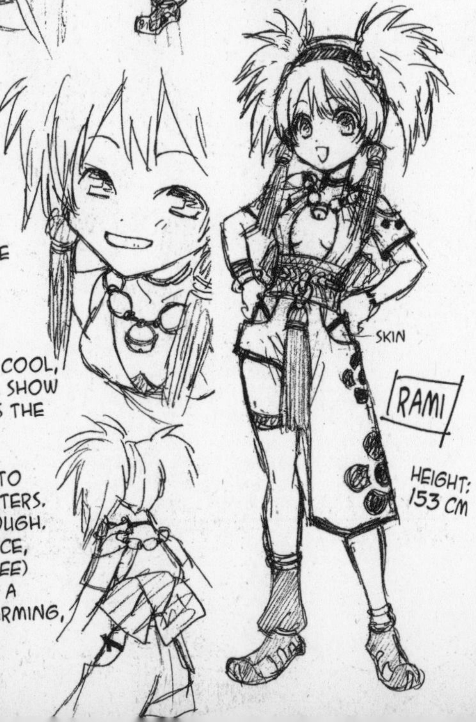
SKIN
RAMI
HEIGHT: 153 CM

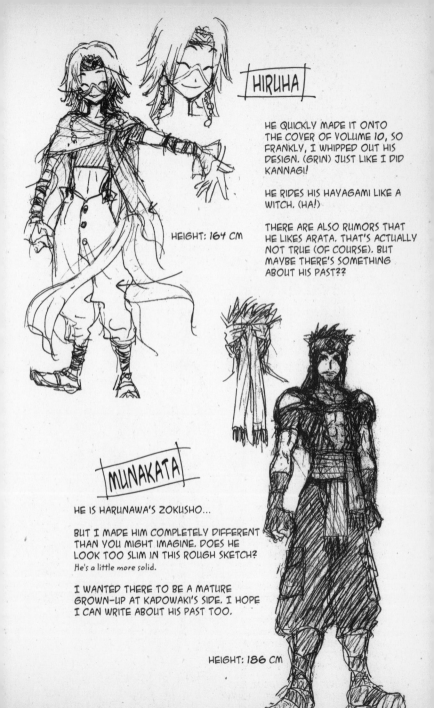

HIRUHA

HE QUICKLY MADE IT ONTO THE COVER OF VOLUME 10, SO FRANKLY, I WHIPPED OUT HIS DESIGN. (GRIN) JUST LIKE I DID KANNAGI!

HE RIDES HIS HAYAGAMI LIKE A WITCH. (HA!)

THERE ARE ALSO RUMORS THAT HE LIKES ARATA. THAT'S ACTUALLY NOT TRUE (OF COURSE). BUT MAYBE THERE'S SOMETHING ABOUT HIS PAST??

HEIGHT: 164 CM

MUNAKATA

HE IS HARUNAWA'S ZOKUSHO...

BUT I MADE HIM COMPLETELY DIFFERENT THAN YOU MIGHT IMAGINE. DOES HE LOOK TOO SLIM IN THIS ROUGH SKETCH? He's a little more solid.

I WANTED THERE TO BE A MATURE GROWN-UP AT KADOWAKI'S SIDE. I HOPE I CAN WRITE ABOUT HIS PAST TOO.

HEIGHT: 186 CM

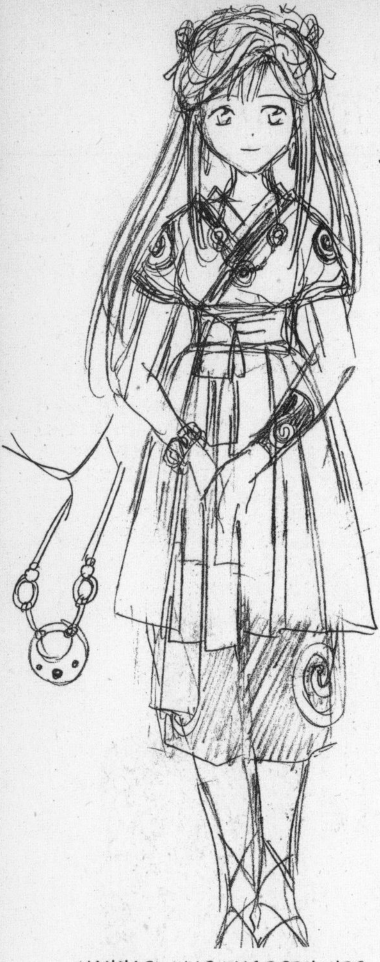

EMISU

AROUND
19 YEARS OLD

I DREW THIS VERY QUICKLY FOR A CHAPTER IN VOLUME 4.

EMISU IS STRONGER THAN SHE LOOKS. SHE'S WILLING TO CLIMB UP A CLIFF IN ORDER TO GATHER MEDICINAL HERBS FOR KANNAGI. WHAT A TRAGIC PAST SHE HAD. (TEARS)

KANNAGI
(18 YEARS OLD)
WHEN HE WAS
CHOSEN TO
BECOME A SHINSHO

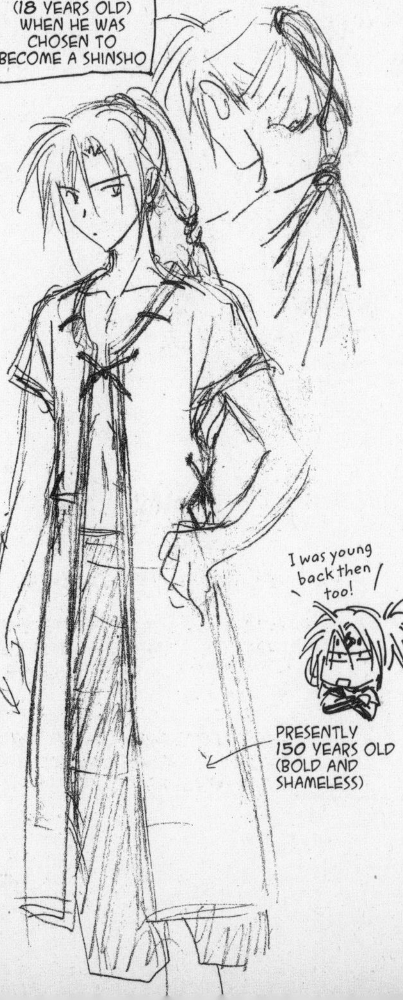
I was young back then too!

PRESENTLY
150 YEARS OLD
(BOLD AND
SHAMELESS)

KANNAGI, WHO WAS BORN INTO A WEALTHY FAMILY, ENDS UP IN A STRANGE LAND CALLED KAGUTSUCHI AND BEGINS TO TILL THE LAND—WORK TO WHICH HE IS NOT ACCUSTOMED AT ALL.

TO LOSE HIS FAMILY, FRIENDS AND HOME IN A SINGLE NIGHT MUST HAVE BEEN A TERRIBLE SHOCK FOR AN 18-YEAR-OLD. FROM THE TIME HE WAS A YOUNG BOY, HE MUST'VE WANTED TO BECOME A BUREAUCRAT SO THAT HE COULD SOMEDAY FREE AKACHI AND EMISU.

THESE THREE TRAGIC CHARACTERS FIND CLOSURE IN THE NEXT VOLUME!

I've moved. My new studio is a little smaller than my last place, but much brighter. I don't even need to keep a lamp within my reach. The only thing is, it's hot. Really, really hot. My desk is near the window, and the scorching summer sun beats down on my back. I have an air conditioner, but the cool air doesn't reach me, so I'm constantly fanning myself by hand. (Why?) I'm waiting for the air circulator to arrive, but I pray that I don't get too dark before that.

This summer is really harsh.

–YUU WATASE

AUTHOR BIO

Born March 5 in Osaka, Yuu Watase debuted in the *Shôjo Comic* manga anthology in 1989. She won the 43rd Shogakukan Manga Award with *Ceres: Celestial Legend*. One of her most famous works is *Fushigi Yûgi*, a series that has inspired the prequel *Fushigi Yûgi: Genbu Kaiden*. In 2008, *Arata: The Legend* started serialization in *Shonen Sunday*.

ARATA: THE LEGEND

Volume 12
Shonen Sunday Edition

Story and Art by YUU WATASE

© 2009 Yuu WATASE/Shogakukan
All rights reserved.
Original Japanese edition "ARATAKANGATARI"
published by SHOGAKUKAN Inc.

English Adaptation: Lance Caselman
Translation: JN Productions
Touch-up Art & Lettering: Rina Mapa
Design: Ronnie Casson
Editor: Amy Yu

The rights of the author(s) of the work(s) in this publication
to be so identified have been asserted in accordance with the
Copyright, Designs and Patents Act 1988. A CIP catalogue
record for this book is available from the British Library.

Printed in Canada

Published by VIZ Media, LLC
P.O. Box 77010
San Francisco, CA 94107

10 9 8 7 6 5 4 3 2 1
First printing, December 2012

www.viz.com

WWW.SHONENSUNDAY.COM

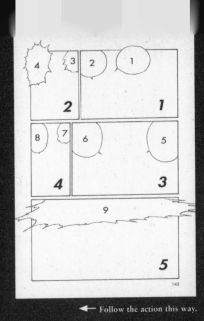

←— Follow the action this way.

THIS IS THE LAST PAGE

Arata: The Legend has been printed in the original Japanese format in order to preserve the orientation of the original artwork.

Please turn it around and begin reading from right to left. Unlike English, Japanese is read right to left, so Japanese comics are read in reverse order from the way English comics are typically read. Have fun with it!